Illinois Central College
Learning Resources Center

Contemporary France

Contemporary France
Politics and society
since 1945

D. L. Hanley, A. P. Kerr
and N. H. Waites

Routledge & Kegan Paul

London, Boston and Henley

First published in 1979
by Routledge & Kegan Paul Ltd

39 Store Street, London WC1E 7DD,

Broadway House, Newtown Road,
Henley-on-Thames, Oxon RG9 1EN and

9 Park Street,
Boston, Mass. 02108, USA

Set in IBM Press Roman by Hope Services, Abingdon
and printed in Great Britain by
Lowe & Brydone Ltd, Thetford, Norfolk

British Library Cataloguing in Publication Data
Hanley, D L
Contemporary France.
1. France – Social conditions – 1945 –
I. Title   II. Kerr, A P
III. Waites, N H
309.1'44'082   HN425.5   79-40090

ISBN 0 7100 0308 0
ISBN 0 7100 0309 9 Pbk

Contents

Preface and acknowledgments · *ix*

Abbreviations · *xi*

Chapter 1 **The French experience since 1944** · *1*

1 The liberation era and the Fourth Republic, 1944-58 · *1*

2 The Fifth Republic: establishment and consolidation, 1958-68 · *15*

3 The events of May 1968 · *26*

4 From Gaullism to Giscardism: 1968 to the present · *39*

Chapter 2 **The structures of contemporary France** · *52*

1 The economy · *52*

2 Social stratification · *69*

3 Political culture · *88*

Chapter 3 **The political framework** · *97*

1 The problem of constitution · *97*

2 Aspects of central government · *109*

3 Central government and local government · *125*

Chapter 4 **Political forces** · *132*

1 The French party system · *132*

2 Parties of the right · *135*

3 Parties of the left · *153*

4 Fringe parties · *167*

5 The parties today · *169*

6 Interest groups · *171*

Chapter 5 **Foreign relations** · *187*

1 Values, purposes and organization · *187*

2 Defence policy: purpose and structure · *200*

3 Main directions of foreign policy · *215*

Chapter 6 **The education system** · *231*
Introduction · *231*
1 The centralized administration · *233*
2 Church and state: Catholic education in France · *246*
3 Primary and secondary education · *256*
4 Higher education · *269*

Notes · *287*
Bibliographical essay · *298*
Index · *315*

Figures and tables

Figures

2.1 Agricultural workers as percentage of total workforce per country, 1900–74 · *53*
2.2 Location of industrial activity, January 1974 · *56–7*
2.3 Penetration of French industry by foreign capital, 1970 · *60*
2.4 French agricultural production per department, 1975 · *64*
4.1 Seating arrangements of deputies in the national assembly, 1978 · *172*
5.1 Decision-making system for defence policy · *207*
5.2 Organization of *gendarmerie* at regional level · *214*
5.3 Organization of CRS · *215*
6.1 The hierarchy of the education ministry, 1978 · *239*
6.2 Map of the *académies*, 1976 · *240–1*
6.3 The hierarchy of the *rectorat*, 1978 · *242*

Tables

1.1 Growth of French production, 1947–58 · *4*
2.1 GDP of developed nations since 1958 · *53*
2.2 Value of French exports since 1962 · *54*
2.3 French energy consumption · *55*
2.4 French firms by size, 1973 · *58*
2.5 French trade with franc zone · *61*
2.6 French agricultural production, 1976 · *62*
2.7 French farm sizes, 1970 · *63*
2.8 Value added by agriculture, 1975 · *65*
2.9 Workforce in commerce, 1962–74 · *66–7*
2.10 Shares of retail market taken by big and small commerce · *68*
2.11 Unemployment trends in France since 1965 · *69*
2.12 Unemployment in France by socio-economic group (CSP) · *69*
2.13 Comparative trends in fertility in Europe, 1861–1939 · *70*
2.14 Average number of births per annum in France, 1945–62 · *71*
2.15 French population by age and sex, 1975 · *72*

2.16 Population decline in rural departments, 1968–75 · *73*
2.17 Population by economic activity, 1975 and 1954 · *74*
2.18 Origin of workers' fathers by CSP, 1964 · *76*
2.19 Income by CSP, 1973 · *80*
2.20 Income per household after tax and transfer payments, 1976 · *81*
2.21 French households, 1973: owners and occupiers · *84*
2.22 Characteristics of accommodation by CSP · *85*
2.23 Annual access to health facilities by CSP, 1973 · *86*
2.24 Life expectancy by CSP, 1971 · *87*
2.25 Cultural activity by CSP, 1976 · *87*
4.1 Majority parties since 1958 · *136*
4.2 Electorate of major parties · *142*
4.3 The right's electorate in the 1960s · *143*
4.4 Main political forces during the Fifth Republic, performance in general elections · *173*
5.1 Defence force comparisons, selected states, 1978 · *205*
5.2 Development of defence expenditure, 1977–82 · *208*
5.3 Exports of war materials from France · *209*
6.1 Teachers' salaries: Paris · *244*
6.2 Teachers' salaries: provinces · *245*
6.3 Percentage of children in private schools · *253*
6.4 Categories benefiting from adult education, 1977 · *264*
6.5 University students according to CSP of parents, 1975–6 · *284*

Preface and acknowledgments

This textbook is designed mainly for use by students in departments of French Studies or European Studies, i.e. those who in addition to learning the French language are studying the social and political structure of modern France. We also hope, however, that it will be of interest to students in politics departments, perhaps by dint of its rather different approach. Our book aims to analyse the working of the French political system and set this into its social and economic context. We give considerable attention to the latter, in fact, and spend less time than some authors on the formal mechanisms of government decision-making; in our view, these are more than adequately analysed in much recent work on French politics (see bibliography) which fits into the 'government and politics' tradition, rather than into the 'politics and society' approach undertaken here.

A second feature of the book is that its approach is historical. This reflects not simply the fact that its authors all teach modern French history, but also a methodological belief common to them all, viz. that a social system can only be understood in any of its constituent parts - political, cultural or whatever - if analysed in terms of its historical development. For this reason we begin with a general historical outline of developments in key sectors - social and economic structures, domestic politics, foreign relations - since 1945. After this, specific aspects of the social and political system are then analysed in turn, again from a historical point of view.

It is hoped that thus equipped students will be able to engage in further exploration of French politics and society. Our book therefore embodies a third distinctive feature, a critical bibliography. At the risk of sacrificing quantity for quality, we have tried to give some idea of what various secondary works involve (degree of difficulty, type of analysis, etc.), rather than giving the undifferentiated list in alphabetical order that some textbooks use. As we assume that any serious student of contemporary France will have a reading knowledge of the language, no special effort has been made to single out material in English.

So far as possible we have tried to avoid jargon and to explain fully our terminology. This may involve being over-explicit in places; but we feel that this is a risk worth taking in a work which aims above

x   *Preface and acknowledgments*

all to initiate. Although there was clearly a division of labour among the authors (D.L. Hanley was responsible for chapters 1(1), 1(4), 2, 3(3) and 4: A.P. Kerr for 1(3), 3(1), 3(2) and 6: and N.H. Waites for 1(2) and 5), this work is to some extent a joint effort, in that it represents several years of dialogue and shared experience. None the less, readers will notice clear differences of emphasis or approach in some parts of the book. There are no apologies to be made for this: it simply reflects the fact that in the social sciences there are in the end no definite answers, particularly in the study of a society like contemporary France, which is clearly in a period of dynamic change. But this does not mean that the book fails to express any opinions; the authors have made their viewpoints and conclusions clear at each stage of the book rather than impose a formal conclusion at the very end. Their intention is to encourage argument and discussion among readers who can formulate judgments of their own on the basis of the text, followed up by the recommended reading.

Our thanks are due to the staffs of several institutions, who helped us greatly with documentation – the Centre de documentation of the Ministère de l'éducation and the Ministère des universités: the Institut d'études politiques: the Institut national de la statistique et des études économiques (rue de Bercy, Paris): the International Institute of Strategic Studies: the Royal Institute of International Affairs: the Service de traitement de l'information et de la statistique industrielle. We are also grateful to the Research Board of Reading University for the provision of money to facilitate our research.

Many individuals helped particularly in the preparation of this book, by giving expert advice or technical assistance, or answering questions. Our thanks are offered to them in alphabetical order – J. Boisson, C. Calvez, S. Cann, G. de Carmoy, P. Collet, A. Duguet, W. Elbro, M. Fowkes, D. Hay, P.M. Jones, V. Laloy, F. Loncle, J. Ouvrier, K. Sainsbury, F. de la Serre, A. Shlaim, M. Vaïsse and P. Woodward. Valerie Andrews was a marvel of efficiency and helpfulness in producing the final typescript. As always, there were many others, too numerous to mention, who helped in many different ways; our thanks are offered to them also. Responsibility for errors remains of course with us.

D.L. Hanley, A.P. Kerr, N.H. Waites

Abbreviations

CD	Centre démocrate
CDS	Centre des démocrates sociaux
CERES	Centre d'études, de recherches et d'éducation socialistes
CES	Collège d'enseignement secondaire
CFDT	Confédération française démocratique du travail
CFTC	Confédération françise des travailleurs chrétiens
CGC	Confédération générale des cadres
CGPME	Confédération générale des petites et moyennes entreprises
CGT	Confédération générale du travail
CIDUNATI	Comité d'information et de défense – Union nationale des artisans et travailleurs indépendants
CIR	Convention des institutions républicaines
CNAL	Comité national d'action laïque
CNIP	Centre national des indépendants et paysans
CNJA	Centre national des jeunes agriculteurs
CNPF	Conseil national du patronat français
CPDM	Centre pour le progrès et la démocratie moderne
CPG	Common programme of government
CSP	Catégorie socio-professionnelle
DATAR	Délégation à l'aménagement du territoire et à l'action régionale
ENA	Ecole nationale d'administration
FEN	Fédération de l'éducation nationale
FER	Fédération des étudiants révolutionnaires
FFA	Fédération française de l'agriculture
FGDS	Fédération de la gauche démocrate et socialiste
FLNC	Front de libération nationale corse
FNSEA	Fédération nationale des syndicats d'exploitants agricoles
FO	Force ouvrière
INSEE	Institut national de la statistique et des études économiques
JCR	Jeunesses communistes révolutionnaires
MAU	Mouvement d'action universitaire

M22M	Mouvement du 22 mars
MDSF	Mouvement démocrate socialiste de France
MODEF	Mouvement pour la coordination et la défense de l'exploitation familiale
MRG	Mouvement des radicaux de gauche
MRP	Mouvement républicain populaire
OP	Ouvrier professionnel
OQ	Ouvrier qualifié
ORTF	Office de la radiodiffusion-télévision française
OS	Ouvrier spécialisé
PCF	Parti communiste français
PEEP	Parents d'élèves de l'enseignement public
PR	Parti républicain
PS	Parti socialiste
PSU	Parti socialiste unifié
RI	Républicains indépendants
RPF	Rassemblement du peuple français
RPR	Rassemblement pour la république
RTL	Radio-télévision Luxembourg
SFIO	Section française de l'internationale ouvrière
SMAG	Salaire minimum agricole garanti
SMIG	Salaire minimum interprofessionnel garanti
SNES	Syndicat national de l'enseignement secondaire
SNESup	Syndicat national de l'enseignement supérieur
SNI	Syndicat national des instituteurs
UCC	Union confédérale des cadres
UDF	Union pour la démocratie française
UDR	Union des démocrates pour la république
UDT	Union démocratique du travail
UDV^{e}R	Union des démocrates pour la cinquième République
UGITC	Union générale des ingénieurs techniciens et cadres
UNEF	Union nationale des étudiants de France
UNR	Union pour la nouvelle république

Chapter 1

The French experience since 1944

(1) The liberation era and the Fourth Republic, 1944–58

The years 1944–58 are decisive ones for the development of modern France. During them France experienced major change in all her main structures — economic, social, political and diplomatic. In many ways the France of 1944 was more like that of 1900 than that of 1958; but by 1958 France was already clearly moving towards the rank she enjoys today — that of a foremost second-rank power. The following pages will outline some of these changes.

Our analysis must begin, however, with some attempt, brief though it may be, to evoke the peculiar atmosphere of liberation France — a moral and political climate which it is quite difficult to understand a generation later. In 1944 France was emerging from a foreign occupation, following on the humiliating defeat of 1940; her economy lay in ruins. Her status as an international power, taken for granted before 1939, was now open to question: the very liberation of French territory had been achieved largely by the force of Allied arms, with the Free French forces and various resistance groups playing an ancillary role. Above all, the field of domestic politics was one of bitter strife, with in the latter stages of the war a virtual civil war being waged between the various groups who collaborated with the Nazi occupier and the resistance, pledged to overthrow the occupier and his supporters. Paradoxically, though, the climate of the liberation was one of exhilaration, almost of lightheartedness, despite the enormous tasks confronting France. The newly emerged élites and many of the great mass of French people seemed to feel that as the country had reached a nadir, it could only set a new and better course. The different resistance groups which provided the forcing-ground, as it were, of the new generation of political and economic élites had already caught the mood of optimism in their various pronouncements which called for a radical shake-up of the whole of the French social structure.

Changes there were to be, of course, and they would be many and far reaching. On the whole, though, they would fall short of what many of the élites and many ordinary Frenchmen expected. In many ways, then, the years after 1944 are a long, slow descent from the peaks of optimism. We shall now try to seize the most important changes as they occurred in the fields of economic and social life, domestic politics and international relations.

At the liberation in 1944 the economy lay in ruins after the defeat of 1940, a Nazi occupation which pillaged French resources systematically and the effects of Allied bombing and invasion. Much infrastructure (ports, roads, rail) was destroyed or unusable; there was a chronic housing shortage: energy and industrial output were below the level of 1938 and much industrial plant was in any case antiquated, due to pre-war failure to invest in new equipment. There was insufficient food available to feed a population which had lost 600,000 killed or missing and a further half million of whom were still in German prisons — a grave loss to a country whose population decline had been a source of worry even before 1939. Finally, France faced acute inflationary problems connected with money supply. Given these accumulated difficulties, the economic and political leaders of 1944 had very much the feeling that they were starting from zero — which helps perhaps to explain the bold nature of some of their reconstruction policies.

Their strategy had two axes: first, structural reforms of certain areas of the economy and second, use of limited economic planning. As regards structural reforms, nationalizations were to play a key role. The Renault car company was the first, in January 1945 (its owner had collaborated with the Nazis, which made the operation more acceptable politically). It was followed by the major part of the aerospace industry, the coalmines and Air France: in January 1946 came gas, electricity and the four main deposit banks, plus a large part of the insurance sector. The state now employed directly one-tenth of the workforce and was responsible for one-quarter of all investment: indeed thanks to its control of banking it was in effect directly influencing some 47 per cent of all investment by 1949.

The state could not rebuild the economy on its own, however; clearly, the co-operation of the working classes and of employers was crucial. To enlist the aid of the former, the post-war governments created, like their counterparts in much of western Europe, the nucleus of a welfare state. By April 1946 a system of social security had been extended to all wage-earners, replacing the previous rather patchy system of private or co-operative schemes and giving protection against the major hazards of sickness, accident and old age. It was supported by a generous system of family allowances, aimed at raising the birthrate, which was crucial if France were to have a labour force capable of expanding production. The policy would pay off handsomely, with population rising by 5.6 per cent by 1954 and by 8.8 per cent in the eight years following. Inside the workplace, the decree of February 1945 set up the *comités d'entreprise* and the *délégué syndical* was given official recognition. The latter's task was to transmit workers' grievances to management; the former body, where labour and management sat together, was supposed to discuss the general workings of the firm (it was restricted to large firms). In practice its powers would turn out to extend no further than organizing social activities within the firm; and the hope that workers would participate in the running of industry remained no more than a hope.

To secure the help of private industry, governments adopted the system of five-year plans advocated by J. Monnet, who would be the first Planning Commissioner. Unlike the Soviet plans, which set compulsory targets for industry, French plans were indicative. They brought together in committee employers, state experts and in the early stages at least, representatives of organized labour. The committees were to assess the resources and possibilities of their sector of the economy and propose targets which might realistically be achieved given the co-operation of all partners, especially government. The latter had, in fact, extensive statutory powers at its disposal, whereby it could requisition goods and services from firms if required; but these were never used. Collaboration was forthcoming, because the plans were modest in their aims and suited a wide spectrum of interests. The first (1947-53) aimed to rebuild the infrastructure vital for basic economic activity – coal, electricity, transport, agricultural equipment. The second (1954-7) continued on the same lines, but branched out more into housing and regional development.

It is important to point out that although during the decisive period of reforms from 1944-6 socialist and communist influence was strong both in government and administration, the reforms described did not mean that France was embarking upon a socialist economy, with control of the means of production in the hands of workers. The presence of General de Gaulle at the head of the provisional government until January 1946 and of the strong christian democrat party MRP in the governing coalition were insurance against that. Rather the reforms of 1944-6 are symptomatic of a desire for renewal arising in the resistance organizations which had fought against the occupiers and had hoped for a new republic after the war. The charter of the main resistance organization CNR (*conseil national de la résistance*) had spoken in 1943 of 'une véritable démocratie économique et sociale, impliquant l'éviction des grandes féodalités économiques et financières de la direction de l'économie'. But such a project requires that power be firmly in the hands of socialist forces with unambiguous aims, and this was not the case in 1944. Post-war economic reconstruction is really the prolongation of an old French tradition of *dirigisme* (the state giving clear and precise leadership to the private sector), to revive a moribund capitalism. But as such the operation succeeded very well.

Table 1.1 shows the steady rise of French GDP (and within it, of industrial production) during the Fourth Republic. It is a rapid growth of around 5 per cent per annum and a fairly even one overall. Unfortunately it was marred for some years by monetary problems.

Table 1.1   Growth of French production, 1947–58 (indices)*

Year	Total GDP	Industrial production
1947	109.9	113.4
1948	113.2	118
1949	107.5	106.5
1950	107.9	108.7
1951	106.4	109.6
1952	102.3	102
1953	103.1	102.4
1954	105.4	104.7
1955	106	106
1956	105.1	109.1
1957	106.3	105.8
1958	102.6	103.8

* Each index takes the previous year as 100.
Source: M. Parodi, *L'Economie et la société française de 1945 à 1970*,
        Colin, 1971, p. 64.

At the root of the inflation lay the fact that too much money was in circulation at the liberation; in the run-down economy of the period, with less goods available, this inevitably meant higher prices. Governments were reluctant to grasp the nettle, either by reducing the value of the currency or by soaking up the excess with stiff taxation; either of these measures would have upset some of the better-off, though they would have prevented an inflationary spiral. As it was, wage-earners could only press for higher wages to cover higher costs of living, and so the spiral began. All sectors of the population lost confidence in the value of money. The only actions taken by government were attempts at wage and price freezes, which were unsuccessful and only aroused the hostility of capital and labour alike.

The loss of confidence was compounded by another related problem, the inadequacy of government finance. As well as the usual state debts, the post-war liberation governments inherited the legacy of reparations paid to the occupant, the cost of maintaining a war effort through 1945 and a major share of reconstruction investment. As economic activity was at a low ebb and it was in any case difficult to evaluate resources available, the government could never raise enough by taxation. Moreover, French governments had long preferred indirect tax to direct; in other words they had taxed the poorer end of the population proportionally more heavily than the rich. There was little real change in this policy for several years after 1944, with the result that the budget was in constant deficit — a factor which hardly encouraged non-inflationary behaviour in the population at large.

To bring down the spiral it took the injection of Marshall Aid from the USA[1] and some classic deflationary policies applied after 1948 by governments of more conservative hue (in particular reducing expenditure, raising rents and costs of some public services and selective taxation). By 1949 these measures, together with the effects of post-war investment that were beginning to show through, meant that prices could remain fairly stable while real expansion got under way. Although this situation would be perturbed in the 1950s (especially as a result of the Korean war), it did mean that the economy had turned a corner. But the modernization had been achieved by inflation, and this meant that the wage-earners had carried a major share of the burden.

There is no doubt either that the nature of the economy was now changed. Before 1939 it was often described as 'Malthusian': the family firm predominated, modest in scale (though there were exceptions, notably in steel and motors), fearful of expansion, and prone to hiding behind tariff barriers. Instead of profits being ploughed back into expanded production, they were often immobilized in safe but unproductive outlets, like government stock. The modernizers aimed to break this structure, and part of their strategy was to encourage mergers so as to give bigger units of production. This process was well under way by 1958: Parodi shows that for limited companies in the period 1950–60 there was an average of eighty-five mergers per year.[2] The other axis of the modernizing strategy was to open up the economy to international competition, with the aim of forcing it into greater rationalization and efficiency. Thus it was that in 1950 France joined the European Coal and Steel Community and in 1957 a much wider trade area, the European Economic Community.

This streamlining and directing outwards of the economy had inevitable repercussions on social structure. Growth implies always a move away from the primary sector (agriculture and fisheries) into the secondary (manufacturing) and tertiary (commerce, services, administration). France was typical of this after 1945. Before 1939 the peasantry had been the largest and most inert class in France; after 1945 it declined by 1 or 2 per cent annually. By 1958 the percentage of workforce on the land had fallen from 35 to 23, and 300,000 farmers had disappeared. In 1947 agriculture still took 25.4

per cent of the national income; after 1951 it would take between 11 and 14 per cent.[3] Post-war growth told against the farmer. There were limits to how much produce he could sell (families spent progressively less of their income on food) and at the same time the price of machinery (tractors, etc.) rose faster than the prices he received. Modernization meant in fact that only the bigger farmers using advanced techniques could be assured of survival; many of the smaller ones could linger on for a few years at the level of subsistence farming (G. Wright estimates that half of them were in these straits by 1958), or else leave the land and go to work in one of the new factories springing up, perhaps selling off their land to a bigger operator. Thus agriculture underwent concentration of productive units as did industry. The process was resisted by farmers, sometimes violently; but the rural exodus went on, with governments reluctant to tackle the problem of agricultural structures till the 1960s.

The other main victims of modernization were also old social groups, the *artisans* or craftsmen (especially those in the older trades, whose skills were made obsolete by mechanization) and the small shopkeepers, squeezed by the growth of co-operatives and supermarkets, and finding taxes difficult to pay once inflation had slowed down. Like the peasants, such categories were too numerous for a developed economy, and a certain thinning-out was bound to occur. A shopkeeper from the Lot, P. Poujade, organized resistance to tax inspectors, which developed into a political movement. Battening on the discontent of the self-employed and of the poor farmers, especially in the centre and south-west, Poujadism was the violent and anarchic protest movement *par excellence*. Although it had over fifty deputies elected to the 1956 parliament, they were able to do little about the structural problem which explained their presence there, viz. that of obsolescent economic groups, squeezed out by a developing economy.

Other social changes included the emergence of new managerial strata (*cadres*), whose numbers rose sharply and whose self-awareness was reflected in the creation of their own professional organization, the CGC. Beside them there emerged, in the advanced industries, highly skilled types of worker, whose knowledge and sophistication seemed to contrast increasingly with the subaltern roles assigned them in the productive process. By the end of the 1950s, observers were wondering if they might not be the beginnings of a 'new working class'.

The social and economic changes of the period were not accompanied, however, by a similar renovation in the field of politics.

Politically, liberation France was in a vacuum. The Third Republic had committed suicide in July 1940, when most of the deputies and senators, panicked by the French collapse, voted the abolition of the republic and passed over full powers to Marshal Pétain. The latter ruled over the *état français* (the part of France not occupied by the Nazis); this was a régime of personal power, based largely on the prestige and moral authority of the Marshal. It collaborated fairly willingly with Nazism in all domains, even to the extent of helping the Nazis implement their policies of genocide. Its own domestic policies were an odd mixture of cultural archaism and economic dynamism, with an increasingly fascist influence predominating in the later stages. By 1943 the Vichy régime, as it was called (Vichy being its capital), was engaged in virtual civil war with the resistance, those who had decided to oppose the occupant and his allies by armed force. This explains the savagery with which collaborationists were punished when France was liberated.[4] When the Nazis withdrew in 1944, Vichy collapsed. In its place was installed a provisional government, based on personalities and groups from the resistance and the Free French forces which had fought outside France; this included representatives of the political left as well as followers of de Gaulle, widely recognized as head of the resistance. De Gaulle was head of the provisional governments (until he resigned in January 1946) but his authority was moral. To obtain the legitimacy conferred by universal suffrage the government had to organize elections for a constituent assembly, which would devise a constitution and submit it to the French people in a referendum for approval or rejection. In this way regular political life could restart.

In fact it proved hard to devise an acceptable constitution. A constituent assembly was duly elected in October 1945, but its draft constitution was rejected in May 1946 by 10.5 million to 9.5 million votes, mainly because it had no provision for an upper chamber. A second constituent assembly elected in June 1946 produced another draft, which was voted on in October. This time it scraped the barest measure of popular approval with 9 million for, 8 million against and 8.5 million abstaining. But France now had a constitution and elections for a national assembly (lower house) were held in November 1946. Thus was the Fourth Republic born with grudging approval; it is perhaps unsurprising that it was only to last twelve years.

Its politics fall into several phases. First there is *tripartisme*, with government shared between socialists, communists and MRP. This is a period of social and economic reform and inflation; it ends in May 1947 when the socialists evict the communists from government as the Cold War begins. Governments now need an alternative basis, which means that Radicals and conservatives now enter ruling coalitions; their influence helps bring some financial stability. We are now in the period of the 'third force', i.e. groups supporting the republic and opposed both to communism and a new challenger, Gaullism. The 1951 elections give the right a majority, and governments are now based mainly on conservatives and radicals; economic growth continues, but problems of foreign policy loom larger, as France adjusts traumatically to its new role as a second-rank power. Social discontent from the victims of modernization takes the shape of farmers' revolts and Poujadism. The 1956 elections give a majority to the socialists and their allies in the 'republican front'; but by now the dominant problem is the colonial war in Algeria. This will tax both the economic resources of governments and their political authority to a point where in 1958 the republic will emulate its predecessor and call in a saviour, de Gaulle. We shall now explore in detail the political failure of the republic.

Discerning observers had seen that the new constitution promised to be very like that of the late Third Republic, which many still blamed for the collapse of 1940. It had been characterized by a clear lack of governmental authority, which was due to several factors. One was cultural. It was widely felt among republican politicians that firm government was only one step away from the authoritarianism (*césarisme*) which has often marked French political life. Weakness or at least pliability was almost a civic virtue: energetic personalities with strong ideas about policy were kept carefully away from office, unless needed in times of crisis. But behind this lay a more structural factor. French society, economically underdeveloped and with deep cultural divisions, had spawned a great variety of political opinions and sectional interests, which all found their expression in political movements. In other words, the chamber of deputies was never dominated by one or two parties, as in Anglo-Saxon systems; it was a place where several groups of roughly equal strength confronted each other. Governments were always coalitions, which meant compromises between their members (and these were often hard to achieve) or plain immobilism (by doing nothing, one offended nobody). Premiers were weak, hostages of their party colleagues, of deputies from other groups and ultimately of the pressure groups outside parliament, who pushed their demands vigorously. The parties themselves were mostly undisciplined and unstructured, having little contact with their supporters outside election time. Now, such a system can last a long time, provided that (a) social change proceeds slowly, so that there is no unmanageable discontent from displaced groups and (b) there is no external threat. The Third Republic lasted seventy years on this basis, though it did have periodic recourse to heroic leadership, the deputies scenting trouble and passing their prerogatives briefly to a strong premier. But the economic crisis of the thirties, followed by the Nazi invasion, found the Republic too weak to riposte. *Gouvernement d'assemblée* stood condemned: hence the anxiety when the Fourth Republic seemed likely to develop on similar lines to its predecessor.

To begin with, the occupation and resistance had had little effect on the fragmentation of political opinion. No united left-wing party emerged, and the right was still as untidy as ever. The centre was occupied by an apparently new force, the MRP. Later on, new movements such as Gaullism or Poujadism would mushroom in response to various grievances. Even the change in the electoral system from the old single-member system (which favoured local dignitaries and thus encouraged fragmentation) to proportional representation had little effect: there were still some six major groups in the parliaments. Their demands were as conflicting as ever, at least on paper. Communists and socialists could agree about nationalizations, but not on wage controls or foreign policy. Socialists and MRP both favoured European political and economic integration, but could be split on a question like state aid to catholic schools. Radicals might agree with socialists about schools, but would quarrel with them bitterly over how to deal with nationalist movements inside the empire. Parties were often split internally on these and other questions. In short, no durable consensus was possible.

In addition, the president of the republic was still a figurehead without authority; at most he could be an 'honest broker' between party leaders. A premier wishing to confirm his authority dare not follow an option open to his British equivalent, i.e. dissolve parliament and call elections, even though he had the constitutional right to do so. The one premier who did dissolve, Faure, never became prime minister again. A premier could not, incredibly, plan his legislation by controlling the parliamentary timetable; this was the prerogative of party leaders. If he wanted too much authority in some matters, deputies might delay voting the budget and eke out money supply to the government in monthly *douzièmes provisoires*. And there was still a last obstacle before bills got on the statute book – the senate. Dominated by rural interests, it had a long tradition of obstructing and occasionally overthrowing upstart governments. In short, the deputy still ruled, and behind him the pressure groups were as active as ever, urging him to obtain concessions and favours: the North African lobby and the wine and alcohol producers are the classical ones, but there were a host of others. Scandals involving greedy or corrupt parliamentarians continued, as they had done under the previous republic.

The result was that by the mid-1950s the 'system', as many now called it, seemed to work in a vacuum, cut off from the voters and very much the preserve of the professionals from the political class. Attempts were made to give governments some authority but they came to little; increasingly canvassed was a presidential solution, whereby the clear focus of authority would be a president with some sort of electoral mandate and power to dissolve the lower house if need be.

De Gaulle suggested this as early as 1946, and his RPF challenged the republic on this basis. Increasingly, then, the republic seemed unable to deal with the urgent problems of France – less her economic ones, perhaps, than her political ones. And foremost among the latter were those of foreign and colonial policy.

The domestic politics of the Fourth Republic were always overshadowed by foreign questions in fact, which compounded differences already existing between parties. These questions come under two headings: relations with (a) Europe and the USA, and (b) the empire.

The Yalta treaty of 1945 effectively split Europe into two spheres of influence, the east falling under Soviet hegemony, the west under American. Some time was necessary for both politicians and public to realize that a new map of the world had been drawn and that for the older powers, especially Britain and France, their role was now reduced. They could at best aspire to that of second-rank powers behind the two super-powers, the USA and the USSR. Tension grew between the latter after 1945, as the extent of Soviet influence over the new communist-dominated governments in the East became clear. Marshall Aid and the Prague coup of February 1948 (when Czech communists seized full power in an insurrection) confirmed that the wartime alliance had broken down and that capitalist and Soviet blocks confronted each other in a 'cold war'. French governments recognized this by their decision in 1949 to join NATO, the alliance of western states under US leadership, formed to confront what seemed to be a threat of Soviet expansionism. Within NATO lay a delicate problem for French governments, though – that of Germany. When West Germany was admitted to statehood by the Allies in 1949, the question of adding its military and economic potential to the Western alliance was clearly acute. It became even more so the following year when the cold war became a hot one. In Korea, the USA and its allies intervened to save the régime in the south from a Soviet-backed invasion by the communist north. One consequence of this was that Western governments felt obliged to re-arm, thus putting an unwanted strain on the new resources that post-war growth was beginning to produce; but the other was political. How could Germany be admitted into NATO? French foreign policy had, for obvious reasons, always seen Germany as a major threat: and this was still so after 1945 (cf. French demands for the dismemberment of Germany at the end of the war). This clearly made the admission of Germany into the alliance very hard to swallow, despite the fact that the balance of forces in Europe had now been changed drastically.

An ingenious way around the problem was proposed by R. Pleven, premier in October 1950. This was the European Defence Community (EDC) – a sort of European army into which would be incorporated soldiers from all NATO countries, along with Germans, under a centralized, multi-national command. German soldiers would thus be disguised as European ones, as it were, and the spectre of German rearmament somehow concealed. The Pinay government signed the EDC treaty in 1952, but it needed parliamentary ratification. For two years governments procrastinated, because opinion in country and parliament was extremely divided. Eventually in 1954 the energetic Mendès-France forced the deputies to a vote, and ratification was refused. It made little difference to France, because eventually the USA was able to force acceptance of German rearmament and admission into NATO as a full member. But it did make for further division inside French politics, giving a boost to those who were increasingly dissatisfied with what seemed to be lack of independence from outside (read US) pressure and who were anxious about France's status in the world.

Similar feelings were bred in the other crisis area, that of colonial policy. In 1945 the French empire was second only to the British, covering much of North, West and sub-Saharan Africa and including, in Asia, Laos, Cambodia and Vietnam. Like other colonial powers, France soon faced demands for autonomy or independence from nationalist forces inside her empire. Her reply was negative: the Brazzaville conference of 1944, called by the Gaullists to discuss the future of the empire, spoke of economic development for colonies, but eschewed any idea of independence. The reasons for this attitude are complex: certainly the idea of assimilation is important (according to this official philosophy, in time all indigenous populations were supposed to develop into French men and women). So too are the activities of various colonial lobbies. Whatever the reasons, though, France was the slowest of all imperial powers, Portugal apart, to learn that decolonization must be carried out in the end. The two main arenas of decolonization were Indo-China and North Africa.

At the end of the war Vietnam was mostly under the control of the nationalist Vietminh.[5] The Japanese occupation during wartime had displaced the former colonial officials, and the Vietminh had filled the vacuum left by the Japanese surrender. France had thus a choice: either to find an arrangement with the Vietminh or begin what was in effect a war of reconquest. Although the Vietminh was led by Ho Chi Minh, head of the Vietnamese communist party, it was by no means exclusively communist, grouping together other types of nationalists under a common umbrella. Moreover, its demands were modest — recognition by France of a unified Vietnamese state inside the French union (as the empire had been prudently rebaptized) but with its own government, parliament, defence and finances. Ho and Sainteny, the French negotiator, agreed on the above terms in March 1946, and the agreement was to be submitted to government and parliament for approval; the nature of Vietnam's diplomatic relations and her future status (whether the agreement was a stepping-stone to total independence or not) was left vague. But what had been agreed was a useful basis. It was never to be incorporated into a formal treaty, though: the ill-will and cowardice of governments in Paris and the provocative actions of local administrative and military chiefs saw to that. In the summer of 1946 Thierry d'Argenlieu, whom de Gaulle had appointed Commissioner for Vietnam, proclaimed — quite illegally — a separate republic of Cochin-China. This was a deliberate attempt to split off the Catholic south from the rest of Vietnam. In November the French fleet shelled Haiphong, killing several thousand people, on the slimmest of provocations. Neither action was countermanded from Paris, and war became inevitable. The Vietminh began an armed struggle that would last seven years, and in which France would pay dearly for the missed opportunity of 1946.

The war of reconquest meant increasing expenditure and heavy commitment of men and material, despite an influx of US aid after 1950 as part of their wider anti-communist strategy. It also brought military and diplomatic defeat: even by 1950 large tracts of territory had been abandoned to the Vietminh and were run by them as 'liberated zones'. In their search for support inside Vietnam, the French were forced to offer first autonomy and then total independence to alternative nationalist forces, based on the wealthier sections of Vietnamese society and headed by the hereditary monarch Bao Dai. But even this, which was more than Ho ever received, proved too little. New techniques of rural guerilla warfare, perfected by General Giap and combined with skilful building of political support among the local population were crucial. Eventually in May 1954 a large part of the French forces was trapped and defeated, despite its superior equipment, in the base at Dien Bien Phu. The war was lost, and in the resultant peace conference at Geneva during July it took the energy and lucidity of Mendès-France to secure reasonable terms for French withdrawal. Vietnam was cut in two, with the north left to the Vietminh, by now much more communist and dependent on Soviet aid. The south was left to clients of the USA; one imperialism replaced another, with results known to all. France escaped cheaply in fact. Vietnam was far from home and there were few settlers to repatriate. Conscript troops had never been used. Even the drain on the economy had been palliated by US aid, and Mendès-France's skill at Geneva had avoided excessive diplomatic humiliation. Unfortunately, then, the real lessons were never learned. Few saw the danger of abandoning policy initiatives to local officials or the trauma that the army had experienced. Many soldiers, captured by the Vietminh and admiring their tactical and political skills, could still never understand how they had lost: the temptation to blame others — 'the politicians' — was strong. In these circumstances France faced her next colonial ordeal in Africa.

France was able to disengage with relative ease from her protectorates of Morocco and Tunisia, with their small settler populations, in 1955 and 1956. The outline-law of G. Defferre in 1956 also set decolonization in motion in Black Africa: it would result in the creation of a series of new states, most of them clients of France, which would become first members of the French union, then fully independent by 1960. If there was comparatively little opposition to this strategy, then Algeria was a different matter. It was legally part of France, under the jurisdiction of the interior minister. Its nine million people included a million white settlers, *colons* or *pieds-noirs*, of French nationality (most of whose parents had in fact come from parts of the Mediterranean other than France). The other eight million, Arab Muslims in the main, enjoyed few political or civic rights, the commanding heights of the Algerian economy being firmly in white hands. The *colons* had the ear of local officials sent from France and powerful friends in parliament. They were thus easily able to stifle attempts to improve the political and economic lot of Arabs, such as the 1947 statute (parts of which were simply never applied and parts of which were adapted, by devices such as intimidation and electoral fraud, so as to preserve the status quo). In November 1954 the nationalist FLN (*Front de libération nationale*) began an armed rising that would lead to Algerian independence in 1962.

Few French politicians were inclined to concede anything to the FLN. Most favoured a military solution, i.e. defeat of the FLN by force of arms; though some, notably the left and some MRP, would follow this up with a package of political and economic reforms. No one, not even the communists, admitted independence. The consequences of this attitude would be fatal for Algeria and for the Fourth Republic.

First, France had to mount massive repression: by 1957 some 400,000 troops, including conscripts, were needed to maintain order in Algeria. Military service was extended. From 1954 to 1960 the cost of the war was reckoned to amount to some 28 per cent of the budget. There were nasty side-effects: hundreds of thousands of Arabs were herded into internment camps: urban civilian life was subjected to sophisticated and degrading techniques of military surveillance: torture and murder of Algerian nationalists and European sympathizers went unchecked. In France itself, governments suppressed opposition papers and jailed suspected FLN sympathizers arbitrarily. These tendencies reached their peak in 1956–7 when government was dominated by socialists and Radicals, who were drawn, despite good intentions, into the implacable logic of colonialist nationalism. Observers coined the phrase 'national molletism' (after G. Mollet, the socialist premier) to describe the feeling of national decline and frustrated impotence which seemed by now to be widespread in France, and which found expression in the Suez expedition of November 1956. Here French and British combined to invade Egypt in a classic piece of gunboat-diplomacy, the French because of alleged Egyptian support for the FLN and the British because Egypt had nationalized the Suez canal (where the majority of the share capital was British). The warnings of the two super-powers and the condemnation of the United Nations were necessary before the expeditionary forces withdrew in humiliation and it was realized where real power lay in the modern world.

The crucial effects of Algeria were on domestic French politics, however. Increasingly governments in Paris shut their eyes to events in Algeria, leaving policy to local forces — a collusion of settlers' leaders, pro-settler administrators (of whom the socialist minister-resident, R. Lacoste, was to become particularly notorious) and above all the army, desperate to retrieve honour lost in Vietnam. Orders from Paris were disobeyed or disregarded. In 1956 the FLN leader Ahmed Ben Bella was illegally abducted from a Moroccan aircraft. Presented with the *fait accompli* by his secret services, Mollet merely gave his approval. In February 1958 the airforce bombed illegally a village in Tunisia, Sakhiet (allegedly a shelter for FLN troops) and killed sixty-nine civilians. The premier Gaillard by now did not dare to condemn this. When he resigned soon after over Algerian policy, no one could form a government for thirty-eight days — the longest ministerial crisis in a republic that had known plenty of them. The system was grinding to a halt. When P. Pflimlin, leader of a liberal tendency in the MRP who was reputed to be less severe on Algerian nationalism than some, was eventually appointed prime minister, the pent-up forces in Algiers exploded.

On 13 May 1958 *colons* and soldiers staged an open insurrection in Algiers, setting up para-governmental bodies called, with appropriate nostalgia for earlier centuries, committees of public safety. Corsica was already under the control of insurgent troops: there were rumours of an invasion of Paris. The Fourth Republic had lost control, and the only alternative to civil war seemed to the political class to be an appeal to a figure whom they believed capable of placating all sides (and whose supporters had certainly been hard at work amid the Algiers insurrectionists) — de Gaulle. The General accepted office as prime minister, but only on the understanding that he could devise a new constitution. This would be drafted and approved by referendum at the end of the summer. Civil war was thus averted, but the Fourth Republic was dead.

Its unfortunate end might make us forget its achievements. It had an impressive record in economic and social modernization, and in foreign policy it took the NATO and EEC options clearly and decisively. Later governments would benefit from its work — much more than they ever admit. Its failure was political, with its lack of authority being cruelly exposed by the colonial crisis. Some explanations have been suggested for this, mainly of a structural order; though as Julliard says, the cowardice and weakness of the political class, and its failure to bring party politics closer to the public, are also important. It remained to be seen whether the new republic would deal any better with the major problems still facing France.

(2) The Fifth Republic: establishment and consolidation, 1958–68

The crisis of 13 May became the matrix for the birth of the Fifth Republic. On 1 June General de Gaulle was voted the last prime minister of the Fourth Republic by 329 to 224 deputies in the national assembly. His coalition government containing SFIO socialists and conservatives was handed a basket of special powers for six months, mainly to restore public order and resolve the Algerian problem but also, on de Gaulle's insistence, to propose changes to the constitution so as to get rid of what he saw as weaknesses in the public powers in France. Thus the deputies were induced to issue a death sentence for the Fourth Republic in their anxiety to end the Algerian crisis. Nevertheless, the basic socio-economic structures developing in France since 1945 were not likely to be revolutionized by a formal change of régime in 1958; nor were the issues at stake in the Algerian war.[6]

Although legal power could be conferred by the national assembly in Paris, real power lay in Algeria. The army had joined with *colons* to form the committees of public safety, in Algiers and other large cities, which continued to rule local affairs for several months. Colonels in the parachute regiments were particularly determined to recover military pride and to keep Algeria French by winning the war. Older generals, however, feared army disunity if civil war broke out in France; their caution opened the minds of Massu and Salan to persuasion that perhaps de Gaulle would guarantee a French Algeria. The loyalties of General Salan hung in the balance for he was military commander and head of the civil administration in Algeria while at the same time acting as nominal leader of the rebellion.

De Gaulle had no ready-made Algerian policy any more than his predecessors.[7] But he was careful during several flying visits to Algeria to maintain his acceptability to the rebels by making vague but sympathetic speeches such as the one at the Forum in Algiers on 4 June which began 'Je vous ai compris!'; at Mostaganem on 7 June he even cried for the first and last time 'Vive l'Algérie française!' Moreover, he reaffirmed the authority of General Salan. But he usually preferred to adopt sphinx-like attitudes while appointing new and trusted administrators. By the middle of October, army officers were withdrawn from the committees of public safety which were finding themselves increasingly by-passed by administrators from Paris. Thus was quietly severed the umbilical cord attaching de Gaulle to the rebellion of 13 May; but his survival would remain precarious for another four years.

The search for a solution to the Algerian problem went through four stages. Initially, between June 1958 and September 1959, de Gaulle's policy was to float trial balloons to test public opinion while also introducing reforms to improve the climate for a settlement without making any commitments on the future status of Algeria. At Constantine early in October he outlined a plan to spend 100,000 million francs per annum over five years on a programme of social and economic reform to benefit Moslems and enable them to participate in Algerian administration. That this was not enough in itself to win Moslem confidence was apparent when de Gaulle's appeal for a *paix des braves* in his first press conference on 23 October was rejected by the FLN who regarded it as merely a cease-fire without guarantees. Just as the army and *colons* in Algeria waited anxiously for reassurance, so did Moslem doubts persist. Even if they achieved military success, the Algerian nationalists feared that the French might resort to partitioning the coastal area and the oil-producing regions of the Sahara. Such fears were justified, for de Gaulle's first prime minister, M. Debré, was suggesting a partition policy as late as June 1961.

The search for a settlement entered a second phase on 16 September 1959, when de Gaulle admitted the right of all Algerians to eventual self-determination, while clearly hoping that they would choose to retain close links with France. A storm of protest culminated in a revolt in Algiers in January 1960 by *colons* aided by some army officers. De Gaulle survived this crisis with a successful broadcast appeal for army loyalty and then moved some dangerous officers to metropolitan France. Having restored order, de Gaulle made secret preparations leading to negotiations with FLN leaders at Melun in June 1960. The talks soon broke down, but having now recognized the FLN as a representative Algerian organization, de Gaulle put his plan to prepare for self-determination in Algeria before the French people in the form of a referendum, in January 1961. He was encouraged by the 75 per cent vote in favour of his plan, but the result provoked another revolt in Algeria in April led this time by four generals whom de Gaulle had recently retired. Generals Challe, Jouhaud, Salan and Zeller won support from only part of the army, and after only four days their insurrection collapsed in confusion. Secure once more, de Gaulle had further abortive negotiations with the FLN between May and July, this time held at Evian, a French spa town on Lake Geneva.

There followed a third phase during the summer of 1961, a period of reappraisal when there were serious doubts whether de Gaulle was capable of solving the Algerian problem, which was the task for which he had been given power. Public opinion had become increasingly critical of the war and its brutalities, and the previous September a *déclaration des 121* signed by well-known intellectuals had even proclaimed the right of national servicemen to refuse to fight in Algeria. Meanwhile on the extreme right the *Organisation de l'armée secrète* (OAS) mounted a campaign of assassinations and plastic bomb attacks intended to break down law and order by terrorism and thereby prevent a settlement in Algeria. To meet the challenge the FLN tightened its organization and redefined its aims to combine socialist revolution with the fight for independence.

The way was cleared for the final phase of the crisis when de Gaulle renounced the possibility of partition at his press conference on 5 September 1961 and thereby based his hopes on association between France and a unified Algeria. The FLN responded on 24 October by suggesting provisions to serve the interests of France and *colons* remaining in Algeria after independence. Secret preparations led to more negotiations at Evian which resulted in a cease-fire agreement on 18 March 1962, accompanied by a complex settlement labelled 'independence in co-operation with France', which was approved by 91 per cent of French voters in a referendum on 8 April and by almost 100 per cent of Algerians on 1 July. The settlement provided for minority rights for *colons* if they chose to stay; it provided for French interests in Saharan oil, atomic tests and the Mers-el-Kebir naval base, but only for a limited period; it provided for a major role by the FLN in organizing the referendum; and most important it provided for absolute sovereignty in internal and external affairs for an independent Algeria. By means of an aid programme on a similar scale to the Constantine Plan the French hoped to keep a special relationship with Algeria, but after eight years of war and in view of differences of ideology and national interest, it was unlikely that a spirit of co-operation would prevail. Both before and after the settlement of 1962 most of the million *colons* in Algeria moved to metropolitan France. Last desperate efforts at sabotage by the OAS merely made the break more complete, their bomb attacks driving *colons* out and their assassination attempts against de Gaulle enabling him to win support to entrench himself in power.

Apart from returning to power to restore order and solve the Algerian problem, de Gaulle and his coalition government were empowered to draft a new constitution according to five principles embodied in a constitutional act passed on 3 June 1958. To meet de Gaulle's wishes, the executive should be strengthened and separated from the legislature. To meet the wishes of the leading Fourth Republic politicians both legislature and executive should be based on universal suffrage, the government should be responsible to the legislature, an independent judiciary should be maintained, and relations between France and her overseas territories should be reformed. Accordingly, de Gaulle's legal advisor, Debré, drafted a text that was slightly amended by a committee formed by both government and parliament before being published on 4 September and submitted to a referendum.

The subsequent campaign paid little attention to constitutional details because most French people feared that a rejection of the constitution would cause de Gaulle to resign, leaving them with little hope of peace in Algeria and the strong possibility of civil war in France. In any case, the absence of clear proposals for an alternative constitution left the opposition weak and disunited. It was in these circumstances that the referendum on 28 September 1958 resulted in 79 per cent of the vote in metropolitan France being cast in favour of the constitution. The opposition vote of mainly four million communists was much lower than anticipated. For the overseas territories the constitution offered a choice between secession and co-operation that would involve devolution of power; only Guinea voted for secession, but when the snags involved in the terms of co-operation with France became clear during the following year, most of the other territories followed the path towards independence, so that the worldwide French empire had largely disappeared by 1962.

The most significant features of the new constitution were the presidential powers to dissolve the national assembly (but not more than once a year), to hold a referendum under certain conditions, to appoint the prime minister and other ministers, and to assume full powers when he deemed that there was a state of emergency; for its part the government had power to extend legislation by means of decrees and ordinances, and could control parliamentary agendas during the relatively short sessions of the national assembly; finally parliament had power to refuse a vote of confidence in a new government and to pass a motion of censure to force an existing government to resign. There was considerable debate at the time as to whether it was a presidential or a parliamentary régime, but in reality the 1958 constitution had to be hybrid to satisfy de Gaulle and the politicians in his coalition government.

Following provisions in the new constitution, national assembly elections were held in November to fill 532 seats (including 67 in Algeria) by means of single-member constituencies decided by two ballots failing an overall majority in the first ballot; this reverted to a Third Republic practice, instead of the proportional representation of the Fourth Republic. The Gaullists formed a new organization, the *Union pour la nouvelle république* (UNR), and surprised everyone by increasing their seats from 20 to 189; with the dependable support of 132 conservative deputies in the *Centre national des indépendants et paysans* (CNIP) the Gaullists would be able to form a reliable majority. Likely to be in opposition on the other hand were thirty-four radicals and other centre groups, fifty-seven MRP, forty SFIO, two other socialists and ten communists. Apart from the communists, who polled over a million votes less than in 1956, the opposition parties maintained their vote; but they all suffered from a disproportion between votes and seats, partly due to new constituency boundaries but mainly due to fragmented strategies exposed by safety-first voting for the UNR and CNIP in the second ballot. Three-quarters of former deputies had not been returned to the national assembly which was therefore revolutionized, though many former deputies subsequently managed to win seats in elections to the senate.[8]

Encouraged by this evidence of public support, de Gaulle proceeded to contest the presidential election held on 21 December with an electorate of 81,764 deputies, senators, local mayors and councillors. He duly won 79 per cent of the poll against 8 per cent for a centrist and 13 per cent for a communist. Now securely in power, de Gaulle announced drastic financial and economic reforms including a 17 per cent devaluation of the currency; the gradual introduction of a new franc worth 100 old francs; a major reduction in tariffs on foreign imports, particularly from countries in the new European Economic Community (EEC); increased budgetary expenditure for military and other purposes; reduced subsidies on public services and family allowances, and finally new taxes that would meet about half the increase in expenditure. De Gaulle could now afford to dispense with the socialists, who refused to serve in the new government in protest against his economic policies, though promising to continue to vote for his Algerian policy. Confident of a safe majority in the national assembly, de Gaulle could appoint Debré prime minister in January 1959, together with the conservative Pinay as finance minister, in terms that emphasized presidential power while paying scant regard to the need for the government to win a vote of parliamentary confidence.

Now president instead of prime minister, de Gaulle nevertheless wished to keep personal direction of government policy in Algeria and foreign affairs to an extent that exceeded the presidential role of arbiter according to the constitution. The Gaullist party congress in 1959 justified the creation of a *domaine réservé*, a presidential sector of policy; but the extent and nature of the sector was not defined by de Gaulle and was likely to vary according to the president's interests. Moreover, de Gaulle assumed special powers in 1961, when he declared a state of emergency from 23 April to 30 September, even though the generals' revolt lasted only four days. He was aware of considerable speculation that he might be manoeuvred out of power when the Algerian war ended and that the OAS were attempting to bring his rule to a rather more sudden end, and his greatest concern was that the essentials of presidential power in France should be upheld beyond his term of office. He therefore decided that election by universal suffrage would be the best means to give the president a national authority at least as great as that of the national assembly. Fears of political instability were widespread due to persistent OAS terrorism, particularly following de Gaulle's narrow escape from assassination at Petit-Clamart in August 1962. De Gaulle chose this opportunity to propose, by means of a referendum, that the presidential electoral system be changed from a restricted to a universal suffrage. The politicians in the national assembly objected that it was constitutionally unjustifiable to make such a change by referendum and they passed a motion of censure against the government on 4 October. In the referendum on 28 October, of the 77 per cent who went to the polls, only 62 per cent voted to support the government's proposal; but rather than change his government to suit the national assembly, de Gaulle chose a dissolution. In the elections in November 1962 the Gaullist UNR, with its left-wing *Union démocratique du travail* (UDT), won 230 seats out of 482 and could rely on support from 35 Independent Republicans plus a few other conservative allies. Indications of doubt and opposition among the electorate were that only 69 per cent voted in the first ballot and that the parties campaigning for a 'no' vote in the October referendum raised their votes from eight to eleven millions, against seven millions for the Gaullists and their allies. But incoherent programmes and strategies resulted in the opposition groups occupying only 189 seats, of which the SFIO had 66 and the communists had 41.

Thus de Gaulle had not only strengthened the presidency through success in the referendum, but even more by the unexpected triumph of the UNR in the elections. He had replaced Debré in March, partly due to differences over Algerian policy, and appointed a new prime minister, G. Pompidou, who was regarded as a nonentity and who lost a vote of censure within six months. But after the elections had returned a safe majority, Pompidou was reappointed for the next six years to become the longest serving prime minister in French republican history. Freed from the Algerian incubus and with a firm power base, de Gaulle was able not only to pursue his foreign policy ambitions to the full but even to win re-election to the presidency in December 1965, in spite of opposition efforts to combine more effectively against him in the meantime.

In his speeches and writings de Gaulle had always attached the greatest importance to French influence and independence in world affairs.

On his return to power in 1958 he proceeded to interpret articles 5 and 15 of the new constitution, which made the president guarantor of national independence, territorial integrity, and respect for treaties, as well as commander-in-chief of the armed forces, as authority for him to take control of all aspects of foreign affairs and defence policy.[9] But he shared the same problems that handicapped his predecessors, whatever the formal powers he assumed; the constraints arising from the cold war and preoccupations with the Algerian problem also affected him during his first four years in power. This was anticipated by allied powers who tended to disregard French interests. De Gaulle's ambitions were largely ignored in June 1958 when American and British troops moved into Jordan and the Lebanon, a traditional French sphere of interest, and again in September when his request for a French share in the direction of NATO met with no reply from Washington. His one moderate achievement during these early years was to develop French participation and influence in the EEC. By devaluing the franc he cushioned the French balance of trade against the scheduled tariff cuts laid down by the 1957 treaty of Rome; and by exchanging friendly visits with Chancellor Adenauer, beginning in July 1960, he cultivated West German support in order to create a political base from which he could prepare to launch an attack on the existing international power structure.

Nevertheless, it was not until 1962 that developments at home and abroad significantly increased French freedom of action in world affairs. In France de Gaulle's power was strengthened by the ending of the Algerian war and by the election of a stable majority to the national assembly. Abroad there was a cold war crisis in October 1962 when the United States refused to allow the siting of Soviet missiles on the island of Cuba; although they came close to war, the two super-powers resolved the crisis peacefully in a way that indicated their agreement to co-exist. Friction was reduced by a clearer demarcation of interests. The Soviet Union withdrew its missiles from Cuba, but it had proceeded from August 1961 to build a wall to divide East and West Berlin, the area of greatest tension in Europe. Co-existence instead of conflict brought a sigh of relief from the world, followed by the dawning recognition that *détente* between the super-powers might provide scope for lesser powers to take initiatives in their own interest, rather than lining up automatically with Moscow or Washington. This view was most clearly articulated in France where traditions of great power status made cold war constraints particularly objectionable.

De Gaulle broke the conventions of American leadership at a press conference on 14 January 1963. A recent Anglo-American meeting in the Bahamas had reaffirmed their long-standing co-operation in producing nuclear weapons, while perfunctorily suggesting that France might buy some sea-to-air Polaris rockets. Now de Gaulle rejected the offer, pointing out that France had neither the submarines nor the warheads to use such rockets; he also rejected American proposals for a multilateral Atlantic nuclear force, which he believed might undermine French plans for a nuclear force of their own. At the same press conference he indicated that he considered it impossible for Britain to enter the EEC, his veto thus bringing to an abrupt end negotiations begun in October 1961. He did not refer directly to Anglo-American military agreements, but by expressing concern that their economic links might adversely affect the EEC if Britain joined, he indicated his belief that Britain was an American 'Trojan horse'. Thus de Gaulle declared a war of independence from 'Anglo-Saxon' overlordship.

At the same time he strengthened his power base in Europe by signing a treaty on Franco-German co-operation on 22 January, which involved links in foreign affairs, defence and education by means of regular meetings between heads of state and relevant ministers. Close West German relations with Washington meant that the timing of the treaty with France was an embarrassment to the Germans; Adenauer's visit to Paris to sign the treaty had been arranged before the 14 January press conference and he decided to go through with it, though the subsequent terms of ratification by the *Bundestag* set limits to co-operation with de Gaulle. Suspicion of his personal friendship with Adenauer lay beneath the surface in German politics, until the latter's retirement in March 1966 allowed an open assertion of German interests diverging from those of France.

The decision taken under the Fourth Republic in 1956 to develop a French nuclear weapon system was upheld enthusiastically by de Gaulle, who greeted the first successful atomic test in the Sahara in February 1960 with the acclamation 'Hourra pour la France!' But his ambition would not be satisfied until there was a nuclear striking force under independent French command. This became official policy in spite of the great expense involved, and it survived a motion of censure which had the support of more than two hundred deputies in the national assembly on 25 October 1960. De Gaulle also resisted constraints from abroad by refusing, in July 1963, to sign a nuclear test ban treaty sponsored by the United States, the Soviet Union and Britain; he regarded it as an attempt to protect their existing privileges to the detriment of China and France, the newest nuclear powers.

De Gaulle was convinced that an independent French foreign policy was restricted by the integrated military command structure of NATO. As early as March 1959 he withdrew the French navy from NATO command, though the decision was interpreted as mainly serving special French security needs in the Mediterranean during the Algerian war. In spite of de Gaulle's efforts to develop friendly relations with communist powers, firstly by recognizing the Chinese People's Republic in 1964, and then by negotiating several commercial and diplomatic agreements with the Soviet Union in 1965, many Frenchmen remained convinced that national security required the firmest possible alliance with the United States. Therefore it was only after being safely re-elected to the presidency in December 1965 that de Gaulle announced in February 1966 his decision to leave the NATO military system, while remaining in the Atlantic Alliance as a purely diplomatic agreement. The decision meant that American forces had to leave French soil within twelve months, together with NATO headquarters which had to be transferred from Paris to Brussels. De Gaulle then visited the Soviet Union in June 1966 and agreed to consult regularly and to construct a direct telephone link between the Kremlin and the Elysée. He insisted, however, that his aim was not neutrality but rather to make France an independent power within the western alliance.

Contacts with the Soviet Union and subsequently with other states in eastern Europe were part of a European policy not confined to the six members of the EEC but geared rather to a Europe stretching from the Atlantic to the Urals. De Gaulle appreciated the economic benefits of the EEC, particularly those derived from the Common Agricultural Policy which solved the problem of French farming surpluses; but he objected to supranational integration, as proposed in the treaty of Rome. Between 1960 and 1962 he presented plans to the EEC through Fouchet, his ambassador in Copenhagen, which purported to strengthen political co-operation in the Common Market but were rejected because they ruled out genuine integration by leaving full sovereignty with each member state. A loosely-knit political co-operation was the kind which de Gaulle hoped would be ultimately acceptable to eastern European states. As he was attempting to bridge east and west, the other five EEC members proposed to go ahead with integration by means of qualified majority voting procedures on the council of ministers which were laid down in agreements under the treaty of Rome. For seven months there was deadlock while French delegates boycotted EEC meetings, until the Luxembourg agreements in January 1966 enabled France to keep a veto on issues involving her vital interests. The French veto was exercised yet again, in spite of opposition from the other five members, when a second British application for membership was blocked in May 1967.

During his presidency de Gaulle travelled to most parts of the world. He offered his creed of national independence to the developing countries, particularly those subjected to neo-colonialism at the hands of the United States. He was bitterly critical of American policy in the Vietnam war. Convinced that American influence in the world was artificially maintained by privileges derived from the Bretton Woods monetary system created at the end of the Second World War, the gold exchange standard which gave the dollar equal status to gold, de Gaulle recommended at a press conference on 4 February 1965 a return to a straightforward gold standard without privileged currencies. The subsequent French practice of converting dollars into gold amounted to a 'gold war' that proved an irritant to the United States though not actually defeating their policies. Nevertheless, at the cost of considerable isolation, de Gaulle had succeeded in creating world-wide awareness of a distinctive French policy and influence. Its durability would depend, however, on how long conditions at home and abroad continued to allow scope for French freedom of action.

De Gaulle's electoral successes and general popularity were partly due to the prosperity of the influential sectors of French society derived from economic growth since the Second World War.[10] An average 5 per cent per annum growth rate meant that by 1965 the French gross national product was twice that of 1950. The régime in power benefited politically from the general feeling of prosperity. Inflationary tendencies, however, were as endemic under the Fifth as under the Fourth Republic. The 1958 devaluation eased the problem for a time, but unlike his predecessors de Gaulle attached pride and prestige to maintaining the value of the new franc. In September 1963 the finance minister, Giscard d'Estaing, leader of the independent republicans supporting de Gaulle, introduced a deflationary *plan de stabilisation* involving cuts in public spending and tighter controls on credit which lasted well beyond 1965. This coincided with the Fourth Plan (1962–5), whose social investment priorities for items such as schools and hospitals were jeopardized; the priorities remained, but corners were cut by means such as jerry-building. The planning commissariat was overridden by the ministry of finance with its short-term budgetary priorities, and this continued to be so under the Fifth Plan (1966–70). The pursuit of economic growth was maintained by giving tax-rebate incentives to business corporations. But, if inflation was to be controlled while high industrial investment was accompanied by high social investment, then the sole remaining target for a credit squeeze had to be consumer spending. In these circumstances it was hardly surprising that the trade unions objected to planning discussions that tended to focus on wage controls, or that they were impelled to produce a counter-plan of their own in 1965. Expectations of full employment and increasing incomes were now shaken by pressure on wages and a significant rise in the unemployment figures by 1968. It was against this background that the government decided to rule by ordinance in the economic sphere for six months from April 1967. Harsh measures such as price increases in the public services became the focus of attack from the increasingly combative French left.

From 1964 the opposition to de Gaulle became more coherent and effective. Undoubtedly his foreign policy was generally popular; his

ability to score points off the United States contrasted with the insecurity and ignominy of the war and post-war years. But his economic
and social policies on the other hand met with increasing criticism,
particularly as de Gaulle clearly regarded foreign and defence policies
as being vastly more important. His paternalistic declarations at press
conferences and in appearances on state-controlled television provoked
all the more resentment because the attenuated role of the national
assembly left public opinion with few outlets.

In May 1964 the French communist party decided on various
changes in organization and strategy that would facilitate co-operation
with other parties of the left in the period leading to the presidential
election in December 1965. Disorganization in the non-communist
left, however, was not resolved until Mitterrand emerged as the leader
capable of creating a framework to meet the interests of diverse tendencies. He became the candidate of a united left on 9 September,
having won communist backing and at the same time organized the
SFIO, the Radicals and socialist clubs, into a new *Fédération de la
gauche démocrate et socialiste* (FGDS). Although this achievement
came rather late, it did enable Mitterrand to force de Gaulle into a
second ballot before he won with a 55 per cent to 45 per cent majority
on 19 December 1965. It was a lively campaign in which access to
state television for the first time enabled Mitterrand, and the centrist
candidate Lecanuet, to rival de Gaulle briefly as public personalities.
Moreover debates on the economy such as one between Mendès-France
and Debré in November revealed attractive possible alternatives to
government policies. Public interest resulted in an 85 per cent poll.

Preparations soon followed for the national assembly elections due
in March 1967. The structure of the non-communist left was maintained and the FGDS published its election programme by July·1966;
its critique of government social and economic policies lost some of
its impact, however, when attention was diverted during the campaign
towards constitutional conflicts between president and parliament.
Rivalries on the left resulted in the five million communist and four
million FGDS voters only forming an alliance in the second ballot on
12 March 1967. Nevertheless the eight million Gaullist voters needed
to recuperate all possible support from centrists and independent
republicans, whose leader Giscard d'Estaing had only grudgingly offered
qualified support, before they could emerge with a knife-edge majority
– 244 seats in an assembly numbering 485. Faced with opposition from
73 communist and 116 FGDS deputies, apart from possible defections
among the 43 independent republicans, the government chose to rule
by ordinance in economic and financial affairs from April to October
and thereby exacerbated a tense and potentially unstable political
situation.

De Gaulle had to cope with problems abroad in 1967 as well as in

France. Although he had emerged from EEC disputes in 1966 with the French veto intact and the Common Agricultural Policy firmly established, opposition from other members was increasing. He became particularly isolated after March 1966 when Adenauer's successors in West Germany pursued policies less sympathetic to French interests; with a considerable growth of economic power behind them, they felt able to adopt more independent policies such as negotiating directly with the Soviet Union and eastern Europe, and maintaining the value of the mark to preserve their favourable trade balance. It was not merely that de Gaulle resented being upstaged in international diplomacy, but also that West German economic and financial strength placed competitive pressure on France.

At this difficult time 'perfidious Albion' increased the isolation of France within the EEC by submitting a second application for membership in 1967. Although de Gaulle promptly issued a veto in May, the British left their application on the table. This meant that the issue remained on the agenda of subsequent EEC meetings and provided a focus for anti-French criticism and resulted in deadlock in all important Common Market negotiating.

De Gaulle continued to cultivate support in the developing countries of the third world, partly to extend the *rayonnement* of French civilization. But his travels abroad showed an increasing tendency to play to the gallery, so much so that foreign governments became wary of offering him invitations. During a visit to Canada in July 1967 he was asked to leave after proclaiming 'Vive le Québec libre!', and a subsequent visit to Poland gave rise to anxiety that he might ignite Russo-Polish relations. The French public, too, were increasingly critical of his fascination for the world stage at the expense of French problems at home.

Of all the problems facing French society in the aftermath of the 1967 elections, the most deep-seated and intractable arose from a massive increase in population over twenty years, together with a huge migration from country to town. France needed to give high priority to resolving attendant socio-economic problems such as shortages in housing, hospitals, schools and recreational facilities. Action had been delayed until the Fourth Plan in the early 1960s which in any case had been undermined by changes in government policy. It was not surprising, therefore, that a challenge to de Gaulle's régime in 1968 should come from young people, particularly school-children and students.

(3) The events of May 1968

Student unrest since the war had been concerned with practical considerations, unless stirred by political events such as the Algerian and

Vietnam wars. The unrest which immediately sparked off the events was generated at Nanterre, one of several university institutions built in the 1960s to cope with the ever increasing student population; in this case specifically to take up some of the overspill from the Sorbonne. Although of modern design, there seems to have been little thought as to the suitability of the site (it had originally belonged to the defence ministry), nor had any provision been made for cultural facilities — the building of the library was only begun in 1968.[11]

Yet students at Nanterre enjoyed better material conditions for their work, and from an academic standpoint the situation should have been easier than at the Sorbonne. A number of teachers were attracted by the new complex and by the possibilities that it offered of a new approach to teaching, and to staff-student relations. They were encouraged in this attitude by the dean, P. Grappin, whose efforts had succeeded in creating a more human and liberal atmosphere. Why did things go wrong? One cause was the growth of student numbers which at Nanterre had been phenomenal (1964 (opening year) — 2,000; 1967 — over 11,000), with the inevitable over-straining of the academic facilities; but all university institutions were in a similar position. Two other factors, specific to Nanterre, added to the unrest.

First, there was a strong sociology department, with between 600 and 700 students mainly in their first and second years. Sociology students have always played a central role in student protest movements, whether in France or elsewhere. They study society, which gives rise to a critical attitude to their own society. In practical terms also, students of sociology had reason to be dissatisfied with contemporary society, since it offered little in the way of jobs to sociology graduates, who were thus particularly vulnerable at a time of general unemployment.

The second factor was the comparatively liberal climate of Nanterre; it was at once too extensive and too limited. 'Le libéralisme de la faculté fut assez grand pour tolérer certains actes, mais trop limité pour remettre activement en cause une situation universitaire qui empêchait des initiatives autonomes.'[12] The liberalism of Nanterre can thus be viewed as a provocation in that it promised but could not perform, given the centralized organization of higher education in France.

Unrest had broken out in Nanterre in autumn 1967. This was caused by the Fouchet reforms of 1965 which were then due to come into effect. There was uncertainty about how these were to operate — which was particularly worrying for students who had begun their studies under the old dispensation, and had now to change over to the new. It was enough to cause a ten-day strike of about 10,000 students, under moderate leadership. The demands at this stage were moderate, dealing with size of classes, examination standards and student representation in university councils. The last of these demands was perhaps the most significant. A committee composed of both staff and students was indeed set up to propose changes which would be put to the ministry of education. However, since it had no powers itself to make changes, it achieved very little. Students were thus made to realize that partisans of mere reform were likely to get nowhere, and moderate demands were therefore fruitless. The more moderate student leadership thus lost its following to those of more radical persuasions (such as Daniel Cohn-Bendit, a second-year sociology student), whose criticisms went far beyond the French university system and who wished to see an entirely new form of society established in France and elsewhere.

After the notorious exchange between F. Missoffe, minister of youth and sports, and Cohn-Bendit on 8 January, when the swimming-pool at Nanterre was opened, the rumour became current that the student — a German national — was likely to be expelled by order of the ministry of the interior.[13] Another rumour, never proved, about the existence of a 'black list' of militant students, served to poison the atmosphere yet further, and P. Grappin, the dean, became the object of personal attacks. On 6 January, a number of militants demonstrated in the sociology building. Strictly speaking, political activity on the campus was forbidden, and when members of the administration asked the students to stop they were roughly handled. Grappin called for police assistance to restore order. A fight took place between police and students and the former were chased off the campus.

In common with other faculties throughout France, Nanterre was involved in protests over visiting hours in student residences in 1968 — a protest symbolic of the students' desire not to be kept in a kind of artificial minority by the authorities, but to be treated as adults with all the liberties which that implies. An issue of more immediate significance was that of American involvement in south Vietnam.

The war in Vietnam aroused not only the political consciousness of students, but also that of the *lycéens*, via the organization of the *Comité Vietnam national* in 1966 by the JCR and the PSU. Many CVN committees were formed in the *lycées* and these were to form the basis of the *comités d'action lycéens* (CAL), which were to be very active during May, bringing many *lycéens* out on to the streets in support of the students. The Tet offensive in spring 1968 caused demonstrations in Paris which became more violent in mid-March. Members of the CVN (among them one Nanterre student) were arrested after bombs were exploded outside some buildings which housed American organizations. On 22 March a meeting was held at Nanterre to protest against these arrests, which were regarded as repressive action by the police. After the meeting, Cohn-Bendit led a move to take over the conference chamber in the administration building, where lengthy discussions were held late into the night. Thus was born the *mouvement du 22 mars* (M22M). A teach-in on the struggle against imperialism was proposed for 29 March, but when this news became known to the administration, Grappin closed Nanterre from 28 March to 1 April.

During April, it became increasingly clear that the administration could not control the campus at Nanterre — in part, at least, because it could not decide what tactics to adopt. It seems to have been neither authoritarian enough to take up a hard line and stick to it, nor liberal (or independent) enough to make concessions; and the student militants, gauging this to a nicety, knew very well how to prey upon it.

> The originality of Nanterre lay not in the environmental conditions of the students there, but in the tactical sense of Daniel Cohn-Bendit and some of his fellow-students. Their genius lay in drawing the conclusions from the failure of traditional forms of protest. Their answer lay in taking, and keeping, what they demanded, and so forcing the authorities to choose between total surrender or forceful repression. (J. Gretton, *Students and Workers*, p. 77)

Later on, similar tactics were to be equally effective on a much grander scale.

The short Easter vacation was punctuated by the news that selection was to be introduced at university entrance (instead of the 'open door' policy hitherto practised) and of the attempted murder in West Berlin of Rudi Dutschke, the socialist student leader, which provoked left-wing student protest in France. At the end of April, fear of reprisals by the right-wing commando groups, principally *Occident* (an up-dated version of the pre-war *Action française*), caused a further heightening of tension at Nanterre, and on the night of 1–2 May, preparations of a quasi-military nature were made by students in case of attack. Matters were not improved by the knowledge that eight students — all members of M22M — had been ordered to appear before a disciplinary committee at the Sorbonne on 6 May. Further disorders occurred, and on 3 May all teaching was suspended at Nanterre.[14]

The focal point of activity was now the Sorbonne, where, on the morning of 3 May, a demonstration took place to protest against the closure of Nanterre and the possibility of disciplinary action to be taken against the eight students. The main student organizations were represented: UNEF (vice president/acting president: J. Sauvageot), JCR (founded and led by A. Krivine), FER, MAU (formed by Sorbonne graduates in March 1968) and M22M, led by D. Cohn-

Bendit. These people, together with A. Geismar, leader of SNESup (part of the FEN), were to be the most prominent amongst the leaders of protest during the May events. A similar meeting was held in the afternoon, but there were again fears of a clash with the right-wing groups. The Sorbonne authorities were consequently very anxious for the demonstrators to leave, but initially they declined to do so. The *Occident* forces did try to reach the Sorbonne, but were repulsed by the police, who were present in force outside. Since the danger of a left–right clash had been averted, it might have been thought that no further police action was necessary. The *recteur*, J. Roche, possibly under pressure from the education minister, A. Peyrefitte, seems to have felt the need to have the police evacuate the Sorbonne, which was done only after written instructions had been given to that effect. The police entered the Sorbonne, and after discussions with the student leaders, it was agreed that the students would leave quietly. However, on quitting the courtyard, they found that they were all (over 500) put into police vans and driven away to have their papers verified.[15] Outside was a crowd of about two thousand, comprised partly of militant students, partly of others who had left the Sorbonne earlier, on the suspension of their classes. At the sight of their comrades herded into police vans, there were jeers and shouts, and anger soon turned to action – paving stones were thrown at the police who responded with tear gas and truncheons. Several hundred people were injured, of whom 80 were policemen, and 590 people were arrested.

It seems clear from all accounts that not only was the student reaction spontaneous, but it was also very violent (it took 1,500 policemen a long time to bring 2,000 students under control). This violence caused the police to over-react, which was to assist in bringing the forces of law and order into disrepute. Moreover, the police had had to enter the Sorbonne, which was seen as a violation of the academic freedom of France's most ancient university. Previously uncommitted students had consequently become very partisan. This would not perhaps have affected the non-student population at all, but it was the police 'mopping-up' operations which did the most harm in terms of public opinion. Many innocent passers-by suffered from police attack and arrest, and these arbitrary actions inevitably gave the impression that the students were the victims of police oppression. There seems little doubt that the police were at a later stage guilty of violent and at times sadistic attacks on demonstrators. However, the point must in fairness be made that, for a few weeks following 3 May, the police would have been guilty in the eyes of the public, whatever they had done.[16] By 8 May, 80 per cent of the Parisian population was pro-student.

On the afternoon of 6 May there was another violent clash between police and students who were pressing for the release of four students sentenced by the courts over the weekend to two months' imprisonment for their actions on 3 May. The fighting lasted for twelve hours; 422 arrests were made, with several hundred people injured on each side. Further protest demonstrations against the violence occurred on 7 and 8 May.

At this stage the student demands were simple enough: the re-opening of the Sorbonne, the withdrawal of the police from the Latin Quarter and the release of students sentenced by the courts.

Hitherto the students had been regarded as 'faux révolutionnaires', guilty of 'aventurisme gauchiste', who would without fail bring disrepute on the genuine revolutionary movement pursued by the working class (see *L'Humanité*, 3 May 1968). On 8 May, communist attacks switched from the students to the government, not only in *L'Humanité*, but also in the *assemblée nationale*.

For the government, too, 8 May was a significant moment. The politicians were in difficulties; G. Pompidou, the prime minister, was on an official visit to Iran and Afghanistan from 2 to 11 May. Interim authority was in the hands of L. Joxe (justice minister and acting prime minister), A. Peyrefitte (education) and C. Fouchet (formerly education, now interior minister). Such a divided authority was difficult to exercise, since the essential power lay with the president of the republic. Furthermore, the triumvirate appear to have had differing views on what should be done. Fouchet seems to have taken a hard line throughout, whereas Peyrefitte, possibly less consistent, seems to have been more flexible in his approach. During the debate in the *assemblée nationale* he let it be known that if calm were restored, both the Sorbonne and Nanterre could soon be re-opened. While not complying with all the student demands, Peyrefitte's statement was vaguely conciliatory; but on 9 May a tougher line was imposed on him by de Gaulle himself, and the minister was forced to announce that the Sorbonne would remain closed, much to the dismay of many liberal-minded university teachers, whose hopes had been raised by his earlier pronouncement.[17] An opportunity to defuse the situation was lost, causing a hardening of the students' attitude, not without significance in view of the violence to come on the night of 10–11 May.

The fighting on 10–11 May in the Latin Quarter was by all accounts savage, particularly in the rue Gay-Lussac (see Gretton, op. cit., pp. 110–12). Prior to it, there had been vain attempts at negotiation and much hesitation on the government's part which, incidentally, gave time for the building of barricades. The order to clear the area was not given until early on 11 May; fighting began around 2.30 am and went on until about 6 am. CS gas and tear-gas were used by the police and hand-to-hand fighting occurred in an endeavour to take over the barricades. Many of these were set on fire before their defenders retreated; 367 people were wounded, 460 arrested and 188 cars were either damaged or destroyed.

It was inevitable that excessive violence would occur in such a situation, with the students trying to repel police attacks with paving-stones and molotov cocktails. What caused greater shock were the police attacks on Red Cross volunteers, on people already wounded, on spectators looking on from their flat windows (some were dragged from their homes). Certainly some onlookers did render assistance to the students, taking them in to avoid arrest, providing food and generally giving moral and practical support. M. Grimaud asserts[18] that objects were thrown at the police from flat windows; this may explain, if not justify, certain actions, but the police were the object of virtually universal blame.

This was the situation confronting Pompidou on his return to France; but he, unlike his ministers, was able to persuade de Gaulle that a policy of conciliation might work. In his television broadcast of 11 May, he announced that student demands would be met (including the release of students after an appeal court hearing). The worst seemed to be over, but the change of policy had come too late. There was to be a twenty-four-hour general strike and demonstration, called by the CGT, CFDT and FEN on 13 May to protest against police brutality. Circumstances had forced the communists to adopt a more positive attitude to the students, but the student-worker alliance was never an easy one. Negotiations over the organization of the demonstration were difficult.[19] The atmosphere of distrust and resentment was not lessened when, after the joint demonstration, a reference was made by Cohn-Bendit, whom the CGT had wished to exclude, to 'Stalinist filth'. Such a gross insult to the communist leadership may account for the continued hostility with which he was regarded.

The demonstration was massive; calculations range from half a million to a million. Student protest could no longer be brushed aside as the work of a few trouble-makers. There were also echoes in the provinces, where similar demonstrations were held — notably in Marseille, Toulouse, Lyon and Nantes.

After the demonstration the Sorbonne, re-opened as promised, was occupied and an occupation committee elected. Thus was born the 'commune étudiante' of the Sorbonne (and its extension in the Odéon theatre, taken over on 15 May), which lasted until 16 June. This was certainly the most picturesque of the May events, if perhaps less than wholly positive. All power stemmed in theory from the daily general assembly, but it was the occupation committee (in theory re-elected each day) which held effective power and dealt with the logistics and organization, while debates on every conceivable issue went on incessantly. The 'commune' was an immense talking-shop, with an aura of festival about it. It was also perhaps a kind of *défoulement*, where each individual re-discovers the pleasure of communication, of escaping from society's strait-jacket, of the freedom to speak, to work out ideas without any constraint. 'Everywhere spirits were unmuzzled, and intellectual dykes burst in a splendidly wasteful release of youthful energy.'[20] Splendid it may have been, but there was a negative side to it. Up till then, there had been virtual unity among the students, moulded by what was viewed as state repression; once the Sorbonne was occupied, the luxury of disagreement was again possible. *Groupuscules* apart, there were two main currents of thought, one concerned principally with university problems and the other which viewed university reform as of secondary importance, when compared with the need to bring about a total revolution in state and society.

After 13 May begins the second phase of events, when the emphasis shifts from students to workers. De Gaulle left France on 14 May for a state visit to Romania, leaving Pompidou in charge, but announcing that he would address the nation on 24 May. In the few days of his absence, drastic changes occurred. Young workers were attracted to the ideas of worker participation or control, and all had seen that forceful action had compelled the authorities to react. It was clearly a good opportunity to obtain redress of grievances, of which there were many. Between 13 and 20 May, factory after factory was occupied until, by about 23 May, many millions of workers were on strike.[21] Even then the unity which the students sought so eagerly between themselves and the working class was not assured. Attempts made by the students on 16 and 17 May to link up with the workers occupying the Renault factory at Boulogne-Billancourt were frustrated by the watchful and suspicious shop stewards of the CGT, anxious to prevent any ideological 'infection'.

One of the most interesting aspects of the strike was the involvement of professional people (usually assumed to be essentially middle-class and consequently conservative). In many cases they showed themselves to be more radical than the workers in their demands for the structural reform of their professional activity, for a greater degree of autonomy. Demands of this kind were made throughout France in areas such as the cinema, medicine, teaching and the arts. One strike which was particularly serious for the government was that of the ORTF, where a complete reorganization of the media was demanded, to make it independent of the state and safeguard freedom of expression.

With the country virtually at a standstill, de Gaulle decided to return from Romania earlier than planned. Exceedingly angry with his government for having let matters get out of hand, he was only persuaded with difficulty from having the Sorbonne and the Odéon forcibly evacuated. Pompidou was preparing for negotiations with the CNPF.

On 21–22 May the government faced and survived a censure motion in the *assemblée nationale*. For over a week there had been little street fighting, but the news that Cohn-Bendit, then in Germany, was forbidden to return to France, provoked an upsurge on 23 May and again on 24 May (which the student leadership tried vainly to prevent), with the inevitable score of wounded; 110 demonstrators, 78 policemen. On 24 May also, de Gaulle addressed the nation on television, promising a referendum: 'la voie la plus directe et la plus démocratique possible' (see *Le Monde*, 26 May 1968). It would be centred on renovation of the education system and of the economy. He made it clear that if the referendum went against him, he would resign. The address was, unusually for de Gaulle, who is said to have recognized the fact, a 'flop'; reaction to it was at best lukewarm. It was now up to Pompidou to see what negotiations with the unions and the employers could achieve. These lasted from 25 until 27 May; the outcome was the following package, known as the *accords de Grenelle*: a 35 per cent increase in both SMIG and SMAG (now 3 NF per hour – a monthly increase on a theoretical forty-hour week from 384 NF to 520 NF, and on an actual working week of forty-five hours, nearly 600 NF per month); a general wage increase of 10 per cent (7 per cent immediately and 3 per cent in October); an agreement in principle on a shorter working week; the proportion of medical expenses not reimbursed by social security reduced from 30 to 25 per cent; strike pay at 50 per cent of normal wages; a government promise to introduce legislation giving greater rights to unions on the shop floor. Not all union demands had been met, but the CGT, with its emphasis on practical improvements, was probably better pleased than the CFDT which was more interested in the reform of structures via participation or workers' control. Substantial gains had however been extracted from the employers, and it was thought that the strike would soon end. With the rejection of the package by workers at Boulogne-Billancourt when it was presented to them, G. Séguy, the CGT leader, had no option but to accept, and to make his own, the decision to continue the strike. Other large factories followed suit, and it seemed as if nothing could save the Fifth Republic from the fate of its predecessors.

Inevitably, members of the opposition considered the possibility of stepping into the apparent power vacuum, which would have required the existence of a united left; and it seemed, with the rally at the Charléty stadium on the evening of 27 May, organized by UNEF, the FEN and the PSU, as if a new left-wing revolutionary, but non-communist, movement had been born. Although no clear strategy was formulated, the meeting was critical of the CGT's attitude: there were calls for Séguy's resignation, and an enthusiastic welcome for A. Barjonet, an ex-CGT official who had resigned in protest at what

he viewed as betrayal of the socialist cause by the CGT. The link
between the 'new left' and the conventional political world was provided by P. Mendès-France, one of the few real statesmen of the Fourth
Republic, and a member of the PSU. He declined to speak at the
rally, but received a considerable ovation.[22] At a press conference
on 28 May, F. Mitterrand, leader of the FGDS, proposed the formation
of a provisional government headed by Mendès-France, in the event
of the government's fall. He would himself be a candidate at the presidential elections which would ensue if de Gaulle resigned. This did
not suit the communists, always suspicious of Mendès-France's atlantic
sympathies, and now outraged by his presence at Charléty on the
previous evening.

All this came to nothing with the news, on 29 May, of de Gaulle's
'disappearance'. Ostensibly wishing to spend a quiet day at his home
in Colombey-les-deux-Eglises, he in fact went to Baden-Baden to
confer with General Massu, commander of the French armed forces
there. It seems reasonably certain that de Gaulle did, in various ways,
assure himself of military support (which was later paid for by the
release of General Salan and his associates), but also that his disappearance was merely a tactical manoeuvre, designed to turn attention
away from events in Paris. On his return on 30 May he made an energetic radio broadcast to the nation. He would not resign, nor change
his prime minister. The referendum was deferred, the *assemblée
nationale* dissolved, and elections would be held (this last decision
included at Pompidou's specific request). That evening, a vast anti-
communist demonstration (300 or 400 thousand people) organized
in advance by leaders of the Gaullist party and the various Gaullist
organizations took place. This show of strength was perhaps less important than the disarray of the left in the face of a government which
had regained its confidence. For differing reasons, the unions were,
on the whole, opposed to any demonstration against de Gaulle's policy
as revealed in the 30 May address. UNEF therefore, supported by the
PSU, decided to go it alone, in the teeth of a round condemnation by
the CGT, now only interested in the elections. The split between
students and unions was now self-evident, a factor which would be of
weight during the electoral campaign. The UNEF demonstration of
1 June was a large one − 35,000 people − but there was now a feeling
of lassitude and defeat.

The workers' strike, too, began to fade during June; although some
did not return to work until the second half of the month. Strikes
ended through lack of money, or a feeling that public opinion was
no longer sympathetic, which allowed various types of pressure to
be used. Force was used against strikers in two car factories, at Flins
(Renault), where a *lycéen*, Gilles Tautin, was drowned on 10 June
while trying to escape from the police, and at Sochaux (Peugeot),

where two workers died on 11 June. These deaths brought one final protest demonstration on 11 June, in which the street fighting was very violent; but this time the students, not the police, were blamed. A frightened public opinion had become hostile to the students, and this in turn allowed the government to act decisively. On 1 June it banned demonstrations until the elections, and outlawed a number of extreme left-wing groups. On 14 and 16 June respectively, the Sorbonne and the Odéon were cleared of their last occupants.

It is perhaps in its electoral campaign that the government showed clearly its move to the right, in spite of the presence in Pompidou's revamped administration of several left-wing Gaullists. Taking its tone from de Gaulle's broadcast of 30 May, it was dominated by the theme of law and order, and the threat of a communist dictatorship. All the parties of the left were lumped together by the Gaullists for electoral purposes. This was an effective strategy, but was unfair not only on the PCF and the CGT (which could, in Gaullist terms, have taken advantage of an apparently crumbling Fifth Republic, and did not do so), but also on Mitterrand (and the FGDS) who had acted in a perfectly legal manner.

From a Gaullist standpoint the calling of elections was a masterstroke. It gave a scared electorate the chance to express an opinion, at the same time doing away with the justification of revolutionary action, since the elections could not be viewed as anything but democratic. While the students did their best to persuade the electorate that it should boycott the elections, rather than accept a bourgeois form of legality, i.e. the existing political framework and its mechanisms, the electorate did not accept such a view, as the election results proved. After the second ballot, it was clear that the Gaullists and their allies had won 358 seats out of 485, a victory which paradoxically owed its existence to the events which had almost destroyed the régime a month earlier.

The causes of the May events, though complex, may be looked at from two main standpoints — educational and social. If we look first at the educational aspect, one cause is clearly a long-standing dissatisfaction with inadequate facilities: overcrowding caused by rising student numbers (136,700 in 1949; 508,199 in 1967 — of which 153,865 were students of literature); the inadequacy of the grant system which forced students to pay their own way through university, and the inevitable wastage that ensued.[23] Education, which provided qualifications, was increasingly viewed as a passport to financial and social advance, but the system was defective. In 1967, for example, 57 per cent of the children of top management and the liberal professions attended university, whereas only 3.4 per cent of working-class children did so.[24] There thus seemed to be a self-perpetuating upper-class élite, maintained by the educational system, which was therefore considered socially unjust. Unemployment, which had risen to almost 400,000 in 1967, was also a factor.[25] The post-war population explosion was in part responsible, with many young people, graduates amongst them, seeking work. These problems caused students to think deeply about the purposes of education, which seemed on the one hand to keep a small class of people perpetually in power, and on the other to be governed solely by market forces.

Yet, had student unrest encountered no echoes in the rest of French society, it seems unlikely that the events could have taken hold of the country as they did; and here, students and other workers had similar grievances. That society was suffering from a malaise is demonstrated by the reaction, not only of students, but of numerous categories of professional people as well as some of the younger industrial workers (those not yet 'set in their ways'), against the hierarchical structures of their own professional activities. It was suggested, shortly before the events began, that France was bored (P. Viansson-Ponté in *Le Monde*, 15 March 1968). This can well be accounted for by the centralization of French society, administratively and, to a lesser extent, politically. 'The constitution created and interpreted by General de Gaulle has done much to exclude the citizen from government. He has downgraded the Assembly, which at least offered the voter a share in public affairs by proxy, and has bypassed it with the referendum which offers the citizen only the primitive choice of saying "yes" or "no" to loaded questions' (C. Serpell, 'Participation', *Listener*, 27 June 1968). This may help to explain the significance of a number of key words for people in very differing walks of life – *participation, autogestion, autonomie, contestation*. The use of these words reveals a thirst for responsibility, for personal involvement, and for communication and discussion, which France's institutions did not provide, and which was not satisfied by de Gaulle's alternatives of national independence and policy of 'grandeur'.

It might perhaps be thought that the May events achieved nothing, in view of de Gaulle's devastating come-back. In the short term, they brought about an attempt to change the higher education system (*Loi d'Orientation*, November 1968). They also hastened the radicalization of the CFDT, with its emphasis on total change of industrial structures via workers' control and hence of the whole of society. They also brought about a change of leadership and changes in policy. De Gaulle's promised referendum on participation (regional reform and reform of the senate) was rejected in April 1969, and his resignation followed immediately. Some changes had already taken place; although the *accords de Grenelle* had not been accepted overall, they had formed the basis for subsequent agreements in numerous industries. This, together with the effects of the long general strike, put France in a weaker economic position, forced her to abandon her

monetary policy (the *étalon-or*), and brought her within a hairsbreadth
of devaluation, while de Gaulle was still president. De Gaulle's policy
of national independence also, based as it was on co-existence between
east and west, seemed less credible in view of the Russian invasion of
Czechoslovakia in August 1968 and the Brezhnev doctrine of 'limited
sovereignty'.

In the long-term, its effects are not easy to define. It cannot be
said that the structures of society have in any way altered. Yet possibly
some changes of approach may be discerned. There is perhaps a greater
concern with social justice, however limited, which can be seen in
more recent legislation on education, and in matters such as the reduction of the age of majority to eighteen, more liberal legislation on
abortion, divorce and radio and television. 'Il faut voir qu'aujourd'hui
toutes les formations politiques s'occupent des questions qui, au-
paravant, étaient tabou. Les jeunes, les femmes, les immigrés, les
prisonniers, l'écologie: ce sont les produits de Mai 68 . . . Mai 68
a imprégné profondément tous ceux qui ont eu une responsabilité
dans ce pays' (P. Mendès-France in *Le Nouvel Observateur,* no. 695,
4 March 1978). A very limited move in the direction of decentralization and participation may possibly be seen in the regional reform
of 1972, although matters still appear to be left firmly in the hands
of the government, in the person of the prefect. The parties of the
left have also had to accept some of the lessons of May 1968 (even
the CGT admits the need for participation), and to endeavour to come
to terms with other, more radical, left-wing groups, who still consider
the ideas of May as the pattern for the future ideal society. On a very
small scale, some of these ideas can be seen at work in attempts to
work out new forms of education, the *écoles nouvelles, écoles paral-
lèles*, where an attempt is being made to bring up children according
to a different set of values — the basis for an alternative culture (for
more details see *Autrement*, no. 13, April 1978, and *Le Monde de
l'éducation*, May 1978, pp. 8–13).

Certainly some values have changed, for better or worse, according
to opinion. Yet May 1968 has also brought politics and violence into
the universities, which may prove in the long run to be something of
a poisoned chalice. We may ask, over and above some fairly obvious
changes, if structures in society and administration have been in any
sense transformed. If this is not the case, then we may perhaps conclude with M. Jobert (*Le Monde*, 6 May 1978) that May 1968 could
well repeat itself, and consequently, that the Fifth Republic may
yet have similar trials to undergo.

Finally, what were the events of May? How should they be described? From what has already been said, two interpretations may
be made, namely that they were the outcome (a) of a crisis in higher
education, and (b) of a crisis in the institutions of the Fifth Republic.

Further interpretations include the consequence of subversion with massive financial resources, undertaken by the left. This has been adequately refuted by M. Grimaud,[26] as far as foreign subsidies were concerned. The economic crisis has also been indicated as the source of the troubles, as in the case of earlier revolutions. It has further been suggested that the events constitute a kind of mass liberation, a psycho-drama, where the students acted out a revolution.[27] This interpretation has aroused some hostility but it must be admitted that, in the past, a certain revolutionary mythology has influenced the leaders, even although this time the influences may have been less than wholly French in origin. For Alain Touraine, the May events present the first example of a new type of class struggle, against the technological society, undertaken not by the working class, but by the students and the professional classes. One, however, which may embrace all of these interpretations (which undoubtedly all contain some element of truth) is that which sees the events of May as one example of a crisis of our civilization. It could well be suggested that, with the decline of organized religion, which lies at the basis of western civilization, the values which it imposed became somewhat eroded and were replaced by an indiscriminate materialism and a consumer society, so strongly condemned in May '68.

How fresh values are to be found and accepted is, at present, a problem for all western societies. Part of this might well be sought in the idealism of May '68, stripped of its intolerance and propensity for verbal and physical violence.

(4) From Gaullism to Giscardism: 1968 to the present

1968 had ended in apparent triumph for Gaullism. The Grenelle agreements, the electoral victory and the intelligent concessions of Faure's education law seemed to have brought the régime out of danger. But in the spring of 1969 de Gaulle made an attempt to confirm his authority that was to misfire and to open up a new era in French politics: this was the April referendum. In it the General offered voters a package deal: they were asked to approve a regional law providing for some small measure of decentralization away from Paris and, in the same vote, to approve changes in the composition and powers of the senate, long a thorn in de Gaulle's side (especially since its opposition to the 1962 referendum on presidential elections). The senate was now to lose its legislative powers, and henceforth only half of it would be elected — the other half being nominated by interest groups. The stick was thus combined with the carrot, and the French asked to give a single yes or no to two quite different proposals, which in any case contained several dozen sub-clauses. Opinion polls and de Gaulle's advisers suggested that there were limits to how far the public's arm could be twisted, but he went ahead with the referendum, making a 'yes' vote the condition of his staying in office. Whether this reflected his belief that he could coerce the electorate or whether, as some have claimed, it was a kind of deliberate political suicide, the General lost his referendum by 53.2 per cent to 46.8. Decisive in his defeat were not merely votes from the left, but also those of the centrists and most of all, the Independent Republicans of V. Giscard d'Estaing who were allied with Gaullism, but whose leader had been dropped from government in 1966. On 24 April de Gaulle resigned, to die the following year. A new chapter in politics had been opened.

The June presidential election saw the Gaullists present G. Pompidou as their candidate – a clear admission that the victor of 1968 was heir-apparent. He faced opposition from A. Poher, centrist senator and acting president of the republic until elections could be held. There were also two challengers from the left, as socialists and communists were still feuding. The former ran G. Defferre, considered one of their more moderate figures, and the latter presented the veteran J. Duclos. On the first ballot Defferre was beaten badly and Duclos did well, pulling in all the available communist votes. Poher did better than expected for such a mild gentleman with a Fourth Republic image, and Pompidou came first. The second ballot was thus between him and Poher, and he won easily (57.5 per cent to 42.5), as not many left supporters were ready to vote Poher rather than Pompidou (it was, as Duclos put it, a choice between 'blanc bonnet et bonnet blanc'). Pompidou thus began a presidency that would last till his untimely death in April 1974: this period forms a whole to some extent, so we shall deal with it as such, leaving the presidency of Giscard d'Estaing till later.

Pompidou's presidency was no period of dramatic social and economic change. By now the broad lines of French development were clearly fixed and Pompidou continued the course set in the sixties. France aimed to become a major economic power, which meant greater efficiency and productivity, plus a heavier commitment to exports. It also meant more French investment abroad and greater penetration into France of foreign investment (by 1971 there would be more of this in France than in Germany). Inside France the number of industrial mergers would continue: the number of self-employed, especially in agriculture, would decline and that of wage-earners rise steadily. Pompidou's reign saw no great change in foreign policy, either: if there was slightly less frigidity with regard to the USA, then France still maintained privileged links with Eastern Europe. And if Britain was admitted to the EEC, then traditional French hostility to supranational initiatives remained strong. What is interesting about Pompidou's presidency is domestic political development and we shall concentrate heavily on this.

Pompidou had two premiers — J. Chaban-Delmas from June 1969 to July 1972 and P. Messmer until his death. Chaban saw himself as the progressive type of Gaullist, eager to innovate and broaden the bases of governmental support; the dour Messmer believed that what France needed was order and stability. That Pompidou used both is significant.

Any examination of his policies should begin, however, with an attempt to situate him in the context of Gaullism. Clearly Pompidou could never have the charismatic authority of de Gaulle: he admitted as much by his careful cultivation of the image of a shrewd Auvergnat, dependable and undramatic. While the Gaullist barons (Debré, Foccart, etc.) had been closely involved in all the heroic periods of Gaullism, as well as in the 'traversée du désert' (the long years when de Gaulle was out of power), Pompidou had been working quietly in banking, occasionally giving the General financial advice. If he had risen in the hierarchy after 1962 thanks to his political skills, this did not mean that he was popular with historic Gaullists, or indeed with the General, who had in the end sacked him for being right in 1968 against the General's own point of view. But these personal and historical differences were compounded by a more serious one, namely the differing analyses of French society which Pompidou and the older Gaullists had. The latter had a dynamic view of the state: it was to give leadership and drive in the modernization of France, and make her a great power again. It has been shown how the 'technocrats' of the Fifth Republic pursued vigorous industrial policies, encouraging the private sector to expand — to such an extent that some analysts have spoken in terms of a state capitalism, animated by aims of national grandeur. Now, such policies have their social costs: modernization hit at large sectors of the peasantry, as well as shopkeepers, craftsmen and small businessmen. De Gaulle and his associates believed that these categories could be carried along on a tide of economic growth and nationalist rhetoric; but Pompidou was clever enough to see the extent of their hardship (manifest in the emergence of militant organizations such as CIDUNATI) and to try and placate them. For their electoral weight (worth up to four million votes, according to how one calculates) was clearly vital to Gaullism and arguably to the régime. In 1968 Pompidou had appealed pretty directly to the fears of such categories: increasingly his presidency could be seen as an attempt to steer between concessions to them and modernizing imperatives.

There was another twist to Pompidou's Gaullism, however, which involved an attempt to broaden its support in another direction. At its peak in the nineteen-sixties, when the economy was booming, the UDR had pulled in an increasing number of working-class and lower white-collar votes, many of which the left might normally expect to claim. It seemed possible to Pompidou to try and reconcile them more durably to the régime, however, even though their claims might differ radically from those of the categories just described. This thinking probably lay behind the appointment of Chaban-Delmas, with his project for a 'new society'. Chaban was as keen a modernizer as Pompidou, and he believed it possible to build a very wide consensus inside French society on the basis of economic growth and political stability (both of which could be attributed to the Fifth Republic). Such a consensus could be found by a series of reforms, thought Chaban; if it did not already exist, then this was because (a) the administration was out-dated and arbitrary in its practices, and (b) too many people had an ideological (therefore wrong) view of social relations, which stressed conflict at the expense of consensus. In fact this mixture of pious hope and shrewd political calculation proved hard to translate into practice. In industrial relations, Chaban achieved some small changes: manual workers began to be paid increasingly on a monthly, not weekly basis; the guaranteed minimum wage, SMIG (dating from 1952), was indexed to the cost of living and became SMIC (the C standing for 'croissant'). In the Renault works, a small percentage of dividends was redistributed to workers (Pompidou's version of de Gaulle's participation involved turning workers into small capitalists). More importantly, in the public sector Chaban was able to sign *contrats de progrès* with unions (detailed agreements covering wages and prices). Whether these measures would suffice to rally more lower-class support to the régime without frightening off some of its more comfortable supporters remained to be seen.

Certainly in other areas of policy where he might appeal to a more progressive audience, Chaban was less successful. The regional law of 1972 created bodies with no power, hence incapable of dealing with grave problems of economic imbalance faced by regions like Alsace-Lorraine, with its declining coal and steel industries, the Vosges, with its obsolescent textile production, or the south-west with its industrial under-development and inefficient farming. In the field of civic liberties, Chaban's attempts to liberalize the notoriously pro-government news broadcasts were killed at birth by Pompidou's private office. All this suggested that part at least of the Pompidolian majority was not in favour of trying to broaden the régime's appeal towards more popular or more progressive groups.

Pompidou's modernizing tendencies were seen in his use of the state as industrial spearhead. The building of the Fos port and industrial complex near Marseille used government funds to cover the first one-sixth of the costs: the two steel giants of Usinor and Wendel were then persuaded to amalgamate and the remaining cost was covered by a 25 per cent participation by foreign capital. This is a good example of heroic state leadership to the private sector. On another level, the acceptance of British entry into the EEC served notice that Pompidou was fully committed to the ultimate logic of economic expansion, exposure to foreign competition.

Yet such policies had their counterpart: if Pompidolism favoured the development of big capital, it had also to make concessions to small. Thus in agriculture, although the Common Agricultural Policy, with its guaranteed prices and insurance against market risks, was especially favourable to the big farmers of northern France, it also slowed down the exodus of the smaller farmers, because of both the price supports and the structural reforms agreed by the EEC on the basis of the Mansholt Plan. Thus Pompidou did not run the risk of too rapid a rural exodus and the alienation of farmers' support. Similar steps were taken in commerce, where the small shopkeepers were struggling against competition from larger units by the early 1970s. To keep the support of this numerous and vocal category, J. Royer, minister of commerce, passed in December 1973 a law which effectively gave small shopkeepers blocking power over the granting of building permits for commercial premises – this despite the claims of finance minister Giscard d'Estaing that the whole of the commercial structure still needed considerable modernization.

Another category favoured by Pompidolism was property-development. Developers enjoyed something of a golden age in the early 1970s, when Paris and many other towns were covered in concrete, which was lucrative for them, if less pleasant for those who had to live in or look at their buildings. Given the extent of the housing crisis, it was perhaps inevitable that there should be a property boom. What was more surprising was the extent to which the Gaullist machine became involved in it, even though certain developers were known to be enthusiastic contributors to UDR funds. Gaullist favouritism extended from granting developers planning permission in green belts to involvement by a number of deputies in schemes where housebuyers were the victims of distinctly sharp practice. Some of these deputies resigned or were expelled from the UDR. This helped to spread an atmosphere of scandal, redolent of previous republics, which did no good to the general reputation of the UDR: nor did the publication in 1972 of documents showing Chaban's skill at tax avoidance.

By this time indeed 'le système Pompidou', as hostile observers called it, was beginning to creak. The crisis with which all are familiar since 1974 had not yet fully broken, but there were disturbing signs. Unemployment was over half a million; prices were rising steadily; some regions and sectors stood out in sharp decline; housing was inadequate. Pompidou's 1972 referendum on British entry to the

EEC turned out to be a very damp squib, with 46.6 per cent of the electorate abstaining. To prepare for the 1973 elections, Pompidou replaced Chaban with Messmer. In so doing he had almost certainly been swayed by his private advisers – P. Juillet and M. -F. Garaud – who wanted to move Gaullism on to an increasingly conservative course. They believed that reformism of the Chaban type (anodine as it might seem to outsiders) was already a concession to the op-position left. As such, it would never win wider support but merely antagonize 'la France des profondeurs' – the rural, the aged, the religious, the reactionary pure and simple, many of whom fitted into the declining economic categories described above and whose votes were increasingly necessary to Gaullism. Such people wanted not dynamic change, but preservation of their own status; not workers' participation in industry, but measures against trade unions and com-munists; not liberalization of media or mores, but rather 'law and order'. Whether Pompidou could satisfy their demands is dubious: but the dismissal of Chaban signified a step to the right and set the tone for the 1973 parliamentary elections.

Pompidou and his allies fought these defensively, on a platform of anti-left, and especially anti-communist, feeling. There was a reason for this. Since 1969 the socialist party had renewed its organization, its leaders and its policies. It had also moved closer to the communists after the freeze of 1968. In 1972 the two signed, for the first time, a common programme of government (CPG), which committed them, if victorious at the polls, to making certain changes within precise deadlines. In the constitutional field, they were pledged to abolition of the special presidential powers and creation of a supreme court; in economic policy, as well as a large give-away element (wage rises and improved benefits), the programme promised higher growth and looked to more intensive planning, based on a number of strategic nationalizations, as the means of achieving this. Differences in foreign and defence policy (e.g. over NATO and the EEC) and in economic policy (how to run nationalized industry) were disguised with reason-able skill.

The attractions of this package, plus discontent with long years of 'l'Etat UDR', were likely to mean a swing towards the opposition. Hence the defensive campaign of the government and Pompidou's special appeal on the media just before polling – both of them on the themes of the dangers to France implied by the 'adventurist' and 'irresponsible' economic strategy of the left and the fundamental incompatibility of socialists and communists. The mixture worked well enough for the UDR to remain the leading party, though the socialists gained considerably. But the three years of peace to which Pompidou had looked forward before the 1976 presidential elections were not to be. He looked increasingly ill and seemed progressively less in command of government; thus few were surprised when, after a painful illness, he died in April 1974. Once again, there was turmoil at the prospect of unexpected presidential elections.

In the May election, three major candidates stood at the first ballot, along with a wide spectrum of others, from the feminist and Trotskyist candidate A. Laguiller to ex-minister Royer, whose appeal was very much to 'la France des profondeurs'. F. Mitterrand was again candidate of the united left (though not pledged to implement the common programme in its entirety); V. Giscard d'Estaing, with his long experience as finance minister, competed with the ex-premier Chaban-Delmas for the votes of the right. The latter pair were rated fairly evenly by opinion polls until there occurred an event which had more implications than many realized. Forty-three UDR deputies, led by J. Chirac, had doubts about whether Chaban (a 'fragile' candidate because of his recent sacking and the publicity about his tax affairs) could beat Mitterrand in the run-off at the second ballot. They therefore declared publicly in favour of Giscard (a non-Gaullist). Chaban's rating in the polls collapsed drastically, once it was known that some of his own party considered him a loser. At the same time Giscard secured the support of the opposition centrists of Lecanuet (worth, as the latter boasted on BBC television, some three million votes). This effectively meant a second-round duel between Giscard and Mitterrand, with the former scraping home by 50.6 per cent to 49.4. The left could lament the missed opportunity, and Giscard now had to govern with a majority (in parliamentary terms) which was broadly sympathetic, but whose dominant party was not his own. This fact he recognized by making Chirac his premier. Gaullism had paid dearly for not having a successor to Pompidou ready in the wings.

Giscard had placed his campaign under the sign of 'change without risk': he promised voters an 'advanced liberal society'. His approach, then, was more along the lines of Chaban-Delmas than the conservative course lately set by Pompidou. It implied broadening the power-base of the government — a task doubly necessary given the slimness of Giscard's victory. But as with Chaban-Delmas, there were limits to how far Giscard could go. Nothing in his background or that of his party suggested any radical disagreement with the workings of French capitalist society in the seventies. It would rather be a question of making this society work less conflictually, by reconciling as many social groups to it as possible. This would involve reforms, but not far-reaching ones: it might also involve a good deal of publicity, to suggest that more was being changed than was actually the case. We shall now examine some of the policies of the advanced liberal society.

It began with a wave of reforms affecting civic liberties. Abortion was legalized, divorce made easier to obtain, and the age of majority lowered from twenty-one to eighteen. These reforms were voted with the help of the left in parliament, which had demanded them for a long time, and against some of the Giscardian and UDR deputies. Other areas of civil liberties have received more cavalier treatment, however. M. Poniatowski, long a close associate and adviser of Giscard, was made minister of the interior, where he proved just as tough and illiberal as his predecessors. Outbursts against 'soft' magistrates, use of police dogs to clear workplaces occupied by strikers, and a relish for noisy polemics against the communist party shed some doubt on the liberal intentions of the new president and eventually led to Poniatowski's removal. The way in which the government broke up the 1975 national servicemen's movements in favour of trade-union rights for conscripts (which are recognized in more than one west European country), by use of a special military tribunal, again made one wonder how far civil rights could be extended.

One area widely admitted to be in need of reform was local government. Here Giscard restored Paris to equality with other French towns by granting it an elected mayor, in December 1975 (previously it had been under the authority of two prefects, i.e. government appointees). But he made no move towards strengthening the regional assemblies, despite previous support for this idea.

In party politics, the new president deplored the division of France into two and called for a relaxing of the hostility between left and right. *Décrispation* was a slogan much used in the media; but how it was to be translated into practice was not clear. Giscard would have liked some arrangement with the socialists, detaching them from their communist partners and at the same time allowing his own supporters to escape from the Gaullists. This was never likely to be forthcoming, though, and Giscard would probably have been happy with the kind of polite relationship that prevails in Britain between government and opposition, with regular exchanges of views between party leaders. Despite his numerous overtures in this direction, all he had managed to achieve by the summer of 1978 was to win over one or two personalities from the fringe of the opposition (with the prospect of some others to follow, no doubt) and to have had talks at the Elysée with the trade-union and opposition leaders, following the left's defeat in the election of March 1978. The oppositions in French politics run deeper perhaps than Giscard or some commentators realize. Perhaps the comment of the veteran Gaullist Sanguinetti is appropriate in this context: 'Qu'est-ce que Giscard? C'est Guizot, c'est la grande bourgeoisie libérale d'émanation protestante, quant à la mentalité, même si elle est en pays catholique. On veut gouverner ce pays comme s'il était anglais ou allemand. C'est une erreur qui peut coûter cher à la France.'[28]

The crucial test of the advanced liberal society is its economic policy. Since 1974 the west had been plunged into what is commonly termed 'the crisis'. By this is usually meant the effects of the Yom Kippur war of 1973 and the discovery by Arab states of the 'oil weapon'. Since then, the determination of OPEC countries to extract higher prices for their oil has perturbed the balance of payments of the importing, industrialized countries and greatly fuelled inflation there. This compounded defects already existing in western economies. Britain, with its declining industrial base, high level of public expenditure and poor trade balance was particularly affected. So too was France, despite having a renovated industrial structure. She has been plagued by inflation, unemployment and balance of payments problems. Faced with this pressure, Giscardian policies have been indeed liberal, but not particularly advanced.

During 1975 and early 1976, under Chirac, public expenditure was allowed to rise, which helped restrain unemployment to some extent, but at the cost of a rise in wages and prices and a deterioration of the foreign trade balance. A more surgical approach was adopted with the appointment of R. Barre as premier in September 1976. The major strategy has been to try and cut inflation and the balance of payments deficit. The different Barre plans have used deflationary measures such as price controls and pressure on wages, increased taxation and social security contributions. While the balance of payments position improved, the run-down in economic activity implied by the plans meant that this result was achieved at the cost of rising unemployment, despite measures to help smaller firms (which might be expected to use a higher proportion of labour). Nor has inflation slowed down as fast as was hoped (it was still 9.3 per cent in August 1978). Barre's austerity measures have not been accompanied by any great attempt to spread the burden of sacrifice more evenly across French society. One way to do this might be to change the tax system, generally recognized to be one of the most unfair in Europe, because its high proportion of indirect tax penalizes the worse-off. In 1976 Fourcade, the finance minister, presented a capital gains tax bill, which was a modest beginning to reform of the tax system. The president's own parliamentary majority effectively destroyed it. Even those who believe (and they are not all on the right) that workers might be content with less material gains if offered a greater share in decision-making within the firm have been disappointed. The Sudreau report of 1975, which recommended some worker representation on management boards and was certainly an advance on the *comités d'entreprise*, was shelved after pressure from employers and parliamentarians close to them. The most that the president has been able to offer in this context is a junior ministry under L. Stoléru, dealing with 'la revalorisation du travail manuel'. This has resulted in some provisions for early retirements and shorter hours, but its major contribution to reducing unemployment has probably been Stoléru's proposal of giving lump sums to immigrant workers prepared to return home! Probably the one sector which has benefited from Giscardian social and economic policy is the old, whose basic pensions have been doubled; though it is true that these were at a pathetically low level before 1974.

In foreign policy the presidency has been marked by a desire to innovate; though as in domestic affairs, results have sometimes been hard to obtain. Breaking with Gaullism, Giscard has stated his commitment to European political and economic integration: clearly the road towards this has not been easy, given the climate of economic recession and the numerous political and economic reservations of some European leaders. Monetary union might have been one way forward, but France was obliged to withdraw from the 'snake' (an arrangement whereby the values of different currencies are not allowed to diverge beyond agreed limits), and it remains to be seen whether the 1978 Bremen proposals will revive the movement towards monetary integration. But probably the main Giscardian thrust towards integration will come not from monetary policy, nor even the direct elections to the European parliament (which the Giscardians eagerly endorse). Rather, it will come through the regular meetings of EEC heads of government and state, where common policy initiatives might be taken and presented to the European parliament. At any rate, Giscard's commitment to Europe is firm; it emerges constantly in the form of his close personal and political ties with H. Schmidt and in his repeated support for the enlargement of the EEC to include Spain, Portugal and Greece.

In a wider context, Giscard has posed as a champion of the third world (i.e. the under-developed capitalist countries), especially in Africa, where he continues a long Gaullist tradition. He was instrumental in convening the North-South conference where under-developed and industrialized countries met, with the hope of finding a more just arrangement of the world economy. The project suffered from the same problem as Giscardian domestic initiatives, viz that good intentions are no substitute for economic and political reality: in this case the fact that the prosperity of developed countries depends to a large extent on Asia and Africa remaining relatively impoverished suppliers of men and material and serving as outlets for western goods and capital. Indeed, direct Giscardian initiatives in Africa have usually been on the side of régimes that few would call progressive. In 1976 the French airforce flew Moroccan troops to Zaire to save the Mobutu régime; similarly, France has helped Mauritania repress the Polisario movement in the ex-Spanish Sahara which Mauritania and Morocco seized in 1975.

As regards the USA, Giscard has long been considered pro-American. But he has held to the principle of an independent French deterrent and has refused to rejoin NATO, however closely French forces continue to co-operate with NATO ones. It is true that in other areas of policy, decisions, such as the abandoning of the computer firm CII to the control of the US company Honeywell, do set a question-mark against technological independence and therefore against the reality of an autonomous deterrent.

Much of Giscardian policy, then, has been characterized by innovatory intentions, but without achieving a great deal of change. What impact has it had on public opinion and on organized political forces?

We shall first consider Giscard's parliamentary allies of the right. If Lecanuet's followers were content to find themselves a niche — and a generous number of ministerial portfolios — within the reformist framework proclaimed by the president, then the Gaullist UDR became progressively alienated. Their support for Giscard had been mainly negative, to keep out the left, and their task was to recover from the weak position in which Pompidou's death had left them. Under the leadership of Chirac, who progressively ousted the barons, they took full part in government for two years, until Chirac's noisy resignation in 1976. He protested that he had insufficient authority to perform his task — an odd complaint from a supporter of a régime which has never exactly been a vehicle for strong premiers. Behind his protests lay some hard truths: slowly the 'UDR state' was breaking up, with UDR loyalists being slowly ousted from key posts in the state apparatus. There was also an objection to Giscard's reforms: they implied too many concessions to the left (shades of Chaban-Delmas) and would only upset traditional supporters. Chirac favoured a much tougher approach to the left, especially the socialists (whom the Giscardians tended to treat gently, never having given up hope of winning them over): and he wanted early elections as a trial of strength. On leaving office, Chirac rebuilt the Gaullist movement as the RPR, which he launched in December 1976: with its very hierarchized structure, it was clearly intended to be the vehicle for a future presidential campaign. The struggle between the two halves of the right was now more open, and they clashed bitterly in the municipal elections of March 1977 over the mayoralty of Paris. The RPR refused to accept a single list of candidates led by the Giscardian d'Ornano; and Chirac, leading an RPR list, defeated both the left and the Giscardians in a campaign where few punches were pulled. After this victory the sniping between the rivals continued, with Chirac making maximum use of the prestige and resources of the capital, so as to display his national (or presidential?) stature, and the Giscardians for their part using administrative techniques of harassment against the new mayor (cf. their forcing him to raise local taxes so as to cover increased police costs — a measure which doubtless displeased Parisians no end).

A more serious threat came from the left. Retrospectively, the efforts of 1974 might be seen to represent the peak of left unity; but the common programme partners continued to prosper, taking 56 per cent of the vote in the 1976 departmental elections. In the municipal contest of 1977 this progress was maintained (157 large towns out of 221 were won by the left, with gains in traditionally right-wing areas). It is true that this unity lay increasingly under the shadow of squabbling, which had its roots in growing communist worries about the development of socialist strength and how it might affect their commitment to the CPG. Doubts initially raised by the disappointing results for communists (but encouraging for socialists) in the by-elections of autumn 1974 were followed in 1975 by a prolonged wrangle about events in Portugal, where since the revolution of April 1974 socialists and communists had been in fairly severe conflict. Nevertheless, the unimpressive performance of 'advanced liberalism' and the dynamic of recent results achieved in partnership kept the alliance well afloat into 1977. Commentators and opinion polls suggested that the left had an excellent chance of victory in the March 1978 parliamentary election, despite Giscard's announcement that he would not resign if this were so. But in September 1977 the left partners met again to update the CPG, now sadly out-of-date thanks to inflation. It proved impossible to reach agreement, the main sticking-points being: wage differentials; the extent of nationalizations (should all the holdings of the original nine large groups also be included? – if not, how many? Should more be added to the list?); the nature of nationalization also (how should these industries be run?); reform of local government and the finance ministry; land reform. Whatever the deeper reasons for the split (which will be discussed in the chapter on political parties), its effects were foreseeable. The left parties fought the election on separate programmes in a climate of mutual recrimination, the communists accusing the socialists of a 'virage à droite', while they riposted with charges of a return to doctrinaire Stalinism. Their credibility as potential partners in government was badly weakened. Thanks as much to this as to the appeal of their own programmes, the majority parties now fought with some hope, aided as ever by their skilful exploitation of anti-communist fears. The president himself spoke twice before polling to indicate the 'right choice', in a way which is becoming customary. Despite overall left gains on the first ballot, the bare 50 per cent it achieved was never likely to be enough on the second ballot. The socialists were particularly put out, as their vote was down 2 or 3 per cent on the figures long and consistently predicted by the polls: clearly many voters had had a last-minute change of heart. On the second ballot, transfers of votes between communists and socialists in favour of the best-placed left candidate did not occur, whereas they did between Gaullist and

Giscardian supporters. There was also a higher turn-out: the combined right scored 51.5 per cent of all second-ballot votes, but this still was enough to give it a majority of eighty-nine seats. Fear of the left, plus its own internal divisions, had saved a situation which seemed lost to the right six months before.

When the excitement subsided, France faced the future with something of a sense of anti-climax. The permanent electoral fever of the last five years, with one contest succeeding another at various levels, was past. Giscard appeared well confirmed in the exercise of his authority, with the next presidential election due only in 1981. The RPR was in no position to challenge him seriously: the left was full of recriminations between and within its constituent parties: the unions were demoralized by the absence of a left victory on which they had counted, and now faced unpromising rounds of negotiations with state and employers. It is true that a series of by-elections held during the summer (the March results having been declared null and void by the constitutional council) were all lost by the government; but that made little difference to the political situation as a whole. Barre remained premier and embarked upon a more offensive strategy of market liberalism, symbolized by the appointment to the finance ministry of R. Monory, a self-made man who owns garages in the provinces — the type of entrepreneur who is deemed to symbolize all that is desirable about free enterprise. Price controls were to be progressively abandoned ('la liberté des prix') and firms to rely less on government aid, the 'lame ducks' sinking or swimming by their own efforts. Unemployment was to be alleviated by the job-creating investments alleged to be forthcoming from increased profitability. Public service charges were raised sharply. The government believed apparently that only such rugged liberalism could help the economy adjust itself to the pressures of international competition. It is obviously too early to see the effects of this strategy; but in July 1978 unemployment ran at 1,241,000 and inflation was unlikely to be much below 10 per cent for the year. INSEE was predicting a loss of 457,000 further jobs by 1983. Many of these would be in crisis areas like Lorraine (where, liberalism notwithstanding, the government had to intervene with a rescue plan for the steel industry) and textiles (where the Boussac empire in the Vosges collapsed, with the prospect of thousands of redundancies). The problems of wine and vegetable growers in the South, facing the enlargement of the EEC, were likely to become explosive. In a report published in August 1978 the national planning commissioners drew attention to regional and sectoral decline and stressed the need for more interventionist policies in favour of the hardship areas. But in the post-March political atmosphere, their appeal was unlikely to carry much weight.

Chapter 2

The structures of contemporary France

(1) The economy

The process of industrialization in France was long and relatively complex, compared with that of other developed countries. Economic historians have some difficulty in singling out any one period of 'take-off', such as is held to have occurred in, say, Britain or Germany, i.e. a relatively short time during which, from being agriculture-based, the economy moved decisively towards domination by industry. In France it seems that from the early nineteenth century onwards the pattern was one of slow but steady industrial advances (especially in the Second Empire, early Third Republic and 1920s) without there ever having been a dramatic industrializing surge. Such industrial growth varied greatly between sectors and regions, and the reasons for the slowness are too complex to be discussed here.[1] A good index of this slowness is to look at the high percentage of the workforce employed on the land, in comparison with other countries. Clearly this high density of peasantry is important not just in explaining France's industrial lag, but also some aspects of her politics; we shall have to refer to this phenomenon later (see Figure 2.1).

Since 1945, though, industrial expansion has been spectacular, and France today is one of the foremost industrial powers. Table 2.1 shows the growth of the French GDP *per capita* over the past years, in comparison with other developed economies. Of the French GDP in 1975, a mere 5.1 per cent was accounted for by agriculture, with industry representing 37.2 per cent. The full measure of French industrial dynamism is given by looking at the growth of the GDP since the full effects of the world recession began to be felt after 1974. During 1974–6 France's GDP grew at 3 per cent per annum, the highest of all OECD countries. Japan could only manage 2.1 per cent, West Germany 0.2, the USA 0.7, and the UK showed a net regression of −0.3.[2]

Another index of industrial strength is exports; France has developed rapidly here. In 1975 she ranked fourth in the world as an exporter; one should note the low percentage of her exports that are made up by services (as opposed to manufactured goods); see Table 2.2.

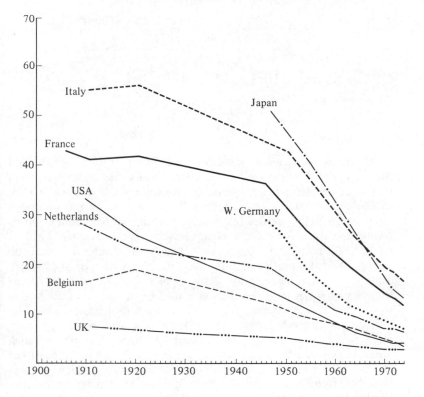

Figure 2.1   Agricultural workers as percentage of total workforce per
country, 1900–74
Source: INSEE, *Les Agriculteurs*, 1977, p.25.

Table 2.1   GDP of developed nations since 1958 (dollars)

Country	1958	1963	1966	1968	1970	1972	1974	1975
West Germany	1,085	1,649	2,026	2,276	3,106	4,244	6,216	6,872
Belgium	1,158	1,507	1,921	2,159	2,672	3,430	5,464	6,350
France		1,756	2,174	2,545	2,788	3,762	5,060	6,364
Italy	599	958	1,186	1,421	1,722	2,177	2,754	3,084
UK	1,254	1,600	1,936	1,874	2,211	2,811	3,409	4,071
USA	2,600	3,166	3,862	4,320	4,788	5,593	6,630	7,090
Japan	344	681	979	1,419	1,914	2,745	4,126	4,437

Source: INSEE, *Annuaire statistique*, 1968 and 1977.

Table 2.2   Value of French exports since 1962 (millions of francs)

	1962	1965	1968	1974	1975
Value	36,345	49,619	62,576	217,181	220,751
Index*	294	378	472	940	907

* The indices take 1949 as 100.
Source: INSEE, *Annuaire statistique,* 1968 and 1977.

At this point we might pause briefly to consider the reasons behind this exceptional economic performance. Clearly the seeds were sown in the immediate postwar years, but historians are divided in their explanations of the ultimate causes. While most admit that the plans were of some importance (especially, perhaps, British commentators trying to explain why the French economy has forged far ahead of its British counterpart), many are reluctant to ascribe overmuch influence to what was after all only a flexible, indicative type of planning. Thus for C. Kindleberger the plans were important only insofar as they helped foster or spread new attitudes among the public; if growth took place it was because the public wanted to consume more and because entrepreneurs were now on hand who were willing to invest more so as to satisfy the new demand.[3] Perhaps the spread of such attitudes is part of a wider revulsion towards the whole ethos of the 1930s, with its economic and political stagnation, which postwar Frenchmen could now see as responsible for the disasters of 1940–4. Kindleberger also draws attention to the role of 'new men' with dynamic ideas, both in the state apparatus and in business. R. Paxton has shown that some of them were not entirely new, in fact; for even under the Vichy régime there were areas where men of an expansionist, 'technocratic' outlook came to the fore, and some of them would still be influential after 1945.[4] M. Parodi insists more on another cause of growth, viz. the role of the state.[5] It provided both the infrastructural improvement necessary for expansion and also strong competition for an ailing private sector, the new nationalized sector serving as a spur to the latter. More crucial was its role as a direct investor, referred to in chapter 1, and its creation of the various social institutions of the liberation era. These were surely vital in creating among wage-earners that climate of security and confidence necessary to any phase of demand-led growth. In more recent years government policy has again been important in streamlining French industry and agriculture, with the express aim of orienting the economy increasingly towards export, i.e. towards competition with other advanced industrial states. Whatever the underlying reasons for three decades and more of economic growth, though, that growth has been impressive, and France's future as an industrial power looks more secure than that of some of her neighbours.

The most dynamic sectors of French industry today are probably chemicals (representing some 23.5 per cent of total industrial production) and certain areas of the metal-working industries, notably motor vehicles and armaments; all of these figure prominently among French exports. Sectors in decline include textiles, especially of the cheaper varieties, shipbuilding and steel (in 1977 the French steel industry showed a deficit of 40,000 million francs, or 115 per cent of its total turnover for the year). All these industries, which are quite long established, have suffered, like their counterparts in OECD countries, from the competition of emergent, more efficient rivals (Taiwan, south Korea, etc.).

A potential weakness of industry in France is its high dependence on imported energy; 'la France n'a pas de pétrole', as government advertising slogans put it. Despite her domestic production of coal, natural gas and hydroelectric energy, reinforced of late by nuclear power, France has seen a steady widening of the gap between the energy she produces and that which she consumes (see Table 2.3).

Table 2.3   French energy consumption

	1970	1972	1974	1975	1976
Home produced energy as percentage of total domestic consumption	35.2	29.1	25.4	27.6	23.3

Source: STISI (Ministry of Industry Statistical Office).

Let us now look more closely into the structures of French industry, however. Figure 2.2 shows the location of industrial activity according to the number of workers employed; in so doing, it clearly reveals some long-standing regional disparities. The heaviest industrial concentrations are clearly in the Paris region, Nord/Pas-de-Calais, the north-east and the Rhône valley; these were the original industrial areas, based on mining, metal-working and textiles. To the west of the Caen–Marseille line, there is much less industry, especially in the south-west (even here the apparently industrialized regions of Aquitaine and Midi-Pyrénées are accounted for largely by the success of two towns, Bordeaux and Toulouse, home of much of France's aerospace industry).

Regional imbalances are paralleled by imbalances in the size of firms. In general, the more developed an economy is, the higher will be the degree of concentration. By this term is meant not just mergers, whereby one firm acquires a controlling interest in another, but any arrangement whereby two or more firms pool their resources in an

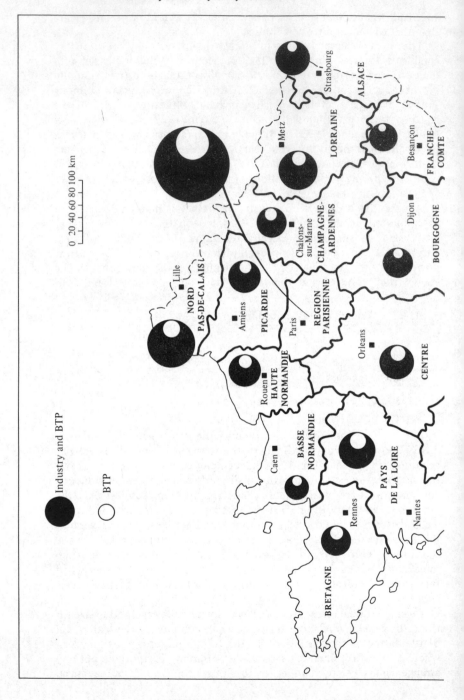

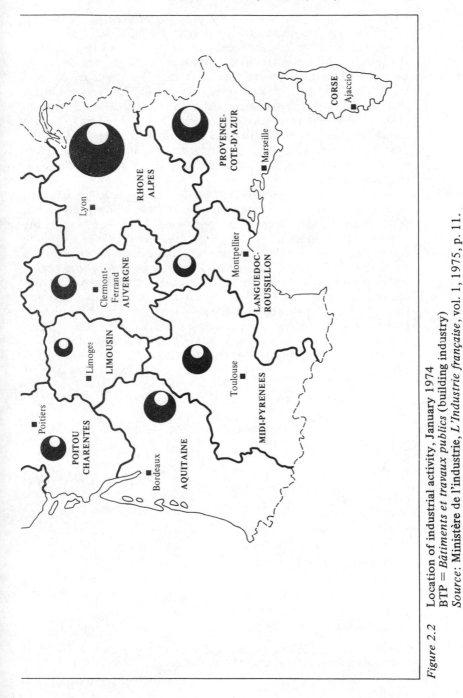

Figure 2.2 Location of industrial activity, January 1974
BTP = *Bâtiments et travaux publics* (building industry)
Source: Ministère de l'industrie, *L'Industrie française,* vol. 1, 1975, p. 11.

attempt to obtain greater efficiency and a bigger share of the market. Concentration thus includes such practices as the creation of subsidiary companies (*filiales*), by one firm or by several acting together, the grouping of numerous firms in different conglomerates or under the aegis of financial groups, the creation of networks of sub-contractors, and so on. In all such operations the aim is to corner a bigger share of the market; hence it is a tendency that is potentially monopolistic. The extent to which concentration has been taken in France shows how far economic structures have changed since 1945; its industrial structure today is a far cry from the 'Malthusian' structure of the 1930s, dominated by the small family firm, largely self-financing and unadventurous.

This means that to some extent France has a dual industrial structure. On the one hand a small number of vast groups, public and private, increasingly dominant in their sector of the economy; on the other a host of small and medium-sized firms, *les petites et moyennes entreprises* (PME).[6] Table 2.4 gives the position in 1973. In 1974 France had fourteen companies with an annual turnover above 10,000 million francs; by 1976 twelve of these figured in the top seventy-five companies outside the USA.[7] Three of them were state-owned and most of the rest candidates for nationalization under the left's Common Programme of Government. Their weight in the economy − and that of the groups of firms immediately below them in terms of size − is considerable. G. Mathieu demonstrated in 1972 that some 1,100 firms (0.7 per cent of the total) accounted for over 33 per cent of

Table 2.4   French firms by size, 1973*

No. of workers employed	No. of firms	Employees (hundreds)	Turnover in francs (millions)	Percentage of national industrial turnover
6–19	16,944	195	18.8	2.9
20–49	12,326	403	38.1	5.9
50–99	5,235	376	39.8	6.2
100–199	3,034	429	43.0	6.7
200–499	2,174	671	72.1	11.2
500–999	837	582	63.5	9.9
1,000–1,999	301	412	50.0	7.8
2,000+	201	1,962	300.3	46.7
Total	41,052	5,030	625.6	100

* Building and food industries are excluded.
Source: Ministère de l'industrie, *L'Industrie française*, 1975, vol. 1.

turnover. At the other end of the scale, 1.5 million firms (93 per cent of the total) accounted for a mere 15.9 per cent of total turnover. To put it another way, 1,300 small firms achieve less than one huge one. Concentration has gone furthest in heavy industry (steel, engineering, chemicals) and in the newer industries (oil, electronics, cars); it is relatively weak in such areas as precision engineering, furniture and clothing – in other words, hardly the leading sectors of an advanced economy.

With its growing degree of concentration, the French economy is like that of other developed capitalist systems. It resembles these in another way also – the extent of its internationalization. There are two measures of this. One is the growth of foreign trade, to which reference has already been made; the other is the penetration of foreign capital into French industry and the export of similar French capital abroad.

An increasing number of French workers are working for foreign capital within France. In 1970 it was estimated at 10.7 per cent of the workforce. Figure 2.3 shows where such capital goes; the further to the right the horizontal lines, the more that sector is controlled by non-French capital. Foreign capital favours, logically, areas where profits will be highest, i.e. industry which is, as INSEE put it, 'qualitativement concentrée, dynamique, moderne'. Until 1968 most of such capital came from the USA. Since then, with the growth of the EEC (and perhaps, to a small extent, Gaullist anti-Americanism?) the percentage of US capital in France has tended to decline in favour of EEC investment.

The countervailing tendency is for French capital to be exported overseas; like Britain, France has had, historically, great expertise in this field. Interestingly, most French capital today goes not so much to the USA or the EEC, but to under-developed capitalist countries, especially former French colonies in Africa. Thus in 1970 some 63.5 per cent of direct French investment overseas went outside the EEC and North America, most of it towards the under-developed world, where it was absorbed mainly in oil and other extractive industry. This economic link that France retains with her former possessions is reinforced by the panoply of military and political agreements which the Fifth Republic has concluded with most of its former dependencies, and the arrangement works very much to France's advantage.

This assertion is borne out when we consider France's trade balance with these countries. In 1977 French trade with the developing world accounted for some 25 per cent of exports, of which some 9 per cent went to OPEC countries; but in return some 27 per cent of French imports came from these countries, of which 17.4 per cent came from OPEC (i.e. oil). In other words, French industry needs to import from the under-developed world most of its energy, considerable

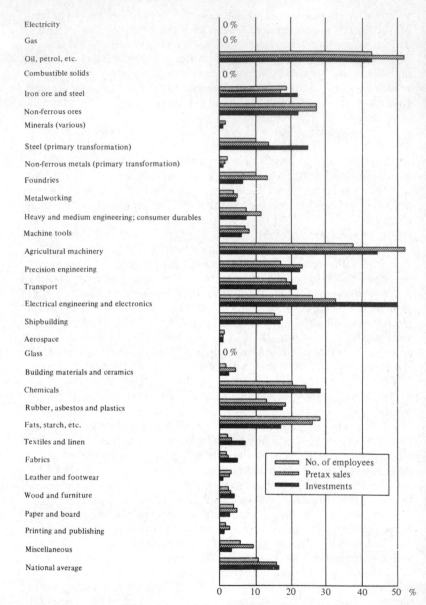

Figure 2.3   **Penetration of French industry by foreign capital, 1970**
Source: INSEE, *La Mutation industrielle en France*, vol. 1,
1975, p. 82.

amounts of raw materials (including some food) and indeed, when the economic situation requires it, quantities of immigrant labour; in return France exports to such countries manufactures (both consumer goods and some capital goods). Such a neo-colonialist or imperialist arrangement is, then, crucial to the running of the French industrial system, as of course are similar deals to virtually every developed economy (see Table 2.5).

Table 2.5 French trade with franc zone (millions of francs)

	1973	1974	1975	1976	1977 (Jan.–Apr.)
Imports	5,841	8,811	7,567	9,301	4,130
Exports	8,145	9,756	11,027	13,628	5,142
Balance	+2,304	+ 945	+ 3,460	+ 4,327	+1,012

Source: *Statistiques et études financières*, nos 343–4, July–August 1977, p. 64.

Agriculture has long occupied a privileged place in French life. For people in Britain where only 2.3 per cent of the workforce is employed on the land and where for two centuries a large proportion of food has been imported from cheap primary producers, with prices cushioned by government subsidies, agriculture is by and large something that one takes for granted. In France it is different, however; some understanding of French agricultural structures is necessary if one is to grasp some aspects of politics and society.

Exceptionally suited to agriculture by her geographical and climatic situation, France has long been a surplus producer of food and drink of high quality – both of which, incidentally, are much more highly esteemed, in every sector of the population, than in Britain. As has been explained, the exodus from the land was slower than elsewhere; even today 9.3 per cent of the workforce still works there (7.6 per cent are owner-farmers, 1.7 are agricultural labourers). Many town dwellers still have relatives in the country to whom they will go (or, more likely, send their children) for holidays. The peasantry has played an important role in French history (albeit usually one of inertia, rather than dynamism) and it has acquired over the centuries a certain ideological stock. The observer should not be misled by references to '*ploucs*' or '*culs-terreux*' that one might hear in Paris; these are more than outweighed by the veritable mythology of rural life that has become an important part of French culture, and which traverses all shades of opinion from right to left. There is in French opinion a vision of the countryman as the epitome of hard work, individual enterprise, frugality and common-sense – a reflection perhaps, even if a crude one, of what many believe to be the qualities of the nation as a whole. This vision is by no means dead, even if it is based on a shrinking reality.

For since the war the rural exodus has speeded up. The causes are those always associated with rapid industrialization. The spread of mechanization on farms, the gap between farmers' incomes and the prices of industrial goods (tractors, combine-harvesters, etc.), the difficulties in obtaining credit to cope with increasing debt – all this made it harder for the small farmer to survive. Increasingly he could either sell up and leave the land for the new factories that were springing up, or group together with neighbours in a similar plight. For only the bigger and more efficient units survived. Even the Common Agricultural Policy and measures based on the Mansholt Plan (designed precisely to humanize this relentless weeding-out of the small man) have not changed this basic fact. Farming is becoming increasingly capital-intensive and industrialized; there will be less and less room for the small producer, as Giscard d'Estaing himself has made plain.[8]

Where does this leave French agriculture today? In 1976 the activity of French farmers could be broken down as in Table 2.6.

Turning from type of production to size of farms, one finds some interesting discrepancies: other figures reveal a steady disappearance of farms at the rate of 2.7 per cent per annum over the last five years (see Table 2.7).[9]

As with French industry one notices a dualistic tendency; there are indeed 'two agricultures' in France. If we take farms of less than 20 hectares as 'small', then we see that they account for 70 per cent of the total of farms but cover only 27 per cent of the arable surface. At the other end of the scale, large farms (50 hectares and above) account for a mere 7.6 per cent of the total of farms, but cover over

Table 2.6   French agricultural production, 1976

Farms producing	Percentage of national agricultural product
Vegetables, cereals and other crops	22.6
Mixed (livestock and some crops)	18.2
Fruit, including vines	11.6
Beef and dairy cattle	28.6
Other livestock	7.1
Poultry	5.1
Miscellaneous	5.2
Total	100

Source: adapted from INSEE, *Les Comptes de l'agriculture française en 1976*, 1977, pp. 160–1.

Table 2.7   French farm sizes, 1970*

Size of farm	Number of farms (thousands)	Percentage of total farms	Percentage of total arable surface
−1 ha.	167	10.5	0.3
1–10 ha.	576	36.3	9.1
11–20 ha.	356	22.4	17.3
21–50 ha.	369	23.2	37.9
51–100 ha.	93	5.9	20.9
100 ha. +	27	1.7	14.5
Total	1,588	100	100

* 1 hectare = 2½ acres (approximately).
Source: INSEE, *Les Agriculteurs*, 1977.

35 per cent of the arable surface. On the one hand, the tendency is towards the family farm ill-equipped, technically, financially and organizationally; on the other, the industrial farm, run impersonally and efficiently, like a large corporation. There is a world of difference between, say, the ageing melon-grower of Lot-et-Garonne, working long hours on his 20 hectares to make a bare and hazardous living and the cereal-grower of the Paris basin, producing massively for the export market.

The geography of French agriculture brings this out even more cruelly. Figure 2.4 shows the strong areas with the big farms: the northern departments, Paris basin, Normandy and some of Brittany (though the latter area has many poor farms also). Equally the southwest, Auvergne, Limousin and the east in general, are all areas, not on the whole favoured by their geography, where the further decline of agriculture seems inevitable.

It remains briefly to set French agriculture in an international context. France is the leading agricultural producer of the EEC, producing 27.5 per cent of the total value added therein.[10] In Table 2.8 the high percentage of GDP accounted for by agriculture in Italy and Ireland should not mislead the reader, for in both cases the total value added is well *below* that of France. In other words, the agricultural sectors of both these countries are too large and too inefficient, compared with the French.

In terms of international trade, France does not figure among the top ten agricultural exporters; but she does occupy third place (after the USA and Canada) in the list of exporters of that key agricultural commodity, cereals.

We must also consider the 'tertiary' sector of the French economy. This accounts for an increasing part of the workforce (currently some 49.2 per cent) and covers such activities as transport, education, banking and insurance as well as the more classical activity, commerce. We

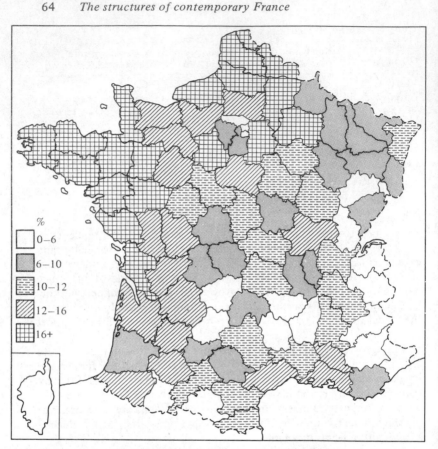

Figure 2.4   French agricultural production per department, 1975
          Source: INSEE, *Les Comptes de l'agriculture française en*
          1976, 1977, p. 115.

shall concentrate particularly on this latter sector here, because of its
rather special place in the economic and political structures of the
country.

Commerce in France bears witness in many ways to the late economic development of that country; it has many features that seem
archaic in a system that in so many other ways is ultra-modern. The
first of these is undoubtedly the very high proportion of self-employed
shopkeepers or *indépendants*, as they like to call themselves. Anyone
who has spent much time in France knows that the French use these
small and often quite specialized shops (*boulangerie, crèmerie, cordon-
nerie*, etc.) much more than do the British. Why this should be so is
hard to say. It has certainly something to do with a culture which
still places a high value on well-made things, as opposed to mass-

Table 2.8   Value added by agriculture, 1975 (millions of francs)

Country	Sum of value added	Percentage of GDP
France	71.46	5.03
West Germany	46.78	2.43
Italy	62.46	8.61
UK	20.66	2.14
Netherlands	16.56	4.83
Denmark	9.31	6.08
Belgium	7.49	2.72
Ireland	5.47	16.33
Luxembourg	0.30	2.88

Source: *Nouvel Observateur, Faits et chiffres, 1978*, p. 13.

produced but less aesthetically appealing ones, and in which stress is placed on rather formal personal relationships (cf. the mystique of 'personal service' which surrounds the shopkeeper/customer relationship). Whatever the reasons for its survival, though, *le petit commerce* has proved remarkably long-lived, even though the percentage of owners is going down steadily and that of wage-earners increasing. That this shrinkage still takes place relatively slowly is due as much as anything to the obstinacy of the *petit commerçant*, who, tightly organized in his professional associations and pressure groups and using his political muscle to the maximum, manages to delay his lingering decline: how this happens will be discussed below in chapter four. In commerce as elsewhere in the economy, the struggle of big and small goes on; here perhaps the small seem to have put up a more effective resistance. In 1974 they could still claim 69 per cent of the retail trade against bigger competitors. One could say that it is harder to classify commerce under the headings of *grand, petit* and *moyen*, as is done for industry. Not all big shops (e.g. hypermarkets) belong to large commercial groups; they may be the property of a successful individual, or group of *commerçants*. Similarly some small shops are branches of big chains. And how does one fit in the various co-operatives and groups of small shops? The essential polarity, though, is still between the big chain on the one hand and the family business on the other, between giant and 'independent'; and Tables 2.9 and 2.10 bring it out succinctly.

   Small commerce is in fact a very volatile sector, where many still feel confident enough to set up in business 'se mettre à leur compte'. None the less, even if the overall volume of commerce increases, along with the number of people employed in it, the trend is, inexorably, towards a decline in the number of small establishments.

Table 2.9   Workforce in commerce, 1962–74 (thousands)

(a) Self-employed

Secteurs d'activité	1962	1963	1964	1965	1966	1967	1968	1969	1970	1971	1972	1973	1974
Commerce de gros alimentaire	56.6	56.2	55.9	55.2	53.9	52.4	52.7	50.6	46.7	45.2	44.7	45.2	44.7
Commerce de gros non alimentaire	12.7	12.5	12.2	12.1	12.0	12.0	11.8	11.5	11.5	11.4	11.1	10.9	10.7
Commerce de gros inter industriel	16.5	16.4	16.7	16.9	17.1	17.4	17.6	17.6	17.8	17.9	18.1	18.8	18.8
Ensemble commerce de gros	85.8	85.1	84.8	84.2	83.0	81.8	82.1	79.7	76.0	74.5	73.9	74.9	74.2
Succursalistes alimentaires	11.9	11.9	12.0	11.9	11.7	11.6	11.5	11.5	11.4	11.4	11.2	11.2	11.1
Coopératives	4.1	4.1	4.0	4.0	4.0	3.7	3.6	3.7	3.6	3.4	3.3	3.2	3.2
Grds mag. mag. populaires, VPC*	11.8	12.2	12.4	12.6	12.8	13.0	13.2	13.5	13.5	13.4	13.3	13.2	13.1
Commerce de détail concentré	27.8	28.2	28.4	28.5	28.5	28.3	28.3	18.7	28.5	28.2	27.8	27.6	27.4
Commerce des viandes	112.7	111.8	112.1	111.3	109.8	109.2	107.5	105.0	102.9	101.3	99.4	97.7	96.3
Détaillants spécialisés alimentaires	167.4	162.2	158.0	153.6	148.5	144.7	137.9	127.8	120.9	116.5	112.2	198.4	104.9
Détaillants spécial. non alimentaires	203.3	204.9	206.4	207.6	207.4	202.8	202.5	205.7	204.5	205.0	205.4	205.0	204.8
Pharmacies	16.3	17.5	18.0	18.5	18.6	17.7	18.2	20.5	21.1	21.4	21.8	22.9	22.4
Commerce non sédentaire	73.9	74.7	75.1	75.6	75.6	75.3	74.1	72.2	70.2	69.7	70.6	70.5	69.2
Ensemble commerce non concentré	573.6	571.1	569.6	566.6	559.9	549.7	540.2	531.2	519.6	513.9	509.4	403.6	497.6
Ensemble commerce de détail	601.4	599.3	598.0	595.1	588.4	578.0	568.5	559.9	548.1	542.1	537.2	531.2	525.2
Ensemble commerce	687.2	684.4	682.8	679.3	671.4	659.8	650.6	639.6	624.1	616.6	611.1	606.1	599.2

(b) Wage-earners

Secteurs d'activité	1962	1963	1964	1965	1966	1967	1968	1969	1970	1971	1972	1973	1974
Commerce de gros alimentaire	186.0	202.1	204.2	209.8	215.4	214.9	213.6	220.5	224.4	224.1	228.6	233.2	235.6
Commerce de gros non alimentaire	121.4	130.9	135.3	140.4	146.5	151.4	154.9	160.2	167.2	177.6	188.3	196.4	201.1
Commerce de gros inter industriel	180.8	197.4	208.9	217.3	224.9	230.0	238.2	254.0	267.7	279.2	293.1	307.7	317.9
Ensemble commerce de gros	488.2	530.4	548.4	568.0	586.8	596.3	606.7	634.7	659.3	680.9	710.0	737.3	754.6
Succursalistes alimentaires	53.7	61.6	69.0	74.3	79.1	85.9	90.9	97.9	106.7	113.3	118.8	124.9	130.1
Coopératives	39.4	39.3	40.1	40.4	40.6	41.9	42.9	43.2	43.6	44.8	45.3	45.7	45.4
Grds mag. mag. populaires, VPC*	89.2	94.1	102.6	110.0	113.5	117.5	118.0	126.0	128.8	121.1	118.0	117.1	116.9
Commerce de détail concentré	182.3	195.0	211.7	224.7	233.2	245.3	251.8	267.1	279.1	279.2	282.1	287.7	292.4
Commerce des viandes	83.6	87.0	85.9	87.9	89.7	90.5	88.1	83.8	81.4	80.7	78.9	76.9	75.9
Détaillants spécialisés alimentaires	50.9	56.3	60.7	65.2	65.3	65.9	68.2	71.3	75.8	79.7	85.6	91.7	94.2
Détaillants spécial. non alimentaires	308.9	329.8	343.4	359.5	367.9	377.5	380.8	385.5	396.5	408.7	424.0	438.5	447.0
Pharmacies	40.5	41.2	42.3	44.4	46.1	48.0	49.5	51.4	54.4	56.7	59.1	63.3	64.5
Commerce non sédentaire	15.2	15.4	15.7	16.8	17.7	18.4	18.3	17.9	17.8	18.0	18.3	18.3	18.4
Ensemble commerce non concentré	499.1	529.7	548.0	573.8	586.7	600.3	604.9	609.9	825.0	643.8	665.9	687.7	700.0
Ensemble commerce de détail	681.4	724.7	759.7	798.5	819.9	845.6	856.7	877.0	905.0	923.0	948.0	975.4	992.4
Ensemble commerce	1169.6	1255.1	1308.1	1366.5	1406.7	1441.9	1463.4	1511.7	1564.3	1603.9	1658.0	1712.7	1747.0

*VPC = *Vente par correspondance* (mail order).
Source: Commissariat général du Plan, *Rapport de la commission commerce, services, artisanat* (Documentation française, 1976), p. 88.

Table 2.10   Shares of retail market taken by big and small commerce
(percentages)

	1968	1969	1970	1971	1972	1973	1974
'Grand commerce' (commerce concentré, plus grandes surfaces indépendantes et mixtes)	24.6	25.3	26.7	27.5	28.6	30.0	31.0
'Petit et moyen commerce' (commerce indépendant traditionnel y compris les grands établissements specialisés)	75.4	74.7	73.3	72.5	71.4	70.0	69.0
Total	100	100	100	100	100	100	100

Source: Commissariat général du Plan, *Rapport de la commission commerce, services,
artisanat* (Documentation française, 1976), p. 100.

The situation in 1978

Although French agriculture still occupies a relatively strong position,
there are underlying problems that could become very serious. Within
the export sector, wine and spirits retain their important place; so
does sugar beet, produced mainly on the big northern farms. But
France is already a net importer of some meat (pork and mutton)
and of fruit and vegetables (350,000 and 250,000 million NF deficit
respectively in the 1977 balance of payments). No doubt the promised
loi cadre on agriculture will have to direct producers into these areas;
it will also have to stimulate the whole of the food industry. This
IAA (*industrie agro-alimentaire*) which backs up the farmers is much
less efficient than its European neighbours, owing to insufficient
concentration. Change must proceed along such lines if French agriculture is to achieve its full potential and become 'le pétrole français'.

There are also deeper problems, notably the inequality between
farmers; differentials between the incomes of big and small probably
run from 1 to 33; land prices, rising faster than farmers' incomes,
make it hard for the small to expand or the young to set up in the
first place. In wine-growing in particular, there is massive disorganization, with over-production of *gros rouge* and producers facing rising
costs, declining markets and competition from cheaper Mediterranean
products. Drastic but subtle surgery will be needed if disturbances
are to be avoided in the south, as the decline continues. All these
problems will require political solutions, and it is not easy to see
where these might come from.

Industry for its part has one notable problem, apart from the sectoral ones outlined above. In recent years, as the recession made itself
felt, unemployment has bitten hard into western Europe – well beyond
the 4 per cent of the workforce that capitalist economists consider to
be inevitable anyway. France has been no exception to this rule.

In October 1977 the government admitted to 1,110,200 unemployed. Such figures are obviously always disputed; thus in March 1977, the government claimed 1,021,000, whereas the International Labour Office said 1,100,000 and the CGT said 1,405,000. Whichever figure one takes, though, it is clear that unemployment is high, and shows no sign of diminishing substantially. Unemployment hits at the young and the less qualified (white-collar rather than manual). But even the managerial strata (*cadres*) are sufficiently affected for their unions to be worried (see Tables 2.11 and 2.12).

The government's answer to such problems after the 1978 elections was a traditional one. By progressively dismantling price controls (an operation referred to as 'la vérité des prix'), the government hoped that prospects of increased profitability would stimulate investment and thereby create jobs. The struggling industrial sectors could not expect much in the way of help. Whether such classical liberal remedies could have the desired effect remains to be seen.

(2) Social stratification

Who are the people, then, who carry out economic activity in France? France has always had a distinctive population structure, compared

Table 2.11   Unemployment trends in France since 1965 (thousands)

	1965	1967	1968	1970	1974	1975	1976
Unemployed	142	196	254	262	498	840	934
Unfilled vacancies	30	32	36	93	205	109	124

Source: OECD, *Economic Surveys, France 1976-7*; INSEE, *Bulletin mensuel de statistique*, November 1977.

Table 2.12   Unemployment in France by socio-economic group (CSP)

	1975		1976	
	Absolute number	as percentage of CSP	Absolute number	as percentage of CSP
Employés	202,790	5.6	259,040	7.0
Ouvriers	381,790	4.7	436,300	5.5
Cadres moyens	79,560	2.6	101,870	3.5
Cadres supérieurs	79,000	2.0	31,660	2.1
Agriculteurs	25,590	1.2	27,740	1.3
Recherche 1e emploi	299,800	–	307,770	–

Source: INSEE, *Enquête sur l'emploi, 1975*, p. 65; ibid., *1976*, p. 53.

Table 2.13   Comparative trends in fertility in Europe, 1861–1939*

	1861–70	1881–90	1901–10	1930–4	1935–9
France	26.4	23.9	20.6	17.0	14.8
Germany	37.2	36.8	32.9	16.3	19.4
England	35.2	32.5	27.2	15.8	15.3
Italy	36.9	37.8	32.7	24.5	23.2

* Birth-rate taken per 1,000, approximately.
Source: I. Thompson, Modern France: a Social and Economic Geography,
    Butterworths, 1970, p. 4.

with her neighbours; in particular, observers have been struck by the
very slow rate of population growth through the nineteenth and
twentieth centuries. Demographers cannot agree as to why this should
have been so; among the many and highly varied explanations adduced
are the effect of military service in delaying marriages, the inhibiting
effects of an agriculture-dominated economy, the desire to limit
property-fragmentation among heirs, or even the generally timorous
nature of élites; whatever the reason, the French were for a century
and a half 'Malthusian', not wishing to procreate. World War I compounded an already serious demographic weakness, and it has been
calculated that if the French population increased at all between
1801 and 1939, then this was only because (a) people lived longer
and (b) immigration was encouraged (see Table 2.13).

   The turn-round began after 1945. Encouraged by the pro-natality
policies of post-liberation governments, especially family allowances
first promoted systematically by Vichy, the French procreated rapidly
for some twenty years in the famous 'baby boom'. At the same time,
as years would elapse before the new babies could join the workforce,
and as expanding industry needed rapid supplies of labour, the
traditional policy of immigration was continued. Now immigrants
came increasingly, not from Italy or eastern Europe as before 1939,
but from the Iberian peninsula, North Africa and later on, Black
Africa. Immigration accounted for roughly one-third of the post-
war population increase. Over the last few years, the fertility boom
has slackened off, and the French seem to be returning to a level of
procreation near to that of the thirties. INSEE has calculated that
by the year 2000 the population of France would still be below 60
millions (see Table 2.14).

   The last census was taken in 1975. It estimated the French population to be 52,599,430 – an increase of 5.8 per cent on the 1968
figure. Distribution by age and sex, together with the proportion of
working population within either of those categories, is shown in

Table 2.14   Average number of births per annum in France, 1945–62

	Total	per 1,000 population
1945	643,000	16.2
1946–9	860,650	21.1
1950–3	825,150	19.6
1954–7	806,300	18.5
1958–62	822,840	18.0

Source: C. Dyer, *Population and Society in Twentieth-Century France,* Hodder & Stoughton, 1978, p. 134.

Table 2.15. Of the total population in 1975, some 48 millions (93.5 per cent) were French; of the 6.5 per cent of foreigners, 1.4 were Algerian, 1.4 Portuguese and 0.9 Spanish. These foreigners represented some 7.3 per cent of the working population (and only 6.5 per cent of the total population), proving that France, like other countries, admits immigrants basically because the economy needs labour.

Since 1968, some long-term trends are confirmed. Inhabitants of rural communes continue to diminish as a percentage of the population; they tend also to become older, as younger country people migrate to the towns and their suburbs. This phenomenon seems most marked in the Massif Central and the south-west, where departments like Gers and Lozère lose population steadily (see Table 2.16).

Turning to the economic activities of the population, we find the classification given in Table 2.17 (the figures from the 1954 census are given so as to show up the rapid change in the socio-economic structure). These figures are in fact based on the socio-economic grouping CSP (*catégorie socio-professionnelle*). The CSP was developed by INSEE as a standard measure of social stratification, and it is advisable for any student of French politics and society to become familiar with it, as it is the basis of most surveys, opinion polls and the like. But the CSP does have its shortcomings as a means of social analysis, for it clearly privileges economic status or the nature of one's employment as a determinant. In so doing, it avoids what is in our view a much more crucial social determinant, class.

Although a much less visible or measurable structure than the CSP, class exists in France, as it does anywhere else. Much of what happens to an individual will in the last analysis be decided by the class into which he/she is born or might move, thanks to various mechanisms of social mobility. This is not to imply that class is a cast-iron framework which produces immediate and visible effects on individuals; rather, the whole process by which people's lives are structured by their class-position is a much more subtle and complex one than rather caricatural views of the above kind would suggest.

Table 2.15   French population by age and sex, 1975

Year of birth	Age at 1.1.76	Total population Both sexes			Males			Females		
		Total	%	No. working	Total	No. working	% (o)	Total	No. working	% (o)
1971–5	0–4	3,424,210	6.5		1,752,645			1,671,565		
1966–70	5–9	4,185,945	8.0		2,138,455			2,047,490		
1961–5	10–14	4,299,265	8.2		2,196,590			2,102,675		
1956–60	15–19	4,242,255	8.1	1,012,235	2,162,380	571,255	26.4	2,079,875	440,980	21.2
1951–5	20–24	4,211,185	8.0	2,884,400	2,127,530	1,508,555	70.9	2,083,655	1,375,845	66.0
1946–50	25–29	4,390,285	8.3	3,465,035	2,264,060	2,132,150	94.2	2,126,225	1,332,885	62.7
1941–5	30–34	3,060,575	5.8	2,350,895	1,594,795	1,550,085	97.2	1,465,780	800,810	54.6
1936–40	35–39	3,022,335	5.7	2,255,620	1,553,940	1,512,070	97.3	1,468,395	743,550	50.6
1931–5	40–44	3,270,555	6.2	2,402,875	1,657,915	1,605,670	96.8	1,612,640	797,205	49.4
1926–30	45–49	3,312,455	6.3	2,409,000	1,663,055	1,586,255	95.4	1,649,360	822,745	49.9
1921–5	50–54	3,203,030	6.1	2,231,685	1,567,415	1,445,380	92.2	1,635,615	786,305	48.1
1916–20	55–59	2,011,740	3.8	1,230,845	971,880	794,625	81.8	1,039,860	436,220	41.9
1911–15	60–64	2,466,590	4.7	990,900	1,148,250	623,945	54.3	1,318,340	366,955	27.8
1906–10	65–69	2,442,120	4.6	343,275	1,093,285	208,040	19.0	1,348,835	135,235	10.0
1901–05	70–74	2,096,545	4.0	118,595	882,345	67,615	7.7	1,214,200	50,980	4.2
1900 or before	75 or over	2,960,340	5.6	79,500	969,895	37,030	3.8	1,990,445	42,470	2.1
Total		52,599,430	100.0	21,774,860	25,744,475	13,642,675	53.0	26,854,955	8,132,185	30.3
1956–75	0–19	16,151,675	30.7	1,012,235	8,250,070	571,255		7,901,605	440,980	
1911–55	20–64	28,948,750	55.0	20,221,255	14,548,880	12,758,735	87.7	4,399,870	7,462,520	51.8
1910 or before	65 or over	7,499,005	14.3	541,370	2,945,525	312,685		4,553,480	228,685	

% (o) = percentage of same sex or age-group.
Source: INSEE, *Recensement de la population de 1975* (1 in 5 sample).

Table 2.16   Population decline in rural departments, 1968-75

	Population 1975	1968	Absolute loss	Loss as percentage
Gers (total)	175,366	181,577	−6,211	−3.4
Urban communes	61,223	58,156	+3,067	+5.3
Rural communes	114,143	123,421	−9,278	−7.5
Lozère (total)	74,825	77,258	−2,433	−3.1
Urban communes	24,131	23,315	+ 816	+3.5
Rural communes	50,694	53,943	−3,249	−6.0

Source: INSEE, *Principaux Résultats du recensement de 1975*, 1977, p. 48.

We shall attempt in the brief space available to try and hint at the importance and the complexity of social class. Classes arise, historically, with economic development. In any mode of production (a structure in which men, tools and materials are brought together so as to transform by their labour natural objects into objects that satisfy needs), there is no 'pure' economic activity, with production taking place in some neutral, technical vacuum; production always involves social relations between those engaged in it. Such relations involve domination by some, and subordination on the part of others; here is where classes have their origin. It is important to realize that they arise, and remain, in antagonism. Now, social relations pivot on the control of the means of production (land, labour, materials and, as development proceeds, capital – which represents the accumulated labour of previous workers). In the capitalist mode of production, currently dominant in the world, the dominant class will be that which possesses or effectively controls the major means of production, i.e. it is essentially a capital-owning bourgeoisie. This contrasts with a working class which owns neither capital nor any other means of production, but sells its labour-power to the bourgeoisie in return for wages. The latter never fully cover the labour input which the worker has contributed to the productive process, however; and it is this extra unpaid labour (taking concrete form as money or capital) that enables the original capital invested to reproduce or to expand itself. Workers and bourgeois are the two fundamental classes of any developed social formation, and all other social groups need situating with reference to them.

But if ownership (or not) of the means of production is the prime determinant of social class, there are others also. Crucial in our view is ideology. As classes emerge, they secrete an ideology, i.e. a certain view of society and of their relation to it; such ideology can go very

Table 2.17   Population by economic activity, 1975 and 1954

CSP	1975 Number	Percentage
Agriculteurs exploitants	1,605,865	7.6
Salariés agricoles	375,480	1.7
industriels	59,845	0.3
artisans	533,635	2.5
maîtres pecheurs	15,835	0.1
gros commerçants	186,915	0.9
petits commerçants	912,695	4.2
Patrons de l'industrie et du commerce	1,708,925	7.8
professions libérales	172,025	0.8
professeurs, professions littéraires et scientifiques	377,215	1.7
ingénieurs	256,290	1.2
cadres administratifs supérieurs	653,755	3.0
Professions libérales, cadres supérieurs	1,459,285	6.7
instituteurs, profs. intellectuelles	737,420	3.4
services médicaux et sociaux	298,455	1.4
techniciens	758,890	3.5
cadres administratifs moyens	970,185	4.5
Cadres moyens	2,764,950	12.7
employés de bureau	3,104,105	14.3
employés de commerce	736,595	3.4
Employés	3,840,700	17,6
contremaîtres	443,305	2.0
ouvriers qualifiés	2,985,865	13.7
ouvriers spécialisés	2,946,860	13.5
mineurs	73,444	0.3
marins et pecheurs	38,280	0.2
apprentis ouvriers	106,690	0.5
manoeuvres	1,612,725	7.4
Ouvriers	8,207,165	37.2
gens de maison	234,355	1.1
femmes de ménage	154,100	0.7
autres personnels de service	855,035	3.9
Personnels de service	1,243,490	5.7
artistes	59,075	0.3
clergé	116,945	0.5
armée et police	347,980	1.6
Autres catégories d'actifs	524,000	2.4

CSP	1954 Number	Percentage
Agriculteurs exploitants	3,983,840	20.8
Salariés agricoles	1,151,520	6.0
Patrons de l'industrie et du commerce	2,295,840	12.0
Professions libérales, cadres supérieurs	554,240	2.9
Cadres moyens	1,139,540	5.9
Employés	2,078,480	10.9
Ouvriers	6,465,100	33.8
Personnels de service	983,870	5.1
Autres actifs	499,040	2.6
Total	19,151,470	100%

Sources: INSEE, *Recensement de la population de 1975* (1 in 5 sample);
Recensement de 1954, pp. 58–9.

deep and have wide ramifications. Often, many members of a class will endorse a whole ideology, or large parts of it, without ever realizing it; many aspects of their lives (moral beliefs, work situations, personal relationships even) they will interpret quite spontaneously in ideological terms. Ideologies exist, and although they vary from one social formation to another, their core can usually be identified. They help to give stability and cohesion to classes and class-fractions.

Ideology as a basis of class seems to us more crucial than other factors sometimes adduced, e.g. income level, life-style, access to various desiderata. Such factors can, however, be useful adjuncts to class consciousness in that they help to reinforce basic feelings of belonging (or not). We shall therefore discuss them briefly later; the ideologies of different classes are probably best left to the chapter on political forces.

Finally it should be stressed that classes are not massively homogeneous. On the contrary, they are differentiated within themselves, probably increasingly so. A century ago 'the capitalists' seemed much easier to identify as a social group; so did the workers and the peasantry. The growing complexity of capitalist development obliges the analyst to be more nuanced, though, and to locate within each class layers or fractions, whose relationships are often quite conflictual, as they contend for overall hegemony. Indeed as new types of economic activity emerge, it can be quite difficult to place those who practice them firmly in one class.

Given these reservations, then, we can perhaps reinterpret the French CSPs of 1975 in terms of social class. This analysis will deal with the working population only.

The pivot of French society is clearly the most numerous class, the working class, some nine million strong in 1975. It includes all those engaged *directly* in the production of material goods and in the auxiliary activities vital to such production. It is located essentially, then, in agriculture, industry, transport, public works and construction and its work is largely manual (though one must beware of over-facile distinctions between 'manual' and 'intellectual' work, as will be seen). Three layers are often distinguished within the class; the top bracket consists of three million OP (*ouvriers professionnels*), or OQ (*ouvriers qualifiés*), as they are often called. These are skilled workers who have served an apprenticeship, and they command higher wages and prestige. Below them come the OS (*ouvriers spécialisés*) – a misleading term, since such workers are specialized in nothing except the execution of one narrow, repetitive task, usually on the assembly-line. For this they require little training; the English term 'semi-skilled' would be a very loose equivalent. Today there are some three million OS located mainly in the key industries (two-thirds of the total workforce in cars and electronics, over one-half in steel). Many of them are immigrants.[11] At the bottom are the *manoeuvres* — over one and a half million totally unskilled labourers.

The working class is a class that largely reproduces itself. Table 2.18 shows the origins of workers in 1964; over one-half had worker fathers. The remainder came mostly from agriculture, and the traditional petty-bourgeoisie, reflecting thereby the decline of those sectors. Very few (some 3 per cent) had fathers from the upper reaches of society.

Increasingly, the working class is female, with a high concentration of women in *manoeuvre* and OS jobs — a reflection of the demand for cheap labour by new, often provincial, industry. Thus in 1975, women represented 26.8 per cent of the total of OS, and 38.1 per cent of unskilled labourers.

Such then is the French working class; its hard core is in the established industrial areas, probably in factories with large numbers of employees. This core tends to provide the union and political élites of the class. But the diversity of the class and the fact that it is continually evolving, should not be forgotten.

If it is easy to identify the working class, then this is not true of its counter-pole, the bourgeoisie. Who does control the major means of production and exchange in France, and how numerous are such people? The census lists some 60,000 industrialists and over 180,000 *commerçants*. Many of these will, however, be in a fairly small way of business and cannot really be counted at the top end of the bourgeoisie. On the other hand, many of the upper reaches of the *professions libérales/cadres supérieurs* could be, either because of their level of capital ownership, their economic decision-power or their expertise, which is necessary to the continuation of the social system. Such professionals (who need of course to be distinguished from the rest of their CSP) would include senior experts (technical, legal, etc.), senior managers (in public and private sectors alike) and certainly the

Table 2.18   Origins of workers' fathers by CSP, 1964 (percentages)

Ouvriers	51.6	
Agriculteurs	19.1	
Petits commerçants, artisans	9.8	
Employés	9.8	
Salariés agricoles	6.7	
Cadres moyens	1.7	
Industriels, gros commerçants	0.7	2.9
Cadres supérieurs	0.5	
Total	100	

Source: INSEE, *Economie et statistique*, February 1970.

top echelons of the different parts of the state apparatus, whether repressive (police, army, judiciary) or ideological (media, education). These figures are sometimes referred to as 'faux salariés', i.e. although notionally wage-earners, as with managing directors, say, they in fact derive most of their income from surplus produced by others. In addition there are still a number of the more traditional type of capitalists, who live simply off dividends from shareholdings; these would appear in terms of CSPs as part of the non-working population! At any rate, in so far as it is possible to identify a ruling class in France, then it is comprised of these groups. They would probably amount to some 300–500,000 people.

Such a class is by no means monolithic, of course. There seems to be one very obvious split between the big and medium-sized bourgeoisie. The latter comprises the owners of medium-sized capital, whether industrial, financial or commercial; to it would be assimilated part of what Gramsci called the 'intellectuals': those from the middle ranks of the professions and state apparatus, as described above, whose activities are cultural or administrative and who are so necessary for maintaining the hegemony of a class or class-fraction within civil society (i.e. the process whereby such groups secure, by non-violent means, the consent of the mass of the population to their rule). By antithesis, the big bourgeoisie comprises the representatives of the biggest forms of capital, plus the very summit of the state apparatus, consisting of a few tens of thousands at most. It is distinguished from the medium-sized bourgeoisie primarily by the extent of the capital that it controls;[12] within its ranks the dominant force is that of finance capital. In the view of theorists such as Quin and Morin, there are some twenty financial groups which effectively control the major part of French industry and commerce; and this phenomenon is at the heart of what the PCF calls monopoly capitalism.

According to this analysis, the tendency within any one sector of economic activity is towards concentration of capital-ownership. This will eventually entail monopolistic domination of that particular sector of the market, for this is seen as the only way in which capital, once invested, can reproduce itself with sufficient profit. One can identify some 200 monopolistic groups in France, and within their ranks, finance capital (banks, finance houses, etc.) has increased its penetration. It should be pointed out that formal ownership is not the only means of assuring effective control over the operations of a concern; thus while monopoly capital has made little direct penetration into such fields as agriculture or construction, it often exercises decisive control here by influencing, say, the supply of materials or the marketing of eventual products. F. Morin has shown[13] the hold of finance capital over many sectors of the French economy. Penetration by foreign capital extends naturally into the monopolistic sector. Thus Quin claims that in 1971 fifty-six of the top hundred companies in France were effectively controlled by non-French big capital. Here lies clearly a major source of potential conflict.

Theorists of monopoly capitalism see this tendency as a long-standing and inevitable one within capitalism; they give the theory another dimension when they speak of monopoly state capitalism. We shall discuss the full implications of this theory later, in connection with the PCF, but briefly, such theorists see the state as a ready and willing tool of monopoly groups. By direct aid (contracts, subsidies, etc.), by economic policy (prices and incomes, taxation), by use of its own economic power (using the public sector as a 'crutch' for private capital) the state is seen as helping the drive towards con-centration of capital and monopoly. Clearly such a theory takes no account of any measure of autonomy that the state might develop with regard to capital.

Such, then, is the bourgeoisie in France. What of the groups be-tween it and the workers? These are not easy to classify. The 3.8 million *employés* (white-collar wage-earners, in industry and com-merce, performing mostly subaltern tasks with little power of initiative or decision) and the 1.2 million service workers are unhesitatingly counted as 'proletarians', along with the working class, by sociologists like Baudelot and Establet. Although they do not enable capital to expand itself, as do workers (rather, their function is to transfer or distribute such capital), they are none the less exploited in their work, as are workers, and often their working conditions are similar. This seems to us however to ignore the cultural or ideological difference between white-collar and productive workers, predicated largely, as Poulantzas has shown, on the distinction between 'manual' and 'intellectual' work. Although this distinction is less and less relevant in reality, it is always likely to induce white-collars to see themselves as distinct from workers.[14] Hence it is advisable to see them as part of the petty-bourgeoisie. With them would need to be counted the bottom end of the professions, the *cadres moyens* and most of the engineers and technicians; these latter categories are mostly wage earners, even if their income and conditions of work are usually superior to those of the lower white-collars. Baudelot and Establet believe that there is a tendency for petty-bourgeois working in the public sector (teachers, lower civil servants, etc.) to develop a different mentality from that of their equivalents in the private sector; but this hypothesis should be treated with some caution.

If such categories comprise the new petty-bourgeoisie, resulting from a development of production that demands more and more auxiliary services, then they still coexist with the old petty-bour-geoisie. This consists of the artisans, the small businessmen and the shopkeepers described above. Although they own their means of production or exchange (shop, small business, etc., usually family-run and employing less than five workers), they are effectively subordinated to bigger capital which allots them their modest place in the economy, usually by controlling either their supplies or their outlets. Clearly there is a parallel between their class-situation and that of the numerous small farmers. And like its newer variants, the traditional petty-bourgeoisie occupies a sandwich position between the capitalist class and the workers.

If we were to redraw the map of French society in terms of class, rather than of CSPs, we would probably get something like this:

bourgeoisie   — *industriels*
                 grands commerçants
                 cadres supérieurs
                 top of *professions libérales* and *agriculteurs*

petty-
bourgeoisie   — rest of *professions libérales; petits*   old petty-
                 commerçants; artisans; (agriculteurs)   bourgeoisie
            — *cadres moyens;* top technicians; *employés;*   new petty-
                 most *personnel de service;* most *autres*   bourgeoisie
                 actifs

working class — *salariés agricoles*
                 ouvriers
                 most technicians
                 some *personnel de service*

If any definition of social class must start with production relations, there are many other factors involved outside the workplace which can help in different ways to reinforce feelings of class. How much one earns: what sort of life-style one can afford as a result: what access to culture or education one has: where one lives. These factors are important in anyone's life and can always impinge on his/her way of looking at themselves and their relation to society. Without claiming that all members of a class experience reality in the same way, it does seem to us that there is a fair degree of similarity in the conditions that most members of a class are likely to experience in their everyday lives, and that this similarity can be measured; in other words there is a material foundation to class present in everyday life, even if individual members of a class perceive it to different degrees, if at all.

At the risk of simplification, one can single out several factors that help solidify French society into classes. Taken on their own, they would not necessarily prove anything. Taken together, though, they show up a consistent pattern which suggests that the famous social 'inequalities' about which so much debate rages in France are not the effects of accident or economic misjudgment, but necessary symptoms of a deep-lying structure whereby the productive system reproduces itself from one generation to the next, allotting individuals places in the classes and fractions that compose society. By way of illustration we shall look at income, education and (in the widest sense) patterns of consumption.

It is a commonplace to point out that economic growth has led to a steady increase in purchasing power *per capita* for all sections of the population (roughly 3.3 per cent per annum since 1960). This overall increase conceals a big hierarchy, however. Just looking at wage-earners, the average yearly wages per CSP in 1973 were as in Table 2.19. For the self-employed, the figures were as stated in the same table (though they are not fully accurate, because less is known about them than about the income of wage-earners. In particular, the members of families of farmers and shopkeepers, the *aides familiaux*, contribute large amounts of notionally unpaid labour).

It will be objected that the modern welfare state irons out these discrepancies by taxation, allowances and the like. Even after such transfer payments have been completed, though, and despite a small narrowing of differentials between groups and within any one group over the past ten years, the overall hierarchy of income is still clear enough (see Table 2.20).

A significant point here is the high incomes not just of the self-employed but also of *cadres supérieurs*, most of whom belong, as

Table 2.19   Income by CSP, 1973 (francs)

(a) *Wage-earners*

Cadres supérieurs	101,200
Cadres moyens	49,300
Employés	28,950
Ouvriers	26,400
Salariés agricoles	26,160

(b) *Self-employed*

Industriels	195,000–215,000
Professions libérales	190,000–195,000
Gros commerçants	140,000–150,000
Artisans	70,000–75,000
Petits commerçants	65,000–70,000
Exploitants agricoles	c. 40,000

Source: CERC, *Les Revenus des Français*, 1977, pp. 300–1.

Table 2.20   Income per household after tax and transfer payments, 1976

	Average pre-tax income per household per annum (francs)*	Tax deducted as percentage	Transfer payments as percentage of compensation	Disposable income (francs)
Professions indépendantes	157,000	−26.5%	+18%	127,500
Cadres supérieurs	159,000	−42	+11.5	100,500
Cadres moyens	92,000	−44.5	+20	69,300
Agriculteurs	81,000	−23	+19.5	78,000
Employés	72,000	−45	+23	56,500
Ouvriers	68,000	−49	+29.5	54,500
Salariés agricoles	55,000	−46	+34	48,000
Inactifs	20,500	−48.5	+150	41,000

* The differences between column 1 of this table and the previous tables are explained by the fact that the previous tables are based on individual income, whereas this one treats the income of households. Also, the label 'professions indépendantes' is an amalgamation of numerous *bourgeois* and *petit-bourgeois* categories under one heading.
Source: CERC, *Les Revenus des Français*, 1977, p. 303.

we saw, to the top bourgeois stratum. If we take the average wage of the top 10 per cent of non-working-class wage-earners (mainly *cadres supérieurs*, in fact) and the bottom 10 per cent (*employés*), we will find that the ratio between the two is 5 to 1 in France, compared with 2.8 to 1 in the UK or 2.3 to 1 in West Germany.[15] So even on the level of income the bourgeoisie, or part of it, stands out. The same is true of the petty-bourgeoisie (e.g. *cadres moyens*), as compared with workers; the difference between the average wage of each group being 63 per cent higher than that in the UK and 57 per cent higher than that in West Germany.[16]

Similar hints are provided by examination of French taxation. A tax system usually provides insights into the political and social structures of a country. The most striking thing about France is that a high proportion of tax receipts comes from *indirect* tax (mainly VAT); this percentage was calculated at 65.6 in 1972, as against 33.5 per cent from direct taxes on incomes (in Germany the figures were 50.9 and 48.7 per cent respectively[17]). As indirect tax, unlike a progressive tax on incomes, covers most basic items such as food and clothing, it hits all social categories equally. In other words the French state has always preferred to raise its revenue by penalizing the lower classes more than the higher.

Even within the income tax hierarchy, there are some striking discrepancies. One could cite those of the spectacular kind that can probably be found in most developed countries, though perhaps not

quite to the same extent as in France, e.g. the ratio of 1 to 105 between the income of an old age pensioner (479 francs per month in
1974) and one of the top 10,000 taxpayers. (The real gap is probably
bigger for it is universally admitted that opportunities both for legal
evasion and actual fraud are high at the top end of the tax scale.)
But more significant perhaps is the fact that the bottom 42.4 per
cent of taxpayers (representing some 21.5 per cent of the total population) held 21.1 per cent of taxable income in 1975; what they paid
in tax represented 8.7 per cent of government receipts. At the other
end of the scale some 4.43 per cent of taxpayers, representing 2.23
per cent of the population, held 19.1 per cent of taxable income;
but what they paid in tax came to 43.5 per cent of total receipts.
To put it another way, some 470,000 households (the core of the
bourgeoisie, surely) accounted for over half the receipts, whereas
22.8 million others (working class and different *petit-bourgeois* fractions) paid in only one-third. Of the latter, 10.7 millions did not in
fact earn enough to be taxed.[18]

So the fiscal system again sheds light on class structure, both by
the way in which it privileges indirect tax and by the hierarchy within
taxpayers. But if this suggests a certain material basis to class, what
can we learn from other areas of everyday life?

We might start by considering the availability of a commodity
that most people consume at some time in their lives, viz. education.
The intention here is not to give a detailed breakdown of the education
system in France (this will be done in chapter 6) but to show how
education contributes to the reproduction of social classes across the
generations. Inspired by the euphoria of rapid growth, some observers
assumed that this growth would necessarily increase social mobility,
i.e. people would be able to rise more or less freely out of the class
or CSP of their parents, thanks to the 'equality of opportunity' af-
forded by an expanding education system. The higher your qualifications, the better your job; all you had to do was obtain these qualifications. But that would happen if you were good enough to deserve
them. Recent theorists have argued, however, that although a few
people might rise socially in accord with this meritocratic vision, they
tend rather to be the exception that reinforces the rule. Parkin suggests
that much social mobility in western Europe takes place on the margin
of the lower petty-bourgeoisie and the upper reaches of the working
class, often between generations; moves from very high up the social
ladder to very low down are rare.[19] By and large it emerges that in
France, as elsewhere in the developed world, education is mainly a
process whereby, in Poulantzas's phrase, individuals are assigned places
in the relations of production, or if one prefers to put it thus, are
prepared for insertion into one class or another.

It has long been realized that upper-class children are abnormally highly represented in higher education, with a corresponding under-representation of the children of lower groups, notably workers and farmers. But we know now that this process has its roots in the second-ary school. This is the place where future careers are effectively chosen and where, for all the apparent egalitarianism of the CES, bourgeois children will mainly tend to get into the academic streams, leading to university and better jobs; most working-class and white-collar children will gravitate towards the technical streams, which lead mainly to work in industry and services at the age of sixteen. Various explanations were initially given for this (pressure from teachers, ignorance of parents about the relationship between qualifications and employ-ment, etc.) but increasingly these came to be fitted into a deeper sort of analysis. Theorists such as Baudelot and Establet realized that the process of guidance (or selection?) of children was much more systematic; the school was seen as the place where the productive system allotted roles to the rising generations, where the future bour-geois, petty-bourgeois, workers (and unemployed?) were to be shaped. They claimed that there were really two education systems, running in parallel – PP (*primaire/professionnel*) and SS (*secondaire/supérieur*) – and that most children would be firmly embarked on one or the other by the last year of primary school. PP led through the technical stream to worker or low-white-collar jobs; SS led on to university and a position of *cadre* or above. Although there were exceptions, most lower-class children tended to be PP, most upper-class ones SS. In between the two main streams it was possible to discern a third stream, producing mainly *petits-bourgeois*; in it one found most of those working-class children who did better, and the less successful bourgeois children. In other words, this was the place where such limited social mobility as existed would occur. At any rate, in 1966 a working-class child had a 54 per cent chance of being PP and only a 14 per cent one of being SS; for a bourgeois child the odds were almost the exact reverse.

The Bourdieu school laid emphasis on the hidden constraints within education, showing how much success is not a matter of mastering a neutral body of knowledge, thanks to one's innate ability, but more of an ideological matter, involving implicit skills. They stressed the acquisition of what they called 'cultural capital', i.e. a whole series of codes, social and linguistic, which teachers and, later on, others in authority will expect 'good' pupils to know. To put it crudely, success in education is not so much what one knows as how one expresses it. What teachers call 'gifted' pupils are really ones who have an articu-late mastery of these codes, which of course are transmitted mainly through family mechanisms. Thus bourgeois children are obviously best placed to inherit this cultural capital, essential if one is to climb to a high place within society, because only their families possess it in the first place.

Even the few who make their way out of the lower classes to university are not guaranteed a brilliant social future. For the job market steadily demands new qualifications, which only those in the know will be aware of. Thus for some years degrees in arts and pure science have been losing value, whereas economics degrees seem to lead to good jobs. Yet of the lower-class children in university, a high percentage are to be found precisely in arts faculties. Moreover, as access to the best economics courses depends on having the maths *baccalauréat* C, the competition to get into this stream is acute; indeed for Alain Touraine this is one of the key points where social reproduction takes place. It is legitimate to suppose that lower-class children are by and large not preponderant in the C stream.

One is led to conclude then that the education system is a place where classes compete for the life-chances of their children but where, *pace* the ideologists of social mobility, the privileged position of the dominant class and its ability to reproduce itself are not greatly threatened.

Where people live can often influence their view of their place in society, as can their ownership (or not) of their home. Table 2.21 shows that property ownership does tend still to be the preserve of the

Table 2.21   French households, 1973: owners and occupiers (percentages)

| CSP | Renting accommodation | | Housed free | Owners | Owner-occupiers |
	Total	Incl. HLM* tenants			
Agriculteurs exploitants	2.5	(0.1)	26.3	56.4	14.8
Patrons	34.5	(2.9)	4.9	35.1	25.5
Inactifs	34.5	(6.3)	12.8	48.1	4.6
Salariés agricoles	27.9	(2.7)	41.7	18.7	11.7
Personnel de service	55.4	(15.2)	18.5	14.8	11.3
Autres actifs	51.2	(15.1)	30.1	5.2	14.5
Professions libérales, cadres supérieurs	41.5	(5.6)	8	16.3	34.2
Cadres moyens	37.1	(14.7)	9.9	10.3	29.7
Employés	58.3	(20.6)	7.6	12.9	21.2
Ouvriers	55.7	(18.7)	7.7	14.3	22.3
Moyenne nationale	43	(11.3)	11.5	28.1	17.4

* Habitations à loyer modéré: corresponds roughly to British council housing.
Source: INSEE, *Données sociales, 1978*.

Table 2.22   Characteristics of accommodation in the 1970s by CSP (%)

	Uncom-fortable	Over-crowded	Far from workplace	Second homes
Agriculteurs exploitants	64.5	11.4	–	1.6
Salariés agricoles	60.0	17.2	–	–
Industriels	3.7	3.9	5.6	17.7
Petits industriels et artisans	26.4	6.3	3.4	12.1
Patrons pêcheurs	25.4	3.6	7.1	–
Gros et moyens commerçants	17.5	3.8	3.5	17.7
Petits commerçants	36.3	8.2	3.5	10.0
Professions libérales	2.3	3.2	5.9	30.6
Professeurs et professions littéraires et scientifiques	7.4	4.2	14.4	9.2
Ingénieurs	3.7	3.7	15.5	28.3
Cadres administratifs supérieurs	3.9	2.8	13.2	19.9
Instituteurs et professions intellectuelles diverses	12.7	5.5	11.7	6.6
Services médicaux et sociaux	14.5	2.4	12.5	6.6
Techniciens	10.8	8.0	19.0	13.8
Cadres administratifs moyens	10.8	5.9	15.7	13.0
Employés de bureau	24.8	8.5	18.0	7.7
Employés de commerce	25.9	10.2	14.4	16.6
Contremaîtres	18.3	9.0	12.7	3.5
Ouvriers qualifiés	31.8	14.7	16.0	4.8
Ouvriers spécialisés	40.8	15.7	15.3	
Mineurs	48.0	4.8	13.8	6.2
Marins et pêcheurs	23.3	12.7	8.5	
Apprentis et ouvriers	53.0	8.5	–	–
Manoeuvres	54.5	20.1	15.2	2.4
Gens de maison	61.7	8.5	8.7	
Femmes de ménage	65.3	4.1	13.3	6.5
Autres personnels de service	38.3	12.1	12.5	
Artistes	19.1	11.5	12.1	9.2
Clergé	34.7	4.7	5.4	6.6
Armée et police	16.0	6.7	11.3	9.9
Etudiants et élèves	39.5	16.2	11.1	12.6
Militaires du contingent	28.9	30.2	16.4	
Anciens agriculteurs	80.1	4.8	1.0	2.9
Retirés des affaires	33.1	1.1	1.0	
Retraités du secteur public	41.3	2.0	1.0	5.2
Anciens salariés privés	68.0	5.7	1.0	2.9
Inactifs de moins de 17 ans	60.1	0.0	0.0	–
Inactifs entre 17 et 64 ans	48.1	11.0	2.4	1.2
Inactifs de plus de 64 ans	61.2	1.9	0.3	2.6

Source: *L'Expansion*, March 1978.

upper groups in society, though the number of owner-occupiers among workers and the newer *petits-bourgeois* is growing, as France develops the mortgage system familiar in the English-speaking countries. Again, these figures say little about the different quality of housing available to social groups, or the fact that for the upper groups a second home is increasingly prevalent. Table 2.22 shows figures that do bring out the hierarchy that exists in this domain.

Recent research has also confirmed that the area in which people live has much to do with social class.[20] The authors distinguish several possible ways in which the areas of a town can be divided among bourgeois, petty-bourgeois and workers, and indeed among the subgroups thereof; what is always certain, though, is that towns are divided along these class lines, and measurably so, with differential access to various amenities for social groupings.

There are many other factors of life-style that point up the way in which social classes are structured and structure their members. Let us consider access to medical services (cf. Table 2.23). As well as enjoying unequal access to medicine, social classes are unequal before death (cf. Table 2.24).

Patterns of cultural consumption show a similar hierarchy, even if one refers to things as anodine as visits to the theatre or reading newspapers (Table 2.25).

What emerges from all this is that social classes are quite clearly structured in France; there is a clear hierarchy within and between classes. J. Marceau sums up well the ways in which class structures people's lives when she says of the workers, small farmers and white collars that they earn least (but contribute most to social transfer payments), have least income security (and the highest risk of unemployment), have the least capital, the fewest consumer goods and

Table 2.23   Annual access to health facilities by CSP, 1970

	Visits to specialists	Prescriptions
Agriculteurs exploitants	66	1,375
Salariés agricoles	38	1,087
Patrons de l'industrie et du commerce	95	1,504
Professions libérales, cadres supérieurs	177	1,866
Cadres moyens	123	1,884
Employés	122	1,808
Ouvriers	78	1,328
Inactifs	112	3,122

Source: INSEE, *Données sociales, 1974*, p. 213.

Table 2.24 Life expectancy by CSP, 1971

CSP	No. of survivors at 75 years for every 1,000 at 35 years	Life expectancy at 35 years
Instituteurs	574	40.9
Professions libérales, cadres supérieurs	551	40.5
Clergé catholique	524	39.5
Cadres moyens (public)	518	39.3
Techniciens	507	39.0
Cadres moyens (privé)	489	38.5
Agriculteurs exploitants	473	38.0
Contremaîtres	472	37.8
Ouvriers qualifiés (public)	446	37.3
Employés (public)	448	37.2
Artisans et commerçants	460	37.6
Employés (privé)	448	37.4
Ouvriers spécialisés (public)	406	36.0
Ouvriers qualifiés (privé)	380	35.6
Salariés agricoles	356	34.8
Ouvriers spécialisés (privé)	362	34.7
Manoeuvres	310	32.9
National average	412	36.1

Source: G. Desplanches, *La Mortalité des adultes suivant le milieu social*, INSEE, 1976, p. 13.

Table 2.25 Cultural activity by CSP, December 1974 (%)

	(a)	(b)	(c)	(d)
Agriculteur	61.2	21.1	8.7	1.5
Patron de l'industrie ou de commerce	60.2	17.2	20.8	14.6
Professions libérales, cadres supérieurs	61.1	57.2	65.3	35.8
Cadres moyens	57.9	34.6	48.9	33.5
Employé	60.4	18.8	36.3	12.0
Ouvrier qualifié/contremaître	54.3	10.7	24.7	7.4
OS/manoeuvre/personnel de service	50.0	12.2	26.3	6.0
Femme inactive de moins de 60 ans	41.5	9.0	28.9	13.1
Inactif de 60 ans et plus	66.3	14.1	19.9	8.6
National average	55.1	16.6	28.4	12.1

(a) reading a daily newspaper; (b) reading a social or political periodical; (c) reading twenty books per annum on average; (d) having visited theatre once in past year.
Source: INSEE, *Données sociales, 1978*, p. 310.

the shortest holidays. They participate least in leisure and cultural activities, and above all they know very little about their position of deprivation compared with other social groups.[21] Of such realities is class, in France and elsewhere, made.

(3) Political culture

In any social system, we can identify what is often called a political culture. By this is understood a set of political values (beliefs about the nature of that particular society and the ways in which it runs – or should run – its affairs). Such a culture is an historical product and depends on the classes and fractions that make up the society in question; it is in fact a distillation of different ideologies that has taken place over a period of time.[22] Hence it is more appropriate to speak of a series of sub-cultures in any one society, rather than to imply the existence of one uniform, national political culture. Amid these contending sub-cultures, however, one can see a number of common threads running. A bourgeois may have a concept of the nation, say, that is different from that of a worker; but both do have a concept of nation. It is this common core of concern that we shall try to identify in this section.

Such an exercise is essential if one is to have an understanding of French political behaviour; there is after all a strong connection between what people feel about politics and how they are likely to act in the political system. Indeed we would say that for France the political culture is doubly important. In most areas of French life, not just in politics, discussion and argument are more prominent than in Britain; the French are less ready to concede a point and can usually defend their ideas articulately. Often too the level of such debate is different from that of Anglo-Saxon countries in that people are much readier to conceptualize and to analyse – and this is valid for many sectors of the population, not simply for intellectuals. In short, much French political debate takes place at a higher level of explicitness and self-consciousness than in Britain. Thus the outsider needs to become familiar with the assumptions and values of those conducting the debate.

Given this, we can now try to identify some of the constants of French political culture – all of which are refracted in different ways and for different purposes, by the ideologies of the different groups and classes of French society. Most of these constants have their origin, logically enough, in the period that saw the birth of modern France – the Revolution of 1789. This affected the social and economic structures of France, her political system and her ideological structures. Socially, the Revolution confirmed the loss of hegemony within civil society by a declining nobility, to the advantage of what one is obliged to call a bourgeoisie of property-owners, timid and fragmented though it was; at the same time, the peasantry, acquiring noble and church lands, emerged as a class in its own right, the most numerous and the most inert in France. In the later stages of the Revolution, the movements of the *sans-culottes* and *babouvistes* showed that the urban population of small traders, artisans and manual workers was beginning to emerge as a social force to be reckoned with. Politically, the Revolution saw the change from the *Ancien Régime* (personal power of a monarch, based on divine right) to something approaching a constitutional monarchy, and then to a republic with an attempt at parliamentary government. This gave way, under the pressure of foreign invasions, to the 'patriotic dictatorship' of Jacobinism (highly centralized rule by a small élite, supposedly incarnating the national will). Later, when the emergent bourgeois fractions could not reconcile their differences by any of these systems, Bonapartism arrived to guarantee order. Based on personal power and the creation of a powerful and efficient type of state machinery, it combined in a unique mixture the support of the new propertied élite and the peasant mass. Although its duration was brief it gave France a series of basic institutions – administrative, legal, educational – that would prove remarkably long-lived.

In short, in the quarter-century after 1789, France saw the emergence of a socio-economic structure that would change only slowly over the next 150 years (although the struggle between social classes was unrelenting and often more violent than elsewhere in Europe), and of a series of political régimes (republic/constitutional monarchy/ Bonapartism) that would alternate with regularity. Needless to say, at the level of ideology or value-systems, similar bases were laid. The Revolution saw the emergence of a number of ideologies which express the aspirations of different classes or fractions. Leaving aside the *ultra* theories (total opposition to the Revolution and return to a divine-right monarchy), which were steadily losing influence from the early nineteenth century onwards, the two main ones could be clearly seen to be liberalism (for economic freedom, based on property: for political and civil liberties and political participation, though by no means extended to all), and, in a crude but recognizable form, socialism (opposition to a régime based on property and demands that individual welfare be taken in hand by the collectivity). Of course these value systems would undergo modification throughout the succeeding centuries, in the light of social and economic change, as well as of political experience. None the less the Revolution is the fountain-head of these value systems which are still very vigorous (as witness their bitter clash in the 1978 general election).

As well as changing social and political structures and secreting these value systems, the Revolution also raised two other issues which seem to cut across class cleavages. One is the question of the Catholic church and its role in the French social and political system; the other is the problem of the nation. What is the nation? What values does it stand for? Who incarnates these? On both the religious and the national questions, the Revolution began a debate that is still going on.

Let us now look in detail, then, at these problems which the Revolution raised and which have become constants of French political culture. First, the question of the régime. Textbooks on French politics, especially those written by Anglo-Saxons, delight in pointing out the number of régimes France has enjoyed since 1789 (fourteen, not counting the provisional governments in between régimes) and contrasting this lack of political consensus unfavourably with the solid basis enjoyed by the monarchy in the UK or the presidency in the USA. Why is there this lack of agreement about the régime?

Discounting the racial or cultural type of explanation that one sometimes still hears (i.e. the French, like other Latins, are volatile and unstable by temperament, and this inevitably comes out in their political behaviour), it seems to us that there are sound historical reasons for this uncertainty. Ideally, each change of régime would need a full analysis of all the short- and long-term factors that contributed to its demise, but in the brief space available, some general hypotheses can be put forward. The first of these concerns the type of bourgeoisie that emerged from the Revolution: composed of professionals, administrators, commercial and financial elements, which had increased their strength under the *Ancien Régime*, it had been above all an acquirer of land. Gains realized in commerce and various forms of speculation during the revolutionary period were promptly immobilized in landed property, which became the key to political influence (access to the electoral register was proportionate to the amount of property owned until 1848). What did *not* emerge was a dynamic, industrializing bourgeoisie. Frightened by the chaos of the revolutionary years, content with the comfort and power it had acquired, this 'Malthusian' bourgeoisie wanted not further change but stability. Having taken power illegally itself, it felt insecure and was always looking over its shoulder, as it were, to see if there were other social forces ready to supplant it in its turn. This bourgeoisie was also divided as to the nature of the régime. If most of the July Monarchy *notables* favoured the constitutional monarchy with restricted suffrage, others favoured the republic based on universal (male) suffrage; it would take until 1870 for the latter view to prevail.[23] These internal differences were of course subordinated to what the various bourgeois fractions had in common, viz. defence of property; hence their readiness to accept a *régime d'exception* (Bonapartism) when threatened from below. But on occasions (notably

1848) their differences could be serious enough to endanger the régime and their own class-domination for a while.

It is probably this timidity that explains the reluctance to broaden the political basis of the early régimes (in 1848 there were only 250,000 electors from a population of 36 million). It also explains why any economic or political demands from lower classes, such as those of the emergent working class in the 1830s, were repressed, either by legislation (combination laws) or violence (use of the armed forces in 1834–6). The coalition of bourgeois forces that ruled France in the early nineteenth century had, then, some difficulty in assuring its hegemony (i.e. securing passive assent to its rule and thus making reliance on force unnecessary); a symptom of this is the chronic difficulty which it experienced in forming a party or parties to canalize its parliamentary strength. This meant that any concessions had to be wrung out of the political system by force; hence very often the régime had to collapse before concessions were obtained (e.g. the July Monarchy falls in 1848, after which universal male suffrage was conceded; the Second Empire collapses in 1870 as the price for the return to a fully parliamentary régime).

Such changes were often facilitated by three other factors. First, the high specific weight of Paris within French life. All major aspects of French life − culture, politics, administration, business − had their source in Paris, which dominated the passive and largely under-developed provinces. Crises occurred first in Paris, where it was possible for a revolutionary élite to mobilize the high number of under-privileged inside the capital and seize power. This could not last long, however, for soon the dead weight of peasant France, rallied by the overthrown *notables* would make itself felt and repression set in (June 1848, May 1871).

That this pattern could be repeated in the nineteenth century proves the importance of another factor, the slow rate of industrialization, to which reference has already been made. This meant that there was no sudden arrival on the political scene of a proletariat (i.e. a large manual working class, employed in big units of production and developing a strong class-consciousness and political organizations to correspond to it). On the contrary, rural exodus was slow, the growth of working-class consciousness and organizations tardy and fragmented. Hence the sense of political stagnation and *déjà-vu*, and the possibility for the ruling fractions to recover situations that seemed to be escaping from them.

A third important factor is the foreign invasions which France has experienced and which have often compounded domestic tensions to produce the reversal of a régime (cf. the collapse of the Second Empire in 1870 or the installation of the Vichy régime in 1940).

In short, these frequent changes of régime are best explained by the nature of the post-Revolutionary ruling class and the type of opposition, domestic and foreign, which it faced. Now, such uncertainty about the régime has had much to do with determining political stances, and it is far from being dispelled. If it is true that the republic has had general acceptance since 1870, and that since 1958 economic modernization, the emergence of a presidential executive and the increasing bipolarization of party politics have apparently forced most Frenchmen to accept the logic of the Fifth Republic, then it is equally true that this Republic has worked so far only because the right has enjoyed uninterrupted power. Who can guarantee that had the left won the 1978 general elections, the much-vaunted consensus of the past twenty years would have continued? Perhaps France might already be moving, *de facto* if not *de jure*, into that Sixth Republic of which so many commentators have spoken.

The role of the church in French politics is also a long-standing issue. In Britain the relationship between religion and the state has been relatively easy for a century and a half, the established Protestant church coexisting comfortably with the state, as does the large Catholic minority. In Ireland of course — a country whose political culture is in many ways more similar to that of France than to that of Britain — the problem is posed more acutely. The French church was, before the Revolution, a privileged ally of the monarchy, occupying key positions in the state apparatus in return for moral and ideological support. The Revolution made an attempt to make the church more subordinate to the political authorities and in so doing began a battle which has never entirely finished. It centred on control of the education system, and it entailed an ideological quarrel which is part and parcel of the political culture. Because the church or its leaders at least tended to favour anti-republican régimes, republicans (and later on socialists and communists) built up an image of the church as a kind of anti-republic, a sort of lay version of Antichrist. Intellectual bases for this opposition were provided by the 'positivist' or 'scientiste' doctrines of early republicanism, which laid stress on human reason and implied that all phenomena could be explained scientifically, thus doing away with any need for the supernatural, or 'superstition' as they often called it. Such doctrines also pointed out that Catholic theories implied a natural and immutable hierarchy in the universe, which they contrasted unfavourably with their own theories of natural equality (whatever the shortcomings of these in practice, especially in the economic field). Catholics reacted accordingly, and to the republican stereotype of the Catholic as reactionary, servile and superstitious corresponded a Catholic myth of the republican as socially subversive, dictatorial and atheistic. Now although the Third Republic showed — particularly by the 1905 Act of Separation, which reduced the church from the rank of an ideological apparatus to something ressembling that of a sundry pressure-group – that republican democracy and Catholicism could coexist, the process of rapprochement was to take a long time. It would take the Resistance of 1941–4 and the emergence of a christian democrat political movement to confirm it. Even today, however, it would be simplistic to believe that the 'clerical question' is dead. There are still parts of France where politics are determined primarily by religious alignment or lack of it, and practising Catholics still vote in the majority on the right. In the 1978 elections, for instance, it seems that if the left did less well than expected in the west (one of the most Catholic parts of France) then this failure had something to do with skilfully exploited fears that the socialists had designs on the autonomy of 'free' (read Catholic) schools.

Nationalism occurs in all political cultures. Here the word is taken in a restrictive sense, i.e. a set of beliefs about one's nation and what it represents. In most political systems rulers will use some kind of nationalism to legitimize their rule; it may well be that a polity cannot remain in existence without the propagation of such sentiments. This propagation need not, however, take place directly or obviously – through formal instruction in schools, say. There are many more oblique means whereby nationalist values can be passed on to the citizenry, and the feeling of 'belonging' reinforced.

What is striking about French politics, though, is precisely the openness with which national sentiments are displayed compared with, say, the discrete way in which the British propagate their nationalism (though obviously this latter statement is becoming progressively less true). Today no major French political force dare take its distance publicly from nationalist sentiments (i.e. they all have to proclaim allegiance to the principle of 'France first'), though in private members of the political class can be heard to talk differently. It is true that what France incarnates for a Gaullist is not perhaps the same as what she represents for a communist; but both seem to employ nationalist rhetoric with equal ease.

The reasons for this go beyond the recent success of Gaullism and its revival of xenophobic sentiments, sloganized as *l'indépendance nationale*. Gaullism was simply building on a capital of nationalist feeling that existed since the Revolution. When the Revolutionaries began to construct a new kind of state, they came into conflict with other European powers attached to the *Ancien Régime*. The massive popular mobilization which resulted and which saved France from defeat succeeded probably because the participants knew that basic patriotic or national feeling (defence of one's soil) was inseparable from defence of a new kind of political system. Already, then, French nationalism had acquired this extra dimension of value.

From its republican and progressive origins, though, French nationalism was to undergo changes. The defeat by Prussia in 1870 led to a revival of the nationalist problematic, but this time on the right.[24] For theorists like Barrès and Maurras, the French decline was attributable to the republican form of government and the equalitarian theory on which it rested. A return to a régime of authority and hierarchy was needed; essential Frenchness lay in these qualities. Nationalism moved away from the left, but remained a burning problem, the more so as France was now acquiring an overseas empire second only to Britain and the schools were busy imbuing the rising generations with ultra-patriotic (and anti-German) values, in preparation for a war of revenge. Every political force had to define itself in terms of nationalism: for or against France? If for, then what sort of France? The problem was given a further twist with the emergence of socialist and then communist movements, in theory supra-national ('the worker has no country'). Even these were forced progressively, however, to present themselves in terms acceptable to an increasingly nationalist public opinion.

Since the Second World War, nationalism has bitten deeper if anything into French political culture. The humiliating defeat of 1940, Vichy, occupation and collaboration: the rise of the USSR and USA as super-powers, with the consequent decline of western European nations: the traumatic loss of the French empire after 1945 have all left their mark on at least one generation. All these events raised the question: what does France stand for? In short, given the peculiar historical experiences of the French over the last two centuries, it hardly seems surprising that the debate about nationalism should be so open and that no one can escape participation in it.

It was remarked earlier that Napoleon created much of the state machinery of modern France. It would be more accurate to say that he continued *Ancien Régime* traditions, notably those of Louis XIV, i.e. the use of a highly centralized administration, headed by a trained élite, capable of carrying the state almost irrespective of the nature or abilities of the government. Centralization means that important decisions are taken in Paris and as little initiative (and resources) as possible are allowed to lower tiers of administration elsewhere. In theory this is supposed to be more efficient because decisions are taken by the most enlightened; in practice, as those who have experienced it at first hand know, the lower one descends the administrative chain, the more frequent are the restrictive practices, blockages and inefficiency. It is certain, as Wright and others have shown,[25] that the potential power of the state is never as great as its real influence; none the less, the average Frenchman is conscious that the state casts a big shadow across his life and his relationship with it is in some ways odd.

Its presence appears in apparently anodine things, such as the use of identity cards, which must be produced on the demand of a policeman. This card is the most important of a series of official papers which French people carry with them in wallets specially made for the purpose. In this respect they are like most of their fellow-Europeans, for the majority of European states, east and west, have developed high degrees of administrative centralization. The author has heard French people say that they felt undressed without '*les papiers*'. This symbolizes in a way the close relationship of state and citizen; the state guarantees, literally, the citizen's identity. The state guarantee is, moreover, the only one that counts. In education, for instance, a teacher applying for a post in Britain would have to show references from someone in the professional hierarchy, but might well not be asked to show a degree certificate. In France, the opposite is true. The state is not interested in the opinion of private citizens as to the suitability of X or Y, only in its own proof of competence – in this case a certificate approved by the minister of education. (Usually the original must be produced; if not, a *copie conforme* is acceptable, provided it is stamped by some authorized state representative.) This is a small point, perhaps; but it does illustrate the difference between two systems, in one of which the state keeps its distance from the citizen, whereas in the other it intervenes more directly in his life.

This relationship with the state is ambiguous. On the one hand the state is seen as a benefactor: it dispenses credits, employs on a big scale and for a long time was seen as the classic means of social mobility by the lower classes. On the other it seems remote: often its local intermediaries are inscrutable or evasive: there seems to be something oppressive about this distant but powerful machine. So there is often a sort of reluctant tolerance of the state, without the individual ever giving it his full loyalty – a state of mind well evoked by the Radical philosopher Alain.

This mentality is often linked up with the fact, much stressed by such as Hoffmann[26] and Crozier,[27] that the French have always taken much less part in voluntary associations than the Anglo-Saxons, preferring to allow the state to occupy a maximum of terrain within civil society and making periodic insurrectional forays against it when it is felt to be deaf to sectional demands or plain oppressive. This is probably less true now than at any time. Wright has shown that the relationship between state and groups is much more fluid than the Hoffmann style of analysis suggests. At any rate, the major current demands of right and left (whether Giscard d'Estaing's plea for a 'décentralisation hardie' or the *autogestionnaire* strategy of the socialists) reflect growing impatience with what is felt to be the all-pervasiveness of the state. Whatever the reality of the relationship between state and citizen, it still looms large in the consciousness of many Frenchmen.

The special historical development of French society after 1789:

the nature of the régime: the problem of the church: the question of the nation: the relations of state and citizen — these would seem to be the constants of French political culture. All groups and forces will in their political activity have to refer, consciously or unconsciously, to these factors. How this process takes place will be seen below.

Chapter 3

The political framework

(1) The problem of constitution

The question of a constitution may seem at first glance to the apolitical student to be somewhat obscure, full of meaningless details which have little to do with any kind of reality. Yet the problem of the constitution has loomed large in French life for the best part of two hundred years. Ever since the Revolution of 1789, France has been searching for political stability and has sought it, via a written text, from several traditions in her history and political thought.

The British reader may ask at this point why a written constitution is necessary, but this is how the French define a constitution. (The dictionary definition being: charters, fundamental texts which determine a country's form of government.) This is the essential difference between the political traditions of Britain and France (and most other countries), in that the British constitution is not written. The average Briton knows that British society is, to a greater or lesser degree, governed by certain institutions (a monarch, a prime minister and his cabinet, a parliament, comprising a lower and an upper house). One who is more politically aware may also know that these have evolved over centuries, without there being any document which specifically confirms their existence as such. Since, too, there has been no revolution in Britain since the mid-seventeenth century, we may not unreasonably describe the British political tradition as being one of political stability. This tradition also has an effect on the political mentality of the British who, by and large, do not feel the need to call in question or to abolish British institutions, however much they may wish to see these altered.

Such is not the case in France which has had a large number of written constitutions since her first one in 1791. This has a number of important consequences: (a) unlike Britain, there is a different political tradition, one of instability and change brought about by revolution and (b) more important, the mentality that is engendered by such a situation. When a constitution has to be written, there is inevitably a need for great clarity of thought, and the choice which is finally arrived at implies a recognition of political values. Sophisticated as this approach may be, it also comprises within it an element of instability, since there can be no absolute conviction that the constitution will last. 'Les Français sont souvent comme le Poète: les pieds à peine sur terre et la tête dans les Etoiles. Spécialement dès qu'ils évoquent la Constitution, dont ils ont si souvent changé: ils rêvent toujours de la prochaine, tout en se référant à la défunte qu'ils ont fini par comprendre, tandis qu'ils vivent présentement avec un autre texte' (M. Jobert, 'Le partage du pouvoir exécutif', *Pouvoirs*, no. 4, 1978, p. 7).

Once a régime is established, it must face up to the supporters of its predecessor, it must inculcate into the nation at large a respect for the new institutions. It may be possible to assume general approval for the new régime, if there has been a referendum, for example, but this does not mean a pledge of undying support from a nation whose history has, since 1789, seen régimes come and go at an average rate of once every twelve years. Consequently, the political parties and groups all have to explain their situation *vis-à-vis* the institutions existing at the time, which cannot be taken for granted, as they tend to be in Britain.

In creating a constitution, both the *form* and the *nature* of government have to be considered. Form here is taken to mean the external appearance of power, as in (a) a monarchy (rule of one), whereby power is, to a greater or lesser degree entrusted to one individual, and handed on to a successor via the hereditary principle, or in (b) a republic, where again, as a rule, there is one individual – a president – holding a greater or lesser degree of power, but who has arrived at that pitch of eminence by process of election for a specific number of years. More important than the form, however, is the nature of government. The first distinction to be made here is also the most fundamental: a government is either free or it is not, which means that it permits or forbids the exercise of the basic human and civil rights. However, such a basic distinction can be modified in various ways. A government, whether republic or monarchy, may be described as authoritarian, if virtually all political power is in the hands of one individual, without there being any checks to limit its use (arbitrary power). On the other hand a government may be parliamentary, i.e. where most power is in the hands of the law-making body of elected representatives known as the legislature or parliament (comprised of one single assembly, or an upper and a lower house) and where the executive derives its authority to act from parliament. Inasmuch as this form of government derives its power from the election of national representatives, it may reasonably be assumed that it will ensure the preservation of the basic freedoms since it must, every so often, face an electorate at the polls. However, although a parliament is an elected body, this does not necessarily imply that the whole nation is involved in its election; there is therefore one further element which a constitution-maker may wish to take into account — democracy, which means that the nation as a whole has a substantial say in the election of its government. Normally we may expect to find in a parliamentary democracy a head of state, with purely formal and ceremonial duties, an executive comprising a prime minister and a ministerial team, taken from the majority opinion in the legislature, and deriving its authority from the legislature, to whom it is responsible. In opposition to this form of government, one might consider a 'presidential' system, with power stemming from the president himself. Furthermore, a government may be composed of varying and contradictory elements and merely tend more in one direction than another. Theoretically at least, an authoritarian government may be democratic as well, and some authorities would claim that a government may be both parliamentary and presidential.

Before the Revolution of 1789, there was no written constitution; France was governed by a hereditary monarchy in which, although there was provision for consultation by the king of the nation's representatives in assembly (the *Etats-Généraux*), the monarch himself was the fountain-head of all power — judicial, legislative and executive. This was particularly the case in the seventeenth and eighteenth centuries, when the monarchy is usually described as absolute. It was in 1789, even before the drafting of a new constitution, that different approaches to government were envisaged, specifically in the *Déclaration des droits de l'homme et du citoyen* (26 August 1789). This laid down a number of basic principles, which future governments would have to bear in mind. It declared that all men were equal before the law and that they had certain rights, such as freedom of thought, whether written or spoken, freedom of the person, the right to resist oppression, the right to own property. At the same time the political rights of the citizens were also defined, i.e. to be involved in the making of laws, directly or by representatives. The fundamental point was made that sovereignty (and hence authority) resided in the nation, consequently, any authority which did not explicitly emanate from the nation could not be exercised by any one individual or group. These statements were from this time on regarded as fundamental, at least in theory, for any constitution and the government which it established.

Between 1789 and 1799 there were a number of fairly short-lived governments, starting off with an ill-starred attempt at a modified monarchy, and thereafter a republic was established under varying forms. It is from 1799 that a clearer picture begins to emerge of French political tradition which, on the basis of her history since the revolutionary decade, and in the terms of the nature of government, has two essential aspects which are undoubtedly paradoxical, if not mutually exclusive, since they concern parliamentary government on the one hand, and authoritarian government on the other. The French parliamentary tradition derives initially in the nineteenth century from two attempts to establish a constitutional monarchy (on the British pattern, where the monarch's powers are very much reduced as compared with the eighteenth-century absolute monarchy). These two attempts, the Bourbon Restoration (1814-30), and the July Monarchy (1830-48) where the Orleans dynasty (younger Bourbon line) was brought to the throne, both failed, and were each brought to an end by a revolution, in 1830 and in 1848. The third attempt at parliamentary government was that of the Third Republic, which was born out of military disaster in 1870, gave itself a set of laws providing for parliamentary government in 1875, and fell in 1940, again as a result of foreign invasion. A further attempt at parliamentary government was made with the creation of the Fourth Republic, which, unlike its predecessor, lasted only twelve years (1946-58).

The second tradition may be described as authoritarian, where most of the power is in the hands of the executive, and where power of the legislature is weak or merely fictional. It could be said with justification that this tradition originates with the absolute monarchy of pre-Revolutionary days, but it is essentially to be seen in the régimes headed by the two Bonapartes. These were the consulate (1799-1804) and the empire (1804-14) of Napoleon Bonaparte: also (to a lesser extent), the Second Republic (1848-52), of which Napoleon's nephew, Louis Napoleon Bonaparte, was president; and the Second Empire (1852-70) in which he took the title of Napoleon III. In each case, the legislature was weak, and the powers of the executive were strengthened by the use of what was then known as a plebiscite (now called a referendum) — an appeal to the people on specific issues, like the establishment of a new régime (which often meant the ratification of a *coup d'état*), or some important change to be made to already existing institutions. The powers of the executive were also strengthened in the Second Republic by the election of the president of the republic by universal manhood suffrage. The use of the plebiscite conferred on these authoritarian régimes an aura of democracy. An appeal to the people, in itself democratic, could be and was used to bolster up régimes which, to a considerable extent, did not accord to the nation at large the basic freedoms as laid down in the *Déclaration des droits de l'homme et du citoyen*.[1]

As far as the form of government is concerned, the French tradition is more straightforward. We have seen that the attempts in the thirty years following Napoleon's reign to establish a constitutional monarchy were unsuccessful, partly because the members of the lower house of parliament (*chambre des députés*) were elected by a fraction of the population, but also because, in their different ways, the monarchs exercised more power than the constitution gave them, and than was consonant with the role of constitutional monarch; hence the use by some experts of the term 'Orleanist' to describe a constitutional head of state who exercised improperly wide powers. It is also a fact that the early attempts to form a republic failed, particularly in terms of durability. The First Republic came under the influence of varying political factions from 1792 onwards, only to end up as the authoritarian consulate of Napoleon Bonaparte. The Second Republic had an even shorter life, being killed off by its first president, Louis Napoleon, who felt that it did not give him adequate powers to govern effectively. The third attempt, the Third Republic, was much more successful in terms of length, and it can be said that this long-lasting, if rather unspectacular, régime consolidated the republican tradition in France. Yet it was republicanism of a parliamentary type (unlike the Second Republic, where the powers of the single deliberative body, the *assemblée nationale*, and of the president had been almost equally weighted); but added to it was universal manhood suffrage, in the election of its representatives.

The situation of the *président de la république* in the Third Republic was unusual, in that his powers were substantial, prior to the voting of the constitutional laws of 1875 which reduced them somewhat; although he still had the task of selecting the *président du conseil* (head of government). However, amongst the ceremonial and formal powers of the president (henceforth to be elected by the two houses of parliament) was one which should have given him some political influence. This was article 5 of the law of 25 February 1875, which gave the president, with the senate's (upper house's) agreement, the power to dissolve the *chambre des députés* (lower house) before the expiry of its mandate. Unfortunately, the second president of the republic, Marshal MacMahon, a royalist, chose to exercise this right against an increasingly republican *chambre des députés* on 16 May 1877 — circumstances which gave rise to such controversy that no president ever dared to use the powers of dissolution again. The significance of this is twofold: first, it gave rise, during the Third Republic, to great ministerial instability, given the number of political parties and the consequent need for coalition governments, since the right of dissolution had been intended as a weapon against the irresponsible overturning of cabinets. Every time a ministry was defeated and had to resign, there ought to have been a general election, when the deputies would have had to face their electorates; but since the right of dissolution was never used, this did not happen. Furthermore, the weakness of the president's powers meant that, in the main, those who sought the office tended not to be men of great personality or of authority. Any attempt to strengthen the office was stifled by parliament, and presidents who attempted to use wider powers were pressurized out of office by an outraged parliament.[2] As it was, the assumption tended to be that the president had no real powers; and at a moment of crisis, the president was left, rightly or wrongly, with an impression of total helplessness.

It would nevertheless be unfair to suggest that the Third Republic fell only because its institutions were at fault; however, the débâcle of 1940 did permit General de Gaulle to press for a very different type of constitution to be set up after the liberation. His concept of the ideal constitution for France was outlined in his speech at Bayeux, 16 June 1946, where he laid the blame for a number of France's problems squarely at the door of the political parties, whose disagreements had caused the national interest to suffer, giving rise inevitably to a lack of respect on the part of the French for their institutions. These therefore should be changed. His demands boiled down to two essential requirements: a strong executive (head of state) with wide powers, elected by a large electoral college (not merely the two houses of parliament), and the separation of executive, legislative and judicial powers. A further requirement stemmed from the separation of powers, namely that the powers of the executive should not, as had been the case in the Third Republic, proceed from the legislature (*président du conseil*, supported by a majority of the *chambre des députés; président de la république*, elected by the two houses of parliament).

These views were not heeded, and the Fourth Republic was established with a constitution very like that of the Third, providing for a head of state elected by the two houses of parliament, with powers which made of him merely a figurehead, the real power still remaining in the hands of the legislature. It was not until 1958, when the Fourth Republic virtually ground to a halt over the Algerian crisis, that de Gaulle had an opportunity to put his constitutional ideas into effect, and the constitution of the Fifth Republic was adopted by a large majority at the referendum of 28 September 1958 (17,668,790 in favour; 4,624,511 against; 4,016,614 abstentions).

The constitution of the Fifth Republic provides for a lower house (*assemblée nationale*), an upper house (*sénat*), a prime minister and a president of the republic with very wide powers. First of all, his role is defined: 'le Président de la République veille au respect de la Constitution. Il assure, par son arbitrage, le fonctionnement régulier des pouvoirs publics ainsi que la continuité de l'Etat. Il est le garant de l'indépendance nationale, de l'intégrité du territoire, du respect des accords de Communauté et des traités' (article 5). This definition is important, because any incumbent of the presidency has a reasonably clear idea as to the extent of his role, and it is in order that he may carry out this task, that powers are allotted to him which presidents of the Third and Fourth Republics did not possess. He has, for example, the power to put to a referendum a proposed piece of legislation, thereby by-passing parliament – the normal law-making body (article 11). He also has the right to dissolve the *assemblée nationale* (article 12) and finally, the right to take special powers in moments of crisis (article 16). These powers represent a very substantial advance on those enjoyed by earlier presidents. Other, more ceremonial powers, remain much the same as for earlier presidents, such as the promulgation (official publication) of laws, and, if deemed necessary, the right to ask parliament to reconsider legislation which it has just passed (article 10), the appointment to civil and military posts in the state, the signing of ordinances and decrees (article 13), the accrediting of ambassadors (article 14) and the prerogative of mercy (article 17). Clearly the president of the Fifth Republic is no longer merely a constitutional head of state – that part of the executive dealing only with ceremonial, what Walter Bagehot would call 'the dignified parts of government', but a head of state who is politically active as well – a key figure in the 'efficient parts' of government.

As the president of the republic's powers have increased, so the role of parliament has been reduced, having suffered under the Fifth Republic what has been described as a 'constitutional assault'.[3] Very precise measures were introduced into the constitution to ensure that the political parties (and, hence, parliament) should no longer hold supreme political power. It is stated in the constitution, for example (article 34), that parliament votes the law, which is then defined in detail. This has a limiting effect, since anything outside the definition given is also outside parliament's competence, particularly when it is made clear (article 37) that matters not comprised within the definition of 'law' have a 'caractère règlementaire', which means that a minister may deal with them, without the need for parliamentary scrutiny. Furthermore, the existence of the *conseil constitutionnel* with powers to decide whether or not (a) a specific subject comes within the definition of 'law', (b) legislation passed by parliament is constitutional, and (c) the election of deputies has been conducted in a proper manner, limits the powers of parliament to conduct its own affairs.

Although in formal terms the government is still responsible to parliament, that responsibility has clearly been attenuated by the provisions of the constitution – representing an unequivocal endeavour by de Gaulle and his advisers in 1958 to reduce the extent of ministerial instability which had bedevilled the coalition ministries of the Third and Fourth Republics. A new prime minister, appointed by the president, seeks a vote of confidence from the *assemblée nationale*, on his political programme. As for censure motions, it is explicitly stated that a censure motion must be signed by at least one-tenth of the members of the *assemblée*, and the vote takes place forty-eight hours later. The only votes counted are those which support the motion (i.e. abstentions are counted as being favourable to the government), and there has to be a majority, not merely of those voting, but of all members of the *assemblée nationale*. Those who signed the motion may not sign another in that same parliamentary session. The prime minister may also ask for a vote of confidence on a specific text, which is considered as adopted unless a censure motion is proposed within the following twenty-four hours and a vote taken thereon as already indicated. It is clear enough that considerable obstacles are put in the way of any *assemblée nationale* wishing to bring down a government: the very precise nature of the procedure to follow, the required lapses of time, the requirement that ten per cent of deputies sign the motion, that they may not sign another in that session, all this means that the opposition, by definition more likely to oppose government policies, and also by definition in a minority, would have to be careful not to fritter away its numbers in vain attempts. The success of this in terms of governmental stability is that only one censure motion has ever been passed in the twenty-year life of the Fifth Republic – on 5 October 1962, when G. Pompidou's government was brought down over de Gaulle's decision to put to referendum the proposed election of the president of the republic by universal suffrage.[4]

In the Fifth Republic's constitution, we have seen that a very decided (and successful) attempt was made to cut down the powers of the parties. It may be asserted that, in support of this, an attempt was also made to deal with what was viewed as the excessive number of parties *via* electoral legislation. During the Fourth Republic a form of proportional representation obtained. This system, thought to be too favourable to the existence of numerous parties, was altered in 1958 to one in which voters, instead of voting for several candidates, could vote only for one. If a successful candidate has an absolute majority (i.e. more than the total votes gained by his rivals), he is elected *député*. If, however, the majority is only relative, then there is a further vote in which those candidates who have gained votes totalling a minimum of 12.5 per cent of the number of registered voters, may stand again for election. In this election, a relative majority is sufficient to be elected *député*. It is at this point that parties in alliance may agree on a policy of *désistement*, whereby one unsuccessful candidate may stand down in favour of another and encourage his supporters to cast their votes in the latter's favour. One further innovation is the requirement that each candidate supply himself with a *suppléant*, to take over the *député*'s seat in parliament, in the event of death, or resignation, thereby preventing by-elections. However, the principal reason for this innovation was the constitutions's insistence on the incompatibility of the office of minister and that of *député*. Any *député* acceding to ministerial office must give up his seat in parliament to his *suppléant*. Such a constitutional requirement is the logical consequence of the separation of legislative and executive powers, and, while it may shed a vivid light on the nature of the Fifth Republic's government, it causes no little inconvenience to the professional politician who, when giving up office, must either wait until the next general elections, or prevail upon his *suppléant* to resign in order that a by-election may be held, which virtually nullifies the principle of incompatibility.[5]

The provisions of the constitution, together with the electoral law, make parliament a much less powerful body than in the past. As a consequence, the nature of the régime is a matter for a great deal of discussion, as to whether it is essentially parliamentary or presidential. The views of the opposition (the left) have been consistent in condemning what they see as the anti-parliamentary nature of the régime (see, for a typical example, pp. 150-2 of the *Programme commun*, Paris, Editions Sociales, 1972). The principal architect of the constitution, Michel Debré, denies this categorically: 'Si les gaullistes . . . condamnent le régime représentatif, ils ne sont pas hostiles au régime parlementaire . . . les constituants de 1958 ont voulu rénover, en France, le régime parlementaire.'[6] It has however been suggested that the election of the president by universal suffrage, approved by referendum in 1962, marked a profound change in the nature of the régime. Nevertheless the change, in his view, does not mean that the prime minister, whose duties are defined in article 21, is stripped of power, but rather that a dyarchy (rule of two) is created – an opinion roundly denied by de Gaulle in his press conference of 31 January 1964 where, in describing the respective duties of president and prime minister, he implied that while the former indicated the outlines of policy, it was the latter's task to put this into effect. However, if we look at the way in which the president appoints and dismisses the prime minister, it may be possible to establish the relative powers of each, and hence the nature of the régime. In a purely parliamentary régime, the choice of prime minister is, as a rule, a very straightforward one: either he is the elected leader of the majority party (in a two-party system), or else he is the accepted leader of a coalition (in a multi-party system, either by presidential choice, thereafter ratified by parliament, or simply by an agreement between the parties concerned).

The prime minister in the Fifth Republic is only very rarely the party leader (as in the case of J. Chirac, who became leader of the Gaullist party while prime minister, but resigned the post with the explicit approval of the president). He is, as a rule, one of the party's leaders – possible exceptions here being Pompidou and Raymond Barre, the latter chosen more for his economic expertise than for his influence in any party. Since the Gaullists have been the majority party (with or without allies) for twenty years, it should theoretically have been possible (barring death or other incapacity) for the same individual to have held the post of prime minister for the whole of that time. This would be technically feasible in a parliamentary situation if one party remained in the majority throughout, and should, on the face of it, be equally possible in the Fifth Republic. Article 8 of the constitution concerning the appointment of the prime minister is couched as follows: 'Le président de la République nomme le Premier ministre. Il met fin à ses fonctions sur la présentation par celui-ci de la démission du gouvernement. Sur la proposition du Premier ministre, il nomme les autres membres du gouvernement et met fin à leurs fonctions.' A strict reading of this text implies that the president of the republic merely receives the prime minister's resignation, but does not provoke it. The only reference to the cause of a resignation is to be found in article 50, which indicates that if a censure motion is passed, or if there is formal disapprobation by the *assemblée nationale* of government policy, then the prime minister and his government must resign. The theoretical inference, in strict terms, is clear: only the *assemblée nationale* can bring down a government. Furthermore, during the elaboration of the constitution in 1958, on 8 August, de Gaulle categorically denied that the president of the republic could dismiss the prime minister (see *Avis et débats du Comité consultatif constitutionnel*, Paris, Documentation française, 1960, p. 118). It is also a fact that proposals tending to permit the dismissal of the prime minister were not accepted. By 1964, however, de Gaulle, in his press conference, made it perfectly clear that the president could not only choose the prime minister, but change him when necessary (press conference, 31 January 1964), and a similar line was taken by President Pompidou during his term of office.

The practice of dismissing prime ministers has tended to follow the 1964 rather than the 1958 pattern. The exchange of letters between president and premier makes it clear that if one sticks rigidly to the texts, the following points emerge: that the resignation of M. Debré was the result of a 'gentleman's agreement' arrived at beforehand between president and prime minister; that General de Gaulle dismissed Pompidou but wished it to appear as if he had not done so; that Chaban-Delmas was dismissed by the president; and, finally, that Chirac felt that he had insufficient powers to carry out his task and therefore asked to be released from office.[7] In none of these cases was parliament in any way involved. It is noticeable, on the contrary, that in the case of Chaban-Delmas, the prime minister had been at pains to obtain a vote of confidence from the *assemblée nationale*; noticeable also that a successor was appointed during the summer recess, and that parliament had no opportunity to discuss the change until the beginning of the next parliamentary session.

It must be evident from these instances therefore, that although the prime minister may be said to have a formal and limited responsibility to parliament in the Fifth Republic, the bulk of his responsibility is towards the president who appoints and dismisses him. Clearly common sense would indicate the difficulty, in practical terms, of two men working closely together if one is uncongenial to the other; but it is not a problem which must be reckoned with in parliamentary government, where the head of state must put up with whatever the majority sends him. It is indeed an indication of how far the régime has travelled since 1958.

The government, as a consequence of the incompatibility principle, must depend much more on the support of the president than on that of parliament. Those who become ministers may have been *députés* but, in certain fields, are just as likely to be 'technocrats', for example in foreign affairs, where career diplomats have frequently been appointed (MM. Couve de Murville, Sauvagnargues, de Guiringaud) and in education, where academics with a career in administration have been appointed (R. Haby, A. Saunier-Seïté). This can be looked upon as a new departure, a step into the technocratic age, or as one more link with tradition (either pre-Revolutionary or Bonapartist), where experts were very often chosen to act as ministers and to aid the sovereign.

One further point must be mentioned, since it is furiously debated prior to every general (legislative) election. What happens if the president of the republic and the parliamentary majority are of different political persuasions; in other words, which expression of public opinion is to be taken as predominant? De Gaulle's answer to the problem was straightforward — the threat (or promise) of his resignation if he did not receive adequate support. Pompidou's response was rather more drastic in his press conference of 21 September 1972 (see *Le Monde*, 23 September 1972) where he made it clear that in the event of an electoral victory of the unified left, he would not call upon its leaders to form a government, and that if the government which he chose (presumably a minority one) were overturned, he would dissolve the *assemblée nationale*. V. Giscard d'Estaing's answer to the problem has been decidedly more subtle, namely to indicate that he would fulfil his term of office and put into effect the programme of the majority, a position which has been described as a *coup d'état*, in comparison with the attitude of his predecessors.[8] This may well be so, but the fact remains that in the event of a fundamental disagreement between president and government, the former has the whip hand, since he can dissolve the *assemblée nationale*, if he so chooses. While it may be true, therefore, to suggest that the constitution of the Fifth Republic may be read as a parliamentary one, this has scarcely as yet been the case in reality, since the majority has remained the same since 1958 and there has been no chance to find out how the machinery of the constitution would function if the left gained a parliamentary majority.

Yet there is clearly a good deal of ambiguity in the very text of the constitution itself, which makes a conclusion on its nature difficult to arrive at. The case of article 8 has already been mentioned. Ministerial responsibility (to parliament), always the hallmark of a parliamentary government, is only mentioned in relation to its very limited application of articles 49 and 50. The president of the republic, however, is said, by virtue of article 68, not to be responsible for actions committed by him during his term of office – except in the case of high treason. The political irresponsibility of the head of state is again the characteristic of a parliamentary government, but, as we know, in the Fifth Republic the president has wide powers bestowed upon him, and, in eight cases (articles 8, 11, 12, 16, 18, 54, 56 and 61) acts without the need of ministerial counter-signature. What is the reason for this ambiguity, which is to be found in the constitution's text rather than in its practice? The answer seems to have been one of political expediency in 1958, since, although at that time the constitutional ideas of de Gaulle were paramount, and those of Debré exceedingly influential, there were other parliamentarians who played a part in the discussions.[9] It can therefore be assumed that, although many of them wished to see the establishment of a more stable government, they might have considered de Gaulle's ideal régime as going too far in the anti-parliamentary direction, and that consequently a certain amount of 'masking' of de Gaulle's ultimate intentions was necessary.

> Certains d'entre nous dans les premières années de la Ve République, se sont parfois étonnés, devant le général de Gaulle, de ce qu'il ait accepté une Constitution plus traditionnellement parlementaire que ce qu'auraient normalement comporté ses prises de position antérieures et sa volonté bien actuelle d'affirmer l'autorité du Président . . . les explications données tournaient toujours autour de deux pôles: les milieux politiques y auraient vu du bonapartisme et le pays n'aurait pas compris. (B. Tricot *et al.*, *De Gaulle et le service de l'état*, p. 148)

Apart therefore from analyses of stronger presidential and weaker parliamentary powers, the controversial use of article 11 in 1962, the subsequent election of the president by universal suffrage, de Gaulle's admission allows us to put aside the 'Orleanist' interpretation, even for the period of 1958–62. It can be said that a substantially wider suffrage (*notables* plus parliament = 80–100,000 electors) represents a step towards universal suffrage; but, more crucially, as Léon Blum foresaw, the logic of the 'Bayeux system' meant inevitably a recourse to universal suffrage to elect a *président de la république*, to whom such wide powers would be given (see *Le Populaire*, 21 June 1946) – much wider powers than those enjoyed by even an 'Orleanist' constitutional monarch. The comparison which springs inevitably to mind is that between the president of the Fifth Republic and Napoleon III, as he would have been, had the Liberal Empire of 1870 not been swept away by the Franco-Prussian war. Provision was made specifically for responsible ministers, but the emperor still retained the right to appeal to the people via a plebiscite. Thus we may consider the Fifth Republic an undoubted descendent of the authoritarian/plebiscitarian tradition rather than of parliamentary government.

One further possibility has been suggested:

Les constituants (of 1958) ont voulu que la Constitution puisse faire l'objet de plusieurs 'lectures' différentes. En fonction de la personnalité du Président de la République et de celle du Premier Ministre, de la composition politique de l'Assemblée nationale et même du Sénat, de la concordance entre la majorité parlementaire et la majorité présidentielle, la Constitution établit un régime qui peut être soit plutôt présidentiel, soit plutôt parlementaire. (J. -L. Debré, *La Constitution de la Ve République*, p. 327)

The very fact that the constitution of the Fifth Republic apparently lends itself to so many interpretations, is in itself a factor of arbitrariness and hence a link with the authoritarian tradition, since the president may decide as he sees fit how he will interpret the constitution's description of his powers. Far from being a factor of stability, such a situation could, in the long run, prove to be a danger at the moment when one interpretation supersedes another, possibly giving rise, not merely to theoretical controversy, but to political and civil strife in a country which easily accepts the legitimacy of revolution and the rise and fall of governments.

(2) Aspects of central government

The foregoing conclusion, arrived at almost exclusively on theoretical grounds, may be considered, for that reason alone, suspect. Since an interpretation of the theory suggests that the Fifth Republic is essentially presidential rather than parliamentary, more concrete proof ought to be adduced as well. This section will therefore attempt to focus on areas of the governmental machine which indicate this tendency.

It is perhaps worth noting in this context the fact that the deputy is no longer regarded by the general public as the all-powerful figure that he had been in the Third and Fourth Republics.

> Le député n'est plus qu'une 'personnalité d'arrondissement', à laquelle on s'adresse pour régler les problèmes quotidiens . . . La division du travail introduite par la Constitution de 1958 déprécie par conséquent dans l'esprit des citoyens la fonction du Parlement, l'exécutif assurant de plus en plus la représentation des citoyens.
> (P. Birnbaum, *Les Sommets de l'état*, p. 79)

Like the simple deputy, parliament also has been stripped of power. The constitutional restrictions on her role have already been noted, but there are other practical restrictions which have been imposed by government regulations. For example, parliamentary sessions, two per year, now have a maximum life of ninety days each, which in fact means that there is invariably insufficient time to cope with legislation; this leads to undue haste and poorly drafted texts. The government decides on the day's business in both houses, the *ordre du jour*, with the opposition having no say in the matter; and it may also force on the *assemblée nationale* a single vote on the text which it has proposed, together with such amendments which it has suggested itself, or of which it approves. This reduces the power of both houses of parliament materially to affect government proposals during their legislative passage. Parliament's power of amendment is also restricted by article 40 of the constitution which disallows any amendment tending to reduce public resources (i.e. taxation) or implying the creation or increase of public expenditure. The idea behind this provision was clearly to deny deputies the possibility of demagogic gestures designed to appeal to their constituents, as well as to embarrass the government. While a measure of this kind could possibly be viewed as an aid to efficiency in the dispatch of government business, its interpretation may give rise to restrictions of the most ludicrous kind.[10]

Proposed legislation must be debated not only in parliament as a whole, but by one of six permanent committees: *commission des finances; commission des affaires étrangères; commission de la défense nationale; commission des lois* (dealing with legal and administrative questions); *commission des affaires culturelles, familiales et sociales; commission de la production et des échanges.* This system is unsatisfactory, since the committees are too large, some of them having well over one hundred members. Also, parliament is required to debate, not the draft legislation as amended by the appropriate committee, but the government's original version, which makes a mockery of the committee's labours. In the case of the budget also, parliament's rights are restricted: if the budget has not been passed in seventy days, the government can enact it by ordinance. Again, the amount of legislation to be dealt with in the short parliamentary sessions, makes proper parliamentary supervision impossible.

Yet with the maintenance, albeit in reduced form, of the government's responsibility to parliament, there must still be at least a measure of lip-service paid to that concept. Consequently, the government must keep parliament informed of its activities, either by statements to parliament, or by the method of parliamentary questions, whether oral or written. The use of questions requiring written answers is extensive, but the possibilities of parliamentary power in question time have not been exploited. As Wright indicates, deputies seem resigned to the fact that government pays little heed to their queries; if parliament is weak, the fault lies, in part, with the deputies who have not used to the full the powers which they have, nor pressed for any increase therein.

Most of these problems have, however, arisen as a result of the long predominance in parliament of the Gaullists, and their allies, and the fact that the first two presidents of the Fifth Republic were basically in agreement with the parliamentary majority. Now that this is no longer so, slightly more heed must be paid to parliament, and some of Giscard's reforms have suffered in consequence, notably the imposition of a capital gains tax. Furthermore, the power of parliament to set up *ad hoc* commissions of enquiry (*commissions d'enquête* or *commissions de contrôle*) has performed a necessary service in bringing various types of malpractice into the open.

In general, however, it is clear that the government enjoys wide powers which have resulted in a corresponding reduction in those of parliament. Even within the domain of law, as defined by article 34 of the constitution, the voting of *lois cadres* (laws indicating tendencies and principles) is often couched in the most general of terms. These can only be put into effect by the use of ministerial decrees which provide in detail instructions as to how the law is to be implemented, and consequently leave to the government, in the person of the appropriate minister, substantial interpretative powers as well as the faculty to choose when (or if) the law should be brought into effect. The complexity of the budget has given rise to an analogous process of *debudgetization*, which has taken certain areas of public spending out of the budget and consequently away from parliamentary surveillance, such as it is.

The government, thus, is powerful in relation to the body to which, in theory, it is responsible, and which has only once succeeded in overturning it, according to the terms of article 49. What must now be considered is the extent to which anything resembling cabinet government exists, i.e. to what extent there is any ministerial solidarity or cabinet responsibility, which is assumed to exist in any British government (leaks and political memoirs apart).

The first point to consider is how ministers are chosen. In theory, the president appoints the prime minister, who then chooses his ministerial team. In practice, the prime minister may well have imposed upon him by the president individuals whom he personally would not have selected. One of the most notable examples here must surely be that of Mme Françoise Giroud, who, having made no secret of her support for F. Mitterrand in the presidential elections of 1974, was asked personally by Giscard to take on the post of *secrétaire d'état à la condition féminine* in J. Chirac's government. At times, too, a cabinet reshuffle may well take place on presidential instructions. In political terms, therefore, there is no principle of unity which obtains. With the principle of incompatibility between the post of deputy and that of minister, the prime minister is no longer obliged to choose or appoint deputies or senators, and there has always been in the Fifth Republic a percentage of ministers without parliamentary experience at the time of their appointment, although they may attempt to have themselves elected thereafter.[11]

Consequently, the solidarity of the government as a whole is not great. While the prime minister is, at the very least, *primus inter pares*, there have been cases where specific ministers have been known to be influential, over and above their ministerial role, as in the case of M. Poniatowski, when he was interior minister in the Chirac cabinet. One other element of disunity is that to be found between ministers and *secrétaires d'état* (junior ministers) whose attributions bring them into conflict, notably in the case of the education ministry and what is now the universities' ministry.

There seems to be considerable divergence of opinion as to the existence in cabinet meetings of any genuine discussion – a prerequisite of cabinet decision-making. Some ministers have indicated that the opinions of any minister outside the area of his own competence were not required, others that it was possible for a minister to intervene, but that few did so. F. Giroud's own description of cabinet meetings, with their procedural formalities, make them sound unutterably boring.[12] She also indicates that when ministers had proposals to make, these had to be submitted to the prime minister, to the president of the republic, and to any relevant minister in advance. Where texts were to be discussed, or read out, these were also invariably handed out in advance.

If the cabinet meetings are to be viewed as an organ of consultation, rather than of decision-making, the same cannot be said of other such meetings. Apart from the regular meetings between president and prime minister, the former has similar sessions with the other senior ministers of foreign affairs, finance and interior. There are also three further types of meeting: (1) *interdepartmental committees*, attended by senior civil servants from the ministries and chaired by one of the prime minister's own officials; (2) *interminis-terial committees*, with the prime minister in the chair, composed of ministers and possibly some senior officials, plus representatives from the president's own staff; (3) *interministerial council* or *conseil restreint*, chaired by the president of the republic, where the principal decisions are taken. These stages are progressively used, if agreement has not otherwise been reached at an earlier stage. Such a system also means that it is possible for a prime minister to leave out a colleague whose presence is not thought desirable at certain meetings.

United, the ministers would seem to enjoy little influence on general lines of policy; within their own ministries, and at the head of their own civil service, at the centre and in the provinces they are relatively powerful figures. The minister is a member of the government, and as such he must make the needs of his ministry known to the president, as well as parliament. He is also at the head of his ministry, aided by his own personal collaborators (*cabinet*). He must not only consider the permanent staff at the centre, but also what are known as *services extérieurs*, field services, of which there are three main categories: cultural and social (education, welfare and health); technical and economic (posts and telecommunications, roads, agriculture) and financial services, concerned with the collection of direct and indirect taxes, and the paying out of sums owed to private individuals by the state, *département* or *commune*. While the officials of these services come under ministerial authority and, more specifically, under that of their departmental director, the *préfet* has the task of co-ordinating them. Where a minister has no field services, he may turn to the *préfecture*, if he requires assistance.

While the field services represent one element of centralization, the *préfet* can be said to represent the other. Although in the past his role was decidedly authoritarian, and although he may still be considered as somewhat of an 'enlightened despot', he has other equally important functions. He acts essentially as the intermediary between the central government and his *département*. He must make periodic reports to the government about the state of affairs in his *département*, of public opinion, how the latter has reacted to specific events, such as price rises or strikes. He may also be required to give his views on the advisability of reforms. This informative role may work two ways, since the *préfet* can also pass on specific requests from individuals to the appropriate ministries, adding his own opinion. It is also his task to ensure that laws and regulations are put into effect in his *département*. Since the *préfet* is appointed by the government and is subordinate to it, his functions provide the main force of centralization in France, and the comparatively recent creation of the *préfet de région* has simply added an extra stage in the administrative hierarchy.

Yet all ministers are limited by their financial means, and their wishes are often blocked by the finance ministry, known, until April 1978 as the *ministère de l'économie et des finances*. The problem relates specifically to the budget, over which many conflicts have arisen between the finance ministry and the main spending ministries — for example education and agriculture. The preparation of the budget is a lengthy process, carried out initially by the directorates of forecasting and the budget (*directions de prévision et du budget*). In the budget directorate, work on the budget begins over a year earlier in November, the calculations being based on the previous year's budget, and on the one actually in operation. The forecasting directorate begins its preparation about the same time, and the first phase of its operations lasts about three months, during which it considers all possibilities, relating to the international situation as well as the state of the national economy. Both directorates present their findings to the minister in March, which gives him the material necessary to begin the first discussions on the contents of the finance bill. Once the government's priorities have been established, there follows possibly the most difficult period, between April and July, when discussions are held between the finance minister and the various spending ministries over running costs. It is at this stage that disputes may well have to go to the arbitration of the prime minister, if officials cannot solve them. The outstanding problems then go before the prime minister, the finance minister, and the relevant spending minister, and the prime minister's decision is final, although an appeal may be made by either side to the president of the republic. In the vast majority of conflicts, it is the finance minister's case which prevails.

While the finance ministry has been accused of inordinate conservatism, which has caused many proposals of reform to be stillborn, its position has perhaps been less assured during the Fifth Republic than under the Fourth. The reason is not hard to find; although de Gaulle may not have been interested primarily in economic and financial matters, they were always of interest to Pompidou; the same can equally well be said of Giscard as a former finance minister, and of Barre, who was chosen as prime minister by the president specifically for his economic expertise. Yet J. Hayward[13] suggests that the finance minister had regained a considerable part of his former powers because of the emphasis between 1963 and 1966 on the need for a balanced budget. It is true that every ministry has within it an official appointed by the finance minister, whose task is to exercise a preventive control over the ministry's expenditure. This is beneficial as far as 'good housekeeping' is concerned, but has caused the finance ministry to be considered as inordinately rigid and excessively conservative.

This was the position when, in April 1978 after the legislative elections, with the formation of Barre's ministry, the finance ministry was split in two, one part becoming the *ministère du budget*, under M. Papon, and the other, the *ministère de l'économie*, under R. Monory. This change has been described as a *coup d'état*, and seems to have been regarded as impossible, given the power of the ministry, which was, undoubtedly, vast. It had twelve principal directorates, and an army of officials − 171,000. The size of the ministry seems to have been one of the reasons behind the change, since the number of directorates increased the possibilities of blocking proposals, either before their realization, or once work was in progress. The present organization puts four directorates into the budget ministry: *direction du budget, direction générale des douanes et droits indirects, direction générale des impôts, direction de la comptabilité publique* (public accounting); the eight remaining come under the ministry of the economy.

At this stage, the results of the change cannot be predicted. It has been suggested that the civil service will do what it can to annul its effects. One point seems clear enough; the two ministries will not together be able to exercise the influence wielded by the single ministry in the past, and will presumably be more vulnerable to pressure from the prime minister. For example, when on 19 August 1978 Monory proposed to cut the price of petrol by between 3 and 10 centimes per litre, he was speedily and rather brusquely brought to order by Barre; but only time will tell if this tendency will be continued.

Two other bodies whose existence tend to shed doubt on the parliamentary nature of the Fifth Republic are respectively the *conseil d'état* and the *conseil constitutionnel*.

The former of these is a Napoleonic creation of 1799 − a renewed version of the pre-revolutionary *conseil du roi*. It had not only administrative and judicial functions in this early period, but also a legislative one, since it was consulted on the drafting of proposed legislation, and was responsible for the drafting of all the organic laws, as well as of the *code civil*.

The present functions of the *conseil d'état* are essentially of two kinds, consultative and judicial. The consultative functions are undertaken by the administrative sections − finance, interior, public works, and a section dealing with social questions. There is also a general assembly comprising all members, who meet at least once a week to consider and take a decision on the texts of draft bills, regulations, ordinances, as well as matters on which a separate section feels that further consideration is desirable. The consultative aspect of the *conseil d'état* is completed by the existence of a *commission permanente* which may pronounce on draft legislation in exceptional circumstances.

While the *conseil d'état* could be viewed as a body allied to the government whose powers impinged on those of parliament, the relations between it and the government were by no means cordial. De Gaulle was highly displeased with its ruling on his decision to use the referendum in 1962 to bring about a change in the election of the president of the republic, which he describes in his memoirs as 'abusive', since it permitted itself to pronounce a political judgment on his actions, instead of merely considering the appropriateness of the text itself. (It is also worth noting that it took the same line on de Gaulle's referendum in 1969.) The *conseil d'état* too may be seen as the protector of civil rights. Again, it incurred de Gaulle's wrath, when its judicial section pronounced the annulment of the military court which had been established in 1962 to try rapidly members of the OAS. One of these, M. Canal, was condemned to death by the court, and sought the ruling of the *conseil d'état*. The ordinance of 1 June 1962, setting up the military court, stated that there was to be no appeal against its ruling; it was for this reason that the decision of the *conseil d'état* was arrived at. In spite of de Gaulle's anger, there seems no reason to doubt that this was a totally unpolitical ruling on a matter of civil rights, and many of the judicial rulings of the *conseil d'état* deal with matters of this kind.

The creation of the *conseil constitutionnel* is a complete innovation, its essential task being to rule on the conformity of legislation to the constitution. It is composed normally of nine people – three appointed by the president of the republic and three each by the presidents of the two houses of parliament. Former presidents of the republic are members *ex officio*.

An appeal to the *conseil constitutionnel* for its decision (*saisine*) is provided for in the constitution, where it may be obligatory or voluntary, according to circumstances. Cases where an appeal is obligatory include regulations of parliament (by presidents of the two houses), organic laws (by the prime minister), the use of article 16 by the president of the republic, irregularity in legislative elections, where the matter may be taken up either by the justice minister or by the *bureau* of either house of parliament. Voluntary appeals to the *conseil constitutionnel* are concerned with ordinary legislation, and may be made by the president of the republic, the prime minister or the presidents of the national assembly and the senate. In 1974 this right was extended to groups of sixty deputies and senators, who now have also the right to query the constitutional propriety of legislation.

Initially, the decisions of the *conseil constitutionnel* were thought to be excessively timid, and orientated in favour of the government. Unlike the *conseil d'état*, it declared in 1962 that it did not have the competence to pronounce on de Gaulle's decision to put the election of the president of the republic to a referendum. Yet latterly its decisions have not been necessarily to the government's convenience, notably over the attempts made to modify the arrangements for deputies and their *suppléants*, which have hitherto failed since the *conseil* has invariably maintained the principle of incompatibility existing between the functions of minister and those of deputy.

Yet there are still criticisms made of its pro-government stance, notably in the matter of irregularity in elections. While the *conseil constitutionnel* declines to pronounce on the intervention of the president of the republic on the grounds that the head of state is responsible only to the *haute cour de justice*, it does have competence to decide on electoral irregularities committed by candidates or their supporters, and consequently there is inequality before the *conseil constitutionnel*, as between the government and opposition. Such is the view of F. Mitterrand (see *Le Monde,* 20-21 August 1978), who would prefer to see a non-political supreme court in charge of these matters. His criticism of the political tendency of the *conseil* is undoubtedly a fair one, the problem going back yet again to the fact that there has been no change in the political colour of the government since 1958. Since nomination rests with representatives of the majority, the political complexion of the *conseil* must inevitably seem suspect to the opposition, particularly when the *conseil* is required to pronounce on electoral irregularities in a constituency where the left has been successful. Yet even this situation is to be viewed as less invidious than that which obtained in the Fourth Republic, when parliament verified the elections.

In the light of this cursory examination, is it possible to assess the tendency of the Fifth Republic? There is clearly no doubt whatever as to the power of the state, at central and local level, even if there is not always unity of opinion in Paris and the provinces. More than that, the state has at its service (and has had for two centuries and more), groups of highly trained officials, technocrats capable of passing from one aspect of government to another, whether it be the *conseil d'état*, or the central administration of a ministry. Equally, a large number of politicians have the same type of training, whether it be as members of the *inspectorat des finances* or the *cour des comptes*. We may therefore be justified in speaking of a political class which, by virtue of the *grandes écoles* and the *concours*, may be largely regarded as self-perpetuating.

If this is so, how may the Fifth Republic be regarded as presidential? It has been suggested, and rightly, that the president of the republic is not able to achieve all his policies, and that the state apparatus is by no means unified. Precisely the same comments could be made about, for example, the supposedly absolute monarchy of the *Ancien Régime*, or the Second Empire, whether in its authoritarian or its liberal phase. Another point which is regarded as significant, is that while the prime minister's staff is a large one, the president's is comparatively small. Yet it should be remembered that it is essentially the prime minister's task to carry out in detail the policy outlined by the president. This seems to have been the case in de Gaulle's presidency when the government was more than once accused of acting arbitrarily; but even this emphasis has changed, and presidential involvement with specific policies and decisions is much more evident. While, therefore, the president may well choose to adopt liberal policies, and, in view of the shaky alliance of the majority, may have to take account of political susceptibilities to a greater extent than in the past, there can be little doubt that the essential responsibility rests with him. While this obtains, the régime will be of an essentially presidential and possibly arbitrary tendency, when, in theoretical as well as in practical terms, the power of parliament is allowed to weaken and consequently, provide less of a barrier against further power being taken by an already powerful state.

As well as political and administrative institutions at the centre and a network of personnel spreading over the whole of the country, the French state has a further string to its bow, in the shape of the use it can make of the mass media. This matter could well be regarded as a kind of appendix to the constitution, since, just as much as the latter, it confers power on the state — a power which régimes in the previous century did not enjoy — namely to communicate information and views immediately to the mass of the population. Such a technological advance may also subject the state to the temptation of abuse, of propaganda, hitherto impossible on such a vast scale. The use (or abuse) of these powers may provide yet another indication as to the essential nature of the Fifth Republic.

Censorship of the means of communication has a long history in France, dating back to the *Ancien Régime*. During the nineteenth century it existed to a greater or lesser degree, depending on the strength or tolerance of successive régimes. Yet the mass media have for long been subject to some control by the state. Before the Second World War, while a state monopoly existed in theory, private radio stations were allowed a measure of freedom to operate on a temporary basis. During the war all radio stations, whether privately run or state controlled, or, as in the occupied zone, taken over by the occupying power, suffered from their financial dependence on the authorities; in order to survive, they gave proof of their total docility by the constant broadcasting of propaganda. Such an experience was unfortunate for future developments, since it clearly indicated to postwar governments the political possibilities inherent in broadcasting, which they were consequently reluctant to let out of state control.

In 1945 the *Radiodiffusion-télévision française* (RTF) was established by decree which provided for a state monopoly responsible to the prime minister and the ministry of information. The RTF was headed by a *directeur général* appointed by the cabinet, and in practice was answerable to the information minister. Clearly, such a framework, together with financial dependence, and a lack of coherence in the administrative organization, meant that the RTF was very vulnerable to political pressure. Various attempts to reform the system were made during the Fourth Republic, but to no avail. However, the political pressures did not begin to make themselves felt until the Algerian war, when broadcasters came under strong pressure, if they advocated a political standpoint on the issue, which was hostile to the government. The broadcasting of news suffered, inasmuch as items relating to the Algerian war which were deemed embarrassing to the government, tended to be omitted.

It was evident that reform was necessary if broadcasting was in any way to revert to its role of honestly informing the public. The problem arose as to what mechanisms might ensure broadcasting integrity. One method might have been to authorize commercial broadcasting, which might have ensured genuine freedom of information, but was subject to other pressures which would not necessarily be calculated to maintain either a high standard of entertainment or the ideal of public service. This possibility was therefore not considered when a reform was introduced by ordinance in the early days of the Fifth Republic (4 February 1959).

Reform might indeed be regarded as too forceful a description, since the changes introduced were moderate. The RTF was henceforth to be a state establishment of an industrial and commercial nature, enjoying financial autonomy, since it would have its own budget. Yet the control of the state was still strong, as the RTF still came under the authority of the minister of information. It was, as before, to be headed by a *directeur général*, appointed by the *conseil des ministres*. While he was assumed to have charge of the organization and its personnel, he could not appoint his deputy, nor the directors of the various services, who were, like himself, appointed by the government. Political influence was equally evident in the two bodies set up to assist the *directeur général*. The *conseil supérieur* was made up of representatives of various ministries and the presidents of the specialized programme committees; the *comité de surveillance*, wherein were to be found parliamentarians and officials, only met at the request of the minister.

The involvement of the state became more evident in the early 1960s, when the numbers of people owning television sets began to rise (60,000 in 1954; one million in 1959; three millions in 1963), with the possibility which this factor bestowed on the government of exercising political persuasion over a substantial part of the population. De Gaulle himself was on the whole a notable television performer, and used his skill to the detriment of his political opponents and to the enhancing of his own relationship with the electorate. Television also provided him with yet another means of by-passing parliament, since important matters of policy could be announced directly to the nation, or to that portion of it that could afford television.

The problem which state control over the media provoked was that, with the Gaullists in power, the media were geared almost exclusively to the presentation of the Gaullist viewpoint, to the detriment of any equity or objectivity. While more autonomy for the RTF might have helped to correct the balance, there were financial and administrative difficulties. A further attempt was therefore made to reform the system by the law of 27 June 1964. Its main innovations were the transformation of the RTF into an *office*, no longer under the authority of the information ministry, but merely under its aegis (*tutelle*) and that of the finance ministry, and the setting up of a *conseil d'administration*, with half its members representing the state and half representing listeners, viewers, the press, and people working in the ORTF; they were to serve normally for a three-year period. They would elect a president and vice president from amongst their number. The tasks of the council were to define general policy, discuss the budget and see that it was put into effect, ensure the maintenance of quality and moral content in programmes, objectivity and accuracy of news and, in general, freedom of expression for the main tendencies of opinion and thought. As before, the men at the top, the *directeur général* and his deputies, were nominated by the government.

The system, while representing some theoretical improvement, fell very far short of what the opposition had wished to establish in the way of controls to safeguard objectivity. The role of the ministry of information was reduced, but the composition of the council was by no means as liberal as might have seemed at first glance. The main problem was that none of the members were elected, and while half were in theory to represent workers in the ORTF and consumers, as well as other categories, they too were selected from short-lists. The council's independence was consequently highly suspect.

In terms of freedom of political expression, the reform changed nothing. The views of the government were still presented to the virtual exclusion of others, and journalists continued to lose their jobs because of their political views. Yet the political dangers to the ruling party itself do not seem to have been apparent until the presidential election of 1965. De Gaulle's poor performances at the first ballot clearly came as a shock to him. All candidates were allowed two hours' time on television in the fortnight before the elections, and some of his opponents, notably J. Lecanuet, proved more adroit than had been expected. De Gaulle, forced to descend from his Olympian approach of the first ballot, used all of his television time in the second, and adopting a different technique, he went on to win an adequate victory (55 per cent of the vote at the second ballot). Television, as well as being a new factor in electioneering, also proved a significant one in that, with a modicum of equity in television time for all candidates, it aroused political interest and helped to maintain a high standard in the electoral campaign.

Yet it was not until well after the events of May 1968 that further changes were made. After the strike of ORTF journalists, many were sacked or put in much less prominent positions. J. Ardagh suggests that attempts to stifle opinion had by this time become much more subtle, in that anything which could offend the susceptibilities of any important group, political or religious, was avoided; which gave rise to self-censorship. However, some positive changes were brought in, notably the abolition of the information ministry, as the consequence of a promise by Pompidou in his presidential campaign of 1969. That some further changes were still necessary, was clear from the so-called clandestine advertising scandal that broke in 1971.

The problem was this: commercial radio and television in France was not acceptable to the government, but the persistent financial difficulties suffered by the ORTF brought a measure of advertising, under state control, into the media. There had been since 1960 what was known as *publicité compensée*, that is, advertising for a type of goods, but not for a specific brand; this was paid for by commercial companies. In October 1968 advertising of specific brands of goods was permitted, to the tune of two minutes per day and by 1972 this had increased to nineteen minutes. However, in 1971 it was revealed that there were very close links between ORTF and an advertising agency and that these were being put to improper use. The names of specific brands of goods were brought before the public in television programmes, allegedly for pecuniary gain on the part of private individuals. The solution for this type of malpractice was felt to lie in decentralization, but such a solution would not have given the state the same hold over broadcasting. A further ominous note was the resurrection of the minister of information under a slightly different name – *secrétaire d'état de la fonction publique et des services de l'information* – in the person of P. Malaud, who was given the job of producing a draft bill on ORTF reform which, in due course, became the law of 3 July 1972. Its main innovation was in the creation of a *président-directeur-général*, still appointed by the government for three years; he not only headed the ORTF but also presided over the *conseil d'administration*, concocted as before. While the ORTF was still under the aegis of the prime minister or his delegate, one change seemed to be of very slightly liberal tendency, namely the right of reply, where an individual felt that his or her honour, reputation or interests had suffered as a result of the content of any broadcast. At the same time, however, another provision gave to the PDG powers to decide who, in the case of strikes, was to be regarded as essential for the continuation of the public service, and who was not — i.e. who could strike and who could not; this was inevitably viewed as as attempt to curtail the right to withdraw one's labour.

All in all, this did little to bring about the fundamental changes, for which successive reports (by Diligent in 1968 and Paye in 1970) had pressed, notably in the area of decentralization. Nor was the appointment of A. Conte, a UDR deputy, particularly reassuring. Yet less than two years later, Conte was to leave his post, making his reasons completely clear. In October 1973, Malaud had demanded the removal of two broadcasters for their political views, stating that unless this was done and unless France-Culture (which, he said, was a hotbed of communists and *cégétistes*) was reorganized, there would be no increase in the ORTF budget. In due course, Conte was sacked in what P. Viansson-Ponté described as 'une forte odeur d'autoritarisme' (*Le Monde*, 24 October 1973) and Malaud moved to another post, although not disavowed by the government.

Up to this point, it can be stated that the authoritarian tendency, inherited partly from Vichy and partly from the desire of the left-wing resistance to have no truck with commercial values and to rely on the democratic state for fairness and freedom of expression, had scarcely been modified over nearly forty years. With the arrival of V. Giscard d'Estaing as president of the republic, the format changes. Pompidou had had no doubts on the official role of the ORTF and its broadcasters. 'Qu'on le veuille ou non, le journaliste de la télévision n'est pas tout à fait un journaliste comme un autre. Il a des responsabilités particulières . . . Qu'on le veuille ou non, la télévision est considérée comme la voix de la France, et par les Français et par l'étranger' (*Le Monde*, 23 September 1972).

While the views of V. Giscard d'Estaing were less clear cut, it was likely that he would not share those of Pompidou. (His brother, O. Giscard d'Estaing, was a prominent supporter of commercial radio.) By August 1974, a law had been promulgated which disbanded the ORTF altogether, and reorganized television and radio in seven bodies: three television companies, one radio company, a company to produce films and plays, another to maintain equipment, and an audio-visual institute. It should be made clear that the state is the only shareholder, so that such competition as exists is simply between one state organization and another.

Opinions vary as to the success of the reorganization; for some, the experience of working in a smaller group of people after the impersonal ORTF system is beneficial; for others, it has brought about a lowering of cultural and artistic standards. Yet one hitherto vexed area seems to have reaped some benefit – freedom of political expression. It has been suggested that Giscard has put the new radio and television companies under his personal aegis, for the liberal reason of protecting them from various political pressures. Any criticisms of programmes made by the Elysée are rare and invariably come after the broadcast.[14] Certainly the law of 7 August 1974 not only states in general terms, as earlier laws had done, the need to provide 'un égal accès à l'expression des principales tendances de pensée et des grands courants de l'opinion' (article 1); it also specifies that regular broadcasting time is made available for that purpose. Furthermore the law specifies that a minimum period of time is allotted to political and professional groups for free expression of their views (article 15), and that equal time is allotted to the parliamentary majority and opposition (article 16). Within the groups, too, the permitted time has to be apportioned on the basis of the greater or lesser parliamentary representation enjoyed by these groups: thus in April 1978, it was agreed that RPR should receive the lion's share, sixty minutes, with forty minutes for the PR, thirty-five for the CDS, fifteen for the CNIP and for the Radicals. It seems therefore that the problem of regular party political broadcasts, as well as broadcasting times for election campaigns, is now an accepted issue, together with regular discussions on political issues.

Yet it should not be forgotten that, while some of this 'liberalization' is due to the splintering of the parties, and the consequently shakier governmental majority, much of it rests still on the good will of the president, which, at the most, may last no longer than his tenure of office. The president himself might be viewed as having broken constitutional practice in that he saw fit to broadcast to the nation on the eve of the poll, when the campaign was closed, and it was not possible for any answer to be made. This action, excusable or not, highlights the extent to which liberal tendencies run the risk of foundering on a long tradition of state intervention.

Strangely enough, the exclusive involvement of the state in the media, dangerous as it is to free government, is viewed by some as the one bulwark, already seriously weakened by the law of August 1974, against commercialization.

> Les progrès de la privatisation au sein du service public sont sensibles; déjà, la société anonyme de production, ouverte indirectement aux capitaux privés, est tout entière livrée aux conditions du marché; quant aux sociétés de programmation, animées par la préoccupation de rentabilité financière et de capacité concurrentielle, elles sont soumises à un statut de société nationale qui risque fort de faciliter l'introduction ultérieure de capitaux privés. (J. Chevallier, *La Radio-télévision française entre deux réformes*, p. 319)

However, government policy towards 'pirate' stations seems to have made this fear groundless. A distinction ought to be made here between 'pirate' and commercial radio companies: Europe No. 1, RTL, Radio Monte Carlo and Sud-Radio, which are virtually in the hands of France anyway, since the company which supervises them, Sofirad, is almost entirely controlled by the government. When, in the summer of 1978, a ruling favourable to a 'pirate' radio station was given by a court in Montpellier, which took the view that freedom of speech was protected by the constitution, and that the law of August 1974 did not prevent pirate broadcasting, Giscard immediately asked the government to prepare legislation to ensure the maintenance of the state monopoly in radio and television. The likelihood of commercial interests being able to break down the monopoly seems slight, if only because of political sensitivity on the issue.

The state's relations with the press are in many ways equally ambiguous if, perhaps, less tortuous. Freedom of the press has formally been recognized by the state since 1881, and the problem has been since how the state may best nurture that freedom.

The main danger in the post-war period was felt to come, not from the state, but from commercial interests. The ordinances of 1944 banned any papers which had appeared during the occupation, which effectively left the field clear for the clandestine publications of the resistance, since only the resistance groups were permitted to publish. A stricter definition of the *entreprise de presse* differentiated it from other types of publication in that its productions appearing at least once a month were essentially informative, yet not solely scientific, artistic, technical or professional. The *directeur de publication* had to be either the owner or the principal shareholder, or the editor of the company. It was hoped, in this way, to prevent the setting up of large press empires, yet in the main it must be admitted that the spirit of the ordinances has not been maintained, since the press groups still exist, the newest and largest being that of R. Hersant, which now owns not only the Parisian dailies *France-Soir* and *Le Figaro*, but ten provincial daily papers as well.

Yet if the anti-monopoly aspects of the 1944 ordinances have not been successful, the provision of state assistance which they initiated has undoubtedly helped to keep many papers alive — the principle behind these provisions being to maintain competition among newspapers and periodicals, and at the same time to guarantee a measure of equality to all these organs. State aid is essentially of two kinds: direct assistance in the shape of subsidies for the purchase of printing material, for export aid, or direct payments to the railways for transporting of newspapers, and to the PTT for the cost of telephones; indirect help, in the shape of reduced rate for postal charges, telegrams, etc., reduction in VAT, exemption, whole or in part, from other forms of taxation such as the *patente* (see below). In 1976 and 1977 this system was increased to take in not only daily papers, but weekly publications also, which have to have a national distribution and also be of such a nature as to enlighten their readers on national and international news, and as such, be in the public interest.

Over all, the aid received by the press from the state in France is higher than in any other western country, totalling in 1977 the equivalent of £2.5 million. This gains for the country, in theory, a press which covers a wide range of political opinions and consequently a genuine freedom of opinion. However, without considering here the problems of censorship as applied to books or films, it is clear enough that the state has that power if it chooses to exercise it, and state-aided as it is, the press is ill-equipped to stand against the state if this should ever become necessary. The weakness of the press is clearly a weakness of the democratic principle in France, should the state choose for any reason to exercise its powers against the press. 'Newspapers which accept help from the state, in money or in kind, are inhibited from keeping the cool watch on the state's performance which is among their main obligations.'[15] Given the slightly tentative emergence of television and radio from its Gaullist cocoon, a stronger press in relation not only to the state, but also to the newspaper empires would be of considerable benefit to France.

(3) Central government and local government

The relationship of local and central government inevitably brings one on to the terrain of myth. The problem is often posed from two contrasting viewpoints — Jacobins and decentralizers. The Jacobin archetype, suspicious of the reactionary provinces and seeing Paris as the sole source of leadership, technique and consequently of material and cultural benefits for the people, confronts his decentralizing opponent, for whom Paris is arrogant and remote, if not to say tyrannical, taking its decisions without knowledge or heed of local realities and desires. For the Jacobin, Parisian leadership is the *sine qua non* of national unity: any weakening of it is the prelude to national fragmentation; for his adversary, Parisian tyranny will in the end, unless power is devolved, produce so much discontent on the periphery that the nation may well break up anyway.

Behind this clash of stereotypes lies a more complex reality. It is true that the Jacobin and Napoleonic founders of the modern system of local government wanted to restrict local autonomy as far as they could, and by a barrage of legal and constitutional means at that. But it is also true that local politicians have long since adapted fairly comfortably to this Procrustean bed and are able to have a fair degree of power and influence within the system. What follows is an outline of the different layers of sub-central government, in terms of structures, responsibilities and resources, plus an attempt to grasp their real relationship to Paris; in conclusion some remarks are offered on the strengths and weaknesses of the system, and possible developments within it.

The lowest level is the *commune* (36,383 in 1978), dating from 1789 and based on the parishes of the *Ancien Régime*. Above it is the *département*, created in 1790; there are ninety-six in metropolitan France. Each of these is sub-divided into *arrondissements* which in turn split into *cantons*; but neither of these levels now has either elected authorities nor provides services. Above the departments stand the twenty-two regions, defined by the law of July 1972, each of them grouping a number of departments.

All communes elect a municipal council (often referred to as 'la municipalité'); these are elected six-yearly, the system varying according to the size of commune. Councils number anything from 9 to 109 (Paris): they are obliged by law to carry out certain services (gas and water supply, roads, etc.) and can expand into other fields unless specifically forbidden. The dominant figure is the mayor, elected by his colleagues after taking office and who cannot then be dismissed by them. He is the representative of the state as well as head of his commune. In his first capacity he thus performs duties such as marriages and electoral registration; but in his second, he represents his commune in dealings with other bodies (especially the prefect), assures its security and cleanliness, appoints its staff, draws up its budget and executes its decisions.

Each department has a *conseil général*, whose members are elected on a territorial basis (one per *canton*). The size varies from 17 to 109 (Paris again, for it is both commune and department). The council serves for six years, half of its members being elected at three-year intervals. It meets for a maximum of six weeks yearly, delegating its affairs to a standing committee between times. Although it has an elected president (usually a figure of national standing), its executive is an appointee of the interior minister, the prefect. He it is who prepares agenda and budget, and implements decisions. Like the commune, the department is obliged to provide some services (roads, school buildings, some social security services) and may expand into other activities, legal and financial possibilities permitting.

The region is not a full tier of local government, so it has no elective authorities. Its role is one of economic development, which it fulfils in association with its constituent communes and departments, mainly by proposals and participation in state projects with its rather limited resources. It has three elements – an economic and social council, composed, like its national equivalent, of delegates from local interest groups, whose role is largely consultative; a regional council, of deputies and senators for the region plus nominees from communes and departments, which votes a budget and debates the allocation of central grants; and the executive, a regional prefect who draws up the budget and agenda, and who also doubles as prefect of the main department within the region.

Communes and departments may raise local taxes, two-thirds of which go to the former, one-third to the latter. Three of these are based on property-values and the fourth, the old *patente* (now re-baptized as *taxe professionnelle*) on business activity; many regard the latter as arbitrary and rather unjust in the way it is levied. Bigger communes will supplement resources with industrial or commercial enterprise of their own. In 1975 such resources brought in 35,000 million NF for all France; local authorities borrowed a further 12,000 million and were granted another 45,000 million. 20,000 million of this is the equivalent of an old local tax on wages and salaries, the VRTS: the rest covers recurrent costs (17,000 million) and new capital expenditure (8,000 million). Regional tax-raising powers are slight, the regions being allowed to raise only 55 NF per head per year. In other words, local resources are slight; state loans and grants are decisive. Moreover, most local expenditure (much of it compulsory) is liable to VAT; it is not unknown for the VAT to be higher than the original grant, meaning that the commune subsidizes the state instead of the opposite.

This scheme hides much of the real centre-periphery relationship in France. Does the legal and financial muscle exerted by the centre mean that local autonomy is inexistent? An examination of the forces involved suggests that the answer should be a nuanced one.

The prefect is often set up as the embodiment of Parisian tyranny. His formal powers are great: he is the state's representative in his department (hence the elaborate uniform he wears on official occasions). He is appointed by the head of local government in France, the interior minister, and as such exercises supervision, '*la tutelle*', over all local authorities. He can dissolve council meetings (though he never needs to, in fact); he can veto a budget; he has the last word on law and order (so can prohibit demonstrations, etc.); he is the 'eyes and ears' of the government, expected to pick up and pass on the views of politically important (or dangerous) people to his superior in Paris. He is helped in his task by field services (*services extérieurs*) of ministries in his department, which will have office staff and a direct labour force also. The most important are from the ministries of finance, infrastructure, labour and agriculture; the prefect is supposed to be overall co-ordinator of these services in his department (except for those of justice, labour and education, which have their own heads). Prefects will also participate, along with their own expert staff and heads of the field services, in the regional administrative conference, where important decisions about regional planning are effectively taken.

In practice there are limits to this power; some of the prefect's formal powers (e.g. *a priori* control of budgets) have been cut back; he has probably never had a great deal of control over the field services, which may well deal with Paris or local notables behind his back. The prefects' career structure is another source of weakness: they are moved frequently, whether as a reward or as a punishment. Above all, the prefect has never managed to shake the hold of local notables in his department, some of whom will be parliamentarians or ministers; they are thus powerful figures whom a prefect will annoy at his peril. Such figures often obtain various favours for their departments (building grants, the location of job-creating public or private enterprise, etc.) over the prefect's head, which gives them at least as strong a local clientèle as the latter. J. Chirac was reputed, for instance, during his premiership to have a full-time staff in Matignon, channelling resources busily into the Corrèze, where Chirac is a deputy and general councillor. In fact the prefect has long been a 'Janus', facing two ways. On one hand, he must try to implement the will of Paris; on the other, he finds himself increasingly the advocate of the local grievances and demands to which he must listen every day. Recent studies have dwelt on the similarity of the prefect and the mayor, both in the sandwich-position between grass-roots pressure and Parisian imperatives, and hence very much objective allies, despite the potential for conflict that their relationship contains. Small wonder that the prefect's is a difficult task; yet the profession still attracts men (there are no women prefects) of the highest intellectual and political skills, remaining one of the most prestigious 'grands corps' of the French administration.

The other main pressure for centralization is alleged to be the atomized structure and the financial dependence of local authorities. The financial structure has already been described, and whatever the ability of notables to channel resources into their departments, dependence on central aid remains a powerful check on local autonomy — and not just in France, one might add. As regards the existing levels of local government, there are again some unpalatable facts for the defender of local autonomy to digest, starting with size. Ninety per cent of all communes have fewer than 2,000 inhabitants; 50 per cent fewer than 300. Some 996 have fewer than fifty people, even. But at the other end of the scale, some 73 per cent of the total population live in a mere 12 per cent of the total communes. Now all communes are supposed to be equal: i.e. Paris has the same legal status as a hamlet in the Lozère with 120 people. In practice there is a huge disparity between big communes like Lille or Marseille, with considerable revenue of their own, and small rural villages which raise precious little revenue. Many big towns are famous for their urban planning, their business enterprise or their cultural activities; many rural communes are too poor to put tarmac around the telephone-box, assuming that there is one. Autonomy, then, is proportional to resources. A big town can afford its own specialists and finance much of its development plans; its small 'equivalent' might have one part-time official (probably the primary school teacher) who does municipal business one evening a week. Clearly, such communes are at the mercy of the prefect for resources and technical expertise.

Of late, attempts have been made to palliate such fragmentation by encouraging communes to merge, more by offers of financial inducement than by legal pressure. But local pride and fear of losing office have meant resistance. In the four years following the 1971 act on mergers, only 779 of these had occurred. One way forward which sacrifices comparatively little civic pride, is via the various forms of inter-communal co-operation: a *syndicat à vocation unique*, when they combine for one particular purpose, such as bussing school-children; *syndicats à vocation multiple*, for any number of common services. In big city suburbs there are *districts*, which group local communes for several services and where the communes pool much of their finances. Nine big towns have gone even further with the *communauté urbaine*, which takes over compulsory services from its member communes and has its own council of nominees from the latter.

It seems then that French communes fall into two categories — the small and fairly dependent ones which have, however, great civic pride and interest on the part of their citizens, and a minority of big and powerful ones. Measures currently under consideration are unlikely to change this imbalance. Guichard's 1976 report on local government canvasses such measures as increasing the fiscal prerogatives of communes (welcome to the mayors, but less so perhaps to their *administrés*), further reductions of tutelary power, greater possibilities for communes to decide for themselves about the allocation of central grants, the creation of a national conference of local authorities (no doubt similar to the present mayors' lobby, the *Association des maires de France*) and especially, encouragement to continue with the type of co-operation outlined above; indeed, increased resources and powers would be transferred from communes to the intercommunal bodies, leaving the former with prestige but little else (a measure unlikely to please mayors). In summer 1978 the government was considering similar projects, such as reductions in VAT, better time off and pay for mayors, an improved career structure for local officials, increased technical aid, a guaranteed minimum income for communes and changes in the reviled professional tax. Although some of these would help rationalize communal structures, they are not far-reaching; and it may be that in concentrating its efforts on the lower echelons, the government has ignored a more significant dimension, the region.

Today's extensive debate on the region has as much to do with economics as with politics. We have already seen the inequalities engendered by economic development, whereby some regions of the centre, south and south-west are falling behind the rest in terms of output, living standards and indeed population. On the periphery of France this economic deprivation and its attendant change in social structures is compounded by older cultural factors; in some cases local or regional identity has been stressed strongly, implying varying degrees of distance from the French state. The two most noteworthy examples are Brittany, where there have long been autonomist movements of varying political complexions and Corsica, where since 1975 discontent with Paris has been expressed by bomb explosions and riots, but, characteristically, little loss of life. Not all Corsican, Breton or other regionalists want complete separation from the French state, like the insurrectionary FLNC (*Front de libération nationale corse*). Some, like the UPC (*Union du peuple corse*) led by the Simeoni brothers, want internal autonomy (self-government in all areas save defence and foreign relations): some might well be happy with more hand-outs from Paris; some, like the various Occitanian groups, have little more than the feeling of a common identity and a mistrust of Paris. And certainly all of them are minorities, for the time being at least. But their existence testifies to the presence of deep and intractable problems; and many people without autonomist sentiments might well feel that these problems can only be tackled at local level — by elective regional assemblies with fund-raising and executive powers. The department is too small and too weak to fulfil this task.

Regionalists would also criticize the results obtained by Parisian regional planners to date. The finance ministry and the planning commissioners have played key roles here, relying on classical techniques to incite investment in the provinces — development subsidies paid to would-be investors, tax exemptions, credit facilities, etc. Some results have been obtained through the DATAR (*Délégation à l'aménagement du territoire et à l'action régionale*), a team of high-powered planners, with development funds at their disposal and more importantly, direct access to the prime minister; their task was to short-circuit the more elaborate processes of economic decision-making and get job-creating activity started as soon as possible. Yet even the energetic efforts of DATAR have led to excessive concentration of industry in the departments near Paris, to the disadvantage of those further out. But most regional criticisms would turn on the nature of the existing twenty-two regions, which have the appearance of power but little else. Their lack of resources — technical, financial and labour — have already been described. Moreover, the regions themselves often have no basis outside bureaucratic rationality: being simple aggregates of existing departments, they do not correspond to what one analyst suggests as the minimum for a viable region:[16] 'une collectivité territoriale géographiquement et historiquement vécue par ses habitants, assurant à tous ses membres le plein épanouissement de leur personnalité'. To take the Auvergne region for example, it is clear that it does not cover the old province of Auvergne (only about a quarter of it). Nor does it cover a balanced area of industry, agriculture or commerce: its four departments show a gross imbalance between a narrow industrial base with abnormally high penetration of foreign capital, dominated by one industry and with narrow trade outlets, and a good deal of inefficient agriculture. For such regions it is not certain, either, that the Parisian imperative of industrialization at all costs is the best bet; perhaps other models of development (specialized agriculture, tourism, etc.) need to be considered.

Why have governments left the regions so weak? The attachment of men like Jean-Jacques Servan-Schreiber to regional power is well known, and there is no shortage of quotations to show that Giscard d'Estaing was also keen until he became president. Yet he has gone no further than to suggest that one day France might like to choose between the department and the region; for the rest, Giscardian regional planning has consisted in the time-honoured technique of the hand-out from Paris, dispensed with electoral considerations in mind (cf. the special plan for the Massif Central, Giscard's own region, or the various carrots offered to Corsica in the wake of violence – increased infrastructural credits, transport subsidies, the creation of an extra department on the island). One explanation for the reluctance is Gaullist Jacobinism: the fears of such as Debré about breaking up the nation are frequently aired. This probably explains why the regions of 1972 were such weak affairs, with as little resemblance as possible to older cultural and political entities, long incorporated into the French state but where loyalties to France, or at least to Paris, might be weakest. But there are also political considerations. If powerful regional bodies did emerge, some of them would be run by the left; no government would be keen to hive off such big sources of patronage and influence to opponents, especially when the latter know how to make good use of existing levels of local government. Thus the right is unlikely to move towards regionalization, though the left remains explicitly committed to it. Such a strategy may have its limits; for if regional decline continues, some old fiefs of the right, such as Auvergne and Brittany, may well begin to wonder about their loyalties.

Chapter 4

Political forces

(1) The French party system

Parties are nowadays deemed essential to the workings of a democratic political system. Their functions are complex; but their prime one is to organize and give coherent expression to the political demands of various groups. The latter may be a single class or fraction, or a wider grouping. Although the origins of most parties are clearly traceable to different class fractions, the nature of a party may well change over time; in particular, it may well come to attract support from other class fractions than those on which it was first based, thus qualifying for the title of a 'catch-all' party. Such a process is usually a long and oblique one, and in general it is safe to say that the way in which parties mirror (or deform) class interests is a complex one. At any rate, parties aim to capture political power or a share thereof, so as to translate their demands as far as possible into public policy. Much of their activity will consist, then, in mobilizing supporters; and such mobilization need not be restricted to electoral competitions, though the latter obviously occupy a privileged place in the activity of most parties. A final function of parties is to produce élites who will be able to govern. In other words parties are essential to the upkeep of what is often called the political class.

In democratic systems, parties always function alongside each other. The way in which they relate to each other, the party system, is thus crucial for understanding the politics of any country. In the UK or the USA, politics are dominated by two large, stable and apparently unshakeable parties, with no really crucial differences between them; commentators contrast this stability, which they see as reflecting or maintaining a widespread consensus about the nature and objectives of Anglo-Saxon society, with France, where the party system seemed for a long time to offer a model of acute instability.

Under the Third and Fourth Republics, governments were coalitions whose member parties were divided on a number of bases: class differences were important, but so were ideological ones and plain sectional interests. It has been suggested that this division gave an artificial and exaggerated image of French society, i.e. that underneath the rhetoric of party professionals there was a high degree of consensus as to the nature of the society that suited France most. But the consensus never made its way into party politics. Parties remained numerous and divided. Even the rise of a relatively well-structured socialist party, and later on a communist one, did not really affect the fragmentation of the party system. Neither of the above was able to enlarge its audience beyond a certain point; and when their initial militant ardour had cooled, they too were admitted from opposition into the coalition system. The older parties of the right never developed much of an organization, but they never needed to, managing even after the advent of universal suffrage to maintain hegemony within French civil society and stop the left from gaining too much support.

By 1958, then, France had a party system of coalitions between parties which could agree provided that little positive action were taken, but not if urgent action were needed, and which could in fact quarrel bitterly about seemingly trivial issues. This contributed of course to the debacle of 1958.

Since then there has been something of a mutation. New parties have appeared; old ones have been forced to tighten up their organization: and all have been forced into durable alliances, with the result that France seems to be moving towards a two-block party system ('bi-polarization'). The Fifth Republic enjoys widespread legitimacy, but its system of government displaces power away from parliament (the natural terrain for parties) towards the head of the executive, the president. This means that their ability to influence policy is lessened. At the very least, a party wishing to influence government must have presidential endorsement in elections, i.e. it must already accept a number of common policies or objectives. The president, on the other hand, needs a sympathetic majority (of one or more parties) in the lower house; for if his legislation were consistently refused by a hostile lower house, his constitutional position could become untenable. Hence the majority in the national assembly must be disciplined; and so also must any opposition hoping to supplant it. Thus there are considerable pressures towards tighter party organization and alliances arising from the presidential function itself.

The president himself, though claiming to rule only in the national interest and to be 'president of all the French', could never win his election in the first place without the help of party machinery. The very existence of the second ballot, which is limited to two candidates, forces parties to line up in two conflicting blocks. So far as legislative elections are concerned, one should note the system of *scrutin d'arrondissement* (single-member constituencies), with two ballots again. Seats are rarely won at the first ballot (over 50 per cent of the votes cast being needed), whereas a relative majority suffices at the second. Parties have thus a clear interest in making alliances for the second ballot with those nearest them, and not getting in each other's way. What usually happens is that the principle of 'republican discipline' (as the left calls it) obtains, and the best-placed candidate on left or right benefits from the withdrawal (*désistement*) of the candidate closest to him; the result is usually a straight right–left duel (this was the case in 96 per cent of the seats in March 1978). In some cases withdrawal is automatic, because in order to reach the second ballot candidates require the votes of 12.5 per cent of the registered electorate, i.e. probably over 15 per cent of the poll. Now, the parties which benefit least from such a system are ones with a strong identity, especially the communists; this is so because 'at the first ballot the voter chooses, but at the second he eliminates'. This also means that there is no connection between the percentage of votes obtained in the first ballot (the truest index of a party's audience) and the percentage of seats which it will win in the end.

Here is an example of the system:

Eure 3 (Louviers), March 1978 (main candidates only)
First ballot: Montagne (UDF) 20,431   Loncle (MRG) 14,775
                   Desbordes (RPR) 6,164   Binay (PCF) 11,820

Between ballots Desbordes withdraws in favour of Montagne, and Binay in favour of Loncle, with the following result:

    Montagne   31,061
    Loncle   30,939

Montagne thus wins by 122 votes, illustrating perfectly the importance of a good alliance. Even municipal elections exert a unifying pressure: in the big towns, lists cannot be altered between ballots, so parties need to have agreed, and preferably unified, lists before the first.

It is also suggested that many other factors which made for party fragmentation in the past are disappearing. Thus economic modernization, the drift from the land, the beginnings of a relative affluence and the decline of religious observance, plus an increasing consensus on the merits of the Fifth Republic are all adduced to explain the trend towards a two-block system. One could suggest limits to how far these processes have gone. As regards the consensus on the régime, it would seem better founded if the régime had passed the acid test, i.e. can the left govern within it? Similarly one might doubt whether economic development has eroded traditional class consciousness as much as some analysts might think. Whatever the causes or extent of the phenomenon, however, Dupeux and Converse noted in the early years of the Fifth Republic that voters' attachments to established parties were not so strong as was believed and that they were much readier to change their votes. This readiness has probably made the drift towards bi-polarization easier, when taken in conjunction with the institutional factors outlined above.

Today, then, two blocks of parties confront each other in France. They are referred to here as left and right – terms which might appear more ideological or polemical than the 'opposition' and 'majority' currently preferred by government and media. For years now it has been fashionable to say that the terms are meaningless: that left governments have behaved like conservatives and that many of the right's policies have been progressive. Whatever the truth of such assertions, the great majority of French people seem to identify with the terms; for many they bear a strong emotional, if not irrational charge. They are part of the political culture, in fact. Historically of course the left has stood for change and the right for resistance to change, hence the tags of 'movement' and 'order' which some analysts use. Clearly the content of the terms has varied from the Revolution, when they were first coined (in the Revolutionary assemblies the most radical elements sat in the high benches on the speaker's left). Thus to be in favour of the republic and universal suffrage in 1815 was to be well on the left; whereas to demand no more today would place one equally firmly on the right. None the less the movement/order polarity exists in France as elsewhere, and today it is not difficult to identify its content. The parties of the right are those which accept the broad social and economic structures of French capitalism. The left in contrast is composed of those who aspire to structural change in the direction of socialism. It follows from this that the room for manoeuvre of any centre force is slight; it can only define itself negatively, occupying such terrain as left and right leave to it. Of late this has become so slight as to be non-existent; bi-polarization has forced the centrists to choose sides and most of them are now firmly aligned with the right.

A final curious point concerns vocabulary. Unlike politicians of the left, who revel in the title, those of the right never like to be described as such. They have always preferred a label such as *modéré, indépendant* or even *centre-gauche*; only the very muscular right likes to call itself *la droite*. Such a curious practice is puzzling only to those who, as Rémond remarks, have not yet plumbed the depths of French political vocabulary; but it does show the odd mystique which political concepts can sometimes take on.

(2) Parties of the right

The parliamentary majority supporting presidents de Gaulle, Pompidou and Giscard d'Estaing has increased steadily in terms of parties, even if the latter represent a declining share of public opinion. But despite being forced into close collaboration by the presidential system, these parties have all striven to keep a separate identity; we shall examine them in turn (see Table 4.1).

Table 4.1   Majority parties since 1958

President	Years of office	Constituent parties of majority
De Gaulle	1958–62	UNR + varying numbers of MRP, SFIO and Independents (only PCF in outright opposition)
	1962–9	UDR + RI
Pompidou	1969–74	UDR + RI + Duhamel Centrists
Giscard d'Estaing	1974–	UDR (RPR) + RI (PR) + remainder of Centrists (Lecanuet and Servan-Schreiber)

Gaullism – le Rassemblement pour la république (RPR)

Development   Gaullism has been the dominant party or 'movement' (as the faithful prefer to call it) of the Fifth Republic. It has had numerous changes of name. If one leaves aside the Gaullism of the Resistance, based largely on personal allegiance to the General as a symbol of the will to fight the German invader, then it can be said to have entered its organizational phase with the RPF (*Rassemblement du peuple français*) in 1947. Despite a massive initial surge of membership and popularity, the movement had broken up long before 1958, over the question of support for Fourth Republic governments. But de Gaulle's return to power in 1958 necessitated speedy rebuilding of the Gaullist machinery. The UNR (*Union pour la nouvelle république*) developed into the UNR-UDT (*Union démocratique du travail*) in 1962, to be succeeded by the UDV^{e}R (*Union des démocrates pour la cinquième république*) in 1967 and the UDR (*Union pour la défense de la république*) in 1968. This changed to the *Union des démocrates pour la république* in 1971, and in December 1976 the movement was refurbished as the RPR.

Beneath the changing nomenclature, the party grew steadily in organization and influence, particularly after 1962 under Pompidou's guidance, as it became steadily apparent that de Gaulle's charisma alone was not enough to obtain automatic compliance from the electorate. During these years it supported presidential policy unflinchingly, often being rewarded with favours to be distributed among the constituencies on a fairly clientelistic basis – a technique which led sarcastic critics to compare the UDR with the other great historical masters of clientelism, the Radicals. Gaullism was the biggest party in parliament, its ministers were most numerous in government: Gaullists were given key posts in ministries and other parts of the state apparatus (media, education, public enterprise, etc.). Small wonder that by the late 1960s opponents denounced the Gaullist 'colonizing' of the state and coined the derisive slogan of 'l'Etat-UDR'.

The 1973 elections showd a relative decline in Gaullist strength, and when the UDR lost the presidency in 1974 its rapid demise was predicted. Energetic action by Chirac, making full use of the resources of his two-year premiership, revitalized the movement. The RPR that he launched in 1976 was already a well-oiled movement, and it was able to win over 22 per cent of the first ballot vote in the 1978 election, running neck and neck with the socialists for the title of France's biggest party.

Ideology   Gaullists like to see their movement as part of a tradition that resurfaces 'when France is in danger'. Less indulgent analysts usually place it within what Rémond calls the Bonapartist right, as opposed to the 'Orleanist' right (see below). The Bonapartist right is essentially nationalist, populist and, within varying degrees, authoritarian. Gaullist nationalism emerges in its foreign policy of independence, whereby France is to play as autonomous a role in world affairs as is commensurate with her strength as a medium-sized power, resisting in particular the hegemony of the USA. In domestic policy, it emerges in the doctrine of national unity at all costs; for Gaullists the ties of nationhood override, or should override, class or sectional interests. Hence *inter alia* their ready acceptance of the Jacobin state and their hostility to anything resembling decentralization. In the Bonapartist tradition, national unity also involves clear and firm leadership; hence Gaullist dislike of parties and of parliamentarianism in general and their preference for personal leadership based on a popular mandate (presidential election, referendum, etc.), which they claim will provide rational and impartial government in the 'national interest'. Such views are often accompanied by strictures on the primacy of law and order, and hostility to any attitudes that could at all be described as permissive, the whole often being expressed in a commonsense and fairly anti-intellectual language.

For the fairly authoritarian Gaullist conception of the state is also a populist one, i.e. it postulates an indistinct mass of *peuple* rather than a society divided into classes or fractions and believes that it can satisfy them all. This explains why in economics, the Gaullist-Bonapartist tradition keeps its distance from liberal economic theory, talking of a 'voluntaristic' economic policy which uses planning mechanisms and gives the (neutral) state an important arbitral role. Another facet of this economic populism is the various attempts at workers' participation, or *l'association capital/travail*, whereby the Gaullist state has tried, unsuccessfully, to persuade employers and workers to sink their differences in the name of national unity. It is this aspect of the doctrine that also accounts for the persistence over the years of left-wing Gaullists, whose influence on the movement has not, on the whole, been great.

This populism has its limits, however. Gaullism is vocal about the sanctity of property and particularly virulent in its denunciation of marxism, especially the communist party.

Given this ideological basis, then, one can see why Gaullism regards the Fourth Republic as a kind of Antichrist. For them its impotent multi-party system was the result of putting sectional priorities before the national interest; its foreign policy consisted merely of cowardly endorsements of American *Diktats*; and even its social and economic achievements, when these are actually recognized, are attributed to the good work of de Gaulle's provisional government before 1946! One cannot underestimate the importance within Gaullist discourse of the ideal antibody, the Fourth Republic, mere mention of which is enough to legitimize Gaullist rule.

None of the above should be taken at face value, of course, especially the claim to be above the interests of any one class or fraction. Historically *régimes d'exception*, to use Poulantzas's phrase, whether of the gentler Gaullist type or the tougher Napoleonic variety, occur when there has been a loss of hegemony, i.e. when dominant social forces and their political representatives lose political control over society, at least temporarily. Now, so long as there are no social forces to challenge them radically (forces which demand a qualitatively different society, that is), political equilibrium can only be restored by some kind of compromise until the old forces recover or renew themselves sufficiently to reassert control. Perhaps Gaullism was such a compromise. Its assumption of power came only two and a half years after decimation at the polls in January 1956; but in the meantime the impotence of the older right, centre and even its allies on the non-communist left had been confirmed, notably by the Algerian fiasco. It was this crisis which let in Gaullism; the political class, not to mention large sectors of the population, wanted a solution. So too did certain advanced sectors of French capitalism, for whom re-orientation of the French economy was paramount. If the established parties of the régime could no longer guarantee the necessary political stability for this, then perhaps Gaullism could (whatever reservations one might have about some non-economic aspects of Gaullist policy). The Gaullist élites, with their ideals of public service and the national interest, were in fact quite favourably predisposed to economic modernization, and thus ready to perform the task required to speed up the modernization of French capitalism. This task consisted in using the power of the state to pressure industry, and to a lesser extent agriculture, into expansion, mainly by concentrating production into bigger units and opening the economy out towards European competition. Such a course involved a certain amount of pressure from the state, and this the parties of the classical right, especially Pinay's CNIP, had been unwilling to exert, even though it was necessary if French expansion were to continue. Now, this does not imply that Gaullism is simply the tool of 'monopoly capitalism' as the communists have alleged; such an analysis does not explain away Gaullist economic and political nationalism, for instance. But one can suggest that there was a convenient symbiosis between the political needs of Gaullism and those of progressive fractions of French capital, which should perhaps make one look with some scepticism on claims to be above class or other interest.

Although it sought, by packing the state apparatus with its own people and by bringing government and administration closer together (*technocratie*) to give the state some autonomy from capital, this autonomy was in the end only a relative one. Gaullism could in the long run only impose its expansionist policies within certain limits; sooner or later it would have to make concessions to fractions hurt by these policies but who still pulled considerable electoral weight. Pompidou's presidency already showed considerable clemency to smaller and medium-sized capital. One might wonder what the future of Gaullism could be, once it had closed the colonial question, brought political stability and expanded the economy as far as possible. Could it retain an identity once these primary tasks had been fulfilled or would it, like earlier Bonapartist régimes which had had similar cleaning-up operations to perform, simply melt away and allow the return of more conventional capitalist forces? Perhaps an examination of the movement's structures might shed light on this.

Structures   The RPR has the vertical structure typical of mass parties. Its basic unit is the constituency union, though smaller groups may meet at the level of the commune or even of the workplace. The constituency union elects two-thirds of the delegates to the federation, the departmental level of the movement; the other third consists of party officials, office holders and ex-officio members. The federation can send policy proposals and suggest candidates for office to the secretary-general in Paris, but the federation secretary can be elected only with the latter's approval. Federations send delegates to the national conference (*assises nationales*) in proportion to their membership and the number of their office-holders. There is another tier of activity between federal and national level, the regional councils, but these do not seem to be very active.

At national level four bodies are important. The two-yearly *assises* are open to all members (40,000 attended the inaugural one in 1976), though only delegates from federations, parliamentarians and members of the Economic and Social Council have voting rights (there were

14,000 of these in 1976). These elect the president of the movement and some 170 members of the *comité central*, which is supposed to run the movement in line with policy approved at the *assises*; the other members of this body are, since March 1978, all deputies and also members of the *conseil politique*. This body advises the president and consists of the secretary-general (a presidential appointee, currently Alain Devaquet), ex-prime ministers, the chairmen of RPR senate and national assembly groups, and other central committee nominees and co-opted members.

If the central committee is the RPR parliament, then its executive is the *commission exécutive*. This veritable shadow cabinet, which is an oligarchy of presidential nominees, has a dozen national secretaries, who specialize in different areas of policy; it includes the best-known Gaullist leaders, as well as rising stars such as Alain Juppé and Jacques Toubon.

Within the top echelons of the RPR, several tendencies may be distinguished. There are the neo-Poujadists, of whom Hector Rolland, deputy for the Allier, is the most vocal; ferociously anti-communist, opposed to moral and political liberalization, they are still very much the voice of a provincial petty-bourgeoisie threatened by moderniz- ation. On the opposing wing of the party are the *chabanistes*, those who still believe in the progressive rhetoric of Gaullism, though their leader's influence has been systematically weakened by Chirac. Between them lies a broad layer of pragmatic politicians, many of whom have held office and who are basically conservatives; if the truth were told they would be equally, if not more, at home inside the Giscardian party. As for the older generation of historic Gaullists, most of the barons accept the necessity of a tough leader like Chirac, even if he has ousted them slowly from positions of real influence; but some of them (notably Debré) could find their influence increasing if Chirac embarks on a course of conflict with Giscardism.

For the moment one can conclude that the RPR structures are in the Bonapartist line, in so far as they allow a large initiative to the leader while at the same time endorsing him through the mass member- ship. Chirac is very much in control of his machine and is generally believed to take major decisions in a 'kitchen cabinet' consisting of Y. Guéna, C. Pasqua (organizer of Gaullist rallies and grassroots activities) and the redoubtable Pompidolians, Juillet and Garaud; it also included J. Monod, the former head of DATAR and first secretary- general of the RPR, who did much to build its machinery. But Monod resigned after the election win in 1978 because, it was rumoured, of personal and political differences with Chirac.

The party press is slight for such an important movement. Local efforts apart, there is only really the broadsheet *La Lettre de la nation*, edited by Pierre Charpy, which is rather hard to get hold of. One can expect a serious effort to produce a party daily soon. On a more intellectual level there are revues such as *Etudes gaulliennes* or *L'Appel*, which are not official RPR publications but are run by militant Gaullists, usually of the more ideological kind.

Two other features are worthy of note. First, in an attempt to raise the political level of activists, the RPR has put a lot of effort and money into party schools, especially for party cadres and candidates; these schools involve both residential and correspondence courses. Also, in an attempt to compete with the left and to show that the RPR is a mass activist party, Chirac has revived the idea of workplace groups – a throwback to the days of the RPF when Gaullism claimed a million working class members. Care is taken to keep party activity separate from trade-union action. It is early to say yet what results this will give, but in mid-1977 there were perhaps 250 such groups.

Finance is a crucial ingredient of any political party, both for running expenses and for campaigning. A would-be deputy probably needs 50,000 to 100,000 NF to conduct a decent campaign; the three main presidential candidates in 1974 spent over five million. One might be tempted to think that the *patronat* finances parties of the right, but this verdict needs some refinement. While it has often had money for certain candidates in the past, and while it still employs a full-time political staff under A. Aubert, whose main task is to give logistic and financial support to chosen candidates, there is no automatic collusion between the employers' organizations as a whole and any one party of the right. Money tends to come from individuals or sectors within the *patronat* and to be doled out rather reluctantly, and very much on the basis of local situations. It is also widely known that there is a *'caisse noire'* of unspecified proportions in the prime minister's office, which is disbursed at election time.

How, then, do Gaullist finances fit into this picture? As with all parties they are hard to assess. There are probably individuals and groups of employers who donate. Monod was particularly concerned to keep the RPR away from easy money, especially presents from property speculators which had sullied the Gaullists' reputation under Pompidou. Clearly Chirac's departure from Matignon has cut the RPR off from any secret funds, and as it now has few ministers, it will find it harder to have civil servants or officials from public enterprise 'seconded' (*en mission*), i.e. working full time on party business while being paid by the state. Crisol and Lhomeau suggest that the figure of twenty million NF advanced by the RPR is too low to pay staff and other overheads and that Chirac, 'le grand argentier', still has access to considerable but unspecified funds.[1]

Compared with the average of the French population, the Gaullist electorate (see Table 4.2) seems very masculine and middle-aged. Sociologically, there is a high percentage of farmers, retired people,

Table 4.2   Electorate of major parties (percentages)

	PCF	PS/ MRG	CDS/ Radical	PR	RPR	French electorate
CSP						
Agriculteur, salarié agricole	4	8	13	10	12	9
Artisan, petit commerçant	3	5	9	8	7	6.6
Cadres supérieurs, professions libérales, industriel, gros commerçant	4	8	17	14	13	9
Cadres moyens, employés	19	24	18	17	19	20
Ouvrier	46	31	11	16	20	28.5
Inactif	24	23	32	35	29	26.9
Sex						
Male	52	51	57	46	50	48
Female	48	49	43	54	50	52
Age						
18–24	17	13	9	9	13	15
25–34	24	26	8	17	18	20
35–49	26	26	29	26	25	25
50–64	20	21	28	20	21	20
65 +	13	14	26	28	23	20

Source: September 1977 poll by Louis-Harris-France, *Le Matin*, 6 February 1978.

petty-bourgeois and top bourgeois. The working class is under-represented, however. It is also worth pointing out the low number of RPR voters who are either irreligious or belong to a union.

If this suggests that much RPR support is conservative, the hypothesis is confirmed when we look at areas of geographical strength — Alsace and Lorraine, with strong Catholic and nationalist traditions, Brittany and the south of the Massif Central. These are all old conservative areas. But Gaullism has also done well in more industrialized areas such as the Paris region and the north. It has never been very strong in the south, with its long anti-clerical and republican traditions.

All the evidence today suggests that the core of RPR support is increasingly conservative. In 1967–8, the structure of the Gaullist vote was very near to that of the electorate at large (see Table 4.3). Since then it is clear that it has lost much working-class support in particular, and the major task for the RPR is to try and win it back.

As regards membership, the RPR gives the following figures. From 285,000 at its inception, it had swollen to 620,000 by April 1978, including an implausible 49 per cent of women. The RPR claims

Table 4.3   The right's electorate in the 1960s (percentages)*

	France as a whole (1968 census)	Gaullists + RI 1967	1968
Age			
21–34	29	29	55
35–49	29	26	
50–64	22	26	45
65 +	20	19	
CSP			
Cadres supérieurs, professions	6	5	6
Commerçants	9	11	14
Cadres moyens, employés	17	16	18
Ouvriers	32	28	25
Agriculteurs	12	16	18
Inactifs	24	24	19

* Includes the votes for RI candidates standing in alliance with Gaullists.
Source: J. Charlot (ed.), *Quand la Gauche peut gagner*, Moreau, 1973, p. 52.

that over 40 per cent of its members are under forty-five; sociologically, workers are still under-represented, but there is an increase of petty-bourgeois categories (*cadres moyens* and *employés*). It remains to be seen whether this relative renewal will be strong enough to pull Gaullism back to its position of the mid-1960s and shake off the image with which the RPR seems increasingly to be stuck — that of a tough right, champion of declining sections of society.

Giscardism — le Parti Républicain (PR)

Development   The ancestry of the PR goes back to the *notables* of the early nineteenth century. Representing the post-Revolutionary bourgeoisie, these politicians were staunch defenders of economic and political liberalism, wanting to restrict the state's role to one of maintaining law and order. Originally supporters of a constitutional monarchy based on restricted suffrage, these 'Orleanist' liberals were able to adapt themselves to universal suffrage and parliamentary democracy, merging imperceptibly after 1870 with new political currents based on the middle and lower bourgeoisie. Such were the origins of the moderates or independents of Third and Fourth Republics. If by ideology and temperament such groups were loose and ill organized, consisting of deputies clustered around one outstanding leader and potential prime minister (Ferry, Poincaré, Flandin, etc.), their members often held key posts in government. After 1945 the Cold War and the break-up of tripartism gave them the chance to refurbish a reputation tarnished by the fact that many of them had collaborated more or less willingly with the Nazi occupier. They thus became a key element of coalitions, especially after 1951 under the leadership of A. Pinay. During the Fourth Republic Roger Duchet made energetic but only partially successful attempts to federate these chronic individualists into something resembling a modern conservative party — the *Centre national des indépendants et des paysans* (CNIP).

Most independents were glad to see de Gaulle back in power in 1958. But while liking his financial orthodoxy, they found his presidentialism opposed to their parliamentary mores; and his moves towards Algerian independence clashed with their colonialist views. There thus ensued a split in their ranks in autumn 1962 (over the referendum on the system of presidential election), most of them going into the *cartel des non* and suffering electoral disaster for it. Some thirty-five of them followed de Gaulle, however, and they were led by the young deputy for Puy-de-Dôme, first elected in 1956 and widely recognized as a Pinay protégé — Valéry Giscard d'Estaing. In 1966 they set up a party of their own, the *Fédération nationale des républicains indépendants* usually known as the RI.

Until 1974 the RI played a useful secondary role in French politics. Always within the majority, they used the Gaullist umbrella to prosper, roughly doubling their parliamentary strength. They held some key posts (Giscard at the finance ministry, Marcellin at the interior), and were fully associated with Gaullist policy during its dominant period. Yet they were never Gaullists by temperament, ideology or origins. Their position was summarized in Giscard's famous 'Oui, mais . . .'; they agreed broadly with Gaullist policy but reserved the right to express differing views — notably on European affairs and on questions of economic and political freedoms. Needless to say their dissent did not go far, except for the referendum of 1969 where their hostile vote (Giscard was temporarily excluded from government by the General at the time) effectively sealed de Gaulle's fate. Many Gaullists still cannot forgive Giscard for this; but it meant his return to power under the aegis of Pompidou. The RI were clearly awaiting the end of the latter's mandate so as to install their leader in the Elysée in 1976, but their wish was granted earlier than foreseen when Pompidou died in 1974.

Since then the RI have struggled to develop a party machine to match that of Gaullism, so as to support the actions of their leader. Despite the much publicized metamorphosis of their movement into the PR in May 1977, it does not seem that they have been too successful. But by the 1978 elections they had managed to unite the non-Gaullist parties of the right into a loose electoral organization, the

UDF (*Union pour la démocratie française*), very much under PR hegemony. In the new parliament the UDF deputies formed a group; but it was too early to say if this meant the beginnings of a new non-Gaullist mass party of the right.

Ideology Today's PR is characterized above all by its style, which could be described as one of moderation. Its spiritual leader, Giscard d'Estaing, is urbane, aloof and coolly intellectual – the very opposite of Chirac, who cultivates an image of hardworking and uncomplicated directness. The style of the parties matches that of their leaders. The RPR goes for what it thinks is a plain man's language, full of appeals to 'common sense'; it is never afraid of polemic and at times positively welcomes noisy public dispute. PR discourse is a more subtle affair, resting on carefully calculated appeals to different categories and not so much on muscular denunciations of 'collectivist' opponents (though these are not to be ruled out in extremis). These differences in style conceal a number of characteristic ideological themes.

First among these is an appeal to individualism against what is seen to be the all-encroaching power of the state – 'donner à l'épanouissement individuel priorité sur l'organisation de l'Etat'.[2] This theme, a constant of liberal thought since the early nineteenth century, contrasts with the more Jacobin view of the Gaullist right, which tends to sublimate individuals into the framework of the nation. In the economic field this involves a greater commitment to free enterprise, with no talk of the voluntaristic planning dear to Gaullism; indeed the PR recommends hiving off sectors of nationalized industry to private capital. The PR has something to offer small businessmen and farmers, promising support to those wishing to set up on their own; but it also admits the necessity of rationalizing further both agriculture and industry, speaking of 'une politique industrielle sélective', so as to increase exports. In other words it attempts, somewhat uneasily, to reconcile the claims of big and smaller capital.

Individualism also characterizes the PR view of social relations, where the accent is put on participation and decentralization of responsibilities. This contrasts with the RPR, which the Giscardians like to present (usually more by implication than by direct statement) as being further to the right than themselves. The PR sees society not as a homogeneous block, and not in terms of class cleavages either; rather it is a loose agregate of groups, with the middle groups between the very privileged and the very deprived becoming steadily more numerous. These middle groups can, the PR hopes, be won over. To structure this society, and to ensure greater participation by individuals in decision-making, the PR counts, like its ancestor Tocqueville, on the *corps intermédiaires* – voluntary or public bodies situated between citizen and central government. The PR proposes to give greater powers to voluntary organizations, but there are limits to how far decentralization and participation will be taken: on the level of sub-central government, for instance, the PR, although it claims that it will abolish the tutelary powers of prefects, refuses the creation of regional authorities with proper powers. In the field of industrial relations, while it promises *cadres* a significant say in decision-making inside the firm, it offers workers merely an increased (but quite unspecified) say in the organization of conditions on the shop floor.

As regards political structures, the PR accepts the presidential régime, but would probably prefer parliamentary elections to be based on proportional representation, despite the possible risks of instability. This should be seen less as an essential part of PR ideology than as a tactical move: with a proportional system the Giscardians would hope to cut back Gaullist representation in parliament, and also perhaps to escape from their uneasy alliance with Gaullism towards a deal with other partners.

Finally, on the level of foreign policy, the liberal tradition has always been less nationalistic than its Bonapartist rival. Thus, Giscardism has always been more favourable to European political integration than Gaullism, and in the current trial of strength over the enlargement of the EEC, the two again find themselves on opposite sides. The PR programme wants increased co-operation between the developed capitalist democracies — 'une communauté de peuples libres' — in an unspecified way; but the tone of this proposition is in stark contrast to the Gaullist stressing of French priorities. The PR is also characterized by a definite lack of the anti-American feeling which was and is an important emotional constituent of Gaullism.

Structures   Despite the presence of its moral leader in the Elysée and the sophistication and ubiquitousness of its publicity, it should not be thought that the PR is a particularly well-structured organization. When Giscard came to power in 1974, he was in roughly the same position as de Gaulle in 1958 — he had supreme power, but in order to use it fully, he needed an adequate party machine. The old RI fell a long way short of requirements and it is not certain how well today's PR fits the bill.

At local level the significant unit is probably the departmental federation, with its centrally appointed secretary; constituency associations would seem to be fairly weak. At national level the network of committees that ran the old RI has been reduced to two — a *bureau politique* and a *secrétariat national*. These are appointed by the secretary-general, himself elected by the three-yearly party congress (though Jacques Blanc, successor to the first PR secretary-general J.-P. Soisson, was simply appointed to his post when Soisson became a minister in April 1978). The secretariat contains eighteen persons who are responsible for different areas of policy and are in effect PR spokesmen on these topics. The *bureau politique* is a more powerful body, 'le véritable exécutif du PR', and it determines the main outlines of policy. Chaired by the secretary-general, assisted by his two national delegates, it contains twenty-four people, all of them notables. Its members in 1978 included R. Chinaud (chairman of the PR deputies' group), M. d'Ornano (minister of environment), J.-P. Fourcade (ex-finance minister) and two women, Nicole Pasquier and Monique Pelletier, who had held special governmental posts, dealing with women's problems and drug offenders respectively. The PR programme has much to say about listening to grass-roots initiatives, but with the long intervals between congresses, the wide powers of appointment accruing to the secretary-general, the PR would seem to be a centralized machine, especially if, as Ysmal claims, party leaders have a monopoly of the congress platform anyway.[3]

Little is known about PR finances; it admits to a budget of eight million NF 'partly covered by subscriptions and gifts'. But as only ten NF of each member's subscription comes into head office, this means that the proportion of gifts from companies and individuals is probably high. Campana recounts the unsuccessful attempts of V. Chapot, a senior PR organizer and very close to Giscard d'Estaing, to raise some finance from industry after 1974 by the device (which most political parties in France use) of floating a company which is largely fictitious but whose services can be paid for generously (and legally).[4] Some running expenses are certainly covered by the 'loan' of full-time staff from the offices of PR ministers to do party work. Soisson had at least three when he was in charge, and there were probably others. Certainly the comfortable offices in the rue de la Bienfaisance with their forty staff (as Frears calculated) and their sophisticated documentation service could not be run on a shoe-string.

In terms of press the PR is badly served, not managing to produce a regular journal. The cynical would no doubt point out that the radio and television in France do a more than adequate job in propagating Giscardian ideals. There are also a number of weeklies, notably *Le Point*, which, though having no organic connection with the PR, present Giscardian views in an intelligent and readable way.

As regards membership, the PR claimed 90,000 in March 1978 — an improbable figure. Some of these will also be members of the youth movement *Autrement* (previously *Génération sociale et libérale*), which claims 15,000 members and which Wright describes aptly as a movement for well-bred youths. More important are the clubs *Perspectives et réalités* who claim 20,000 members; under Fourcade's chairmanship these clubs are 'think-tanks' which contribute policy ideas and more importantly, attract and groom suitable candidates for local and national office from among the educated and better-off sectors of the population.

The PR is proud of the youth of its membership (one-quarter under twenty-five, 69 per cent under forty-five) but rather more cautious about its sociological composition; it uses an analytical breakdown that does not correspond to the normal system of CSPs. Thus some 11 per cent of members are listed as *fonctionnaires*, which could cover anything from a train-driver to a *chef de cabinet ministériel*. One or two features do stand out, however; there are relatively high proportions of lower petty-bourgeois (18 per cent of *employés*) and of retired or non-working people (over 16 per cent). Workers represent a mere 8 per cent of the total, suggesting that the militant audience of Giscardism at least has not penetrated far below the petty-bourgeoisie.

The PR electorate is of interest as it is very close to that of the Gaullists. It is slightly more feminine and has more retired people than the national average, but the PR appears now to attract slightly more working-class votes than its rival. Like the RPR voters, a high proportion of PR ones admit to being practising Catholics or at least feeling a strong religious sentiment. But if one compares the answers given by both sets of voters to various questions (limitation of the right to go on strike, role of the family within society, opposition to structural changes within society), one sees that the difference between the two is minimal.[5] One can say that the PR and the RPR are fighting for the loyalties of the conservative Frenchman (certainly the PR does well in areas of conservative tradition – Normandy and Brittany, the east, the Alps). It may well be that in the first ballot local considerations and personalities decide which party does best; but in the crucial second ballot there is almost an automatic transfer of support both ways. The essential Giscardian gains in 1978 came in Gaullist seats; and one could note the presence of a number of young deputies who have begun to supplant the older type of provincial notable, often inheriting their seats. The Gaullists, on the other hand, were unable to renew their parliamentary strength to the same extent, relying more on well-entrenched notables. But beneath the rivalry of an older and a newer right, the voters are able to recognize a common conservative core.

Giscardian allies

These are the CDS (*Centre des démocrates sociaux*), plus some minor groups. CDS is by far the most significant.

Development   CDS has a long history, inseparable from that of the church. The reader is familiar with the long antagonism of church and republic since the Revolution; but with the consolidation of republican democracy, the church decided to come to terms with the inevitable and encourage Catholics to participate in republican politics, so as to conserve as much influence as possible. The result is christian democracy. Never having much of an audience or organization before 1939, it owed its dramatic start in 1945 to the upheaval of the occupation years and the part played by Catholics in the Resistance. These were the people who launched the MRP (*Mouvement républicain populaire*) at the liberation. It was to become a key party of the Fourth Republic, attracting on occasions up to 28 per cent of the vote and sitting in most governments, sharing power first with the left, then with the right.

This thankless position in the centre of French politics reflected the fundamental contradictions of the MRP, torn between a reformist leadership often close to the socialists on some points (notably social policy and European union) and a conservative electorate. The latter voted for it only because (a) it was Catholic and (b) older conservative parties were discredited by their record during the occupation, and Gaullism was not yet available as an alternative. The revival of both these forces after 1947 took support from MRP, which moved steadily to the right in an attempt to regain this. The MRP was really in a cleft stick; if it supported traditional Catholic demands, such as state aid to church schools, it fell out with the left. But if it turned against conservative vested interests (e.g. that of the home distillers' lobby, responsible for much of the alcoholism in France) it stood to lose votes in vital seats. By 1958 its stock had shrunk steadily, and being identified with the Fourth Republic it shared the opprobrium generally incurred by the régime. Although the MRP supported the arrival of Gaullism and shared in government till 1962, it broke with the General over Europe and the presidential election question; the November election dealt it a death blow, much of its support going over to Gaullism.

After momentary thought about reviving the old alliance with the socialists, the rump of the movement decided to go it alone. It ran a candidate, J. Lecanuet, in the presidential election of 1965 and he scored over 15 per cent on the first ballot. Convinced that there was still a solid bedrock of christian-democrat support in France, he launched a movement, the *Centre démocrate*, in December 1965 to canalize this (the old MRP was wound up in 1967). This 'opposition centrism' fought elections (as the *Centre pour le progrès et la démocratie moderne*) and formed a parliamentary group; but their opposition lacked conviction, to say the least. Some of them joined the majority of G. Pompidou in 1969, under the leadership of J. Duhamel, leaving Lecanuet still in opposition. He joined with another rump-party, the Radicals of Jean-Jacques Servan-Schreiber, in 1971 under the umbrella of *Les Réformateurs*. This coalition scraped together enough deputies to form a parliamentary group (a minimum of thirty is required) in the 1973 elections, but only thanks to Gaullist withdrawals at the second ballot. Giscard's campaign in 1974 was the signal for Lecanuet to abandon his opposition, and he supported the eventual victor right from the first ballot. The reward was a generous share of ministerial portfolios for himself and his friends. It now remained only to unite the two halves of the old CD, as both were now in the majority. This duly took place at Rennes in May 1976, the new formation taking the title of CDS. We can thus summarize its rather untidy evolution in diagrammatic form:

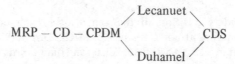

$$\text{MRP} - \text{CD} - \text{CPDM} \overset{\displaystyle\nearrow \text{Lecanuet} \searrow}{\underset{\displaystyle\searrow \text{Duhamel} \nearrow}{}} \text{CDS}$$

Ideology   The CDS has retained much of the character of the mainstream MRP (the members of that organization who took its progressive aspects seriously having long since departed to various parts of the non-communist left). It makes as much as possible of its centrist title, implying that it occupies a happy medium between a 'collectivist' left and a hard, inflexible right (read Gaullism), which is incapable of change. It implies that it is the left wing of the right, as it were, and thus that it is best able to pull Giscardism towards a policy of reforms and even one day (for politics is sometimes made of dreams) serve as a link between Giscardism and the socialists. Lecanuet often casts himself in the unlikely role of siren, attempting to lure the socialists away from their communist partners. CDS discourse is suitably moralizing, and it borrows a lot from a humanistic type of vocabulary developed by the MRP: words like 'justice' and 'responsibility' figure prominently. Yet this is usually mixed with a fairly elementary anti-communism which is certainly cruder than that of the PR. The CDS is clearly reformist, i.e. it does not seek to change the structures of French capitalism but believes that these can be improved by legislative measures, such as income redistribution through the tax system or participation for workers in the workplace (in which they might perhaps go further than the PR). A characteristic theme is the CDS view of the family as the matrix of society and their wish to shape social policy around the family. This and the humanistic discourse are the surest signs of the CDS catholic origins, though the movement denies strenuously that its christian appeal is limited to any one denomination. Politically, CDS favours greater decentralization, especially increased spending power for communes (logically enough, given that its strengths are mainly provincial); though it stops short of demanding full regional authorities. Above all, CDS is committed to European political unity. This has long been its major trademark (and the main source of Lecanuet's opposition to the régime before 1974). CDS leaders can be heard to remark in private that the idea of an independent foreign policy is a myth, although naturally their public pronouncements are more nuanced. A proof of the Europeanism of the CDS is its membership of the *Parti populaire européen*, an international grouping of christian democrat parties set up to co-ordinate the electoral campaign for the European parliament in 1979.

Structures   Apart from traditional Catholic areas (Brittany, Alsace, Auvergne), organizations at constituency level are weak. Departmental federations send delegates to a two-yearly national congress, which elects a president and secretary-general; but in the interim, power resides with the top committees. These are, first, the *conseil politique* composed of departmental delegates and parliamentarians, and theoretically responsible for overall policy guidelines. It also elects thirty members to a *comité directeur*, who sit with various co-optees of the president and secretary-general. Within this latter committee lies the real locus of power, the *bureau politique*, which meets monthly and is composed of president, secretary-general and assistants, treasurer and six others.

Power is thus concentrated in a few hands, mainly those of parliamentary notables; this is an adequate structure for a party whose task is not to put on massive displays of militant activity but to rally the *bien-pensants* of provincial, and mainly petty-bourgeois, France. The personality of its president, J. Lecanuet, senator and mayor of Rouen, looms large over CDS, though his hegemony is now under threat from a generation of rising stars such as P. Méhaignerie (agriculture minister) and J. Barrot (commerce minister).

If relatively weak in terms of deputies, CDS has a strong base in local government with its 4,000 mayors and 355 departmental councillors, 11 of whom chair their *conseil général*. The CDS also boasts a youth wing, the JDS (*Jeunes démocrates sociaux*), which probably contains most of the real activists; some of them confess disappointment at CDS support for the austere policies of recent governments. There is also a women's movement which claims 4,000 members and which, while by no means militantly feminist, is still very critical of the inadequate life-chances which are offered women in French society.

Membership of CDS as a whole is estimated at 35,000, no sociological analysis of membership being made. Federations are supposed to give 10 NF per member annually to headquarters, and members may well pay in 50 or 100 francs above this. Some parliamentarians pay in a percentage of their salary. This would not be enough to pay the forty or so staff and the dozen secretaries which the CDS employs, or to pay the rent on its double office suite in boulevard Saint-Germain. Hence the movement's refreshing frankness in admitting the help of civil servants on loans and gifts from various parts of the business world.

Lack of militants on the ground is compensated by an excellent publicity machine, the best of the right parties. In addition to numerous broadsheets produced by local groups and federations there is a very competent weekly *Démocratie moderne*, which sells 25,000 copies. *Commune moderne* is a specialized review for local councillors: and there is the more theoretical periodical *France Forum*. The ably produced election manifesto *Une Autre Solution* sold 22,000 copies — some of them in a comic-strip version. The documentation centre is well equipped, and visiting foreign academics are received with a courtesy that is by no means frequent with political parties.

The remainder of the Giscardian alliance is made up of random elements, starting with the Radical party, whose history will be recounted at greater length in the following section. It has shrunk sadly from the days when it was the pivot of the republic; today it lives on only through its local councillors and its handful of senators and deputies (most of whose seats are secured by some very subtle electoral alliances); there is also the financial backing of Jean-Jacques Servan-Schreiber (JJSS). Little remains of the old Radical spirit except rhetoric and nostalgia. Probably the party's one characteristic idea, that of regional executives (long a hobby-horse of JJSS), is a historical aberration anyway, in a party that was always Jacobin at heart. The Radicals claim 30,000 members, of whom less than 1,000 are probably paid up. Their share of the popular vote is less than 2 per cent, and their future looks altogether bleak.

Two other minor factions are Emile Muller's MDSF (*Mouvement démocrate socialiste de France*) and Eric Hintermann's PSD (*Parti social démocrate*). Both these are small groups of ex-socialist notables, terrified by the 1972 alliance of communists and socialists and driven to support Giscardism as the best hope of achieving some reform (and of holding their seats). They have little existence outside the small cluster of activists that support their leaders.

Of slightly more significance is the CNIP, that relic of the Fourth Republic which confounded many who had believed it to be dead by doing quite well in the 1978 elections. Here it had nine deputies elected, most of whom, it is true, took the precaution of getting the endorsement of either the RPR or UDF (sometimes both). The CNIP has also conserved a solid foundation in local government, attested to by the presence of thirty senators in the upper house. The CNIP is really the last stand of the notables of earlier republics, very much the representatives of an earlier phase of capitalism, when the small and medium-sized businesses still weighed heavily in the economy. They are too individualistic to join either Chirac or Giscard d'Estaing.

In their numerous brochures and their monthly journal, the independents propound a rugged liberalism. They have never really accepted the welfare state, any kind of government intervention in the economy, women's rights, or moral liberalism; church and family are still very important to them, and most of them regard Giscard as a crypto-socialist. Their anti-communism is the most uncompromising of all the right-wing parties (in an election poster directed against the communists, the main motif was a map of Siberia, with the various *gulags* marked prominently — in red of course). But archaic as they are, they were needed in 1978 to keep the left out of some key seats, and in this they probably succeeded beyond their wildest hopes.

(3) Parties of the left

These are essentially the socialists and communists, which are assumed to be on the left because they seek to transform the structures of capitalist society, instead of reforming or managing it. Since 1972 these parties have been combined in a left union, along with the left Radicals (a small left-over from previous republics, which will be discussed briefly). Stimulated by the common programme of government (CPG), which committed its signatories to a precise legislative programme if elected, the union progressed well in terms of popular support until September 1977, when the renegotiation of the CPG broke down, resulting in a drastic deterioration of relations between the partners and the loss of the 1978 elections by the left. But the left union, though at a low ebb, is not dead; the two main partners still claim to be committed to it, and it is hard to see how in the foreseeable future either could find a realistic alternative alliance. For this reason, we shall insist somewhat in this section not just on an analysis of the separate components of the left, but also on their inter-relationship in all its conflictual dynamism.

Socialism — the Parti socialiste (PS)

Development In 1905 a number of marxist and near-marxist fractions united to form the SFIO (*Section française de l'internationale ouvrière*). The new party was an unstable mixture; its revolutionary marxist rhetoric belied a leadership much more inclined to reformism and the conquest of power through parliament. This contradiction was plastered over, brilliantly, in the theoretical writings and the political action of Jean Jaurès, the effective party leader until he was murdered in 1914. By this time the party's one million votes showed that it had a solid working-class base and was also making inroads into the lower petty-bourgeoisie and peasantry.

A revolutionary party in theory, aiming to establish social ownership of the means of production, the SFIO excluded collaboration with bourgeois governments – at least to the point of joining one. But this temptation grew stronger between the wars under the leadership of Léon Blum, especially as the party was challenged for the working-class vote by a new and intransigent movement, communism. Pressure came to a head in 1934–6, with the worsening international situation. The threat posed by fascism persuaded communists (with the blessing of the Soviet Union), socialists and radicals in several European countries to join together in Popular Front alliances, the object of which was not to promote socialism but to shore up the wavering capitalist democracies for what seemed an inevitable war against fascism. In France the Popular Front alliance scored a clear win in the 1936 elections, Blum forming a government with communist support, but not participation. Though short-lived, the government implemented a number of changes (forty-hour working week, paid holidays, representative status for trade unions) which have retained a nostalgic, almost mythic odour for people on the left; they are seen as an example of what the left can do when united, and in an odd way 1936 marks a peak of left unity that has never been achieved again.

If its first spell as dominant partner in government had been reluctant, the SFIO was to find itself a frequent member of Fourth Republic coalitions, sharing power first with communists and MRP, later with MRP and Radicals of various hues in the 'third force' type of government – this despite having committed itself in 1946 to a rigorous marxist doctrine under its new secretary-general Guy Mollet. The SFIO record up to 1958 was not brilliant; if it could point with pride to its share in setting up the welfare state institutions of the liberation period and the beginnings of economic recovery, then it had also presided over wage freezes and brutal strike-breaking, as part of the policies demanded by French capitalism for its post-war consolidation. Most of all, in colonial policy, the Mollet government of 1956–7 was responsible for the decisive escalation of the Algerian war. It undertook the disastrous Suez expedition, allowed the forces of repression a free hand in Algeria and made a steady erosion of civil liberties at home. In other words it contributed decisively to that weakening of government authority that in the end killed the Fourth Republic. By 1958 the electoral and militant support of SFIO had sunk as low as the prestige of a régime of which it was now a pillar. It gracelessly admitted defeat and helped de Gaulle to power.

The 1960s were spent exploring various alliances to try and revive the machine. In an early phase it was hoped to revive the old centre-left or third force alliance (MRP to SFIO), an idea particularly associated with G. Defferre, who hoped it could be the platform for a presidential campaign of his own. Lack of enthusiasm by Lecanuet (and also by the communists, who were shut out of this deal) ensured that the idea was stillborn. The mid-1960s saw then a dwarf version of the centre-left alliance called the FGDS (*Fédération de la gauche démocrate et socialiste*). This embraced the SFIO, the Radicals and a group of near-Radical remnants from the Fourth Republic clustering under the leadership of F. Mitterrand known as the CIR (*Convention des institutions républicaines*). This alliance did reasonably well in the 1967 elections, with Mitterrand emerging as a leader of national dimensions, but failed to withstand the electoral disaster of 1968. Since then the logic of bi-polarization has told, and the socialists have been pushed back towards the communists. The rapprochement of the two had been getting under way as early as 1962, in fact, when the communists withdrew a number of second ballot candidates in favour of the SFIO. In 1965 the communists took the dramatic initiative of not running their own presidential candidate and supporting Mitterrand as the united left candidate. In 1967 they again stood down in the second ballot for FGDS candidates and in February 1968 signed a joint declaration with the FGDS in which both partners listed policy points on which they agreed and disagreed. There seemed to be the possibility of a common programme of government emerging as the basis of a united left campaign. But the electoral defeat of 1968 and the Soviet invasion of Czechoslovakia, condemned by the communists with no great enthusiasm, again drove a wedge between communist and non-communist left.

The division was not to be durable, though. During 1969–71 the SFIO rebuilt itself, becoming the PS and formally absorbing Mitterrand's CIR and some smaller groups. The unification congress of 1971 at Epinay-sur-Seine elected Mitterrand as first secretary. As well as changing its name, the PS changed its leaders and its ideas: its 1972 programme *Changer la vie* leaned markedly in the direction of the political philosophy of *autogestion* (see below). Visibly taking on new life, the PS felt strong enough to talk to the communists again; in July 1972 a common programme was actually signed. Fighting the 1973 elections with the CPG behind it, the PS did almost as well as the communists. After Mitterrand's narrow failure in 1974, the party drew in new blood in the shape of several thousand members of the PSU at the *assises du socialisme* of October 1974. Since then its strength and prestige have grown steadily to the extent where, the disappointments of 1978 notwithstanding, it is again one of France's major parties.

Ideology   If so much space has been devoted to the history of French socialism, then this is no accident. First, the political and social analyses made by the PS are properly historical, as befits a socialist organization. Second, its own view of itself and its relations with other forces is heavily coloured by memories of its past. The PS sees itself as continuing and extending the old republican tradition, with its attachment to democracy and civil liberties. But it is also a socialist party, believing that capitalism is based on exploitation of the majority and that full democracy and freedom can only be achieved under socialism, when private control of the means of production and exchange is ended. Today the conditions for such a transformation exist: recent monopolistic trends in French and international capitalism have increased exploitation and redrawn the map of society, pushing downwards strata of petty-bourgeois who were previously in a fairly comfortable position. These can be won over, along with the working classes and that part of the petty-bourgeoisie which is employed by the state (and which was for a long time the main activist base of the SFIO), in a 'class front'. This front would seem to involve less of the middle bourgeoisie than the communists' 'anti-monopolist alliance'.

Aware of the poor governmental record of the SFIO, the new PS refuses the label of social democracy (managing capitalism without trying to change its structures, but at the same time trying to redistribute a few social advantages). But it is equally critical of the Soviet type of one-party socialism, with its evident lack of democracy. It has thus developed a third model, *le socialisme autogestionnaire*, derided by some commentators, especially English ones, as naïve and impractical. But if socialist parties are ever to mobilize people for social change, as opposed to merely arousing cynicism and indifference, then perhaps they will have to try and appeal to the imagination – and *autogestion* certainly does that. Its keynotes are decentralization and responsibility, but it goes much further with these than do those parties of the right who are not averse to borrowing some of its themes. So far as possible, in any area of activity, power will be brought nearer to the grass roots – whether in the workplace, the school or university, or the local community. The key area of activity, the economy, will be brought progressively under workers' control, starting with the public sector, and extending, it is hoped, into the domain of private capital; intermediary structures between state and private sector, such as self-managing co-operatives, will be encouraged. The risks of economic fragmentation will be avoided by a revitalized and more democratic form of planning, with inputs coming in from the self-managing firms rather than from central ministries. Politically, decentralization will involve abolition of the prefect's role, and the creation of fully elective regional authorities.

The PS believes that the transition to *autogestion* can be sponsored by a government based on the left alliance to which it remains fundamentally committed and that it can be done without revolution. It also believes that such a project has more chances of success on a European scale than on a French one, hence its attachment, warts and all, to the EEC and its wish to implement common European socialist policies agreed across national frontiers. This also explains its special links with the socialist parties of southern Europe, whose prospects would appear to be bright.

It is easy to criticize such a programme as the result of too many years spent in opposition; and it is true that it underestimates, to put it politely, the resistance of the capitalist state to political and economic change. But the popularity of such ideology has been evident enough in recent elections, although by no means all PS supporters are *autogestionnaires*, as we shall see from a study of the movement's structures.

Structures   Basic units (*sections*) exist at workplace or residential level; their delegates attend the departmental federation, which in turn elects to regional and national bodies. The most important of these, constitutionally speaking, is the two-yearly national congress, where delegates are sent by federations in proportion to membership. Traditionally this has meant congresses dominated by the three largest federations — Bouches du Rhône, Nord and Pas-de-Calais (an alliance often described sarcastically as 'les Bouches du Nord').

Federations also elect delegates to the national convention, which meets twice yearly and which is supposed to check that the sovereign decisions of congress are being upheld by the party executive, the *comité directeur*. This is elected by congress and supervises in the interim the party's office-holders, members and press outlets. People are elected to this body in proportion to the number of delegates which support their motion; at present there are in effect two main *courants* which present motions (though a militant feminist tendency within the PS is trying hard to create a third). *Courant II*, the *Centre d'études, de recherches et d'éducation socialistes* (CERES), got 31 of the 131 full members and 7 of the 27 substitutes, all the rest going to Mitterrand and his allies.

As usual in large parties, the *comité directeur* delegates day-to-day running of affairs to a smaller caucus which it elects, the *bureau exécutif*. This is a locus of considerable power, and its twenty-seven members include all the best known PS leaders, seventeen having the title of national secretary (i.e. they are spokesmen on specific areas of policy). They are helped in this task by a number of general delegates and national delegates. There is no doubt that within the leadership Mitterrand is predominant; he federates the various tendencies within his movement, much as a British Labour leader must do. His authority is founded on his long experience (much of it less than glorious, but far enough removed in time to be ignored by all save those with long memories), the prestige accruing to his presidential campaigns, his skill with the media and his tactical cunning. It is such that he is alleged to control the party in a monarchical way, to use Cayrol's phrase. There is certainly no obvious successor to the ageing leader and this is one of the long-term problems facing the PS.

Within the élites of the PS one is struck by a phenomenon typical of the party at large. This is the way it has absorbed new blood since 1971 to renew the SFIO base on which it was built. Thus a new leadership generation is being groomed beside veterans such as Mitterrand, Defferre and Mauroy (mayor of Lille). Many of the rising stars are well-educated men of comfortable background, such as M. Rocard, L. Jospin, L. Fabius or J. -P. Chevènement, leader of the CERES faction, and indeed many of them are *énarques*. Wright observes that a similar renewal of élites has taken place at the level immediately below (parliamentarians, mayors), with the emergence of young highly-qualified leaders.[6]

Although officially forbidding the existence of organized tendencies, the PS runs its affairs in such a way that these are inevitable (cf. the notion of 'courants' discussed above). This is indeed one of the most attractive and progressive features of the party. Commentators are divided in their attempts to pick out tendencies, for these are very fluid, with political differences often compounded by personal and historical rivalries. At the risk of some simplification, four can be identified, three of them allied against the fourth CERES. At times the leadership has put pressure on CERES, excluding it from the top *sécretariat* after the Pau congress of 1975 and attempting – unsuccessfully – to stop it having its own premises and publications. The other three tendencies are, broadly speaking, the Mitterrandist group of near-Radicals (including such close advisers as Dayan, Mermaz and Dumas), who moved towards a more socialist viewpoint in the 1960s: the 'Bouches-du-Nord' core from the old SFIO, particularly strong in local government, and of whom Defferre and Mauroy are typical: and finally a more *autogestionnaire* group around Michel Rocard, many of whom joined the PS after 1974 and who often have a far-left or trade-union background. Rocard himself tempers his *autogestion* with more regard for financial orthodoxy than some of his followers. These three groups obviously have their own disagreements (the first two, for instance, are probably a good deal nearer to social democratic positions than the third), but in general they tend to be united against CERES by a scepticism about how much can be achieved quickly if the left takes power. CERES is deeply committed to the *autogestionnaire* ideal, however, but believes that the transition to such a type of socialism will take more than a left-wing victory at the polls. Such a government can help the transition by swift and resolute actions, but these must be reinforced by pressure from mass movements, fuelled by labour unions and other popular organizations. CERES sees the PS as the necessary link between government and such movements, and wants it to become more of a militant, campaigning party, like the communists. The latter would in fact occupy a key place in any left government for CERES, which has long argued that the only way to break the rigidity of the communist party is to involve it irreversibly in the dynamic sort of process described. For this, CERES is often accused of being a Trojan horse for the communists; certainly it irks the PS leadership, who see it as frightening away uncommitted centrist voters. But the group does have the merit of asking some awkward questions, raising in particular the whole problem of the transition to socialism – surely crucial if the *autogestionnaire* discourse is ever to become more than electoral rhetoric.

In April 1978, the PS claimed 187,600 members – probably an honest estimate. Some 20 per cent were women. Apart from the 'Bouches-du-Nord', they were most numerous in old SFIO strongholds – big towns like Toulouse, Bordeaux and Lyon, anticlerical areas like the Landes. A feature of the membership is the high proportion of catholics, especially young ones – a far cry from the anticlerical heyday of the SFIO. As membership of a union is obligatory in theory for party members, many join the CFDT. The PS electorate is a fairly popular one, with its 30 per cent of workers showing that it has regained some hold on the class which gave it birth. If it still does best in old republican regions, mainly south of the Loire (especially Burgundy, the Rhône valley, the south-west and Languedoc) and in the old mining and textile areas of the Nord and Pas-de-Calais, it has grown of late in the conservative east and west, but not yet to the point where there are seats to show for it.

As regards finance, members pay in 1 per cent of their wages, and office holders, local or national, a set proportion of their emolument. To pay the fifty-odd staff in the new premises next door to the Palais Bourbon, however (to say nothing of those in Lille or Marseille), extra sources are probably necessary. Campana believes that some reformist-minded employers contribute to funds,[7] and it is suggested that *Urba conseil*, the PS architectural advisory service, is perhaps rather generously rewarded for its services by some socialist municipalities.

The PS has some interesting press outlets. *Le Poing et la rose* is a compact monthly for members, and the weekly *Unité*, under the astute editorship of C. Estier, publishes party documents as well as news and analysis. There is also the *Nouvelle Revue socialiste*, ten times yearly, which aims at a more cultivated public. But the most interesting papers are those with the least formal connection with the PS. Apart from provincial dailies such as *Le Provençal* (owned by Defferre) which support the party, there is the Parisian daily *Le Matin* which achieves the difficult synthesis between readability for a mass audience and reasonably sophisticated political analysis. There is a

stream of lively theoretical reflection from reviews like the CERES
Repères, or *Faire* (produced by some of the keenest *autogestionnaires*).

A final feature is the party's predilection for creating groups,
whether internal study groups (on all levels and on every topic), in
the workplace (over nine hundred claimed in 1977) or elsewhere in
civil society. There are even links with sympathetic army officers
through the CORAN (Convention of Reserve Officers for a New
Army). The PS has its own book and record clubs, its own film shows,
festivals and debates. It even has its own theme song, with music
by Theodorakis. All in all, although its strength can clearly be built
up much more, it seems to have taken on once again the life of a mass
party.

Communism – the Parti communiste français (PCF)

Development   Like most of its sister-parties in Europe, the PCF
began as a split from an existing socialist movement, in the aftermath
of the First World War and the Bolshevik revolution. Thus the SFIO
congress at Tours in December 1920 saw admirers of the Russian
revolution leave 'la vieille maison' to form a new party, the PCF.
Accepting the rigorous twenty-one conditions for membership laid
down by Lenin, the PCF was admitted to the Third International
(Comintern), and for a long time carried the sub-title SFIC (*Section
française de l'internationale communiste*). If its founders were
enthusiastic about Leninism, however, they had still much to learn
about the theory and application of that doctrine. It would take over
a decade to 'bolshevize' the new party and make it something like the
disciplined instrument demanded by Leninism. During this period the
PCF remained a marginal force in French politics.

Its future depended, then as now, on its relations with socialism.
Until the mid-1930s it would attack the SFIO with the slogan of
'classe contre classe', stressing the necessity of a revolutionary break
with capitalism and denouncing the reactionary nature of the SFIO
for implying that this could be achieved without a vanguard party
(like the PCF). In this it was faithful to the policy laid down by the
Comintern, the co-ordinating body for all communist parties under
firm control of the Soviet Union. When the Comintern made its famous
tactical 'turn' of 1934, however, and recommended the adoption of
Popular Front tactics, things changed rapidly for the PCF. Its new
tone of social consensus for class-struggle, patriotic nationalism for
working-class internationalism and defence of parliamentary democracy
instead of denunciation of 'bourgeois freedoms' gave it huge gains
in membership, parliamentary seats and trade-union support – a
base which it has never lost since, in fact.

A good resistance record (especially after the Nazi invasion of

Russia in 1941) helped the party's reputation, and it shared power
from 1944 to 1947 with SFIO and MRP. During this time it made
every effort to preserve political and social stability in France and to
boost production, succeeding so well that de Gaulle acknowledged this
in a letter to the widow of Thorez (PCF leader) on his death in 1964.
This was the party's peak period for electoral and militant strength.
But the Cold War brought its eviction from government and the return
to a ghetto from which it has tried to escape ever since. Permanently
shut out of government, despite holding a steady fifth of the popular
vote, the PCF could at first only retreat into a doctrinaire shell, with
the occasional flexing of its industrial muscle as sole response to its
isolation. But by the early 1960s the start of de-Stalinization in
Russia, the end of the Cold War and the logic of bi-polarization were
all leading to a situation where alliance with the non-communist left
might seem more feasible. The slow genesis of the 1972 alliance has
already been described. But it was always a conflictual one, and from
1974, when it was clear that the PS was the major beneficiary, the
conflict worsened to the point where the PCF was ready to weaken
the alliance and in effect lose the 1978 elections. But in so doing it
held back socialist growth and kept intact most of its own positions
in terms of votes and seats.

This on-off relationship with socialism, characterized by mutual
need but equally strong hatred, has hardly changed at bottom over
six decades. It raises the question: what sort of party is the PCF?

Ideology   Marxism sees historical development as working through
class-struggle: a new type of society only comes into being when a
ruling class is supplanted, probably violently, by a rising one. Under
capitalism the rising revolutionary class is that of the workers: only
it could destroy capitalism and establish a social order not based on
exploitation. Lenin added to this proposition a significant rider, namely
that, left to itself, the working class would probably develop no more
than a reformist consciousness. For it to become revolutionary (i.e.
to see its situation clearly and to realize the task awaiting it), it needed
guidance from an external factor, the party. Formed of those who had
acquired a Marxist understanding of history (and thus an organization
which placed a premium on quality rather than quantity) the party
would organize the class for the seizure of power, the dismantling of
the bourgeois state apparatus and the building of socialism.

The party must thus be disciplined. In Leninist language it would
practise 'democratic centralism' − democratic because the party
hierarchy is freely elected and preliminary policy options freely discussed, but centralized because, once policy has been decided, it must
be implemented by the base without question. The existence of
organized tendencies inside communist parties has been forbidden since

1921. How democratic centralism operates in the PCF will be seen shortly; but such was the Leninist concept which marked it from its outset — hierarchized, disciplined and dedicated to revolutionary class-struggle under the aegis of the Soviet Union.

Over the years a number of factors have eased the PCF away from its purist origins. The evident shortcomings of Soviet socialism: the fact that conditions under French capitalism have never been catastrophic enough to drive huge sectors of the population into the PCF's arms: the division of Europe into two spheres of influence, with France firmly in the capitalist one — all these have led the party to reconsider its role and to move, along with the Italian and Spanish parties notably, towards what is rather sloppily called 'eurocommunism'. For the PCF at least this means that there is no universal model of socialism, certainly not the Soviet one; France must invent its own. Moreover, such a socialism is now considered attainable by non-violent means: electoral victory of the PCF and its allies will usher in a period of 'advanced democracy' where economic and social reform will create conditions for a later stage, socialism, whose characteristics are not specified. The basis of this analysis is the theory of monopoly state capitalism (MSC); it is held that the high degree of interpenetration between the state apparatus and vast industrial and commercial concerns has raised productive capacity to a high level, but only at the cost of increasing hardship and deprivation for many sectors of the population — all, in fact, except the very top layer of bourgeois, 'une poignée de milliardaires insolents', as G. Marchais is wont to put it. This means that an electoral alliance of all the deprived is feasible, 'l'union du peuple de France', under PCF hegemony, of course. The PCF is so committed to the idea of a French socialism that it has made its own the Gaullist notion of independence in foreign affairs, even to the point of accepting the French nuclear deterrent which it opposed for years.

This theoretical revision explains a number of points conceded by the PCF of late. It now admits the possibility of political pluralism during the phase of socialist construction or even of power returning to the right after a period of socialist-communist government; previously it had held to the theory of proletarian dictatorship (which meant in practice irreversible one-party rule), but this was struck off the statutes at the twenty-second congress in 1976. The PCF proclaims its attachment to civil liberties and the necessity to extend these; previously it tended to regard them as 'formal' (i.e. not worth very much). On numerous occasions it has criticized the Soviet Union, timidly at first (cf. the mild reproaches over Czechoslovakia in 1968) but with growing firmness (cf. its obtaining the release of the dissident Plyutsch or its approval of an underground film condemning labour camps in 1976). But this has by no means cleared up the party's problems of identity, either for itself or for others. Perhaps this will become clearer if we examine PCF structures.

Structures   The PCF hierarchy is as follows:

Paris	Congress (elects Central Committee, which elects *bureau politique* (BP) and secretaries)
Department	Federation conference (elects federal committee, which elects *bureau* and secretaries)
Workplace or locality	Section conference (elects committee, which elects *bureau* and secretary)
Workplace or residential	cell (has own bureau and secretary)

The national congress is the sovereign body of the PCF; its authority is delegated to the two-monthly central committee, which leaves day-to-day affairs to the *bureau politique*. In 1976 the CC had 121 members including 24 substitutes; the BP had twenty-one members, seven of whom enjoyed the rank of secretary. G. Marchais is secretary-general.

The organigram shows a pyramidal structure which appears un-exceptional in that the lowest level elects delegates to the next level, and so on upwards. Thus the national leadership, vested in the BP, should be an emanation, albeit indirect, of the grass-roots, and thus amenable to its ideas and proposals. If anything, the reverse is true; it seems that the leadership (and some would even claim the secretary-general) is able to decide changes in policy or tactics (cf. the volte-face over the nuclear deterrent in May 1977) and have them executed by an obedient membership. Revolts do occur in the lower echelons (e.g. after the Soviet crushing of the Budapest insurrection of 1956, or after the electoral disaster of 1978): and in the past, purges were used to restore order. Probably two features explain the relative ease with which the BP runs its machine. One is the party's vertical system of communication: there are no sideways links between cells, which effectively prevents grass-roots discontent from gaining momentum. The second is the hold exerted by *les permanents* (full-time party employees, hence unlikely to cross the leadership) who occupy key positions in the apparatus, notably at the level of federal secretary. Although they are elected, their candidacy has to be approved by the candidates' commission of the CC; in other words they have to have BP approval. Hence this system of filtering ensures that only loyalists win office; and they are expected to 'bien tenir' sections and cells below them. Thus compared with the PS or the parties of the right — although we have seen that one can exaggerate the extent to which the grass-roots influence policy here also — the PCF seems to have perfected a watertight system whereby a small professional élite decides and imposes policy.

Several other features characterize the PCF as a party 'pas comme les autres'. Its strength in the workplace is well known — 9,922 cells in late 1977, with a very strong presence in the public sector. Linked to this is its symbiotic relationship with the CGT (see below). In 1978 eight out of sixteen of the CGT leadership were communists, as were eighty-eight out of ninety-six federal secretaries. It is customary also to remark on the party's influence over other associations in civil society, professional and voluntary alike. The main secondary and higher teachers' unions, the SNES and SNESup, are led by PCF militants; so too is the small farmers' union MODEF. The party's influence spreads across bodies such as the *Mouvement de la paix*, *l'Union des femmes de France* and even ex-soldiers' associations. In all these bodies, communists attain hegemony not because they are 'submarines' or infiltrators, but by hard graft and dedication — qualities for which there are no substitutes in politics.

The party is also important in the publishing world. Its *Editions sociales* produce an impressive range of marxist work at fair prices. There is the party daily *L'Humanité* (claiming sales of 240,000) and one or two dailies based on provincial towns. There are three weeklies — *La Terre* for farmers, *France-Dimanche* which aims at a fairly wide audience and *France Nouvelle* which discusses political and cultural topics. Of the more theoretical reviews one should not forget the *Cahiers du communisme*, which often have important party texts, *La Nouvelle Critique* with a general cultural slant and *Economie et politique*, where party intellectuals develop their particular vein of marxist political economy. In this connection one should mention the immense effort that the PCF puts into education; as well as running many levels of schools for its activists it has two permanent research institutes, the CERM (*Centre d'études et de recherches marxistes*) and the Institut Maurice Thorez.

A good deal is known about party finances. In 1977, 65 million NF were collected in dues and from office-holders (who turn over their salary to the party and are paid back the wages of an OP); a further sixty-one millions came from collections, donations and fêtes. This would not suffice to pay the wages of the several hundred full-time officials which the party uses in Paris and the provinces. The PCF has thus developed a commercial sector of some importance, involving some sixty firms and solidly competing with capitalist enterprise. Its activities include property, printing and agriculture, especially the Interagra export company directed by the 'red millionaire' J.-B. Doumeng. Commentators show some smugness in criticizing the PCF for possessing this veritable capitalist empire; but as, unlike its rivals, it receives no help from government or private capital, it must finance itself somehow. It can hardly be expected today to rely on handouts of 'Moscow gold', for which it was stigmatized in the 1930s.

In March 1978 the PCF claimed 632,000 members; members turn over at a high rate (10 per cent a year). The party has not done a detailed breakdown of membership since Marchais's report in 1967; but some of the trends revealed therein are unlikely to have changed much. It is a young party (47 per cent less than forty years of age), with quite a high proportion of women (perhaps 30 per cent) – a tendency doubtless helped by the PCF's readiness to give women responsibilities (thirteen of the nineteen women deputies in 1978 were communists). There is a high proportion of manual workers (60 per cent, including agricultural workers) and of lower white collars (18 per cent). This strong popular base is sometimes obscured by the presence of many intellectuals of distinction in the PCF, drawn from all the major disciplines.

The PCF vote held steady at 20.6 per cent in 1978. Its bastions are where one would expect them to be, among the working class – Paris suburbs and those of other big towns, Nord and Pas-de-Calais, Lorraine steel area, Bouches du Rhône. But the party has grown in audience in the poorer departments of the south-west, Limousin and Languedoc-Roussillon, thanks to its diligent espousal of the small farmer's cause. Its weakest areas are, unsurprisingly, Alsace and Brittany.

Although 47 per cent of PCF votes were estimated to come from workers in 1978, Colette Ysmal has shown that within its suburban strongholds the party probably lost votes from the better-off parts of the working class and the salaried petty-bourgeoisie; these were disguised by gains from the PS in the more stagnant parts of France.[8] In other words, the PCF might well be missing out on the more dynamic parts of the popular electorate, to the advantage of its socialist rival.

The left Radicals – Mouvement des radicaux de gauche (MRG)

The MRG is heir to a proud tradition. Radicalism was a major force of earlier Republics, notably the Third, where it was in the vanguard of the struggle for parliamentary democracy and the secular state. Perhaps the peak of its achievement was in 1905, when both could be said to have been achieved. Radicalism was based on the petty-bourgeoisie and parts of the peasantry of the provinces: its typical *notable* was the small-town professional man, usually well-entrenched as mayor or deputy and operating on a fairly clientelistic basis, distributing favours obtained from Paris in return for electoral support. The slow rate of change in pre-war France meant that such categories remained important long after the movement had achieved its political aims.

Hence it could only become conservative, winning elections on the strength of its progressive rhetoric and then governing in a timorous way, often in alliance with the right. This led to the joke that a Radical was someone whose heart was on the left but whose wallet was on the right.

The revival of 'third force' politics after 1947 enabled the Radicals to continue this performance under the Fourth Republic, the only exception being the energetic premiership of P. Mendès-France in 1954-5. This capable and far-sighted leader cut several Gordian knots in foreign policy before his appetite for reforms aroused the hostility of the more cautious Radicals and split the party into two. The decline continued through the Fifth Republic and the movement split yet again in 1971, some following JJSS into alliance with Lecanuet (and later Giscard d'Estaing), others joining the left alliance and signing the CPG. These, under R. Fabre, set up a separate party, the MRG.

Although obviously the weak link in the alliance, the MRG played its part loyally enough (apart from the defection of one or two *notables*) until the quarrel of 1977, when Fabre played an important role in precipitating the break-up of the alliance. The defeat of March 1978 split the MRG between its left, led by M. Crépeau who saw no future outside the left alliance, and the remainder, including Fabre, for whom joining the presidential majority (and perhaps reunification with the JJSS Radicals) must now have seemed tempting. Crépeau was elected president of the MRG, but the main financial backer of the movement, M. Diaz, was opposed to him. This rendered its economic future problematical.

MRG discourse continues the republican, 'humanist' tradition. For free enterprise (but against its logical outcome, big capitalism), for private property (so long as it does not become 'gigantisme industriel'), against bureaucracy and for civil liberties, the MRG emerges as what it has always been — the champion of the small man. It likes to suggest that it is the salutary leaven in a dough consisting of doctrinaire communism and socialist adventurism — so much so that one wonders why it ever signed the CPG. The answer is that MRG deputies need communist votes on the second ballot.

For MRG is after all a party of *notables*, despite its claim of 20,000 members and the existence of youth and student movements. The *bureau national* is dominated by national office-holders, though the MRG is clearly losing ground at this level (its sixteen senators now outnumber its ten deputies). At local level there is still some strength, with 200 departmental councillors and 10,000 municipal ones. The main MRG stronghold is the Radical area *par excellence*, the south-west.

Today the MRG has some attractive personalities, some interesting ideas and a certain commitment to the critical/libertarian tradition that characterized the best Radicals of the past. Whether it can survive is an open question. If many MRG go over to the Giscardians, those who remain might have no choice but to close down their movement and join the PS which they despise, with typical Radical defiance, as 'un parti d'intellectuels'.

(4) Fringe parties

On the left

The most notable of these is the *Parti socialiste unifié* (PSU). It began life in 1960 as a refuge for those disgusted with the established left, its early militants including leftish catholics, communists driven out by the rigidity of the PCF, socialists repelled by Molletism and Mendesists alienated from the stagnant Radical party. Always prone to faction-fighting, its role was to gather and to stimulate debate. Its electoral weight was slight (a handful of deputies, Rocard's defeat of Couve de Murville in a by-election in 1969 and his 3.7 per cent of the first-ballot vote in the presidential election of that year); but electoralism was never a PSU priority. It aimed to create a new socialist movement, neither social-democratic nor Leninist. In particular it helped to develop and vulgarize the theory of *autogestion*: and it always saw to it that the PCF was never entirely marginalized in French politics, serving as a bridge between it and the rest of the left. Though critical of the CPG, the PSU supported Mitterrand's 1974 campaign – a sign perhaps that some members felt the PS to be moving towards their policies. Confirmation of this came in October 1974 when Rocard took 3,000 militants with him into the PS after the *assises du socialisme* meetings. But the *pur et dur* minority remained active: in 1974 C. Piaget was the inspiration of the work-in at the Lip watch-factory. In 1978 the PSU fought the elections with feminist, ecologist and pacifist groups under the umbrella of *Front autogestionnaire*. Despite PCF support in two seats against the PS, it won no seats, and its future seems to be that of a small group, sandwiched between a PCF that finds it useful to annoy the socialists and a PS to which it must occasionally give twinges of conscience.

In 1978 the left also counted some opposition Gaullists, for whom Pompidou and Giscard had betrayed what they saw as the essence of Gaullism. Although they had not signed the CPG, the communists supported two of their candidates against the PS in 1978, both unsuccessfully. Neither of the two organizations – the FRP (*Fédération des républicains de progrès*) led by ex-minister J. Charbonnel, or D. Gallet's UJP (*Union des jeunes pour le progrès*) – has much in the way of structures or resources, and the future does not appear bright for these loyalists who still take seriously the progressive parts of Gaullist discourse.

France also boasts a plethora of organizations of the classic extra-parliamentary left, viz. Trotskyists and Maoists. Of the latter, the best known is probably the PCMLF (*Parti communiste marxiste-léniniste de France*), which publishes the paper *L'Humanité rouge*. French Trotskyism is marked by the mutual suspicion and internecine sentiments which characterize Trotskyist movements elsewhere. Of particular note are the *Ligue communiste révolutionnaire*, of which A. Krivine is the best-known spokesman. It has changed its name several times (to avoid police bans) since 1968, when its crash-helmeted activists played important roles on the barricades. It has a daily (*Rouge*) and counts among its members the most courageous and stimulating publisher in France, F. Maspéro. *Lutte ouvrière* is probably associated for most people with Arlette Laguiller, bank clerk and presidential candidate in 1974, where she took one vote in forty on the first ballot.

Small but committed, the far left organizations put most of their energy into campaigning — for conscripts, for women's rights, for tenants, for immigrants, against nuclear power stations. Often they discover themes which are 'recuperated' by the official left for electoral purposes. They also provide many young people with their first experience of active politics and introduce them to a marxist analysis of society — both of which acquisitions may well be put to use later on within the parties of the official left, when revolutionary ardour has cooled somewhat. As such, the far-left organizations may well play within the political system a role somewhat different from that which they intended.

On the right

Like most of her neighbours, France has not been spared from fascism. In the 1930s, a number of semi-fascist 'leagues' flourished, and under Vichy genuinely pro-Nazi elements eventually came to the fore. After 1960 there was a revival of fascism with the OAS, which did not flinch from terrorism in its resolve to keep Algeria French at all costs. The economic recession of the seventies, with its unemployment and tendencies towards economic nationalism, has given fascists in France and elsewhere a new target, the black immigrant worker. In France today there are still people who preach the traditional themes of fascism — the 'strong state', seen as the only barrier to marxist collectivism, total commitment to nationalism, and racialism. The main groups are the PFN (*Parti des forces nouvelles*) run by people close to the newspaper *Minute*, and the *Front national* of J.-M. Le Pen, ex-Poujadist deputy and OAS supporter. Together they claim an improbable 100,000 members, though they polled less than one per cent in 1978. Some analysts claim that the PFN is more moderate than its rival; but looking at the propaganda of both, one is struck by the depressing similarity of their gross over-simplification, violence of tone and overt racialism.

Ecologists

This new force cannot yet be classified in traditional terms. They made a spectacular impact in the 1977 elections (270,000 votes: more than 10 per cent in Paris and other big towns). Even in 1978 they topped 2 per cent in the first ballot. The burden of their protest is familiar – the waste and probable exhaustion of natural resources by industrialized societies, the social ills which result from pollution and other nuisances, the dangers of nuclear power. Clearly such themes can mobilize many people, and not just electorally (cf. the Creys-Malville anti-nuclear demonstration of August 1977, or the eight-year struggle against expropriation of farming land by the army on the Larzac plateau). But it is not clear how ecologism fits into existing political structures. Is it just a self-interested pressure-group, of the type that does not want a motorway in front of its own garden, but has no objection to one in front of someone else? Or can it become a new political movement, traversing existing parties and creating a new politics on the basis of its particular problematic (the use/misuse of nature)? Alternatively, will the movement be 'recuperated' by existing parties, all of whom are rapidly straining to develop an ecological dimension? Ecologists themselves are a heterogeneous collection, as shown by the existence of candidates from two movements (a radical one and a more 'apolitical' one) in 1978, and voting behaviour in the second ballot (some ecologists voting on the right, some on the left). But whatever its uncertainties, ecologism would seem to have an important role to play, at least for the next few years.

(5) The parties today

The situation on the right is one of paradox. The RPR is stronger in organization, finance and office holders; it has a tough and able leader. But its prospects are really quite depressing, for there are limits to what it can do with its strength. The reason is that it has lost its grip on the nerve-centre of power, the presidency, and with it a hold on other parts of the state apparatus. So it is condemned in effect to be a junior partner in the majority, enduring Giscardian policies. Chirac could bring down the government on a number of issues – unemployment and enlargement of the EEC, to name two – but dare he? His deputies might not relish facing the voters so soon again; some of them might drift discreetly towards the Giscardians, who would make them very welcome. The electorate of the right might regard the RPR as a trouble-maker and send back Giscardian deputies in increased numbers; we have seen after all that the two parties' electorates are quite similar. True, the two have differences of an ideological and historical nature (which we have attempted to summarize in terms of a dynamic state-oriented capitalism versus a more liberal traditional one), but this distinction cuts little ice with conservative voters. Nor should it, indeed, as both are agreed on the essential, which is to preserve the basic structures of capitalism; their points of convergence are stronger than those of divergence.

So there are limits to Chirac's room for manoeuvre; his 'oui' will be stronger than his 'mais'. In 1981 he will surely try for the presidency – the key to maintaining his party. Until then he must try and distinguish the RPR sufficiently from Giscardism to suggest that it is a plausible alternative; but short of major confrontation, which is unlikely, this is improbable. The RPR's best hope of victory in 1981 would be a period of growing social tension, which might panic voters into turning towards them as a last rampart – shades of 1958 or 1968. Perhaps it is not too unkind to suggest that the RPR needed the left to win in 1978, so as to engender a climate of fear and uncertainty (on the right, at least). As this did not happen, the movement's future could well be one of slow decline, to the advantage of the Giscardians, coalescing steadily under their UDF umbrella.

The break-up of September 1977 has raised acutely the question of the conflictual relationship of the PCF and PS.

The PCF's desire to break was prompted by simple considerations. It was not simply that the PS was prone to reformism and hence potentially disloyal to the CPG (this was as true in 1972 as it was in 1977); behind PCF allegations of a socialist 'virage à droite' and readiness to strike a bargain with Giscardism, lay the unpleasant truth that the PS was benefiting more from union than the PCF. The PS was growing and appealing to the better-off workers and lower petty-bourgeois, but the PCF seemed incapable of extending its appeal beyond the 20 per cent of its hard-core support. It thus faced the prospect of entering government as a junior partner, with slight influence; it might find it difficult to get the CPG implemented, never mind extended (especially as economic growth, on which the CPG was predicated, had been less rapid since 1974). The PCF thus needed either to get extensive guarantees from the PS (which were not forth-coming in the re-negotiations) or failing that, to make sure that the left failed to win. For marxists, power is not worth having unless one is able to use it to make significant change.

What does the PCF stand for, then, and how does it see its role? Today it has moved further away from the Soviet Union than ever before; but it has still made no detailed analysis of the shortcomings of that system (perhaps because this would involve questioning the role of the Soviet communist party, hence of itself). There are several views of the party: a revolutionary Bolshevik party, still: a rallier of the exploited and discontented: a potential party of government: or even, as Kriegel claims, an 'alternative society' with its own life-style and values. Perhaps the PCF is all of these at once; what is sure is that it is still a Stalinist party, albeit, as Kriegel says, a degenerate one. By this is meant that it is still a blunt instrument, wielded according to the calculations of an entrenched leadership. The leaders may indeed differ inside the BP (cf. the talk of a 'liberal' faction headed by P. Laurent, and a 'sectarian' or Stalinist one, headed by R. Leroy and the late J. Kanapa). But they are united by the desire to keep the party strong at all costs, and if this means wrecking the left alliance, then the liberals will swallow their doubts and go along with the Stalinists.

Up to now the BP has retained control, but the events of March 1978 raised doubts. Many intellectuals and, reportedly, workers and trade unionists began to question publicly the hard, anti-PS line of the leadership, and also the whole way in which party policy is decided. Such protest went beyond the ranks of well-known 'liberals' like J. Elleinstein; it centred on the themes of greater participation and initiative for the grass-roots, and in particular the abolition of the candidates' commission. The PCF has beaten off similar challenges before; only time will tell if internal pressure will lead it away from its rigidity towards the difficult synthesis to which the PS also aspires – that of being a socialist party with a proper commitment to transforming capitalism, while at the same time refusing the Bolshevik party as an instrument of change.

For the PS, the break threatens to exacerbate tensions, particularly between the CERES and the older socialists, who might well feel driven back towards 'third force' options, the logical upshot of which would be an alliance with Giscardism. This is not an immediate possibility; but it could prove hard to keep together a party whose structures are still tender, and which badly needed office to confirm its growth. No doubt the PCF would not be unduly worried if the PS did weaken. But the great beneficiaries of the split remain Giscardism and its allies; it is ironic that the left, which achieved its best score ever in 1978 and now represents half the country, is as far away from power as it has ever been (see Figure 4.1 and Table 4.4).

(6) Interest groups

Political parties compete for power in the hope of translating their supporters' demands into public policy; besides them one finds, in

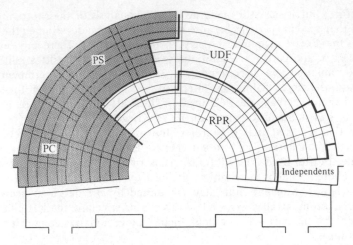

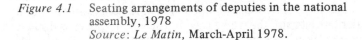

Figure 4.1   Seating arrangements of deputies in the national
assembly, 1978
Source: *Le Matin*, March-April 1978.

pluralistic societies, interest groups. The aim of these is more modest;
bringing together people with common objectives (economic, ideological, etc.) with a view to furthering such objectives by common
action. When they try to influence public policy in this direction
(i.e. by trying to influence decisions within the state apparatus) they
are termed pressure groups.

France has her share of these, but observers have always been
struck by the much looser relationship that they enjoy with the state
than in, say, the Anglo-Saxon countries. In the latter, some groups
appear so well integrated into the process of political decision-making
as to be almost parts of the state apparatus. Much has been written
on French groups, and the current debate has been so well summarized
by Wright that only a few remarks need be made here.[9] Basically,
there is no single model which covers adequately all the possible
relationships between the French state and groups. The latter are not
always natural enemies of the state, prone to violence so as to extract
concessions from a rigid bureaucracy. Nor are they passive clients,
'recuperated' by the government so as to implement its policies more
easily. Nor are they so strong as to dictate policy to certain ministers –
although one could easily find examples of all these situations. There

Table 4.4   Main political forces during the Fifth Republic,
performance in general elections*

		Election date					
		Nov. 1958	Nov. 1962	March 1967	June 1968	March 1973	March 1978
Communists							
	A	18.9	21.8	22.5	20	21.3	20.6
	B	10	41	73	34	73	86
Socialists							
	A	15.7	12.5	19^c	16.5^c	20.7^e	24.7^e
	B	44	66	116	57	101	114
Radicals							
	A	11.5	7.8				
	B	40	39				
Christian democrats							
	A	10.8	16.8^a	17.9^a	10.3^d	13.1^f	
	B	57	55	41	33	64	
Independents							
	A	19.9					21.5^g
	B	192					137
Gaullists							
	A	17.6	37.7^b	37.7^b	44.7^b	36.4^b	22.6
	B	206	268	245	360	238	148

* The percentages in every case do not total 100, as the scores of minor formations are omitted; A = percentage of first-ballot votes; B = number of seats eventually won.
a   combined total of MRP and opposition independents.
b   combined total of Gaullists and Giscardian RI.
c   combined total of SFIO and Radicals allied as FGDS.
d   centrists' group, CPDM.
e   combined total of PS and MRG.
f   30 of these were centrists elected in alliance with the majority: the total also includes those Radicals allied with Lecanuet as *les Réformateurs*.
g   combined total of UDF (PR + all remaining centrists).

are in fact an infinite number of possible relationships between state and groups, and the extent to which groups can extract concessions depends on several variables: their organization, finance, capacity for publicity, access to decision-makers and so on. One point that most observers would concede is that the groups' targets have shifted somewhat; today access to ministers or the Elysée is much more important than access to deputies — a far cry from the deputy-centred republics of old.

Another factor which is sometimes forgotten is that there are obvious limits to what any state can concede within the framework of a capitalist economy. The state's function in such situations is to ensure that accumulation of capital proceeds as smoothly as possible. Now, there is never one unambiguous way for this to occur; there are always strategic and tactical choices to be made (concessions to big capital or to small? or to skilled workers at the expense of unskilled?). Equally there are certain choices which must be ruled out, because they would be damaging to capitalism as a system. One of the interesting aspects of French groups is that some of the most powerful are militantly anti-capitalist.

Bearing this parameter in mind, the next pages will outline concisely the major economic pressure groups, while trying to suggest by what means and with what effect they influence policy.

Working-class unionism

Development   Modern unionism dates from the Second Empire with its modest surge of industrialization. Prior to that the labour movement had known the fate of its counterparts in other countries which experienced industrialization, viz. legal and physical repression. The law of 1864, passed by a régime looking for support among a growing working class, went halfway towards granting freedom of association and was completed by the law of 1884.

A working class that was still small, scattered and divided, both ideologically and in terms of the size of workplaces, might be expected to evolve differently from the UK, where industrialization and urbanization were much quicker. At any rate, in 1895 when the first major national grouping of unions was set up with the title of CGT (*Confédération générale du travail*), it had as its doctrine the theory of revolutionary syndicalism. Largely inspired by skilled workers with a high level of political consciousness, this ideology presumed a high degree of technical and political competence among workers: so much so that they were now able to run the economy and society for themselves, the bourgeois class becoming redundant. Not that the latter would hand over control peaceably, however; a short period of violence triggered by a general strike would be necessary to expropriate them. The *syndicat* (union branch) was seen as the basic political unit, both for the seizure of power and for political and economic decision-making afterwards. Political socialism (the SFIO) was despised as irrelevant or reactionary. Such were the tenets of revolutionary syndicalism, which failed to survive World War I as a living force, but which marked French unionism powerfully. Its most notable legacy is the famous *apolitisme*, enshrined in the CGT's Amiens charter of

1906, which insists on the total independence of the union movement from all political parties; in a different way, the ideology of *autogestion* also owes it something in the way of theoretical ancestry.

Between the wars the CGT was the arena of a struggle for control between socialists and communists, which ended in the victory of the latter; the decisive phase was probably the occupation where the outlawing of the unions by the Vichy régime put a premium on the qualities of resolution and leadership which the communists possessed. By December 1947 the 'moderates' (SFIO sympathizers) were ready to split off; they were helped financially by the American unions and, it was later discovered, the Central Intelligence Agency. The result was a new union CGT-FO (*Force ouvrière*). Since then CGT and FO have gone their separate and antagonistic ways.

The third major union began life in 1920 as the CFTC (*Confédération française des travailleurs chrétiens*). As its title shows, it was for catholic workers and was long characterized by extreme deference (at one point it had an advisory council of clergy). Inevitably its militancy increased as members learned that catholic employers are still employers. After 1945 the movement became more politically conscious, developing a theoretical reflection in which themes of class-struggle and socialism became prominent. This led in 1964 to a retitling of the union as the CFDT (*Confédération française démocratique du travail*); the minority for whom religious convictions remained paramount continuing as the *CFTC maintenue*. The CFDT was heavily involved in 1968, which helped its radicalization no end; it has been in the forefront of the *autogestionnaire* movement and has probably done the most to awake interest in this notion. Yet it has avoided becoming an appendage of the PS; with its radical socialism and its syndicalist mistrust of political parties it seems very much the *enfant terrible* of French unionism today – a role which it has taken over, ironically, from the CGT of seventy years ago.

It is clear, then, that the French labour movement is heavily politicized; and this is logical. For unions always have a political dimension, whatever their members may think to the contrary. This is so for many reasons. Often members are direct employees of the state; even when working for private capital, their everyday demands (wages, holidays, etc.) will have a direct effect on government economic policy. This explains the increasing state involvement in wage-bargaining at all levels. So even when people join unions for non-political reasons (job protection, better rewards, etc.), they are joining bodies that have a political role to play. Now French unions are well aware of this. It is true that they carry out the normal bargaining which members expect of them; but they have also thought deeply about the kind of society they wish to see (a socialist one) and the means to attain it. Clearly at the heart of any such analysis will lie the relationship between unions and political party, to which we shall turn shortly. But let us first examine union structures.

Structures   The following structures are those of the CGT and FO: with slight variations, they are valid for all major unions.

The basic unit is the *syndicat*, organized as far as possible on the basis of one big industry (thus the *fédération des métaux* would group *syndicats* of workers ranging from general labourers to very skilled steelworkers, who in Britain would probably be in specialized unions of their own). The organization of the union is both vertical and horizontal, or to put it another way, both geographical and professional. Professionally, the *syndicats* are part of a federation (a national grouping of all *syndicats* in that particular industry) and the different federations are then joined in a confederation. But geographically they are linked at local, departmental or regional levels with *syndicats* from other industries which share the views of the confederation as a whole. These geographical levels are represented on the national (confederal) bodies, as are the professional levels. The hierarchy thus reads:

confédération

fédération   union départementale

union locale

syndicat

At national level the sovereign body is the national congress (two- or three-yearly), which delegates power in between to other bodies. First of these is the *comité confédéral national*, which is elected by federations and departmental unions and which between its six-monthly meetings passes on power effectively to the *commission exécutive* and *bureau exécutif* (from within the latter's ranks). Thus the CCN is roughly the union parliament, and the CE and *bureau* its executive. The situation in the CFDT is similar, although the names of the top bodies are different.

In general unionization in France is low, compared with similar industrialized countries; it is rated at below 25 per cent of the workforce. Union membership is always difficult to assess in any country, for numerous reasons, but the following estimates give some indication of strength.

In April 1978 the CGT (secretary-general G. Séguy) claimed 2.4 million members. Its strengths lie in mining, the metal-working industries, building, chemicals, printing, electricity and transport, and it is weaker in the tertiary sector. The CFDT (secretary-general

E. Maire) claims 1.15 millions, with special strengths in metal, oil, rubber, textiles, banking and insurance. FO (secretary-general A. Bergeron) numbers around 900,000 and is strong in non-industrial sectors — banks and insurance, transport, commerce and the lower ranks of public employees in general. The CFTC has some 225,000 members.

In terms of resources, Reynaud believes French unions to be the weakest in Europe, along with Italian ones. Most *syndicats* fix dues at 1 per cent of members' salaries, varying parts of which are taken by the higher levels of the union. Unionists who are members of the Economic and Social Council usually turn in their salary, but this represents a small amount (700,000 NF out of a budget of 21 million for the CGT in 1975). There is little advertising revenue from union journals and although the government gives a certain amount in the form of training and research grants, the CGT and CFDT both believe that their more moderate rivals obtain a higher proportional share than is justified by their membership. Also, the grants could be bigger (they covered 19 per cent of the CGT's 1975 budget). This means *inter alia* that strike funds are low and that in prolonged disputes unions must rely on collections and other manifestations of solidarity.

Unions devote an important part of their resources to publicity. There are abundant publications, ranging from local broadsheets to work aimed at specific categories (e.g. papers for immigrants in their own languages). At national level, the most important are the CGT weekly *Vie ouvrière* (in a popular style which sells 200,000 copies) and the more theoretical *Peuple*. The CFDT issues the weekly *Syndicalisme* (55,000 copies) which has important confederal texts as well as practical advice for active unionists and discussion of current problems. There is also the more advanced *CFDT aujourd'hui*. FO publishes the essence of its views in *FO Hebdo*.

Unions deal with the state in various ways. It recognizes only the four major industrial unions, plus the specialized CGC and FEN (see below) as representative. This entitles them to the aid described above and to seats on the Economic and Social Council, its regional equivalents and some public companies. Unions also help to manage a number of bodies in the field of social affairs (vocational training funds, unemployment benefits) and also the *comités d'entreprise*. Since 1968 they have had the right to set up branches openly in large firms, with time allowed for meetings and other business; though there are still large firms where *bona fide* unions are kept out by violence and intimidation. To some extent, union influence can be measured in terms of their performance in the elections for the above bodies, where in the first ballot representative unions have a monopoly of candidacies in theory. Thus in 1976, according to the ministry of labour, of the existing branches in large firms, 40.6 per cent were

CGT, 24.8 per cent CFDT and 12.3 per cent FO; in elections for the *comités d'entreprise* the CGT scored 42.7 per cent, CFDT 18.6 per cent and FO 8.3 per cent.

A more significant measure of strength perhaps is the way in which negotiations are conducted. As regards private employers, these are hardly ever conducted nationally, the employers being strong enough to keep negotiations to the level of the branch, region or even the firm. Only in the public sector have unions managed to sign national agreements since the premiership of Chaban-Delmas, but this practice is by no means universally established. And only in two areas — part of the newspaper industry and the docks — is there a closed shop. There are clearly limits to what the unions can obtain from the state or from private capital.

Ideology   The unions' discourse reveals the double nature of their preoccupations — on the one hand, defence of everyday interests and, on the other, long-term political goals. We shall concentrate especially on the latter.

The CGT is predicated on revolutionary class struggle and aspires to socialism. What such socialism would be is uncertain; if the CGT has recently begun to talk seriously about *autogestion* instead of sneering at it as 'utopian', its own view of socialism would probably centre on what it calls 'gestion démocratique', i.e. a fairly centralized economy with some power of decision devolved to plant level, where the union would pay a key role. This obviously involves looking at the relationship between union and party (a socialist government would obviously be based on the left parties), and confronting the charge that the CGT is merely a conveyor-belt for the PCF. This charge is indignantly refuted by both, in the name of union independence; but it is well known that most of the departmental secretaries are communists and so are half the BE. Séguy and Krasucki are on the *bureau politique* of the PCF. Ross has shown plausibly how the PCF has tried to use the CGT in an aggressive or consensual way over the years, according to its current policy needs; but there are limits to such a process.[10] Any active member of a union knows that members cannot be brought out on strike at the drop of a hat, or even cajoled back to work if they are in dispute; May 1968 was ample proof of that. There is no reason to suppose that this would be any different if the left were in power. There are other unions waiting to welcome the disaffected *cégétistes* who would surely abandon the CGT if it were perceived simply as a means of transmitting unpopular government demands to workers.

If the CGT still appears in some respects to hanker after eastern European practices, then the CFDT presents a frankly leftist image. Although it agrees about extending the public sector, the CFDT wants neither a bureaucratic state capitalism nor an improved private one.

Its self-managing socialism aims at a decentralized economy, with authority in firms exercised by works councils, elected by the whole of the workforce, who would elect and supervise management boards. The latter would negotiate with the national plan, which the CFDT wishes to democratize *à la* PS by placing greater emphasis on inputs from local units. Even the CFDT's immediate demands, such as reduction of all differentials to a scale of one to six have a radical ring about them which distinguishes them from British or American demands. The CFDT stresses intensely the importance of union autonomy from political parties, especially if the left were to take power. This explains its refusal of an organic relationship with the PS, which it has long fuelled with militants and ideas, and its refusal to sign the CPG, although it obviously supported the left union.

FO by contrast has no project for a socialist society, although it occasionally talks about class-struggle. Its outlook is pragmatic and reformist; it sees its task as to extract as much as it can from management and state. It is reluctant to take industrial action and has staked much of its reputation on signing agreements in the public sector (where a good half of its members work); if this policy were to prove impracticable through government austerity, FO could have trouble with its members. FO pays the ritual lip-service to union autonomy from parties, and mixes it with some fairly stiff anti-communism, directed at the CGT; this is logical enough, given its origins. Probably a high number of its members would vote socialist (Bergeron himself is in the PS), but with no great ideological commitment. Certainly, leftist tendencies inside FO have never threatened the hold of the moderate leadership. A final ideological flourish is provided by FO's keen support for European integration: Europe is seen as a framework that can solve problems too vast for individual states to cope with.

French labour unions are thus divided politically and ideologically, as well as by normal competition for members. It took the Barre austerity plans and the imminence of the elections to make the three major ones participate together in the one-day strike of May 1977; more usually, suspicion and hostility are the rule. One can appreciate union pluralism in that it offers workers a choice, keeps debate alive and the union apparatchiks on their toes; but undoubtedly it also means that the employers face a weaker challenge.

Employers' unionism – the Conseil national du patronat français (CNPF)

Employers' organizations in France are as old and as complex as workers'. The CNPF dates from 1946 in its present form, being really an umbrella organization which tries to co-ordinate the activity of employers from all fields (except agriculture, the professions, the *artisanat* and of course the public sector). Its organization is both horizontal and vertical; in other words, it groups geographical organizations embracing more than one economic activity and also the local, departmental and regional organizations of any one individual activity. Individual firms do not join, membership being by geographical or professional bodies. It is estimated that over 80 per cent of these do belong to the CNPF, whose national structures are crowned by an executive council and president (F. Ceyrac), assisted by a number of full-time staff.

This is not to suggest that the CNPF is particularly homogeneous. It has numerous internal tensions, the most important being that between large and smaller capital. The latter has its own organization, the CGPME (*Confédération générale des petites et moyennes entreprises*), founded and led for many years by L. Gingembre, and which has representation inside the CNPF. The smaller employer tends to see himself as being a real boss, closer to the daily realities of the firm, in contrast to the remote and 'technocratic' head of a large corporation. Another split is between reformists and traditionalists, the latter preferring repression of or confrontation with the unions, whereas the reformists are prone to dialogue and consultation (within limits). Many of them are to be found in the *Centre des jeunes dirigeants* and some of them are known to have been enthusiastic about Mitterrand's presidential campaign in 1974, though doubtless less so about the CPG.

Inevitably, then, the CNPF cannot represent all employers' interests because these are so diverse. The most one can say is that of late the authority and prestige of the organization do seem to have grown in employers' eyes, and it seems to speak for the majority of them in some areas at least. The actions of the CNPF are in the main discrete; it provides services to members (expertise in fields such as management techniques or export markets, and also information on unions or political parties). It also has a more public role in that it publicizes heavily the virtues of capitalist enterprise, employing to this end some twenty staff whose task is to insert the employers' viewpoint into as many newspapers and other media as possible. This operation is conducted with increasing success, if one recent analyst is to be believed.[11]

As regards direct influence on government, it would be naïve to think in terms of the latter being teleguided by a clique of employers with clear-cut interests. The reality is more complex than this conspiratorial vision suggests. It is known that the *patronat* disliked some Gaullist policies of the 1960s and that Giscard d'Estaing was for a long while mistrusted by them. But there are limits to political action set by the logic of the capitalist system, from which no right-wing government dare depart, and also certain broad objectives which will suit all fractions of capital. Within these parameters, the CNPF functions as an effective lobby. The reader is familiar with its staff of political experts under A. Aubert; one of its functions is to try and influence legislation at the committee stage and to supply deputies with employers' viewpoints. Of late it would seem to have obtained useful results. The shelving of Sudreau's report, the castration in parliament of the *sérisette* (an anti-inflation tax on 'excessive' wage settlements) and the return to *la liberté des prix* must have been welcome to most employers.

The self-employed: the Comité d'information et de défense – Union nationale des artisans et des travailleurs indépendants (CIDUNATI)

The long slow decline of small commerce has already been referred to, as have the sometimes violent reactions of the disgruntled small businessman. Poujade canalized much of their discontent in the 1950s, but in the 1970s his mantle has fallen on to the shoulders of G. Nicoud and the CIDUNATI. The movement was a fusion in 1970 of groups dissatisfied with the work of their traditional professional associations (which are grouped in departmental chambers of commerce), with regard to government policy on tax and social security. The movement soon made a name for itself by a series of energetic demonstrations, including raids on government offices and seizure of records. Although Nicoud was imprisoned it was not long before the government was engaged in dialogue with CIDUNATI, showing that a delinquent group is still able to frighten Paris into giving something away.

CIDUNATI caters for the small, essentially family business; though members may own up to three or four shops, and there has been an influx of small industrialists also. It is above all for activists, who feel their business threatened and who want safety by all means, even legal ones, as the tag has it. 'Le commerçant ne se rue dans les brancards que quand il se sent le couteau à la gorge': thus did one regional organizer put it, in the down-to-earth idiom typical of the movement. CIDUNATI has a distinct ideology, which stresses the virtues of the small 'independent' man – his hard work, his professional knowledge and care for the customer (compared with the anonimity and shoddy quality of the big supermarket). It is rather impatient with normal legislative procedures, seeing deputies as weak-willed creatures, manipulated by faceless technocrats in the finance ministry. Its basic demands are three: to pay less tax and suffer less interference (read tax inspections: CIDUNATI newspapers often carry stories of honest shopkeepers hounded to suicide by odious tax-inspectors): to have a simpler and more comprehensive system of social security: and most of all, to stop 'unfair competition' from big capital in the shape of the large supermarket or hypermarket.

The movement's muscular actions have wrung a number of concessions, mainly in the pensions and insurance field, but also including the Royer law of 1973 directed against big supermarkets. Royer is the one commerce minister (the member of government who has the thankless task of appeasing small businessmen) who has at all pleased the militants; but the movement is characterized by a perpetual mistrust of all governments. It knows how to use its political weight, however, and its votes are solicited by all parties (Mitterrand has been photographed with Nicoud). CIDUNATI does not give specific support to one party but it can organize a negative vote; in the March 1977 elections, Brousse (then commerce minister) and Durafour (one of the financial ministers) lost their mayor's office as a direct result of a CIDUNATI boycott. Whether this behaviour would occur in a parliamentary election is doubtful, though probably not all members always vote on the right.

CIDUNATI membership is hard to assess, as it deliberately publishes no figures. But it could well be over 200,000. There is an impressive new headquarters in the Isère, Nicoud's department (a gesture typical of the provincial flavour of the movement), and two journals with a style all their own. CIDUNATI claims to have few permanent staff, relying on voluntary work at all levels. The national leadership seems dominated by Nicoud, a waiter turned café-owner, and very much a self-made man; by origins and temperament he is an ideal spokesman for his followers.

Such is CIDUNATI. Whether one regards it as an anachronistic revamping of Poujadism,[12] or a force that is becoming progressively integrated thanks to dialogue with the state, there is no doubt that it will pull a good deal of political weight for some time to come.

Managerial unionism – the Confédération générale des cadres (CGC)

If the traditional petty-bourgeoisie has its own organizations like CIDUNATI, then this is also true of the newer, wage-earning variety. Since 1946 *cadres* have been organized in the CGC, led for many years by A. Malterre until he handed over to Y. Charpentié. There is some doubt as to who is a *cadre* (one who has a position of managerial authority), the CFDT claiming for instance that proper *cadres* are relatively few in number; the CGC recruits its 350,000 members over a rather wide range of white-collar jobs, however, from senior managers and engineers down to foremen, and including such disparate categories as commercial travellers and nurses. The problem, for real *cadres* or sundry white-collars, is however the same one of identity. On one hand they are put off by the mass industrial unions, whose style and image are very much that of the skilled worker; indeed they are encouraged to think of themselves as being different from these. On the other, although culturally they may feel nearer to the employers, they themselves are decidedly not employers; rather their function is to secure compliance with the latter's decisions from workers. CGC unionism reflects the discomfort, in many ways, of this median position. Strictly apolitical, it has no vision of society other than a meritocratic one, whereby rewards go to those with the skill and dynamism to deserve them (i.e. *cadres*). Hence CGC demands are very specific — higher rewards, maintaining wage differentials, greater leniency on tax and national insurance, more consultation by boards of directors, job security (*cadres* have been hard hit by unemployment since 1974). The CGC is not militant, a one-day strike against raising of insurance contributions being the furthest it has gone; it sees the CNPF regularly, but has no such contact with CGT or CFDT. It sees the economy as an arena of 'concertation', i.e. reasonable bargaining between moderate partners, with satisfaction on both sides. The political weight of the *cadres* is important and all parties bid for their support; in general they seem attracted by politicians exuding a certain dynamism — a reflection, no doubt, of the managerial ethos with which they live. Hence the sympathy of many *cadres* for socialists like Rocard, or for the UDF.

There is little doubt that Barre's pre-electoral promises to offer *cadres* more consultation and to put a ceiling on social security contributions were a direct response to CGC pressure. They probably did the trick, as the socialist vote was two or three per cent down on expectations; perhaps many *cadres* felt that the UDF was safest after all.

The CGC is for *cadres* happy with their position between worker and employer. Some *cadres* have joined the special sections of the CGT or CFDT, however, which are called the UGITC and UCC respectively. This means that they have made a political choice, seeing their fate as a class-fraction to be linked to that of the working class. Such a choice clearly involves accepting that in a socialist society the role and privileges of *cadres* might well be changed; they would have to learn, as Maire put it, 'la richesse des relations égalitaires'. For the moment, though, the CGC undoubtedly commands the loyalty of the majority.

Farmers' unionism — the Fédération nationale des syndicats d'exploitants agricoles (FNSEA)

Farmers' unionism reflects many of the contradictions in French agriculture. Chronic peasant individualism and the slow rate of economic development ensured weak and fragmented farmers' organizations, until the depression of the 1930s forced some unity. The Vichy régime with its heavy rural and traditionalist bias attempted to organize and discipline farmers into its peasant corporation. This was not particularly successful, but the idea of a single national farmers' union was revived by the left-wing governments of the after-war period in the shape of the CGA (*Confédération générale de l'agriculture*). Within a few years the FNSEA, which was merely one of the constituent elements of the CGA, had become so strong as to supplant it; in other words, farmers did not want a leftish union imposed from Paris. This clearly tells us something about the character of the FNSEA. Under the Fourth Republic, it liaised closely with the CNIP group in parliament, and from 1951–6 the agriculture minister was always one of its nominees. Since 1958 its contacts with the régime have been at least as intimate; the agriculture minister has weekly meetings with the FNSEA, which is recognized as the only representative farmers' union.

Today the FNSEA claims 850,000 members (some would say 750,000).

Under the energetic leadership of M. Debatisse, it incorporates departmental chambers of agriculture, producer groups (for specialized products, e.g. beef, lamb, etc.) and related bodies like the CNJA (*Centre national des jeunes agriculteurs*), source of many ideas and capable leaders. It is dominated by the big farmers of northern France, its congress being effectively controlled by eighteen departments, because delegates are elected in proportion to dues paid, thus privileging the richer areas. This control explains perhaps the existence since 1959 of the MODEF, more or less under PCF hegemony and claiming some 200,000 members, especially among the small farmers of the south-west. There are also smaller movements of leftish and rightish complexion, but they cut little ice besides FNSEA; in the elections to departmental chambers of agriculture in 1976 it obtained 65.11 per cent of the seats, compared with 17.47 per cent for MODEF and 5.97 for the rightish FFA. But FNSEA is not exempt from internal disputes; at the 1978 congress Debatisse expelled the leftish Loire-Atlantique federation (on dubious constitutional grounds) for criticizing his acceptance of a tax that hit at small farmers in particular.

Although it is supposed to be apolitical, the sympathies of FNSEA lie basically on the right. It has attacked the CPG and is not in disagreement with any of the major farm policies of the régime, though it always wants higher prices for produce. FNSEA has not had to use its muscle (tractor blockades and the like) since the early 1960s to make its voice heard. Governments have made sure that the Common Agricultural Policy of the EEC has been applied in a way that suits the broad mass of farmers; at the 1977 congress the minister Méhaignerie promised to resist any attempt to change this wasteful instrument for the production of unsaleable surpluses. It may be an exaggeration to say that FNSEA makes agricultural policy under the Fifth Republic, but its shadow looms large. The only threat to this symbiosis between it and the government seems likely to come from *ad hoc* action groups of wine and vegetable growers in the south, threatened by enlargement of the EEC, which Debatisse accepts. Only time will tell what results they are likely to achieve.

Teachers' unionism – the Fédération de l'éducation nationale (FEN)

Teachers have by far the highest rate of unionization of any profession in France. Their profession has always had close links with the republican state, which looked towards the teacher, especially in the primary school, to propagate democratic ideals and form the citizens of the future. Public sector teachers have thus long been part of a republican, secular tradition. The counterpart of their loyalty has been higher prestige, better rewards and better conditions than those enjoyed by their colleagues, at least in the UK. After a long struggle for existence (because the republic was not so keen to grant the right of unionization to its own employees as it was to other categories of workers), teachers' unions were incorporated into the CGT. When the latter split in 1947 the teachers avoided the brutal choice between communism and the SFIO by creating a separate organization, the FEN.

Today this 'state within the state' numbers 550,000 members, led by A. Henry. The FEN is in fact an umbrella organization for teachers of different levels. The bulk of its troops are, as always, primary school teachers (320,000) and some 99,000 secondary school teachers, organized in the SNI (*Syndicat national des instituteurs*) and SNES (*Syndicat national de l'enseignement secondaire*) respectively. Teachers in France are radical in their views; a poll in *Le Monde de l'éducation* in February 1978 showed that 59 per cent considered themselves to be on the left, and 21 on the centre-left. Thus within the FEN as a whole, factional struggles are between different shades of left. The movement has officialized tendencies, dominant among which is that of Henry, probably best described as moderate PS or social-democratic; it easily beats off the challenge of communists and extreme leftists. Within SNES, however, the PCF is held to be prominent.

Outside the FEN all the other main unions have their teacher branches, from CGT to CGC; and there are independent unions, especially in the private schools. But their membership is to be counted in tens of thousands, and they cut little ice besides FEN. It is accused of corporatism, i.e. of accepting a consensual role within the state apparatus, in return for rewards given to its members. The claim is only half true. The FEN is recognized as the one representative teachers' union, and the state in practice allows it considerable say in matters such as appointment, promotions and transfers of teachers (especially in the primary sector). It is also true that it has great veto power (cf. its perennial ability to stop governments from cutting school holidays, and its resistance to the Haby reform and its predecessors). But the leftish loyalties of FEN probably make it into something more than a mere corporation.

Chapter 5

Foreign relations

(1) Values, purposes and organization

The foreign relations of a contemporary society such as France are greater in scale and complexity than at any time in history. Their importance for individuals varies according to class, occupation or sub-cultural grouping, but no one can be immune from their impact in an age when energy resources, food, clothing, equipment at work and in the home, cultural and recreational activities, are all more or less dependent on foreign imports and influences. The increase in scale of foreign relations can be analysed quantitatively by using statistics on, for example, mail and telecommunications, foreign travel or inter-marriage; qualitative change is harder to analyse but undoubtedly it has made life both more vulnerable and more fascinating.

A society's foreign affairs relate either directly or indirectly to its political, economic and social systems. Politically there is a basic need for security in peace or success in war. Economically there is a need to ensure supplies of essential food, energy and raw materials; depending on the size and character of the economy there might be further needs, such as foreign financial investment or vital military supplies. Within a capitalist society there are influential groups seeking particular benefits from foreign relations; for example banks and insurance companies profit from external financial exchanges and large companies profit from facilities abroad for creating new branches or market outlets. Finally, the values of a social system, its images of itself and of its place in the world, will influence attitudes to foreigners and preferences for relations with other societies having perhaps a similar language, a similar politico-economic structure, or an historical tradition of friendship.

History has a great influence on France's image of herself and her role in world affairs. It is less than five hundred years since the emergence of the modern nation-state international system. For about half that period, while Europe was predominant in world affairs, France had the largest population, the largest standing army and the greatest cultural influence in Europe, French being the international language. After a period of relative decline in the nineteenth century,

French primacy was revived briefly by victory in the First World War. Experience from the age of Louis XIV to very recent times, therefore, has convinced French people of their political importance in the world.

There have been differing interpretations, however, as to which were the most important international influences emanating from French society. The Revolution of 1789 was the origin of modern French nationalism, with the attempt by Jacobin patriotism to extend France to the 'natural frontier' of the Rhine and to extend principles of republicanism to other societies. Subsequently Bonapartism undertook to export the revolution in a bastardized form. The French, moreover, made significant contributions to the ideology of nineteenth-century liberalism, for instance by introducing universal manhood suffrage in 1848 before other European societies. From another standpoint the French experience in the commune of 1871 was an important stage in the international development of socialism. A different experience, derived from Monarchist and Bonapartist traditions, had laid emphasis on the values of hierarchy rather than equality, the general will of the nation rather than the interests of individuals and groups within it, centralization rather than particularism, the state as actor rather than arbitrator. Such diverse elements in the French tradition have influenced not only Europe but the world at large through the impact of the former French empire.

French nationalism has been particularly self-conscious owing to recurrent struggles for identity in the face of defeat, partition and occupation by enemies during the past two hundred years. Defeat in war or weakness in the face of an external threat has invariably led to a change of régime. Conversely, each new régime has proudly proclaimed its ability to restore national honour, to recreate a sense of security and to defend national interests effectively.

Thus, the Third Republic after 1875 believed that it would regenerate France and her empire with strength derived from liberal principles and possibly persuade Germany to renegotiate the peace treaty of 1871 or, if not, get revenge in battle whenever an opportunity presented itself. By the 1890s many Frenchmen were protesting that the régime had failed to uphold the national interest, but were soon to be proved wrong by the victorious outcome of the First World War. The Fourth Republic emerged from the disasters of the Second World War with a surge of ambition: to reorganize western Europe in such a way that there would be neither the urge nor the opportunity for Germany to attack France again. Whatever its moderate success in Europe, however, failure to deal effectively with problems in the empire led to the Fourth Republic's replacement by a new régime claiming ability not only to reorganize the French community on a new footing, but also to re-establish French national independence in the face of foreign pressures. Within twenty years, the Fifth Republic too was being subjected to bitter accusations that it was failing to uphold vital French national interests in its foreign relations.

Thus the French experience of insecurity, together with political instability, has resulted in patriotic feeling becoming inseparable from the support or rejection of a particular political system. The state is seen as having a specific role to play in world affairs and is always on trial; to put it another way, it is never a neutral but always an ally or an enemy in the eyes of different sections of French society, depending on the way it represents French national interests. Some may judge it according to its pursuit of certain economic or military interests; others may demand that it should uphold a certain ideological tendency; and then there are the simple patriots, lacking political commitment or opportunity for personal profit, who will derive satisfaction nevertheless from the exercise of any kind of French muscle in the world. It is important to recognize, therefore, that assessments of the success, or otherwise, of French foreign policy will always vary according to the optics of diverse politico-economic interests in French society.

In the perennial pursuit of security from enemy attack, French policy assumptions underwent an agonizing reappraisal following the disastrous experience of defeat and occupation in the Second World War. Traditionally, ever since 1870 when Germany had become the dominant land power in Europe, France had depended on allies to restore the balance. This policy had worked well in the First World War when Russia, Britain, and ultimately the United States, helped France to achieve victory and to recover lost territory. The same policy was pursued in the period leading to the Second World War, but in 1940 France had to face the German onslaught with Belgium and Holland trying to preserve neutrality, Britain giving token assistance, and the United States and Soviet Union remaining studiously neutral. Since the bitter disappointment of 1940, therefore, French policy has consistently tended to seek independent means to achieve national security – a policy of 'France first'. Nevertheless the harsh realities of a devastated society at the end of the war, requiring Marshall Aid for reconstruction and the division of Europe into hostile Soviet and American armed camps, requiring a choice as to which bloc France should join, combined to make France more than ever dependent on external support.

This ambivalent collective attitude towards allies was held and articulated most strongly by de Gaulle, who had struggled in exile to recreate French national identity and unity between 1940 and 1944. He found it easier to win the support of various resistance organizations in France than that of the United States, who refused to recognize his provisional government until a very late stage in the liberation of

France in the autumn of 1944. As for the British, in spite of his doubts about their interest in a French recovery, his dependence on outside support led de Gaulle to propose to Churchill on 13 November 1944:[1]

> que l'Angleterre et la France s'accordent et agissent ensemble dans les réglements de demain, elles pèseront assez lourd pour que rien ne se fasse qu'elles n'aient elles-mêmes accepté ou décidé . . . L'équilibre de l'Europe, la paix garantie sur le Rhin, l'indépendance des Etats de la Vistule, du Danube, des Balkans, le maintien à nos côtés, sous forme d'association, des peuples que nous avons ouverts à la civilisation dans toutes les parties du monde, une organisation des nations qui soit autre chose que le champ des querelles de l'Amérique et de la Russe, enfin la primauté reconnue dans la politique à une certaine conception de l'homme en dépit de la mécanisation progressive des sociétés, voilà bien . . . ce que sont nos grands intérêts dans l'univers qui s'annonce. Ces intérêts, mettons-nous d'accord pour les soutenir de concert. Si vous le voulez, j'y suis prêt. Nos deux pays nous suivront.

The proposal was abortive, for Churchill and his successors preferred to pursue a special relationship with the United States, but it articulated poignantly the frustrated ambition of de Gaulle and that of other post-war French leaders who were later to see Britain remain aloof from the European Coal and Steel Community and the treaty of Rome.

Despite the success of socio-economic reconstruction in France by the mid-1950s, the sense of a relative decline in political power in world affairs became increasingly painful. The impact of the Cold War not only forced France to become a satellite of the United States by joining NATO in 1949, but also to accept the rearmament of West Germany within NATO by 1955. Equally unexpected crises in the French empire led to defeat in Indo-China by 1954, subsequent withdrawal from Morocco and Tunisia by 1956, and even the loss by 1962 of Algeria, which had always been regarded as an integral part of France. These reductions in power were made even more intolerable by the reluctance of French allies to treat these crises as part of the Cold War, and by their refusal accordingly to provide sufficient allied help to ensure a French victory. Perhaps the most bitter blow was at Suez in 1956 when American opposition to European colonial ambitions in the Middle East thwarted an Anglo-French military expedition. French decline seemed to be the will of allies and enemies alike.

French leaders had a marked awareness that their interests did not coincide to any great extent with those of the super powers, the United States and the Soviet Union. When the latter reached a state of deadlock in the 1962 Cuba crisis, followed by a period of *détente*, there was a corresponding sense in France that the time was ripe to pursue long-repressed national ambitions. Hence the articulation in the 1960s of a philosophy of national independence.

What were the forces in French politics and society behind the pursuit of an independent foreign policy? Some analysts have traditionally attached excessive importance to the personal influence of de Gaulle (e.g. Newhouse), as if he were able to impose an eccentric policy on a reluctant society. There was, of course, his 'certaine idée de la France . . . (qui) n'est réellement elle-même qu'au premier rang',[2] a conception developed into a fully-fledged philosophy of independence by 1965 in one of de Gaulle's histrionic television broadcasts. After a preamble summarizing the problems involved in the French transition from being 'un peuple colosse' to 'un peuple affaibli', de Gaulle proclaims a total contrast between acceptance of what he disparagingly calls the 'sirènes de l'abandon' before 1958 and the pursuit of independence since his return to power. A policy of independence, he postulates, must fulfil certain rigorous conditions – political, military and economic – and in his view France is managing to fulfil these requirements.

In international politics, he says, while maintaining friendship with the United States, the emphasis in French policy has been to reassert European interests by seeking real solidarity among the six members of the EEC, while also reviving historical links with eastern European states, in so far as they free themselves of their 'écrasantes contraintes'. The ultimate ambition is: 'rétablir d'un bout à l'autre de notre continent un équilibre fondé sur l'entente et la coopération de tous les peuples qui y vivent comme nous'. This vision contrasts, by implication, with an alternative Atlantic community, or an integrated community confined to western Europe. As for the world at large, de Gaulle's view is opposed to hegemony, intervention or repression by one state in relation to another, and favours instead the independence of each nation, free from restrictions and able to receive outside help without being forced into obedience in its policies. On these grounds French policy condemns the American war in Vietnam, while supporting the development of South American and African states, and forging friendly links with China. This, de Gaulle claims, is a distinctively French policy, formulated in Paris.

Military security, he argues, requires that in the nuclear age France should have adequate weapons to deter a possible aggressor so that, while not disrupting alliances, France could ensure that her allies did not hold her fate in their hands. Such a military force, he claims, France is now creating by her own efforts. This project necessitates considerable re-equipment but will not cost more than contributing to the NATO integrated military force which, in any case, would not afford such a secure protection if France remained merely a subaltern member. Thus, de Gaulle contends, France is reaching the point where no power in the world could inflict death and destruction on her without suffering a similar fate in return, and that is the best possible guarantee of security.

In the economic sphere, according to de Gaulle, independence implies maintaining activities essentially under French administration and direction. France must keep up with competitors in the key sectors essential to an advanced economy. If it is advantageous to share inventions and projects with another country, France must combine with one that is not likely to have the power to dominate her. That is why, in his view, financial stability is important in order to avoid the need for foreign assistance. French stability is upheld by, for instance, changing into gold the surplus dollars imported as a result of the deficit on the American balance of payments. He proceeds to list economic successes that meet the above conditions. In recent years research investment in France has increased sixfold; a common industrial and agricultural market is operating jointly with Germany, Italy, Belgium, Holland and Luxembourg; France and Italy have joined to build a tunnel under Mont Blanc; the Moselle canal is being constructed with the Germans and Luxemburgers; France has joined with Britain to build the first supersonic transport aircraft in the world and there is the possibility of further Franco-British co-operation in civil and military aviation; France has recently concluded an agreement to set up her colour television system in the Soviet Union. To sum up he uses a homespun image: however big a glass others may offer, France prefers to drink from her own, while amicably clinking glasses with those around her.

De Gaulle argues that, although the Americans have been disconcerted by French self-assertion, a time will come when they will appreciate the valuable friendship of a France able to stand on her own feet. Now that she has re-emerged as a nation with full sovereignty, the world game begun at Yalta, which seemed to be confined indefinitely to two players, has obviously been transformed. In that world divided between two hegemonies the principles of liberty, equality and fraternity counted for nothing. It is therefore in the interests of peace that a new equilibrium, a new order, should prevail. Who is better able, concludes de Gaulle, to maintain such a new order than France so long as she is true to herself?[3]

De Gaulle's philosophy of international relations clearly favours a diffuse system of nation states rather than a polarized system of integrated alliances or blocs, according to Holsti's definition of different types of international systems. The rejection of the post-war hegemonies of the two super-powers reminds us, not merely that de Gaulle was born in 1890 and was perhaps fond of the good old days, but also that the three fundamental rules for conducting relations between states, namely political sovereignty, territorial integrity and legal equality, originated in the sixteenth century. The rules have been broken with great frequency but remain the conventional practice even today thereby lending substance to de Gaulle's contention that the nation-state is more important than integrated alliances or international ideological forces.[4]

At least one influential French analyst of international relations has tended to support the Gaullist view regarding the importance of the nation-state and the primacy of political over economic relations between states. Raymond Aron has been sceptical towards arguments that EEC economic integration, for example, would prevent a recurrence of Franco-German political rivalry. He has also suggested that pursuit of higher status and independence by middle-sized powers like France will tend to have multiple effects in detracting from status and willingness to assume world responsibilities on the part of a super-power, perhaps driving it to adopt policies of isolationism.[5] The American setback in Vietnam and the failure to maintain a stable currency in the 1970s, lend weight to an interpretation that the US hegemony was in decline. But an alternative interpretation was that such setbacks were merely tactical adjustments leading to the exercise of power by more effective methods, and that super-power hegemony was likely to prevail indefinitely.[6] There was a temptation for those holding this latter view to dismiss pretentions to independence on the part of middle-sized powers as merely self-delusion,[7] without taking into account the significance of the problematic of independence on the level of a vocabulary or semiotic code establishing an identity in relation to a hegemonic force. The actions of a super-power thus generate impulses to independence among other powers as an anti-symmetric image or behavioural paradigm in international society.[8] The importance attached by de Gaulle to verbal style, among his other theatrical characteristics, would account for his ability to articulate the ideology of independence more effectively than others on this level at least. His speeches certainly struck a responsive chord in French public opinion during the 1960s: over half those people consulted in successive opinion polls expressed the view that France should remain neutrally independent in the face of Russo-American rivalry.[9]

Why were many non-Gaullist voters and their political spokesmen attracted by the ideology of independence? To the left of the Gaullists there was a revival of centrist groups by the mid-1960s, who were much more enthusiastic than de Gaulle about European integration in the EEC. One of their principal motivations was that a large economic base in Europe would stimulate growth and maximize business opportunities and general prosperity. This belief carried a particular brand of anti-Americanism that envied the high living standards in the US and resented the profits US companies tapped from branches that had penetrated the European economy. Hence the urge to pursue independence but at a European level, because it was felt that a national economy would be too weak to resist American influence and competition. Centrists like Lecanuet, and independent-republicans like Giscard d'Estaing, went along with de Gaulle's anti-Americanism, but rejected his view that an independent France was worth more than an independent EEC. Their philosophy of dynamic economic modernization was articulated in a best-selling book, *Le Défi américain*, brought out in 1967 by Servan-Schreiber, a publicist who became leader of the Radical party. Describing American investment as a bird of prey feasting on the European economy, he goes on to argue that to regain control will require a new awareness among Europeans that must transcend mere economic nationalism in order to strengthen the economic and political sinews of the EEC.

To the left of centre in French politics, some socialists held to a philosophy that social reform would be most easily achieved as a by-product of rapid economic growth which in turn would be most attainable through European integration. They tended to share the resentment of centre-party politicians towards American influence, as well as sharing their enthusiasm for the EEC as a vehicle for politico-economic progress. Typical of this group were André Philip and Claude Brudain. More left-inclined socialists accepted the EEC while insisting on the need to direct it in the interests of the working class.

Paradoxically the politicians further left had views that had more in common with Gaullism than with those of the centrists. Naturally there was hostility towards the US as the capitalist Mecca. Then there was suspicion that the EEC was serving big business interests and operating beyond the control of French politicians in the national assembly, a view which sympathized with de Gaulle's resistance to further integration in the EEC. Moreover some socialists, and particularly communists, regarded the EEC as an economic reinforcement of western Europe within NATO and therefore as an organization perpetuating the division of Europe into hostile blocs. This too was a view that chimed in with de Gaulle's pursuit of a diffuse international system and an end to polarization so that European links could be forged beyond the confines of the EEC.

Some fundamental requirements of the French economy worked in favour of de Gaulle's independence policy. First and foremost was the need to secure markets for surplus agricultural produce; this was achieved through the EEC common agricultural policy which became firmly established by 1966 as a system protected from competition from the US and other world producers. It made it worth while for de Gaulle to keep France within the shelter of the EEC. Another vital need was a guaranteed supply of oil to fuel rapid industrial growth in France. At first Algeria met the need, but by 1967 the expense of extracting Algerian oil and a degree of political estrangement led

France to look to alternative sources in the Middle East. Good relations with oil-supplying Arab states were created and maintained in the teeth of American and other NATO support for Israel.

Finally, there was an obvious cultural motive for the pursuit of an independent foreign policy that would consequently win the support of most French people. The relative importance of the French language and culture had declined considerably during the previous century and by the 1960s only about 12 per cent of the world's population used French for everyday or business purposes, compared with over 50 per cent who used English. Even if the French community had by then shrunk to only seven member-states, there was a compelling reason for the French government to maintain informal links as closely as possible with the French-speaking world by means of the operations of the franc zone and a foreign aid programme that was on twice the scale of most other countries largely due to its educational and cultural as well as its economic components. The counterpart to this policy was a sustained effort to restrict the penetration of the French-speaking world by the English language. His enthusiasm for *francophonie* and the *rayonnement* of French culture generated for de Gaulle a considerable groundswell of political support.

Conjunctural conditions for the independent foreign policy of de Gaulle to flower fully occurred after 1962 when the end of the Algerian war left him free to concentrate attention on foreign affairs having created a firm political power base including acceptance in France of a presidential policy sector. Moreover, the outcome of the Cuba crisis of 1962 freed de Gaulle of Cold War constraints by revealing that the Soviet Union at least did not intend to push super-power rivalry to the point of nuclear war. In an atmosphere of *détente*, France had scope for divergence from the USA. De Gaulle proceeded with a series of independent initiatives to create links with West Germany, China and the Soviet Union on the assumption that those powers would enjoy as much as he did the freedom and flexibility of a diffuse nation-state system.

De Gaulle discovered, however, that the insecurity of West Germany in relation to eastern Europe first of all made her unwilling to diverge economically or militarily from the US, and furthermore it made her anxious to explore the possibilities of *détente*, not through France as an intermediary but directly through her own *Ostpolitik*. He also discovered that China's interest in containing the power of the Soviet Union made her anxious that not just France but the whole of the EEC should support her policy against Moscow, and ultimately China looked to the United States to use leverage on her behalf against the Soviet Union. Like West Germany, China was looking for a reliably structured system of international relations rather than an unpredictable diffuse arrangement with France. But the most severe blow to de Gaulle's policy came from the Soviet Union, who attached such vital importance to her integrated alliances with eastern European states that she organized military intervention in Czechoslovakia in August 1968 to ensure that a totally loyal régime should replace one subject to doubt. For a time there was fear that Warsaw Pact military operations might escalate into confrontation with NATO and de Gaulle was impelled to co-operate to a very considerable extent with NATO for the purposes of French security, combining operations, for instance, of the French navy with the American fleet in the Mediterranean to monitor the movements of Soviet ships. There were residual trade links with Russia and other communist states but otherwise French bridge-building policies directed towards eastern Europe were in shreds when de Gaulle fell from power in 1969.

If the Czechoslovakian crisis had revealed significant French military dependence on the United States, events in France in 1968 destroyed the financial stability essential to his policy of economic independence. Inflation, and speculative attacks on the franc in world money markets, forced de Gaulle to borrow massive credits from the United States and other powers in his desperate attempt to maintain the value of French currency. A combination of international crises and domestic political problems therefore recreated serious constraints on de Gaulle's foreign policy during his last year in power.[10]

His successors, Pompidou and Giscard d'Estaing, subsequently modified French policy by devaluing the franc and accepting the prevailing world conditions of financial and economic inter-dependence in order to maintain some economic growth and expansion of foreign trade during a period of world recession. Evidence of this more open policy is that whereas American investment in French industry increased by only 55 per cent between 1963 and 1968, it more than doubled in the period 1968 to 1971, a similar rate to that of other EEC states — whereas it had been half their rate in the earlier period. It should be noted, moreover, that the rate of other EEC states' investments in France quadrupled between 1968 and 1971, thus outstripping American investment. The French economy was clearly opened up to international influences once de Gaulle had left the scene. Nevertheless the motivations and ideology of independence continued to be given formal expression throughout the decade after the fall of de Gaulle, thus emphasizing the fact that de Gaulle had articulated a set of beliefs regarding the French image of their role in the world that he shared with a vast number of his fellow-countrymen.

In the 1970s, France was permanently represented by ambassadors or consuls in 160 different states in the world. The responsibilities for the policies they had to implement were defined by the Fifth Republic constitution as follows: article 5 makes the president the protector of the nation's independence, its territorial integrity, its treaties and community agreements; articles 13 and 14 state that ambassadors and envoys are appointed in the council of ministers and are then accredited to foreign powers by the president; article 15 makes the president head of the armed forces and chairman of the higher councils and committees of national defence; article 16 gives the president full powers in a state of emergency arising, for example, from a threat to the independence of the nation or to the integrity of its territory; article 20 states that the government decides and directs national policy and is served by the administration and the armed forces; article 21 makes the prime minister responsible for national defence with power to appoint to a number of civil and military posts; article 35 gives parliament the power to authorize declarations of war; articles 52 and 53 give the president power to negotiate and ratify treaties except for peace treaties involving international organizations, financial obligations, or modification of territorial possessions, which have to be approved by act of parliament; article 86 allows for states to be members of the community while being totally independent. Although articles 5, 15 and 52 give the president extensive powers, there is no mention of a *domaine réservé* and his powers are clearly subordinate to those of the prime minister under articles 20 and 21 while parliament has important powers of decision under articles 35 and 53. The hybrid nature of the constitution could not be better illustrated than in the field of foreign and defence policy.

Nevertheless the experience of the Algerian war, the personality of de Gaulle, and a docile national assembly combined to establish a convention by which the president determined the direction of foreign policy as part of his *domaine réservé*, while the prime minister made it possible to carry out the policy within the context of general government programmes and priorities (in particular the prime minister would have to ensure a majority vote in the national assembly regarding treaty laws or questions of confidence or censure). It was then the responsibility of the foreign minister to carry out the policy in dealings with representatives of foreign powers, a recognizably standard role on the same lines as in other countries.

It is worth looking a little more closely, however, at the role of the prime minister and his office and at their influence on French foreign policy. Although the convention is for the president to have the last word on policy, served by a small group of personal advisers at the Elysée palace, the important process of co-ordinating different issues and policies usually takes place in the prime minister's office at the Hôtel Matignon. The principal official in the prime minister's office, the *secrétaire général du gouvernement*, prepares the agenda for weekly meetings of the council of ministers, takes minutes and keeps a record of decisions taken at those meetings. The rest of the staff in the prime minister's office, particularly the *chef de cabinet*, play a large part in co-ordinating negotiations between ministries which precede and follow each meeting ·of the council of ministers. This process of negotiation is often conducted between relevant ministers in the presence of the prime minister. The latter's close relationship with his colleagues contrasts with that of the president who has weekly meetings with the ministers for foreign affairs and finance separately and never sees the two ministers together except in the presence of the prime minister. Negotiations also take place among officials from various ministries, but again the initiative for convening and presiding over these meetings comes from the Hôtel Matignon. This system gives considerable potential influence to the prime minister in various spheres of policy including foreign affairs. A final point about the traditional system of government established under de Gaulle is that neither prime ministers nor foreign ministers appointed after 1962 were party politicians, and consequently they were unlikely to have an independent power base apart from presidential favour.

During the presidency of Pompidou, the organization of government underwent significant modifications which affected foreign as well as domestic policies. For most of the period 1969 to 1974, the prime minister, Chaban-Delmas, was a leading Gaullist party politician who was therefore a potential rival to Pompidou quite apart from coolness in their personal relations. The result was that the prime minister was virtually cut out of policy-making in various fields including foreign affairs (on one occasion he simply wanted to attend an England-France rugby match at Twickenham but was prevented from going in case he became involved in talks on British entry into the EEC, an issue which Pompidou was determined to handle personally). Normally during this period the president worked with his foreign minister in a tandem relationship, and the Elysée staff took over the work of co-ordinating foreign with domestic policies, thus reducing the importance of the prime minister's office. The secretary-general at the Elysée under Pompidou was Michel Jobert, who, for example, personally arranged a series of Franco-British negotiations regarding the EEC. After the defeat of foreign minister Maurice Schumann in the March 1973 elections, Jobert was appointed foreign minister by Pompidou, whose illness, leading to death in the spring of 1974, incapacitated him to such an extent that in practice Jobert assumed personal control of French foreign policy and had significant influence, for instance, on a resurgence of anti-Americanism in France at that time.

Under Giscard d'Estaing, since 1974, power to direct policy still lies with the president but Giscard's interest and sense of purpose in foreign affairs is more superficial and intermittent than those of his predecessors. His book *Démocratie française* gives very little attention to world affairs and has a bias reflecting his earlier career as finance minister. He replaced Jobert at the Quai d'Orsay with a career diplomat and loyal follower of the president, namely Jean Sauvagnargues, who was not very able and appeared even less so as a result of Giscard's habit of improvising in press interviews and policy statements which left his foreign minister in ignorance so that gaffe followed upon gaffe. (It was not always Giscard's fault — on one occasion the muddle-headed Sauvagnargues welcomed the great pianist Artur Rubinstein as 'Monsieur Toscanini' and was clearly in the same league as President Ford of the United States, who once welcomed the Egyptian leader, Sadat, as 'President of Israel'.) Evidence of incompetence mounted and in August 1976 Sauvagnargues was replaced by Louis de Guiringaud, an experienced diplomat respected for his work in the 'third world' and as French representative at the United Nations, but whose main characteristic was total loyalty to the president. Giscard continued to improvise foreign and domestic policies with the help of his Elysée staff. His appointment of Raymond Barre as prime minister and finance minister indicated the government's priorities and Barre would inevitably have little time to interest himself in foreign affairs.

Thus it was that the troika of president, prime minister and foreign minister that operated in the time of de Gaulle became a tandem of president and foreign minister under Pompidou and then a solo performer under Giscard d'Estaing, with the president and his Elysée staff directing any or every branch of domestic and foreign policy at will. A curious development in view of Giscard d'Estaing's criticism of de Gaulle in 1969 for concentrating power excessively in the hands of the president.

The Quai d'Orsay has suffered a decline in recent years, due not only to some unfortunate appointments to the post of minister, but also to weak organization rendered chronic through inadequate budgeting for reform. Before he was replaced, Sauvagnargues formed a committee to draft reforms. A report in April 1976 proposed that each embassy should have at least three diplomats, that there should be an embassy for each of the 130 members of the United Nations, and that consulates should be given facilities to undertake work on the same level as embassies. The emphasis in representation, it was suggested, should be directed towards countries vital to French interests, namely those supplying oil and raw materials and those providing markets for agriculture, above all the EEC. However, in a national assembly debate on 6 May 1976, Sauvagnargues announced that the prime minister had informed him that no new posts could be created during 1977, and that the Quai d'Orsay budget would continue to shrink in real terms. No reform proposal would be accepted if it required a budgetary increase, he added. During the summer anxiety grew regarding the obvious weakness of the Quai d'Orsay whose staff were disgruntled because they had not been effectively consulted before Sauvagnargues drew up his report.

On 13 October 1976 the president held a meeting of the council of ministers to deal with a wholesale reorganization of the Quai d'Orsay. It was decided that there would be five geographical departments (Europe, Asia-Oceania, North Africa and the Levant, Africa south of the Sahara, America) and three functional departments (political, economic, multilateral). The *secrétaire général* would no longer be head of the diplomatic services, his former role being taken over by the minister for foreign affairs himself, but his new role would be to help the administration of the ministry and to reflect and give new impulses to policy formulation. The traditional role of the Quai d'Orsay in formulation of foreign policy was reaffirmed. Nevertheless, it was recognized that unless these changes were accompanied by acceptance of the five-year plan to improve the budget, the reforms would be abortive. A new *secrétaire général*, Jean-Marie Soutou, was appointed to carry through the reforms.

In spite of all these efforts to improve the Quai d'Orsay's organization and effectiveness, on 9 November 1976 Guiringaud had to submit a budget to the national assembly that was even more disappointing than generally feared. There was an increase of 13 per cent but it would have to face an inflation rate of 11 per cent and a new burden of social security expenses for staff; the budget of 3.5 milliard francs, of which over 1 milliard was spent on staff costs, was condemned by Couve de Murville as 'indigne de la France'.[11] Clearly no real improvement in the organization of French foreign affairs was to be expected for the foreseeable future.

The appointment of Jean François-Poncet, formerly *secrétaire général* at the Elysée and close confidant of Giscard d'Estaing, to replace Guiringaud as foreign minister in November 1978 was likely to have the effect of tightening even further the personal grip of the president on the formulation of French foreign policy.

(2) Defence policy: purpose and structure

A peaceful world does not depend on a sudden change towards benevolence in human nature. It depends rather on methodical procedures to control and reduce tensions before they lead to explosions. In a world where the privilege of some relates directly to the deprivation of others, there must be scope for anger, hostility and violence to show the limits of tolerance. Failure to indicate such limits merely conveys indifference. Anger, hostility and violence are costly, however, and sometimes increase with expression; they therefore need to be controlled and directed at particular causes of tension in order to bring relief without harmful side-effects. To achieve successful management of tense situations, anger, hostility and violence must be accepted as inevitable and expressed so that the other party will make amends; this may require an explanation of the interest or attitude that gives rise to anger. To cultivate co-operation, sympathy and responsibility in others, feelings and requirements should be made clear without insulting or alienating them. If crisis management fails, owing to the determination of the other party to refuse co-operation, an escalation of violence may have to be considered while balancing likely risks and costs against the importance of the need to remove the particular causes of stress and hostility.

Such is a typical contemporary psychologist's approach (actually that of H. Ginott, University of New York) to friction and violence in civil society and international relations. It is perfectly in tune with the 200-year-old dictum of Clausewitz that war is nothing more than the continuation of politics by other means. The French experience of major wars and invasions over the past two centuries had led them to attach vital importance to their security and to the need for armed forces to back up their policies. In the recent history of France the army has been at the centre of passionate debates dividing public opinion almost as much as the schools. It is not possible in France to discuss military questions with sole regard to their technical specificity. Any definition of defence policy automatically relates to a system of political values.

At the beginning of the nineteenth century the revolutionary experience had created a view according to which the soldier was the defender of liberty, and it was among republicans of the left that militarism was most pronounced. Half a century later, however, having witnessed the crushing of the 1848 revolution and the *coup d'état* to establish the empire of Napoleon III, public opinion regarded the soldier as serving order rather than liberty. After the defeat of 1870 there was more consensus on the need for a strong army, and by a new system of universal conscription the politicians of the Third Republic sought to reconcile military strength with political reliability: it was to be a nation-in-arms that would be primarily citizens rather than soldiers, abjuring authoritarianism at home and irresponsible adventurism abroad, but generating an irresistible patriotic dedication to defend the soil of France against an invader, thus following in the tradition of the triumphant *levée en masse* of 1793.

The Dreyfus Affair split French opinion once again over an issue that appeared to demonstrate the incompatibility of justice and military discipline. Consequently one group of Frenchmen regarded the army as incarnating the values of patriotism, social order and respect for hierarchical authority; others saw it as a force for reaction, hostile to the progress and liberty of civil society. These stereotypes of militarism and anti-militarism influenced controversies over military organization. When the socialist leader, Jaurès, argued in 1905 in his book *L'Armée nouvelle* that conscription could be reduced to six months and still provide an army perfectly capable of defending French territory, he was more concerned with making the army politically reliable than with its technical efficiency. In practice a system of three years' service was used at the time of the First World War and proved its value by providing vast reserves of trained manpower. Victory in 1918 ensured the retention of the nation-in-arms philosophy so that proposals for change such as those in de Gaulle's book in 1934, *Vers l'Armée de métier*, were rejected owing to their élitist, apparently anti-republican tendencies, irrespective of the military case for highly trained units using technically advanced equipment that might have been more effective in battle.

In spite of the French defeat in 1940, the same system of conscription prevailed after the Second World War, partly owing to the influence of resistance leaders and partly because conscription had the advantage of being cheaper during a period of perennial budgetary difficulties. By the 1970s a changing French role in world affairs revived controversy as to whether the existing system of conscription for twelve months, possibly even reduced to six or eight months, was more appropriate to French needs than a professional volunteer force. But the debate was still as much concerned with the political significance of military organization and its purposes as with its technical efficiency. Raoul Girardet summed up this persistent French tradition (in *Défense nationale*, April 1977, pp. 21-7) with the proposition that the nature and composition of an army are always closely correlated with the social and political structure of a nation.

The most recent evidence of this tradition was during a period of controversy beginning with the 1973 Debré–Fontanet law, which restricted possibilities of deferment (*le sursis*) for conscripts. This change disrupted the continuity of education and provoked not merely protests and demonstrations against the particular measure but considerable doubt about conscription as a whole. An opinion poll in 1973 found that only 31 per cent wanted a defence system based on conscription, whereas 53 per cent would have preferred a professional volunteer army. For the age group from fifteen to twenty-four, the preference for a professional army was 70 per cent.

In 1974 a *manifeste du soldat* drew attention to the low wages, primitive living conditions and political restrictions in the army; the Trotskyist Krivine was prominent among those campaigning for reform on behalf of the soldiers. But this had the effect of rallying some support for the existing system against disruption by radical reform; thus a 1974 opinion poll found that 34 per cent favoured a conscript system, while this time only 46 per cent preferred a professional army. The then defence minister, Debré, was particularly convinced that conscription was best and therefore had organized an appropriate propaganda campaign to improve the public image of the army.

From the autumn of 1974 there was considerable controversy regarding the political rights and status of soldiers (for example *L'Humanité* was forbidden in the barracks) and unrest was particularly evident at the military bases at Karlsruhe and Draguignan; a number of those involved in the agitation were imprisoned in 1975. Yet public opinion showed a further tendency to defend the existing system against disruption: 44 per cent, when asked in 1975, preferred a conscript army while 43 per cent preferred a professional army, though among young people there was still a marked preference for a professional army. It was interesting, however, that those favouring a conscription system did so on the grounds that it promoted character development and a sense of community rather than that it made any intrinsically valuable contribution to military efficiency.[12]

From 1976 there was a further period of controversy as to whether soldiers might be free to join trade unions, and there was considerable support for this freedom among politicians on the left. But it came up against the traditional fear among older French people, including those in the political class, that national security and social stability might be jeopardized by radical reform of conditions in the army. The government defused tensions to some extent by increasing soldiers' wages. The political parties and trade unions tacitly agreed not to foment controversy during the 1978 election campaign. And in August 1978 the *Cour de sureté de l'état* quietly decided in favour of thirty-five civilians who had been accused in 1975 of joining in activities seeking to bring about demoralization in the army. Thus a period of controversy came to an end with French society still committed to its conscript army which had not undergone any fundamental change. An indication of the consensus was that defence spokesmen from various parties, except the communists, amicably joined together to attend army manoeuvres in the Dordogne region in September 1978; General Bigeard (UDF), who had previously proclaimed that there was *une guerre subversive*, could be seen embracing C. Hernu (PS), while Y. Guéna (RPR) could be seen deep in amicable discussion with M. Faure (MRG) (cf. *Le Point*, 18 September 1978, p. 61).

There remained objections, on grounds of efficiency and suitability, articulated particularly by P. Messmer (RPR), that a professional army was needed to participate in operations in Africa such as the one to uphold the Mobutu régime in Zaire in the spring of 1978, when Moroccan troops were used instead of French. President Giscard d'Estaing's role as *'gendarme'* in Africa seemed to need more specialized men and equipment than the conscript system provided. But the president's answer was to increase the military budget rather than to change the system.

As we have seen, successive French governments since the Second World War were concerned to create an adequate instrument of defence, operating in relation to allied forces but not dependent on allies for vital security. De Gaulle defined an independent policy in April 1965 as one by which France herself should have the capability of deterring a possible aggressor; and in the nuclear age this meant having a nuclear force capable of retaliating against any state in the world that might attack France. How far has France achieved that aim?

Table 5.1 shows the resources and military power of France compared with those of several other states, revealing the nature of her status as a middle-sized power and the gap between her and the super-powers. After 1962 the French armed forces were organized in three sections: the *force nucléaire stratégique*, the *forces de manoeuvre*, and the *défense opérationelle du territoire*. The nuclear force, commonly known as '*la force de frappe*', consisted in 1978 of four nuclear-powered submarines each carrying sixteen ballistic missiles (three vessels had M-20 missiles with a range of 1,800 miles and war-heads about ten times as powerful as the bomb dropped on Hiroshima in 1945; the other vessel had M-2 missiles with thermonuclear warheads hundreds of times more powerful than the Hiroshima bomb). A fifth nuclear-powered submarine was being built to carry sixteen M-4 missiles which would have a range of 2,500 miles and multiple thermonuclear warheads (but budgetary economies were likely to delay its completion, scheduled for 1979) and a sixth submarine originally scheduled for 1982 was cancelled. In addition there were two squadrons in Haute-Provence each with nine intermediate range (1,800 miles) surface-to-surface ballistic missiles, carrying warheads about ten times as powerful as the Hiroshima bomb (soon to be replaced by new S-3 missiles with a greater range and power). Finally, there were thirty-three Mirage IVA bombers carrying bombs about five times as powerful as the Hiroshima bomb. There were plans to replace existing warheads with thermonuclear warheads and to extend the range of missiles, but these were postponed for several years.

Among the operational forces, the army was to be restructured from 1979.[13] There would be eight armoured divisions, each comprising 8,000 men divided into two tank regiments, two mechanized infantry regiments and two artillery regiments; there would also be four infantry divisions, each comprising 6,500 men — divided into three motorized infantry regiments, one armoured-car regiment and one artillery regiment (a fifth infantry division was to be formed later). In addition there were several specialized Alpine, marine and parachute

Table 5.1 Defence force comparisons, selected states, 1978

	France	United Kingdom	German Fed. Repub.	USA	USSR
Population	53,850,000	56,700,000	63,410,000	218,630,000	261,310,000
GNP 1977, estimated in $	374.8 billion	263.6 billion	508.6 billion	1,890 billion	516 billion roubles
Defence expenditure 1978	$17.52 billion[a] (Fr 80.77 billion)	$13.04 billion[a] (£6.92 billion)	$17.26 billion[a]	$115.2 billion	17.2 billion roubles
Military service	12 months	voluntary	15 months	voluntary	2 years
Personnel:					
Total armed forces	493,000 (inc. 266,200 conscripts)	313,253	478,900 (inc. 236,000 conscripts)	1,877,300	2,713,000
army	324,000 (inc. 209,000 conscr.)	160,837	336,200 (inc. 187,000 conscr.)	774,200	1,825,000
navy	68,200 (inc. 18,400 conscr.)	67,770	36,500 (inc. 11,000 conscr.)	532,300	433,000
air force	100,800 (inc. 38,800 conscr.)	84,646	106,200 (inc. 38,000 conscr.)	570,800	455,000
Paramilitary	76,400 gendarmes		20,000 border guard		450,000 KGB & MVD
Combat aircraft	471	511	484	3,400	4,650
Major surface combat vessels	46	72	33	172	243
Submarines	21	27	24 (coastal)	75	243

a approximate.
Source: Compiled from *The Military Balance, 1978-1979*, London, International Institute for Strategic Studies, 1978.

divisions; and five regiments equipped with thirty *Pluton* surface-to-surface missiles for 'tactical' use, each carrying one 20-kiloton warhead equivalent to the power of the Hiroshima bomb. A number of other regiments were equipped with Hawk and Roland surface-to-air missiles.

The deployment of the army in 1978 was as follows: 34,000 in West Germany, plus another 2,000 in West Berlin; 4,000 at Djibouti, 1,200 in the Lebanon as part of the United Nations Interim Force; 1,000 in Senegal; 1,500 in Chad; 450 in Gabon; 400 in the Ivory Coast; another 19,000 men from all services were deployed overseas in Antilles-Guyana, South Indian Ocean, New Caledonia and Polynesia. The remainder of the army was based in France.

The navy was growing steadily in 1978 and it was expected that by the mid-1980s France would have clearly surpassed Britain as a world naval power. To the existing twenty-one submarines three more would be added soon; to the fourteen destroyers three more would be added; and to the twenty-three escort ships five more would be added. Apart from normal deployment of vessels in the Atlantic and Mediterranean, one-quarter of the French navy was deployed in the Indian Ocean (the largest single fleet there, according to Admiral Lannuzel, commander-in-chief of French naval forces).[14]

The air force possessed 471 combat aircraft in 1978. It was divided into a tactical air force comprising seventeen fighter-bomber squadrons equipped with 135 Mirages and 105 Jaguars, and a number of reconnaissance and conversion squadrons; an air defence command with 120 Mirage fighter-interceptors, ten missile battalions and four communication squadrons, then an air transport command and a training command.

Figure 5.1 shows the decision-making structure for French defence policy. The president exercised overall command of the armed forces, assisted particularly by the *Conseil supérieur de la défense nationale*, the *Comité de défense* and the *Comité de défense restreint* which formulated directives for the president's approval. But there was the unwieldy constitutional arrangement by which the prime minister was responsible for national defence and was served by a number of bodies, notably the *Secrétariat général de défense nationale*, which were quite separate from the president and his military advisers. The only institutional liaison, as clearly revealed in the Figure, was in the council of ministers when the president and prime minister met. Otherwise, co-ordination among relevant ministers was achieved in the *Conseil de la défense nationale* which met approximately once every two months under the chairmanship of the prime minister; it was essentially a forum in which other ministers had the opportunity to react to the proposals of the minister of defence. Under de Gaulle's presidency defence policy was separated from other aspects of government, particularly from economic policies. But after de Gaulle, budget-

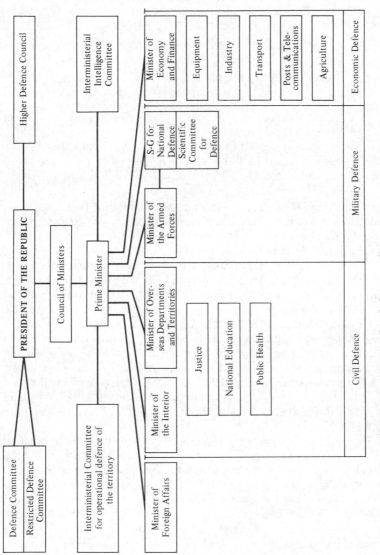

Figure 5.1 Decision-making system for defence policy
Source: French Embassy, Information sheet A/99/6/74, London, 1974.

Table 5.2   Development of defence expenditures, 1977 to 1982
(millions of francs)

	1977	1978	1979	1980	1981	1982	Total
Military research and strategic forces	11,670	13,145	14,795	16,470	18,495	20,570	95,145
Army	18,400	21,080	24,025	27,280	30,975	35,170	156,930
Navy	9,780	11,355	13,200	15,450	17,975	20,955	88,715
Air force	12,225	14,150	16,490	19,405	22,670	26,880	111,820
Gendarmerie (police)	5,925	6,730	7,645	8,655	9,875	11,000	49,830
Total expenditures	**58,000**	**66,460**	**76,155**	**87,260**	**99,990**	**114,575**	**502,440**

Source: *Le Monde*, 7 May 1976, p. 8.

ary problems, added to the character and interests of both Pompidou and Giscard d'Estaing, had considerable influence on defence policy and held up armaments programmes, until 1976 when a new expansion of the military budget was undertaken.

Table 5.2 shows projected expenditure on defence under the fourth military programme from 1977 to 1982. The defence budget, which had traditionally taken up about 17 per cent of the total national budget, was scheduled to rise at a rate of 16 per cent per year until it would take 20 per cent of the total budget by 1982. Such an ambitious programme was significant at a time of international economic recession and in view of French government attempts to curb inflation by cuts in public spending. The most significant feature, moreover, was the emphasis on increasing the strength of the conventional armed forces rather than the strategic nuclear force. Not only the army and air force, but also the navy would be costing more than the *force de frappe* by 1982.

The problem of increasing armaments expenditure without creating budget deficits and domestic inflation would be overcome to a considerable extent by the export of war materials to other countries. By 1978 France had become the third biggest arms exporter after the United States and the Soviet Union. Table 5.3 indicates the rapid increase in French arms exports, particularly after 1972 when arms sales tripled within five years. It was estimated that one-third of armaments industry production was directed towards the export trade, and arms sales in 1975 represented 3 per cent of total external trade. This needs to be seen in the context of global arms sales: between 1965 and 1974, for instance, the United States sold 49 per cent, the Soviet Union 29 per cent, France 4 per cent, and Britain 3 per cent.

Table 5.3   Exports of war materials from France (millions of francs)

Year	Air	Land	Sea	Electronics	Total
1965	1,912	600	50	250	2,812
1966	2,540	320	129	250	3,239
1967	1,686	360	187	380	2,613
1968	2,823	615	143	495	4,076
1969	1,990	400	41	140	2,571[a]
1970	5,242	605	1,055	386	7,288
1971	5,219	1,500	79	324	7,122
1972	3,688	300	80	650	4,734[b]
1973	5,470	2,421.2	234.3	1,310.7	9,436[c]
1974	9,987	5,701	2,224	1,831	19,743
1975	9,210				20,000

Sources: [a] *Le Monde,* 28 February 1970; [b] *Le Monde,* 23 December 1973; [c] *Les Informations,* 9 December 1974.

Nevertheless, French arms exports were the result of an official policy to maintain independence in defence and foreign policies; arms sales were intended to serve the political purpose of guaranteeing an autonomous defence structure and extending French influence in Europe and the world.[15] The continuing success of the policy in an expanding world armaments market could be seen from French sales in a twelve-month period in 1977–8, of which the following were merely examples: fifty-eight Mirage F-1 fighters to Spain; forty Mirage F-1 fighters to Iraq; thirty-eight Mirage 50 fighters to the Sudan; thirty Mirage F-1 fighters to Qatar and ten guided missile fast patrol boats to Libya (see *The Military Balance, 1978–9*, pp. 104–5).

Nevertheless, to achieve such a prolific rate of production and sales for a middle-sized power, particularly in the aircraft industry, it was necessary to get considerable outside support, notably from the United States. It was estimated that in production, operation and maintenance within the French aircraft industry, the American contribution in 1976 was 74 per cent, and the only really significant French contribution was in basic airframe structures.[16] Moreover, to compete in the most lucrative markets for armaments within NATO, France agreed to join, in December 1975, a so-called Independent Programme Group of European nations trying to co-ordinate production and purchase of armaments. Whereas an earlier Eurogroup serving the same purpose without French participation was inside NATO, this new organization was technically outside, but clearly formed and named to overcome Gaullist sensitivity regarding independence.

The emphasis in the fourth military programme on strengthening conventional forces, rather than expanding the *force de frappe*, was in total contrast with the period of de Gaulle's presidency. It also signified a change in defence philosophy as a whole. In de Gaulle's time the philosophy was one of dissuasion, or deterrence, by which any attack on France and her allies would incur massive retaliation from the *force de frappe*. This was carried to its apogee by 1967 when the then chief of the general staff, General Ailleret, proclaimed a defence strategy of *tous azimuts*, a multi-directional system that would be valid against attack from any part of the world. De Gaulle endorsed the strategy in 1968, but politico-economic problems related to the events of May that year made it unlikely that France would have the resources to create a credible multi-directional nuclear force. Moreover, the invasion of Czechoslovakia by Warsaw Pact forces in August 1968 renewed the polarization of the Soviet bloc as a possible threat to western security just at a time when Franco-American relations began to improve. Both before and after de Gaulle's fall from power in 1969, French strategy reverted to a specifically anti-Soviet posture in liaison with NATO. By 1974 General Maurin was chief of the general staff and was speaking in terms of engagement in battle in the framework of the alliance and in consultation with NATO leaders, rather than independent French action.

During the 1960s French strategy was to use the *force de frappe* for three variable purposes: first, to threaten an attacker with unacceptable levels of damage; second, to act as a 'trigger' to ensure use of American nuclear forces in a situation where there was doubt about their commitment in a crisis; third, to obstruct American plans for a 'flexible response' to aggression in Europe by which conventional forces would be used initially in the hope of preventing escalation to the level of nuclear warfare without sacrificing vital interests (the French fear was that the Soviet Union might be tempted to attack in the hope that some areas of western Europe would not be regarded as of vital interest to Washington). Many American and European analysts criticized the French *force de frappe* for involving dangerous proliferation of nuclear weapons and for being prone to obsolescence owing to the apparent inability of middle-sized powers to keep up with super-power technology. Nevertheless, some French analysts believed the *force de frappe* would have sufficient credibility to act as a deterrent to an aggressor, if only on psychological rather than logical grounds, regarding deterrence as a matter of risk rather than certainty.[17] The political debate involved opposition from the left on the grounds that a French nuclear force increased proliferation and the risk of war and that it wasted resources needed in other fields, opposition from the centre on the grounds that the French force should be integrated in a European or Atlantic force, and support from Gaullists and their allies on the grounds that it increased French political prestige and military security, while also having spin-off value in raising the general level of French technology. Variations of opinion in France in the 1960s settled into a consensus in favour of maintaining the *force de frappe* in the 1970s; to reverse policy by scrapping it would involve waste of many years of national investment. Moreover it had two attractive political advantages: first, it ensured a French superiority over the growing power of West Germany, and second, it apparently offered some possibility of independence from the United States.

In the 1978 general election campaign, not only had the left ceased to dismiss the *force de frappe* as 'la bombinette', but the communists were even advocating renewal of the *tous azimuts* strategy in order to make it possible to adopt a neutral stance between the Soviet Union and the United States. There was considerable communist criticism of Giscard d'Estaing for not maintaining de Gaulle's policy of independence by means of an appropriate nuclear strategy. This view was expressed more forcefully, of course, by Gaullist diehards.[18]

French government emphasis on developing conventional forces was in response to criticism that a strategy of massive retaliation reduced freedom of choice, and therefore independence, in a war crisis involving French allies. Was there not a similarity between the *force de frappe* and the Maginot line of 1940 in that they both left France without alternative means to influence hostilities beyond her frontier and involving other kinds of weapons (cf. the view of J. Huntziger, right-wing PS)? Just as France might upset American flexible response strategy by 'triggering' a nuclear response, so might West Germany upset French strategy by engaging in military operations that left France the choice between massive retaliation (and suicide) or doing nothing. Moreover, developments in Africa revealed a possible need for conventional armed forces to operate outside France. Whereas de Gaulle had adopted the position that a Soviet attack on West Berlin, for example, would automatically meet with massive retaliation from France, by 1975 Giscard d'Estaing was asserting French freedom to assess a crisis with a view to ensuring 'à tout coup la sécurité de nos frontières'. It was pointed out to him that, although compatible with the Atlantic Alliance of 1949, this attitude diverged from the Brussels Treaty of 1948 which required automatic assistance to be given to allies; moreover, it would hardly reassure West Germany of French reliability in a crisis (see the article by A. Grosser in *Le Monde*, 17 November 1975).

The deployment of *Pluton* tactical nuclear weapons from 1974, nevertheless, made it possible, even necessary, for France to develop a strategy of flexible response to aggression. The 1976 military programme indicated the change of strategy; and both General Méry, chief of the general staff from 1975, and Giscard d'Estaing explained that the use of tactical nuclear weapons served the vital purpose of showing the adversary that he had reached the threshold beyond which he would incur the threat of strategic nuclear weapons (see article by P. -M. de la Gorce in *Le Figaro*, 3 March 1978).

Once the concept of flexible response was adopted it was inevitable that co-ordination of French and allied conventional forces should be discussed regarding operations in Europe and possibly in the Mediterranean, the Indian Ocean and Africa. Thus the enlarging of French security areas, *la sanctuarisation élargie*, involved closer co-operation with NATO, which met with intense political criticism for departing from de Gaulle's decision to become independent of NATO in 1966. But General Méry insisted that there could be no effective European defence without a European Union complete with a European government. He further argued that in a European defence system France should have strong conventional forces to counter-balance those of West Germany so that unity would be as stable as possible. For Gaullists, of course, integration in Europe would be as unacceptable as in NATO; but many centre and centre-left politicians were attracted by Méry's concept of independence from the United States through promotion of European unity. Moreover, although Giscard d'Estaing had not ventured to speculate as much as Méry, there was little doubt that he too favoured developments towards European integration. The question remained, however, whether the EEC or even France in 1978 were sufficiently independent of American influence and protection to create any real freedom of action.

After the onset of the cold war, and even more after the Algerian war, a major French preoccupation had been security against communist subversion within French frontiers. To achieve this a number of overt and covert activities were regularly pursued. First of all there was the domestic intelligence organization controlled by the ministry of the interior, called the *Directoire de surveillance du territoire*, essentially the French equivalent of the American FBI. Second there was an external intelligence service under the ministry of justice, the *Service de documentation extérieure et de contre-espionage* (SDECE), which was very much the equivalent of the American CIA in that, although officially restricted to an external role, there was criticism in 1978 that 80 per cent of its work has been within France in recent years, including spying related to tax returns — the worst possible offence according to conventional French values — and carrying out 'witch-hunts' against some radio technicians whose membership of the CGT was equated with 'communist penetration' of the intelligence service. Half a dozen men in the SDECE were replaced by the ministry of defence but there was residual public resentment that the organization had overstepped its bounds and was extravagant with its large budget.[19]

There are two more overt organizations active in internal French security. First there is the *gendarmerie nationale*, serving the ministry of defence. Figure 5.2 shows its organization in relation to the division of France into seven defence zones, seven military regions and twenty-one territorial sub-regions, each involving co-ordination of civil and military authorities. There were in 1978 76,400 men serving in the paramilitary force of the *gendarmerie*, including 4,800 conscripts. The force was equipped with 38 light tanks, 160 armoured cars and 100 helicopters (see *The Military Balance, 1978-9*, p. 24). In April 1977 the director of the *gendarmerie*, J. Cochard, announced the formation of seven new *pelotons d'intervention rapide*, one in each military region, each *peloton* consisting of eighteen men with highly sophisticated equipment and a high degree of mobility; the ultimate aim was to provide such a *peloton* for each of the 400 companies of the *gendarmerie* (see *Armées d'aujourd'hui*, July 1977).

The second internal security force was the *Compagnies républicaines de sécurité* (CRS), serving the ministry of the interior via the *direction générale de la police nationale*. As distinct from the *gendarmerie*, the CRS had the normal right of the police to form a trade union but not to strike. The CRS in 1977 had 15,800 men divided into ten groups and sixty companies. Figure 5.3 shows their organization, indicating particularly that just as their numbers were lower than the *gendarmerie* they were also less widely dispersed; moreover their equipment was limited to individual weapons and two light machine-guns for each company. In emergencies, however, such as during the Algerian war, they can be specially equipped with heavier equipment and armaments. The CRS was essentially a flexible force capable of rapid intervention, by order of the minister of the interior, to prevent civil disorder effectively without a provocative show of force such as involvement of the *gendarmerie* would entail; though the CRS trade union had unsuccessfully sought guarantees that in civil disorders where firearms were used the *gendarmerie* would be called in rather than the CRS. The roles of the two forces were therefore not as distinct as their organizations would suggest. In addition to dealing with civil disorders such as occurred in February 1934 and in May 1968, the internal security forces would also be expected to organize resistance in France to an invasion such as that of 1940; this is the wider significance of the division of France into seven zones of defence, so that internal and external security forces are organized to support the various aims of French foreign policy.[20]

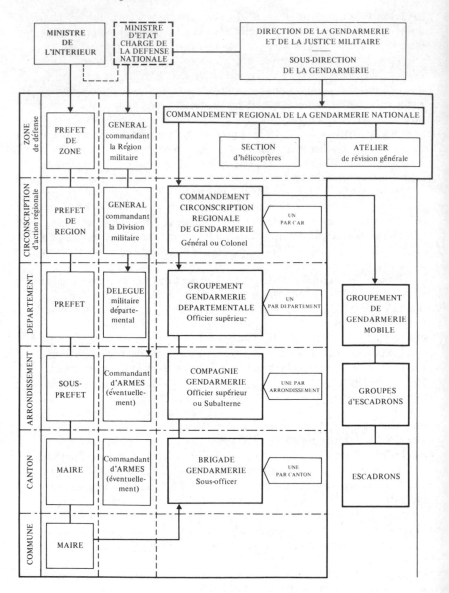

Figure 5.2   Organization of *gendarmerie* at regional level
        Source: L. Mandeville, J. -L. Loubet del Bayle and A. Picard,
        'Les forces de maintien de l'ordre en France',
        Défense nationale, July 1977, p. 68.

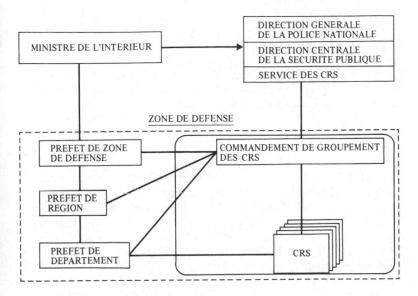

Figure 5.3   Organization of CRS
Source: L. Mandeville, J. -L. Loubet del Bayle and A. Picard,
'Les forces de maintien de l'ordre en France',
Défense nationale, July 1977, p. 70.

(3) Main directions of foreign policy

France has a long tradition of vital interest in relations with both
super-powers, the United States and the Soviet Union, and has a
tradition of bridging or balancing their influence rather than becoming
merely a satellite of one or the other. In the First World War, for
example, France began with an alliance with Russia which saved her
from defeat on a number of occasions between 1914 and 1916, then
she finished up in close association with the United States which
assured victory in 1918. Neither power joined France at the beginning
of the Second World War, but both played their different parts in the
eventual liberation of France in 1944; thus, although physically more
directly attached to the American government and its armies in western
Europe, de Gaulle hastened to Moscow to sign a treaty of non-ag-
gression with the Soviet Union in December 1944 on behalf of the
provisional French government, believing that Franco-Russian solidarity
was in harmony with the natural order in view of the German threat
and the Anglo-Saxon attempts at hegemony (see C. de Gaulle,
Mémoires de guerre, vol. 3, p. 54). But the 1945 Yalta conference,

which mapped out spheres of influence in east and west, and the ensuing deterioration of the cold war, detached France from the Soviet Union and entrenched her firmly in the western sphere dominated by the United States. When a period of relative *détente* eventually began after 1962, de Gaulle had returned to power in France and resumed his earlier policy of seeking freedom of manoeuvre between the super-powers, thus creating an ideology of independence to which his successors have also formally subscribed. What effects did this policy have on relations between France and each of the super-powers after 1962?

In pursuit of political independence from the United States, whose role according to de Gaulle should be to provide a security umbrella for Europe but otherwise to leave her alone, French policy was to propose (in the 17 September 1958 memorandum[21]) equal power-sharing in NATO or otherwise a progressive French withdrawal of her forces from that integrated structure under American command. This policy, culminating in February 1966, was characteristic of de Gaulle's essentially negative achievements during those years; other examples were preventing the American 'Trojan horse', Britain, from entering the EEC in 1963 and 1967, and refusing to sign the 1963 treaty sponsored by the United States, Britain and the Soviet Union banning nuclear tests on land or sea. American governments during that period were constantly frustrated by de Gaulle's blocking tactics regarding initiatives not only in Europe but, for example, in the Congo or Laos.[22]

De Gaulle's concept of political independence, judging by his speech on 27 April 1965, seemed to focus on developing friendly relations with West Germany, eastern Europe, the Soviet Union, China and states in Africa and South America. But his intention to handle the German problem in a purely European context was rebuffed by the Germans themselves who were the third most important trading partner of the United States, and who preferred to trust American security guarantees in NATO rather than a less credible protection from France. The Franco-Soviet consultation agreement in 1966 did not enable France to do anything to forestall the Warsaw Pact invasion of Czechoslovakia in 1968 which destroyed French assumptions that a free dialogue was possible with eastern Europe; and by the end of de Gaulle's rule, France was co-operating with NATO once more against a possible Russian threat. Technical problems required French reliance from September 1968 on NATO naval surveillance and radar networks. In fact this was related to dependence on the United States in advanced technology; in spite of de Gaulle's efforts to minimize American penetration of French industry he was not very successful as shown by the 1963 takeover by General Electric of Machines Bull, the leading French computer firm, and the subsequent evasion of de Gaulle's obstructive policy by General Motors who built one of the largest European car factories in Belgium and were then able to penetrate the French market from across the frontier. West Germany was warned off joining in de Gaulle's obstructionist policy, and France alone could do very little.[23]

The fact that de Gaulle's stand for independence merely amounted in practice to a *'politique déclamatoire'* indicates the limitations on the freedom of even middle-sized powers to initiate change in the world politico-economic system, beyond frustrating initiatives taken by others. This is not to argue, however, that the aim declared in 1965, to work for the freedom of all nations from outside intervention, restriction and domination, was not worth while, but merely that France alone did not have the necessary power to fulfil de Gaulle's ambition.

It is often stated that, whereas under de Gaulle foreign policy had priority over domestic policy, under his successors the opposite priority applied. Although in general this was true, foreign policy continued to have great importance for French governments after 1969 for two reasons: first, that Gaullist politicians, with communist support, kept a close watch on any divergences from independence in world affairs, particularly *vis-à-vis* the United States, and second, that the pursuit of economic growth in France had internationalized the economy to such an extent by the 1970s that foreign economic policy inevitably proved to be a major preoccupation.

Problems for France arising from the events of May and the Czechoslovakia crisis in August 1968 brought about an improvement in Franco-American relations. During the 'gold war', France had refused to sign a Group of Ten financial proposal to increase international liquidity by means of special drawing rights, but eight months later, in November 1968, France borrowed two thousand million dollars from the Group of Ten. On 5 December defence minister Messmer made it clear to the national assembly that there was no question of French neutralism and that France was in the Atlantic alliance to stay. General Ailleret was replaced as chief-of-staff and his successor, General Fourquet, accepted in March 1969 the American nuclear doctrine of 'graduated response' directed specifically at the Soviet Union to the east.

Certainly there was the encouragement for France of a more flexible policy in Washington: American forces ceased to bomb north Vietnam at the end of March 1968 and on 5 May Paris was chosen as the centre for Vietnam peace talks (hardly the most peaceful place to talk at that time). The newly-elected president Nixon visited France in February 1969; in April de Gaulle attended General Eisenhower's funeral in Washington and had a further round of cordial conversations with Nixon. When de Gaulle's successor, Pompidou, devalued the franc in the summer of 1969, American policy co-operated in helping to stabilize the French currency at its new level, while the French reciprocated by ending their doctrinaire resistance to US sales and investment in France.

There was a general expectation in Europe that after the Vietnam war, which ended in 1973, American foreign policy was likely to be more cautious and less domineering. The devaluation of the dollar in 1971 and its further weakening after 1973, accompanied by persistent American balance of payments deficits, all made it clear that successive American administrations were in deep trouble, quite apart from the Watergate affair in 1973-4 which led to the resignation of president Nixon. There was considerable speculation about possible American decline from power and withdrawal into isolationism. It therefore became much more acceptable to French public opinion to see Pompidou and his successor, Giscard d'Estaing, discussing co-operation with the American government in efforts to control the effects of a major world economic crisis after 1973.

The immense scale of American power, nevertheless, meant that it took only the nervous muscular reflexes of weak government to maintain the essentials of world political control. Moreover, the social pluralism and diffuse economic dynamism characteristic of American capitalism enabled it to recover from excessive dependence on short-term state contracts connected with the Vietnam war and to expand other profitable business interests. Although recession and unemployment hit some sectors of American industry, such as steel, there was remarkable buoyancy in other sectors such as plastics, electronics and even consumer durables; furthermore, profits were maintained through manipulation of overseas assets in American multi-national companies.

The American government preserved its grip on the world currency system by means of policy co-ordination between foreign ministries and central banks between 1973 and 1976. A set of guidelines for indefinitely floating currencies were agreed. France changed her policy in December 1974 to agree that currencies would not necessarily be linked to gold and that there would be no official international gold price; for its part the American government agreed that gold should be realistically valued according to market price and made available to governments with balance of payments deficits. By January 1976 a new international monetary regime had emerged to replace the 1944 Bretton Woods system: first, floating rates were legalized according to a set of conditions over which the United States had a veto; second, special drawing rights were made the principal international reserve assets in order to reduce the role of gold; third, the International Monetary Fund had powers of firm surveillance over exchange rate policies and was to lay down certain guidelines; fourth, a trust fund was established for poor countries to liberalize credit facilities (the caucus of underdeveloped countries made acceptance of the whole system conditional on that point).[24] This system involved a degree of Franco-American co-operation inconceivable in the time of de Gaulle. The importance of the dollar remained such that its subsequent devaluations were as much an American lever to manipulate world trade as a sign of instability or weakness.

Faced with an unprecedented threat to oil supplies in 1973, the United States reacted by forming an International Energy Agency as a pressure group against oil producers. France alone among EEC members declined to join the Agency, preferring a wider arrangement with producers as well as consumers of oil to ensure French supplies. There was a brief period of friction between Jobert, acting for the sick Pompidou, and Kissinger in 1974; but by 15 December Giscard d'Estaing had restored tentative agreement with the United States on the desirability of some joint action by oil consumer states. American muscle, including a threat to use military action against Arab states to prevent any embargo on vital oil supplies, restored the flow of oil at more stable prices.

By 1976 there was increasing speculation about 'eurocommunism', a tendency among western European communist parties to seek power by accepting fuller integration into local political systems by means of liberal democratic methods. Some observers anticipated the possibility of communist parties coming to power in Italy, France and Portugal. The American government reacted firmly in April 1976 with the Sonnenfeldt doctrine to reaffirm that the United States accepted Soviet predominance throughout eastern Europe, and at the same time a Kissinger doctrine declaring United States opposition to any communist participation in western European governments. In spite of protests about US imperialist interference, it was clear that the polarization of power in Europe between the two super-powers would continue indefinitely. Moreover, France joined with other EEC members to reinforce this situation. At Puerto Rico on 27-28 June 1976, France, Britain and West Germany reached agreement with the United States that international financial assistance to countries such as Italy should be conditional on there being no communists in the government.[25] By 1978 it was clear that the 'eurocommunist' movement had petered out, if ever it had been more than a mirage, and that America was enjoying its best relations with Europe for twenty years.

Co-operation in politics was paralleled by significant developments in the economic sphere. The takeover of the French computer firm CII by the American Honeywell-Bull company was blessed by the French government in November 1975, with a subsidy of a milliard francs over four years; and at the same time the French atomic energy commission decided to use the American pressurized water process under licence from Westinghouse who would thereby have a dominant relationship with the French firm Framatome. In its battle to maintain at least some economic growth during the world economic crisis, the French government was clearly prepared to compromise its independence policy in order to get maximum benefit from American investment and technology. The French role was that of a semi-peripheral power within the United States's orbit rather than the independent middle-sized power that had been the ambition of de Gaulle.

As one would expect, French relations with the Soviet Union were the converse of those with the United States. Relations had appeared to be good in the 1960s when de Gaulle left NATO and obstructed the expansion or integration of the EEC. During the last year of de Gaulle's rule, however, French policy retreated from *rapprochement* with the Soviet Union owing partly to the Czechoslovakian crisis, but also because a Russo-German dialogue was in progress as part of Brandt's *Ostpolitik* and de Gaulle was finding financial relations with West Germany particularly difficult after May 1968 when the franc came under pressure. It was the Russian turn to show anxiety in 1969 when the newly elected Pompidou showed enthusiasm for integration and expansion of the EEC and for improvement in Franco-American relations. Nevertheless Pompidou maintained friendly relations with Moscow, particularly in the form of trade agreements. As the Soviet Union began to develop a policy of *détente* with the United States in the 1970s it began to treat the earlier *rapprochement* with France as a model for relations with other western states. To develop this approach Brezhnev paid a state visit to France in October 1971. Paradoxically, this was just at a time when France was obdurately opposing proposals for mutual and balanced force reductions in Europe on the grounds that it tended towards a Russo-American condominium at the expense of the Europeans. But the Russians pressed ahead, emphasizing the importance of the Grand Commission founded with de Gaulle in 1966 to foster trade and scientific co-operation. They had since formed similar commissions with other powers including the United States. In October 1970 they had persuaded Pompidou to create a political counterpart to the Grand Commission, a protocol providing for regular consultations on international issues every six months and at other times when international tension might develop. In October 1971 Brezhnev proposed that they codify the principles of their co-operation. Clearly the aim was to make up for the break in relations in 1968 and to maintain apparent French determination not to re-enter NATO nor to allow the EEC to become closed to the east.

But this muted form of *rapprochement* came to an end in 1973 when French policy perceived fully the risks involved in a Soviet-American condominium. It is possible that strident anti-Soviet criticism came at the same time as attacks on American oil policy as a result of Pompidou's illness and Jobert's impetuous handling of French policy during 1973–4. Whatever the reason, Jobert warned the Helsinki conference on European security in June 1973 against a 'moral disarmament deadening the spirit of resistance, deceiving vigilance, and leading to servitude'. This was followed up by the French declaring that they intended to keep up their own military development, and appealing to the United States to maintain their existing conventional and nuclear forces in Europe. At this stage French anxiety regarding a super-power condominium was as much directed at the United States as at the Soviet Union; thus, on his visit to China in October 1973 Pompidou resisted the temptation of his hosts to fulminate against the Soviet Union. Back in Paris, however, Jobert continued to castigate both Washington and Moscow for ignoring European interests in the Middle East crisis of that autumn.

When Giscard d'Estaing was elected French president in 1974 anxiety increased in the Soviet Union that he was likely to commit France to integration in the EEC and to be influenced by colleagues like Lecanuet towards Atlanticism. Moreover, Giscard brought Servan-Schreiber into the government, who was regarded in Moscow as a friend of the United States, a Zionist, and director of a weekly magazine, *L'Express*, that paid considerable attention to the problems of Soviet dissidents. In spite of this, the Soviet Union hoped that relations with France could be maintained, still describing the relationship as a model for *détente*. But relations deteriorated rapidly as Soviet interest in the Mediterranean, Indian Ocean, and Africa expanded. French concern with security in those areas, their rearmament programme from 1976, and their active intervention in various parts of Africa, including Zaire, in 1978, all served to harden Soviet convictions that France had become Atlanticist almost to the point of rejoining NATO. Thus, *rapprochement* had given way to mutual recrimination in Franco-Soviet relations by 1978. As for trade links, the outstanding examples being eastern European adoption of French colour television, nuclear energy co-operation with Czechoslovakia, motor vehicle co-operation with Romania, Hungary and the Soviet Union, they were only half the value of West German links with the east during the period 1966–71 which was supposedly the heyday of Franco-Soviet *rapprochement*. Once the political incentive to improve relations withered away, economic interest alone was not sufficient to maintain them.

The idea of European union has a long history related to early ideals of Christian unity and to efforts to prevent recurrent outbreaks of war which, by the eighteenth century, were already seen to involve greater losses than gains. France was involved in the problems of Europe as the leading power over a long period and was naturally the source of some of the concepts of unification. The prevalence of

Monarchism, however, prevented the European idea from making institutional progress until at least the mid-nineteenth century, by which time the emergence of democratic and liberal thought encouraged a more systematic approach. Hence Victor Hugo's call for a United States of Europe in 1848. But this approach was short-lived as the consolidation of nation-states and politico-economic nationalism diverted interest in France and elsewhere, from the European idea.

It took the suffering of two World Wars and the discrediting of nationalism to bring the European idea back to the surface. The first time it was taken up seriously by a statesman in power was by Edouard Herriot in 1924, and his thoughts were developed tentatively by Aristide Briand into a plan for European union in 1929. But the onset of the depression of the 1930s, fascism and war killed the plan at birth. By 1945 not only was nationalism discredited, but also the machinery of the nation-state had been smashed. International principles involved in communism, socialism and Catholicism, among others, had more scope in the immediate post-war period than ever before; from another point of view, the development of capitalism as a system, and the scale of economic reconstruction problems facing Europe, encouraged serious thought on methods of international co-operation. American influence encouraged federal concepts, but ruled out communism as the cold war set in. Christian democracy and socialism were therefore the two principal movements that proceeded to promote the European idea.

Why did France play a leading part in promoting European unity? First, the two most important political parties under the Fourth Republic were the socialists and the christian democrats. Second, French national interests were to create a security system that would remove both the urge and the opportunity for future German aggression against France, and furthermore to achieve economic reconstruction in harmony with France's natural trading partners in western Europe. So far as timing was concerned, external American pressure in favour of German reconstruction and the organized sharing of Marshall Aid made the creation of some kind of western European institutions a matter of urgency.

Initially the British were involved, having strong interest in European security and stability. The Dunkirk defence treaty of 1947, followed by the 1948 Brussels treaty for mutual assistance against aggression, involved the British not only in military matters but also in discussion of socio-economic and political methods of co-operation. But French policy became attached to the concept of supra-national institutions designed to prevent the danger of Germany recovering the independence and power to threaten France once again. The federal ideas of J. Monnet and R. Schuman proceeded to lead the French government to propose the European Coal and Steel Community, and ultimately to join the European Economic Community, while leaving out the British who gave priority to relations with the Commonwealth and the United States for both economic and cultural reasons. The new West German state was willing to enter into federal agreements in Europe partly because it was shakily built on a divided society, and therefore needed outside political support during its early years, but even more because firm backing from western Europe was considered essential to avoid becoming submerged in the Soviet bloc to the east.

There were countervailing attempts to adopt confederal methods of co-operation between independent states in the 1950s. One example was Western European Union, which included the British, with a view to improving defence and other systems; but lack of political interest on the British side allowed such institutions to remain empty shells. When de Gaulle returned to power in France he did in fact favour confederal rather than federal methods, as shown by his Fouchet Plan launched in 1960; but at the same time he was anxious to avoid weakening the EEC in the face of what he regarded as 'Anglo-Saxon' hegemony, moreover he found it possible to work in harmony with West Germany under Adenauer. The result was a veto on British entry into the EEC during a period when de Gaulle otherwise obstructed further progress towards federalism and created so much ill-feeling that his own confederal ideas made no progress either.

Quite apart from differences of view in France and Europe regarding the form of European unity, there were different conceptions of the purpose and role of Europe in the world at large. Socialists in France were of widely differing tendencies, but generally regarded western Europe as a possible 'third force' developing a distinctive socio-economic system and pursuing independent political interests from those of the United States and the Soviet Union. The christian democrats and many of the Radicals, on the other hand, saw western Europe rather as a second western force, co-operating fully with the United States and sharing Atlanticist economic and political principles while also creating a bulwark against Soviet power and communism. These currents of thought and political tendencies converged, however, in the belief that a united Europe should maintain and develop close links with the under-developed world, thereby sustaining the influence of the French empire: 'Eurafrica' was one of the evocative catchwords of the 1950s. There was a further point of convergence in French opinion, which was appreciation of the importance of the EEC in providing an outlet for French agricultural surpluses and as a dynamic force for economic and social change.

By the end of de Gaulle's rule, in 1969, there were two problems that were preventing the EEC from progressing as smoothly as originally expected. First, there was a deadlock between de Gaulle and the other five member-states which had centred on the issue of British entry. Second, the fact that there was a deadlock at all was an indication of the growth of West German power and independence since the signing of the treaty of Rome. French policy under Pompidou from 1969 undertook to find a solution to both problems at once: the British would be brought in to provide a possible counterweight to West Germany, but on terms that would prevent her from disrupting the EEC organization in any way harmful to French agricultural interests. Thus Pompidou proposed a three-stage programme to achieve a *relance européenne* at the EEC summit conference at the Hague in December 1969: *achèvement* (involving completion and consolidation of the common agricultural policy, CAP), *approfondissement* (involving plans for complete economic and monetary union by 1980) and *élargissement* (involving the entry of Britain and several associated applicant states). This formula was intended to secure the interests of France and the EEC as a whole before British entry. In the event, British acceptance of the CAP and agreement to run down the independent role of sterling as a reserve currency, together with a favourable French referendum in April 1972, cleared the way for enlargement of the EEC in 1973. Nevertheless, this was made possible essentially by an informal understanding reached by Pompidou and the then British prime minister, Edward Heath, at a meeting in Paris in May 1971, and much of this personal understanding proved ephemeral when both men ceased to hold office in 1974.

Unexpected difficulties were encountered by France and the EEC as a result of the world financial and economic crisis which began with the Middle East war of October 1973. During the crisis, France, who was heavily dependent on imported oil for her energy needs, made full use of her special status as a state friendly to the Arabs and consequently received privileged oil supplies; in contrast, Holland was denied supplies of oil for a time and received no support from France. A common energy policy in the EEC proved impossible to achieve and all members except France accepted US leadership in the oil consumers' International Energy Agency. Moreover, world financial confusion disrupted progress towards monetary unity in the EEC. A 'snake in the tunnel' system had been created in September 1972 allowing member currencies to move 2.4 per cent above or below a normal parity. This was complicated when the dollar was floated freely during 1973 and France had to leave the system in January 1974, returning the following year, but leaving again in 1976. Moreover, Britain, Italy and Ireland had even earlier left the 'snake'. Considerable friction arose during this period, particularly as the German mark was clearly the strongest currency and attracted the envy of neighbouring states, including France. Thus, when Pompidou died in 1974, his policy was in shreds: although technically completed on a permanent basis, the CAP had been severely weakened by financial instability; monetary union had been thwarted; and British reactions to the economic crisis had tended towards solidarity with the United States rather than the EEC.

Giscard d'Estaing undertook from 1974 to stabilize and strengthen the French economy within the context of greater EEC co-operation. Disappointed with British policy, which was a source of instability in its demand for renegotiation of terms of membership in 1975, Giscard decided to seek progress on the basis of close relations with the West German chancellor, Schmidt. Franco-German relations became smoother than at any time since the early 1960s, though there was underlying French anxiety regarding the growth of West German economic power and political independence, which was most clearly demonstrated in a monetary policy geared to maximizing the benefits of German trading advantages. The EEC summit at Rome in December 1974 decided to pursue the possibilities of monetary union by 1980 and development in its institutions, particularly the assembly. Initially, there was not much prospect of harmonizing national policies, but recurrent crises affecting the dollar had generated sufficient sense of urgency by 1978 for EEC leaders to propose a European monetary system (EMS) that would have a wider membership and greater flexibility than the 'snake'. Whether the new system would have more success in withstanding world financial crises and speculative attacks on weaker currencies was a problem that preoccupied a number of EEC members, particularly the British; but the French and West German governments were convinced that it was worth trying to make the EEC an island of monetary stability in the shifting sands of the capitalist financial system.

Progress was also made towards institutional change in the EEC by means of a directly elected European assembly. The assembly had begun to improve its status when it was allowed some control over the EEC budget by an agreement signed in April 1970. This budgetary control, allowed by Pompidou, was significantly increased by an agreement of 22 July 1975 with which Giscard d'Estaing complied. The assembly had not used its powers under the treaty of Rome to pass a motion of censure on the Commission in order to dismiss it, but once directly elected in 1979 it would be possible for the assembly to extend its role in accordance with an increase in status.

In 1978 French opinion was divided on a number of issues affecting the EEC, though the French government continued to favour its development as the most favourable context for French economic and political interests. The direct election of the European assembly was resisted by the Gaullists on the right and by the communists on the left because it increased the risk of economic and political power passing out of specifically French control. But the emergence of a stronger centre and centre-left from the French elections in 1978 gave greater freedom to Giscard d'Estaing to pursue further enlargement of the EEC to include possibly Greece, Spain and also Portugal, to accept the EMS as a move towards monetary union, and to develop a closer relationship between the EEC and the United States within an Atlanticist economic and security system.

Although the process of political decolonization was virtually complete by the end of the Algerian war in 1962, France negotiated such terms for independence that it proved possible for her subsequently to maintain extensive cultural, economic and military connections with her ex-colonies and with the 'third world' as a whole. About thirty states in the world with more than two hundred million people continued to use French as their official language and this provided France with a basis for the policy of *mondialisme* adopted by Giscard d'Estaing in 1974.

Although the involvement of the French economy in the EEC and in relations with other developed nations had the effect of reducing its dependence on trade with ex-French colonies, it still derived valuable sources of raw materials from them. Moreover, their fundamental poverty, and particular weakness during a period of world economic crisis, had increased the dependence of ex-French colonies on French support. It is true that Algeria had become increasingly estranged from France after 1962 and had avoided excessive dependence on the French economy by finding a regular and lucrative market for natural gas exports in the United States. Similarly, Morocco, although politically and economically close to France, had achieved some freedom of manoeuvre by establishing a market for phosphate exports in the Soviet Union. But other ex-French colonies such as Gabon, Senegal and Chad continued to be extremely dependent on French support.

French foreign aid took three forms: cultural and technical aid from the state budget, private aid from French business companies, and collective aid under the auspices of the EEC. Public aid from the French state had traditionally been at a higher level as a percentage of gross national product (GNP) than that of other developed states. In 1963, for example, French public aid was 1.33 per cent of GNP at just under one billion dollars, which was double the British figure. In that year the Jeanneney report on foreign aid policy recommended that 1.5 per cent of GNP should be maintained for the next ten years and that to have maximum effect aid should be given to countries best equipped to use it profitably, perhaps to South American countries rather than necessarily to the franc zone countries. Subsequently, however, world aid programmes declined generally and the Jeanneney report remained a dead letter. In 1971 the seventeen western members of the international Development Assistance Committee agreed to give

0.7 per cent of their GNP to developing countries but the average aid actually given in 1977 was 0.3 per cent of GNP. The national figures were: US$4.1 billions, West Germany $1.31 billions (0.26 per cent GNP), Britain $907 millions (0.38 per cent GNP), France $2,394 millions (0.63 per cent GNP). Nevertheless, at least two-thirds of French aid still went to the franc zone countries, and the aid figures included grants to overseas territories like Réunion which were otherwise supposed to be integral parts of France. Furthermore, much of French aid was cultural with the understandable intention of maintaining the world-wide influence of French civilization; for example, the forty thousand teaching and technical assistants sent by France to 'third world' countries amounted to about half those sent out by all the developed nations. Then, like most other aid donors, France tended to attach strings to aid so that, even if it were not repayable with interest, it often required the use of French equipment and personnel. Thus it was hardly surprising that the debts of ninety-four developing countries increased from $71.7 billions in 1970 to $216.6 billions in 1976.[26]

Responsibilities for aid distribution by the French government were divided. The ministry of finance dealt with trading agreements and subsidies, though money was often sent out by other ministries directly concerned. After 1966 the ministry for foreign affairs organized co-operation with all parts of the under-developed world. There was a *secrétaire d'état* dealing with economic aid to the sixteen African francophone states. Then there was a *directeur des affaires techniques et culturelles* to organize educational and technical assistance to all countries receiving aid from France. Altogether the Quai d'Orsay normally spent up to half its budget on co-operation programmes.[27] Within the French government as a whole there were also the activities of the *ministre d'état* for overseas French *départements* and territories, and then of course the activities of the ministry of defence. In terms of trade there was a tremendous decline in the importance of the franc zone to France over a twenty-five-year period: in 1954 about 30 per cent of French trade was with the franc zone countries; by 1964 it was down to 17 per cent; and by 1975 it was down to less than 5 per cent. It was significant, however, that it provided France with an increasingly favourable balance; for example exports in 1975 were worth over three milliard francs more than imports from the franc zone.

The EEC, from its birth in 1957, organized a number of aid and development programmes with the 'third world'. This was important to France in helping to support the French empire and subsequently the independent states in the franc zone. In 1975 the EEC signed the Lomé convention with forty-six states in various parts of the 'third world'. But the agreement did not improve significantly on the existing

EEC generalized system of preferences, in terms of tariffs. For example, it did not allow for goods to have tariff-free entry unless at least half their value was created in the signatory country concerned (thus blocking the development of finishing processes in 'third world' industry); there was, moreover, a safety clause enabling EEC members to block access to 'third world' products if they seriously disturbed a sector of their economies. Financial provision to help stabilize 'third world' countries' export earnings in the face of world market fluctuations was no more than £50 million approximately in any one year for a particular country's commodity (in fact the total aid provision under the convention was only £1,500 million approximately over a five-year period). The Lomé convention was signed by forty-six countries because it was the best available programme of trade assistance in a period of declining levels of aid; and it did encourage a few incipient 'third world' industries in spite of its general emphasis on trade in agricultural products and raw materials. The free trade provisions in the convention were characteristic of the relationship between an advanced and a dependent economy, allowing penetration by the former without much risk of competition from the latter.[28]

Apart from cultural and economic relations with the French-speaking countries in Africa, France had equally extensive military connections. Ten years after their independence in 1960 many African ex-colonies were beginning to reduce their dependence on French military assistance, and president Pompidou had not concerned himself about that tendency. But after 1974 Giscard d'Estaing re-established close relations with ex-colonies. The third summit of French-speaking African states in May 1976 in Paris was attended by nineteen members compared with only eleven at the summit in 1973. At the fourth summit in Dakar in April 1976, president Senghor of Senegal welcomed renewed French interest in Africa, saying that if Europe did not appreciate the security risk in Africa other continents would take control. This reference to Chinese and Soviet intervention in Africa was echoed by a number of African leaders seeking military aid which they very often used for the internal security of their personal power base. Whatever the reason, France renewed military pacts with Congo-Brazzaville, Gabon, Ivory Coast, Cameroun and Senegal; and new technical military co-operation agreements were made with Benin, Chad and Togo. A force of 5,000 French troops was permanently stationed in the new republic of Djibouti, a situation which facilitated links with the large French naval force in the Indian Ocean and with another military base in Réunion. The most notable French military interventions in Africa were in the western Sahara in 1977, to support the Mauritanian government against Polisario guerrillas, and in Chad in 1976, to support the government against Libyan-backed rebels; Giscard d'Estaing was given the title 'gendarme of Africa' in April

1978 when he provided transport aircraft for Moroccan troops to intervene to preserve the government of president Mobutu in Zaire. The most significant point is that France was the only one of the ex-colonial powers to maintain permanent military bases in Africa.[29] The reason for the importance of Africa to French security was explained by the French chief-of-staff, General Méry, in a statement of policy on 3 April 1978:[30]

> il existe entre ce continent et la France un ensemble de liens établis par la géographie et l'histoire, que la complémentarité de leurs économies fondées sur les matières premières pour l'un et sur leur transformation pour l'autre, vient encore renforcer. Or, il règne actuellement en Afrique un climat d'instabilité qui ne peut, en conséquence, nous laisser indifférents et cela pour deux raisons principales que je rattacherai aux deux notions de sécurité et de responsabilité.
>
> La sécurité de la France ne dépend pas, bien sûr, uniquement de la sécurité de l'Afrique, mais elle est, me semble-t-il, très fortement liée à celle-ci. Elle l'est, en premier lieu, parce que le territoire français est proche de l'Afrique en Méditerranée, proche aussi dans le canal de Mozambique avec Mayotte, et à la Réunion. Elle l'est ensuite, parce que 260,000 ressortissants français vivent et travaillent en Afrique, pour l'essentiel en Afrique du Nord et en Afrique Occidentale. Elle l'est enfin et peut-être surtout, parce que les routes maritimes qui entourent l'Afrique servent à acheminer la plus grande partie du pétrole et des matières premières dont nous avons besoin et sont donc vitales pour notre pays. Ces routes passent au plus près du continent africain en plusieurs endroits et sont alors à portée des moyens aériens et navals des pays riverains: à cet égard les zones de Dakar, du Cap, de Tunis revêtent une importance toute particulière, car elles constituent autant de passages obligés et 'singuliers', plus faciles à contrôler que les longs couloirs du Mozambique ou de la Mer Rouge.

He went on to speak of military aid agreements with a number of African states made by their own request and which involved a responsibility France was willing to fulfil in order to contribute to the development and stability of Africa.

Soon after he became president in 1974, Giscard d'Estaing spoke of the need for a new international economic order and subsequently initiated a north-south dialogue (*la conférence sur la coopération économique internationale*) in Paris from December 1975 until June 1977. The emphasis of his approach was on the need for new mechanisms in world markets to ensure a better balance in world trade. His ideal was to remove political and economic obstacles to the evolution of a natural economic order in the world. Nevertheless,

Giscard d'Estaing admitted to the existence of structural imbalance in the existing world economy, and suggested in 1976 some kind of 'Marshall Plan' for Africa. The traditions of French government — *dirigisme* and post-war economic planning — were clearly relevant to African needs. Nevertheless, his apparent anxiety to help in the progress of black African states did not carry conviction while France continued to supply arms to South Africa. Those supplies were suspended in 1977, though France continued to supply nuclear power plant through the Framatome company in accordance with a contract in 1976.[31]

The nature and success of French policy in Africa and the 'third world' as a whole was open to question, but of its importance there was no doubt.

French foreign policy pursued an ambitious role in both Europe and Africa under the Fifth Republic as it sought to maximize cultural and political influence while establishing the most advantageous trading links. Not all sections of French society were committed to or benefited from the policy of *mondialisme*, but the electoral success of Giscard d'Estaing in 1978 ensured that it would be maintained. The potentialities for French initiative in some directions, and the constraints facing French initiatives in others, illustrated the essential characteristics of a semi-peripheral, middle-sized power such as France in the prevailing conditions of the world politico-economic system.

Chapter 6

The education system

Introduction

It might perhaps be thought that education is a topic which has little to do with politics, yet it is one which, in recent years, has become the object of an increased political interest in France (as also in Britain). One reason for this is plain enough in economic terms: in a technological society, such as France, it is no longer sufficient for a worker to sell his unskilled labour; if he wishes to command an adequate salary, he requires a technical qualification, which only education can provide. It has been calculated that in October 1977 out of 22,510,855 men and women forming the working population, 5,802,439 had no qualification whatsoever, and 5,623,435 had only the *certificat d'éducation professionnelle* (INSEE, Microfiche, October 1977).

At the level of government and the higher administrative echelons also, it is higher education which provides the requisite personnel, from the present president of the republic downwards. In every respect, therefore, as W. D. Halls says, 'education in modern society is about power',[1] and the distribution of power is the natural preoccupation of political parties.

This is not to say that there was no realization in the past as to the political usefulness of education. Napoleon, for example, laid down as one basis of education 'la fidélité à l'Empereur, à la monarchie impériale, dépositaire du bonheur des peuples, et à la dynastie Napoléonienne, conservatrice de l'unité de la France et de toutes les idées libérales proclamées par les constitutions' (Decree of 17 March 1808, Titre V, art. 38). This endeavour to gain political support via education may be viewed as indoctrination. Subsequent régimes do not appear to have regarded education in quite such a 'party political' light, even though education was considered a means whereby the social order might be maintained without violence, by including in the curriculum teaching on morality and on the values accepted by society. However, the need to adapt education to republican principles seems to have dominated the legislation of the 1880s.

Yet other opinions on the purpose of education, some going back to antiquity, are today not without significance; i.e. the need to bring up good citizens in general, to teach discipline, devotion to duty, to provide character training, and also to train individuals of superlative ability to serve and lead the state. Such views have exercised a considerable influence on the education systems of Europe, and should not wholly be disregarded. To these should perhaps be added, particularly from the sixteenth century onwards, the more aristocratic concept of the man of culture – a concept regarded by many as outdated, narrow, and over-literary, but still able to wield some power over the content of the curriculum.

The question of what should be regarded as culture is of particular importance. At a time of greater illiteracy when the teacher was the sole purveyor of information, he was viewed with greater respect, and the information which he had to convey was accepted accordingly. Today, in a period of mass communication, the teacher is only one of many providers of information, and his is often considered less relevant or interesting than the others', and undoubtedly less up-to-date. Whereas in 1954, only 1 per cent of French households possessed a television set, in 1976 85.8 per cent did so; and in 1974, 94.3 per cent possessed a radio. The printed word, the most habitual medium for the teacher, fared less well, a total of 73.1 per cent of households possessing books, and of these only 12.2 per cent possessing over 250 books in 1974.[2] Pop music, jazz, science fiction, sport, all these have a claim to be regarded as part of any national culture, but are not necessarily so regarded in scholastic terms

The education system influenced by age-old theories, adjusting with difficulty to the needs of mass society, finds itself criticized for its conservatism and narrowness in relation to what it teaches. Since it is now viewed also as a means to social advancement it is criticized for its inadequacies, or, more accurately, for its success. On the one hand, it is alleged to block the access of the working classes to higher education, in order that the necessary work force for the capitalist economy should still be available;[3] on the other, it is held to transmit the dominant culture from one generation to another, which in turn ensures not only the dominance of the upper classes (from whom the dominant culture proceeds), but also the preservation of the established order.[4]

In view of the criticisms made of the system, the uncertainties surrounding it, and the hopes (often disappointed) which it arouses, education undoubtedly warrants the political interest with which it is now regarded. What follows does not claim to be exhaustive, but is an attempt to provide a survey of the essential aspects of the subject. While French education has undergone major reforms over the last two decades, some elements in its make-up seem hard to shift, or even to reform. In this context, not only education at school and university will be considered, but also some of the more intractable problems left to present-day educators by centuries of history, notably that of centralized administration, and of Catholic education in France.

(1) The centralized administration

The organization of French education owes its present framework to Napoleon, although centralizing tendencies may be seen at the end of the preceding century. If the French Revolution was unable to put its reforms into effect, some of the ideas propounded at that time were to be particularly influential. For example, Condorcet's proposals for reform in 1792 stated that education should be national (provided by the state). Its essential purpose was to give to each citizen the possibility of developing his talents to their utmost, in order to render effective the political equality recognized by the law. The vicissitudes of the Revolution made it impossible to implement these views on a large scale, if at all, and it was consequently left to Napoleon to interpret them as he saw fit.

Napoleon devised a system which followed one part of the Revolution's principles, whilst wholly neglecting the other. A state education system was established, but the need to supply education for all was disregarded. Between 1806 and 1808 the *université* was established which comprised the whole of French education at all levels. The monopoly was absolute in theory but in practice left primary education and women's education to the church; secondary and higher education was Napoleon's main concern, but here too, it was possible for private secondary schools to exist, if authorization were obtained.

The state 'monopoly', such as it was, may be said to have consisted of two elements: the conferment by the *université* alone of all qualifications, at that time the *baccalauréat* at the end of secondary education, the *licence* (either in letters, law or science), the first university degree and the *doctorat*, the post-graduate degree, together with the obligation for all teachers to obtain the appropriate qualification; the surveillance exercised, not by the state itself, but by the *université*, in the person of its own officials. Such a surveillance, extending over primary schools, secondary schools (whether *lycées* with a six-year course of study or *collèges* with a less extensive programme) and the *facultés* for higher education, required an administrative network to cover the whole country, which was divided up into twenty-seven *académies*, each headed by a *recteur*, appointed for five years. This official was aided by one or more *inspecteurs d'académie* and a *conseil académique*, and his task was to supervise all levels of education within his *académie*. He was directly responsible to the head of the *université*, the *grand-maître*, by whom he was appointed. The *grand-*

maître, appointed by the emperor, was himself assisted by a *conseil de l'université*, the members of which were appointed for life, and a number of *inspecteurs généraux*, whose task was, simply, to inspect all levels of teaching. He had at his disposal a wide range of patronage, since he appointed to administrative and teaching posts, and all matters pertaining to the *université* were within his province.

The purpose of this administrative system was to ensure, as far as possible, a high degree of uniformity both in pedagogical and political terms. Napoleon was very conscious, after the disuniting effects of the Revolution, of the need to weld the country together, and education seemed to him to provide the means to that end. This meant inevitably that the education system was used for political propaganda. Among the bases for teaching required in the university were 'la fidélité à l'Empereur, à la monarchie impériale, dépositaire du bonheur des peuples, et à la dynastie Napoléonienne . . .' (Decree of 17 March 1808, Titre V, art. 38). Education, for Napoleon, was essentially a political aid, one which would provide him with the educated personnel to assist him in the running of his empire, and, at a more general level, to provide the state with 'des citoyens attachés à leur religion, à leur prince, à leur patrie et à leur famille' (ibid.).

It is perhaps important to state that, in order to bring about this happy state of affairs, Napoleon endeavoured to create a *corps enseignant*, that is, a body of individuals, imbued with the same spirit, but also with its own hierarchy, from the *grand-maître* downwards. This concept of a 'teaching order' meant that there was a kind of autonomy in the teaching profession, in as much as the state, *per se*, did not interfere. Nevertheless, with the type of guide lines given as to political guidance, the establishment of such an authoritarian and centralized administrative framework, and finally, the fact that the powerful head of the organization could be dismissed at the discretion of the head of state, made the distinction between state and *université* less than wholly assured.

Overall, the administrative system established by Napoleon was retained in the nineteenth century and for a good half of the twentieth. At some periods, the *conseil de l'université* enjoyed more power (July Monarchy), at others the minister of education (the subsequent title of the *grand-maître*) and the administration (Second Empire). In spite of criticisms levelled at the *université*'s centralized administration (less strong than criticisms of the prefectural system), commentators seem to have assumed that its authoritarian origins were not incompatible with the more liberal forms of government, and that the latter's ethos would prevail. 'Ce grand établissement eut ses vices, ses lacunes, témoignage de ce qu'il y avait de vicieux et d'incomplet dans le régime impérial . . . Enfin les maximes d'autorité et de centralisation absolue, qui caractérisaient tout le gouvernement impérial, tenaient là aussi une place exagérée et nécessairement transitoire' (Guizot, speech of 1 February 1836, *Archives parlementaires*, vol. 100, Paris, Imprimerie et librairie administratives et des chemins de fer/P. Dupont, 1899, p. 85). Such optimism seems to have been a little misplaced, since the administrative system has remained, while parliamentary régimes have come and gone. In this context, it is perhaps worth noting the attempts made in the 1880s and 1890s to bring to higher education an element of decentralization and independence. This initiative began with two decrees of 25 July 1885 which re-affirmed the *personnalité morale* of the faculties, i.e. their right to accept gifts and bequests made to them, and also to receive subsidies from towns, departments, *communes*, etc. – all gifts and subsidies to be noted under a specific heading at the ministry of education, and to be used as the faculties thought desirable. In December of the same year, a decree provided for the composition and powers of the representative bodies of the faculties: the *conseil général des facultés*, presided over by the *recteur* and comprising the deans of the faculties, and two academics elected from each faculty: the *conseil de faculté*, composed of professors, dealing in general with finance: and an *assemblée de faculté*, comprising all teaching members of the faculty and concerned essentially with pedagogical matters. In 1890 the faculties were given the responsibility of organizing their own budget, within limitations.[5] In April 1893 *personnalité civile* was bestowed on groups of faculties within the same *académie*, and the crown of the edifice was put in place with the law of 10 July 1896, which gave the groups of faculties the name of *universités* – but this change of title appears to have altered little in fact.[6] In the face of a centralized administrative system, covering all aspects of higher education not explicitly mentioned in the reforms, the latter had little chance of succeeding, given that their terms of reference were so limited. At all events, they seem to have remained enough of a dead letter for C. Fouchet, then education minister, to have stated in 1966 at the *colloque de Caen* on higher education that the texts of 1885 and 1890 provided adequate autonomy if the faculties were capable of profiting therefrom. Yet Georges Vedel, an academic of great experience, is of the opinion that at the level of higher education, centralization was very much less than is commonly supposed. 'La décentralisation et l'autonomie . . . ont existé sous le régime de ce qu'on appelle, chez ceux qui ne l'ont pas connue, l'Université "napoléonienne". Le ministre était à l'Université ce que la reine d'Angleterre est à l'Etat britannique: il signait tout et ne choisissait rien. Tout s'y décidait entre universitaires dans les conseils nationaux et locaux'.[7]

It is possible that for academics higher education was less centralized than it appeared to be. Yet May 1968 is there to give a totally different picture of the administrative system up to that time. 'Virtually no powers of decision are in local hands; all administrative decisions, all budgetary allocations, all staff appointments, are the exclusive prerogative of a distant and faceless bureaucracy in Paris. A French university . . . works to norms ordained by the centre. All 23 universities in the country are state-run, on rigidly standardized lines, like a government department. The local administrative staff is impotent, the students resentful, their mutual relations hostile. Discussion is pointless seeing that decisions are taken elsewhere.'[8] Even if the students held totally erroneous views on the degree of centralization (and the consequent lack of participation) which obtained in French education, their views would still have to be taken seriously, as the *image* of itself which the system had conveyed. Yet the substance of such opinions received indirect backing from a sociological study which indicated that students prior to 1968 were by no means well integrated in society. There was little in the way of corporate life as between students of one faculty or of another, no encouragement from the universities.[9] Such problems could well arise from a situation where a centralized system made the student feel alienated and solitary.

As a result of May 1968, the *Loi d'Orientation* was pushed through parliament in an endeavour to reform the education system, where it had given cause for complaint. In this context, the centralized system was one element considered by E. Faure to be in need of reform. 'La conception napoléonienne de l'Université centralisée et arbitraire est périmée.'[10] The *Loi d'Orientation* will be looked at in more detail below, but at this stage, it should be sufficient to see how far the present post-Faure system can be considered a decentralized one. At the present time, the minister of education is placed at the head of a large army of employees (957,072 in 1978), teachers and officials of all kinds, with a budget of 69,718.4 million francs, representing 17.5 per cent of the total budget of the state. The minister's tasks are many: appointment of officials (*fonctionnaires*), which includes teachers, decisions regarding organization and policy (this is of particular importance since legislation concerning education tends to be of the *loi cadre* variety, which indicates the general lines to be followed, and leaves the ministry to work out its practicalities and interpretations), the signing of official documents. He presents and defends his budget and his policies to parliament. He must also receive deputations from unions and other organizations, give interviews, press conferences and the like. He has, to assist him in his decision-making, a body which he can consult, the *Conseil supérieur de l'éducation nationale* (CSEN). This comprises a maximum of twelve *ex-officio* members, representatives of the ministry; the unions and other interested bodies have at least thirteen representatives, and there are twenty-five elected members from the teaching profession and five from private education. While it is a consultative body, although the minister is free to reject its advice, it also acts where necessary as an appeal court in disciplinary matters.

The minister chooses his own immediate advisers (his *cabinet*) which ceases to exist when he himself resigns. There is also a central body of officials, re-organized by decree in 1975. One directorate general for programming and co-ordination controls eight separate directorates, some with their own sub-divisions. Some elements of central administration are directly linked to the minister – such as the general inspectorate (see Figure 6.1). The minister may also have a secretary of state; the last two ministers, J. Fontanet and R. Haby, gave their *secrétaires d'état* specific duties, but the present minister, C. Beullac, has let it be known that J. Pelletier, his *secrétaire d'état* will replace him in his absence, and no specific duties have been allotted (see *Le Monde*, 18 April 1978).

As in the time of Napoleon, an administrative network covers the whole of France, which provides for the passing down of ministerial directives to all levels. There are now twenty-seven *académies* (including Corsica – a separate *académie* since 1975) each with a *recteur* as its head (see Figures 6.2 and 6.3). The *recteur*, appointed by the government, is the minister's representative in the *académie*; he passes on ministerial instructions to the relevant areas, and sees that they are carried out. He also acts as the minister's informant, as to what problems have arisen as a result of decisions implemented; his opinion may be sought by the minister, and he may make suggestions to the latter when appointments are to be made. It is his task to supervise all state schools, and private schools under contract in his *académie*, in terms of teaching, administration and finance. He is assisted in his task by *inspecteurs d'académie*, one for each *département* within the *académie*. At *académie* level, his role is similar to that of the *recteur*, in that he passes on orders from the *recteur* and the minister. He, too, provides information to his superiors as required. His role at primary level is particularly important, where it is his task not only to suggest appointments, but also to assess and mark the primary school teachers. In this task, he is assisted by *inspecteurs départementaux*.

Thus it is that an element of supervision which is organized from the centre covers the whole of the education system, and gives to the top of the pyramid (the minister) apparently wide powers.[11] It might be thought that creation of an independent *secrétariat d'état aux universités* in June 1974 (since promoted to a ministry in its own right) would have reduced the degree of centralization, but it has simply given the administrative complex two heads instead of one. The universities ministry, dealing with all aspects of higher education and research, has its own *cabinet* and organization. It shares with the ministry of education two directorates (*personnels administratifs* and *administration générale*) and the information and statistics service. As necessary, it also has the use of the general administrative framework of the *académies*. Since the *loi d'orientation* each *recteur* has become *chancelier* of the university in his *académie*. The existence of an elected university president has reduced the scope of his activities in relation to higher education, but he still has powers to alter the university budget if it does not meet with either his, or the ministry's approval (see the Decrees of 14 June 1969 and 5 August 1970).

In general, therefore, administrative centralization is still substantial, and its effects are very marked. For example the heads of schools, with whom the administration communicates, are themselves likely to be as much administrators as teachers. Administration is considered an essential part of their duties which they are not permitted to shirk (see on this point *Le Monde* of 18 May 1978, on the suspension of Vincent Ambite, head of a *collège* at Cassis (Bouches-du-Rhône) caused at least in part by his unwillingness to act as an administrator). The same thing applies in the *lycées* where the triumvirate of *proviseur, censeur* and *intendant* is essentially an administrative one.

This administrative predominance has a considerable effect on teachers too. While they may hope to be sent to a specific area, and to a specific type of school, there is no guarantee that their aspirations will be realized, and the centralized method of appointments at secondary level can give rise to ludicrously inapposite consequences:

> Telle jeune femme 'capétienne' [i.e. with the CAPES teaching qualification] qui désirait vivement enseigner à des adolescents du deuxième cycle est nommée dans un CES (premier cycle uniquement), alors que son amie, reçue en même temps qu'elle et qui préfère les plus jeunes enfants, se voit attribuer un poste dans un lycée ne comportant qu'un deuxième cycle. Un CES, dans une localité donnée, reste un an sans professeur de musique, alors qu'une jeune femme habitant la localité, enseignant la musique, a été nommée par le rectorat dans une ville éloignée.' (S. Citron, *L'Ecole bloquée*, p. 22)

Teachers not only receive a mark, *la note administrative*, from the head of their school (for their general attitude, punctuality, conscientiousness, etc.), but also a mark from the inspectorate on their pedagogical competence, which seems very often to mean simply the extent to which a teacher follows the 'ministerial line'. The following description of an inspection will give some idea of the difficulties which an inspection may cause a teacher. 'Il [the inspector] m'interrompait à peu près toutes les dix minutes pour me reprendre et me rappeler les directives ministérielles. "Pas plus de dix minutes sur ce genre d'exercice"; "La lecture après"; "Il faut faire les choses en

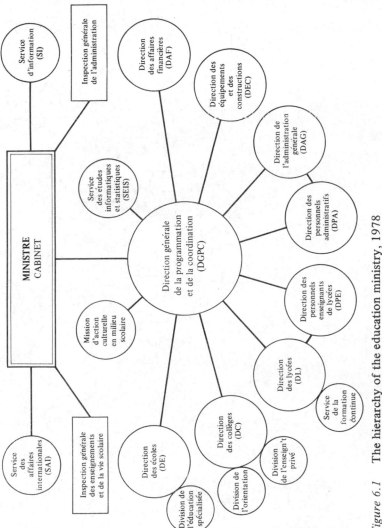

Figure 6.1 The hierarchy of the education ministry, 1978
Source: Ministère de l'éducation.

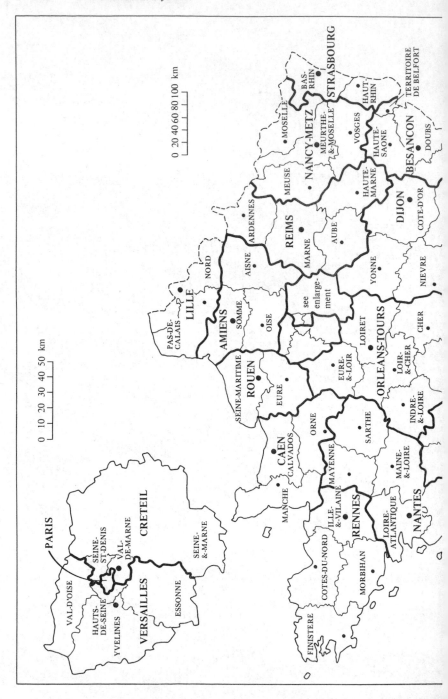

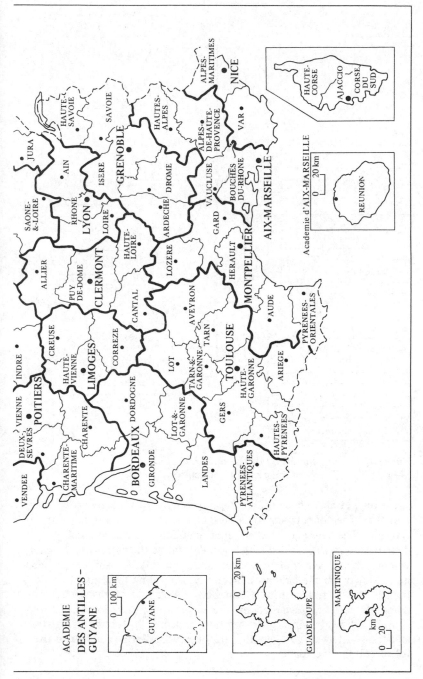

Figure 6.2   **Map of the *académies*, 1976**
Source: Ministère de l'éducation.

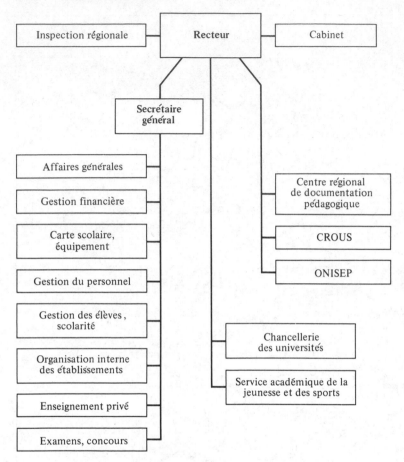

Figure 6.3   The hierarchy of the *rectorat,* 1978
Source: Ministère de l'éducation.

situation", et ainsi de suite.'[12] The impression often seems to be given that the inspector is trying to catch the teacher out, by arriving without warning. The consequences of an inspection are crucial, since on it depends the mark awarded which will determine the career of a teacher, whether he or she will gain promotion quickly, or simply proceed more slowly up the ladder of hierarchy, according to years of service; it may also at times prove a stumbling block for any teacher seeking work, if the marks awarded by the inspectorate have been unfavourable. It is true that inspectors are now expected to be 'the stimulators and transmitters of new ideas',[13] but the authoritarian element of their role is still fairly evident.

Centralization still makes its presence felt in the organization of time-tables, which is still theoretically the concern of the minister himself; although some effort has been made recently to give more freedom in this domain at school level. If we take two examples of the minute detail into which the minister is expected to go, the weight of centralized authority and the consequent difficulty for a teacher to use his own initiative should be clear enough. In a circular published in the *Bulletin officiel* on 1 September 1977, R. Haby, then minister of education, stated that in future the organization of school work would not be decided at national level, provided certain norms were respected, i.e. school work should, in term-time, occupy a minimum of five mornings per week, a minimum of two and maximum of four afternoons per week. This meant that a school head could, after obligatory consultations with other school heads and other interested persons, decide whether to leave Saturday or Wednesday free of classes. A further innovation was the reduction of each lesson from 55 to 50 minutes, the extra five minutes to be used by the teacher to become better acquainted with his or her pupils. Such measures can certainly be viewed as tending towards a measure of decentralization, but they have still required ministerial authority for their realization and ministerial authority could presumably take back these concessions if a future minister ever thought it desirable (see *Le Monde*, 3 September 1977). The second example concerns the organization of swimming lessons, where each child must have the possibility, according to the minister, to 'construire sa natation' (see *Le Monde*, 11 August 1977). Very detailed instructions are given as to the length of lessons, the water temperature, the size of classes, and the number of square metres of water which each child should have to itself. Matters such as this would be left, in Britain, to the common sense and expertise of the swimming instructors, and while important, they scarcely seem to warrant such high-level attention. Centralization such as this not only hampers the teacher's own initiative, but must also encumber the ministry with much detailed work which could well be delegated.

One further effect of the centralized system is an enduring respect for the hierarchy of seniority and of qualification. The marking of teachers by the school head is one such indication, particularly in view of the fact that an *agrégé* will invariably obtain a better mark than a less qualified colleague *for that very reason* (see N. Delanoë (note 12), pp. 19–20). Another indication is to be found in the difference in salary between teachers according to qualification (see Tables 6.1 and 6.2), coupled with the fact that the higher the qualification, the lower is the number of hours required. The situation thus arises that the lowest paid have the heaviest timetables. An extension of this respect for hierarchy may also be noted in the nature of teaching methods, particularly prior to 1968, where an emphasis at university level on the

Table 6.1   Teachers' salaries: Paris (NF per month), as at 1 February 1978

Grade	Start of career	End of normal career	End of career (with change of grade or function)
Instituteur	2,892.08[a] 3,125.37[b]	4,887.86	5,132.58 (directeur d'école) 5,376.38 (instituteur spécialisé) 5,491.20 (directeur d'école spécial.)
Professeur d'enseignement général de collège	3,343.98	5,408.57	5,895.41 (chef d'établissement)
Professeur de CET	3,343.98	5,522.24	7,082.59 (chef d'établissement)
Professeur certifié	3,749.44	6,770.13	8,964.98 (chef d'établissement)
Professeur agrégé	4,410.98	8,492.58	11,106.53 (chef d'établissement) 10,095.60 (professeur de chaire sup.)
Maître assistant	4,342.51	8,677.25	
Maître de conférences	6,978.13	10,300.27	
Professeur d'université	8,717.25	14,401.89	
Maître d'internat	single scale: 2,593.08 (housing included)		
Surveillant d'externat	single scale: 2,616.08 (housing not included)		

a up to 3 months; b   after 3 months.
Source: Ministère de l'éducation.

Table 6.2 Teachers' salaries: provinces (NF per month), as at 1 February 1978

Grade	Start of career	End of normal career	End of career (with change of grade or function)
Instituteur	2,633.41[a] 2,866.70[b]	4,577.69	4,925.65 (directeur d'école)
			5,051.94 (instituteur spécialisé)
			5,273.76 (directeur d'école spécial.)
Professeur d'enseignement général de collège	3,221.40	5,229.23	5,723.56 (chef d'établissement)
Professeur de CET	3,221.40	5,335.14	6,879.79 (chef d'établissement)
Professeur certifié	3,614.77	6,546.43	8,717.75 (chef d'établissement)
Professeur agrégé	4,256.76	8,218.32	10,808.74 (chef d'établissement)
			9,774.19 (professeur de chaire sup.)
Maître assistant	4,195.74	8,402.99	
Maître de conférences	6,754.53	9,978.86	
Professeur d'université	8,442.99	13,960.43	
Maître d'internat Surveillant d'externat	single scale: 2,507.16		

a up to 3 months; b after 3 months.
Source: Ministère de l'éducation.

cours magistral, and at secondary level on the lesson without possibility of discussion, tended to be the rule. Changes have undoubtedly occurred in this area in the last ten years.

Yet, although all this may amount to a kind of authoritarianism, it is perhaps cumbersome rather than genuinely dictatorial. It is by no means perfectly efficient, since in order to fit certain abstract norms, practical problems are not always taken into account by the administrators (see S. Citron, op. cit., pp. 14–23). It must further be remembered that the minister of education must keep within his budget. He may also be subject to union pressure, as in the case of aspects of the Haby reform. Finally, some efforts have been made to 'deconcentrate' the administrative system, so that the *recteur* and the *inspecteur d'académie* have had powers delegated to them. Yet if the weight of centralization is to be lessened, much more will have to be done to shift the possibility of initiative away from the centre and into the schools.

(2) Church and state: Catholic education in France

This question goes back beyond the Revolution of 1789, to the France of the *Ancien Régime*, when the Catholic church and the French state were closely intertwined. One of the former's recognized and traditional duties was education, of which it had virtually sole charge. During the Revolution, this task was taken away from the church, which suffered greatly from persecution and eventual suppression. The Revolution had laid down the principle that it was the state's duty to provide national education, which implied that in the future France would be a secular state, with a correspondingly secular education.

Although Napoleon distrusted intellectuals, and felt that education could be dangerous, he nevertheless had a clear idea of its value as an inculcator of political values, and of the consequent need of a body of suitably trained teachers. 'Il n'y aura pas d'Etat politique fixe, s'il n'y a pas un corps enseignant avec des principes fixes' (Napoleon, *Pensées politiques et sociales*,[14] p. 213). The church was excluded from the monopoly which he established in secondary and higher education (except for institutions known as *petits seminaires* in which novices were prepared for the priesthood). This is not to say that the church had lost all influence; Napoleon was prepared to entrust to it those areas which he did not consider important – namely, primary education and the education of women. Yet the whole, paradoxically, formed part of the *université*, under state supervision. A thoroughly secular state however was not established, since the church was useful to Napoleon as a factor of social and political stability, even although it had been much disorganized and weakened by the Revolution. By the terms of an agreement between France and the papacy (the Concordat of 1802), the Catholic church was reorganized and reintegrated into French society. Religion as such was by no means excluded from schools; according to the Decree of 17 March 1808 (Titre V, art. 38), which established the *université*, it was required of all schools comprised therein that the precepts of the Catholic religion should form part of the curriculum. Yet the church, by the terms of the Concordat, was placed in a position of subservience to the state, its paymaster, the clergy now being salaried state officials. Even then, Napoleon still felt that organized religion, in its internationalism, could present a danger to his régime. 'Le clergé est romain, parce que son chef est à Rome; c'est une nation à part au milieu des nations. Pour les prêtres, c'est à Rome qu'est la patrie' (Napoleon, op. cit., p. 152). From this deliberate exclusion of the church from secondary and higher education, and the church's unwillingness to accept it, was to come a reaction against the state's 'monopoly', claiming freedom of education, freedom here meaning not only the right of the private individual, but also of the church, to have their own schools.

In spite of the inherent anti-clericalism of Napoleon and of the system which he established, the church was not in fact excluded as much as he would have wished.[15] This situation also applied during the Bourbon restoration to an even more marked degree; the same system was maintained with some modifications, whilst the church was permitted to infiltrate it. This close alliance between throne and altar, redolent of the *Ancien Régime*, raised such feeling that when the restoration fell, the church, its strong supporter, found itself politically compromised.

The July Monarchy saw the first innovation in terms of primary education with the *Loi Guizot* of 1833, which also changed relations between church and state in this area. The change lay in the fact that state primary schools were to be established. Yet private individuals also were allowed to open primary schools if they could prove that they were suitably qualified and of good conduct and morality. This law is of interest, for, while on the one hand it represents an inroad of the state into primary education, hitherto always regarded as a prerogative of the church, it also marked a departure from the principle of state monopoly into the beginnings of dualism, with the co-existence of private and state schools. However in all primary education, a marked emphasis was put on religious and moral instruction, which, in the legislator's view was of great importance. 'Par l'instruction morale et religieuse, il pourvoit déjà à un autre ordre de besoins tout aussi réels que les autres, et que la Providence a mis dans le coeur du pauvre, comme dans celui des heureux de ce monde, pour la dignité de la vie humaine et la protection de l'ordre social' (Guizot, *Moniteur universel*, 3 January 1833). Religion, and hence the church, still had a part to play in the maintenance of social stability, and the co-operation of the *curé* was necessary for this. The law stated that he or the local protestant *pasteur* should be a member of the *comité de surveillance* of the local state primary school, which would give him some influence in its affairs, and, it was hoped, prevent him from setting up his own school in opposition. In reality, the *instituteur* (primary school teacher) tended to be very much at the beck and call of the *curé* (see G. Duveau, *Les Instituteurs*, Paris, Seuil, 1961). This compromise did not please the catholics, who had to accept that even at primary level, children could not be forced to receive religious instruction against their parents' wishes. Morality also was no longer wholly the domain of the church, since a form of philosophy, known as 'eclecticism' was also taught, which admitted the existence of God, but arrived at this concept by reasoning, and not by an acceptance of revealed truth; it also professed a number of fundamental truths taken from various currents of philosophic thought. Catholics, who considered such teaching to be atheistic, objected to it. Nor was this their only grievance: although they had gained their 'freedom' in primary education by virtue of the *Loi Guizot*, secondary education remained out of reach, since it changed little during the July Monarchy.

The freedom sought by Catholics did not come to secondary education until after the 1848 revolution. It then became clear to the governing classes that the church provided an excellent means of keeping the masses in check, and was therefore a useful ally. The outcome was the *Loi Falloux* of 1850; by its terms, the freedom provided at primary level by the *Loi Guizot* was extended to secondary education, which gave Catholics their chance. In other ways too, this law provided for greater Catholic influence via academic councils at departmental and national level. During the first decade of the Second Empire this legislation permitted a substantial expansion in Catholic education.[16] Although in the second decade it was thought advisable to curb this, French education was split in two ways as a result of the *Loi Falloux*, a consequence which was to have its effect later in the century.

Yet it cannot be asserted that this legislation was universally acceptable to Catholic opinion.[17] For the most extreme, it did not go far enough, since it did not reinstate Catholic education to the exclusion of all else, nor did it allow freedom in higher education. This last was not achieved until the law of 12 July 1875 was passed — the final triumph of the nineteenth-century dualist system.

Thus, during the nineteenth century the church was viewed as an element of social and political conservation, even if its motives were sometimes distrusted. Although Catholic opinion contained some liberal elements, it was mainly conservative (whether moderate or extreme) and consequently tended to support conservative govern-ments. The Third Republic, in its earlier years, had to face an un-reconciled church which would have favoured a return to a form of monarchy — more likely, in its views, to favour Catholic interests. An education system, of which a large part was Catholic, represented therefore a *political* threat to the republic, which was already weakened by the ideological split fostered by the effects of the *Loi Falloux*. The legislation undertaken by Jules Ferry in the 1880s was the logical answer to the republic's problems. This made primary education secular, obligatory from age six to thirteen, and free of charge. If parents wished their children to receive religious instruction, it was for them to arrange this out of school hours, although moral instruc-tion still was a high priority on the curriculum. The secular principle (*laïcité*) was thus assured in state education, although teaching orders wishing to continue their work in France were required to obtain authorization in 1886. Relations between church and state did not improve up to the beginning of this century, when, between 1901 and 1904 all teaching orders were banned, and in 1905, the separation of church and state was enacted. This simply did away with Napoleon's Concordat (apart from Alsace-Lorraine, which, as a German territory in 1905 was not subject to French legislation, and to this day is still under the *régime concordataire*). The French state was now totally neutral as between one religion and another, its only duty being to ensure freedom of conscience. The clergy were no longer state salaried officials, nor was the choice of bishops in any way the state's concern; church buildings reverted to the state but could still be used for religious worship. This legislation was hotly contested by Catholic opinion, and by the papacy itself, although in the long run it was of benefit to the church, and the issue ceased to be politically explosive.

The issue of Catholic education however remained controversial during the inter-war period, with the Vatican solemnly denouncing the neutral or secular school as irreligious in the encyclical *Divini Illius Magistri* of 1929. During the Second World War, the Vichy régime clearly indicated its support for the church in 1940 by re-introducing optional religious instruction in state schools, by lifting the ban (hitherto more honoured in its breach than in its observance) on the religious teaching orders, and by the provision of state aid for private schools, either via the communes or via grants to pupils from private or state schools. The Catholic church's involvement, particularly that of the hierarchy, with Vichy[18] was to prove an embarrassment after the liberation, since it yet again made the adherence of the church to the principle of republicanism suspect, in so far as the church seemed once more to have given way to an instinctive predilection for authori-tarian régimes. However, the precedents set by Vichy in state aid to private schools were to have a second birth during the Fourth Republic, and were to be politically very divisive. The *Loi Marie* and the *Loi Barangé* of September 1951 provided respectively credits for the education minister to award to the most pupils attending either state or private secondary schools, with priority for the former, and allocated a special amount at the treasury for parents with children attending state or private school (1,000 old francs per child per term). This legislation was opposed by communists, socialists and some Radicals and was supported by Gaullists, some Radicals and the MRP. The *Loi Barangé* in particular aroused great hostility, and an attempt was made to repeal it in 1956, which failed by only nine votes. By 1958, over one and a half million pupils were attending private schools, of which the substantial majority were Catholic.[19]

The Fifth Republic went further towards a dualist system with the *Loi Debré* of 1959 which offered to private schools a number of alternatives, in which aid would be made available (or not) according to the choice made. A school could opt:

(a) for complete integration into the state system – becoming thus a state school, and the teachers state employees;

(b) for the *contrat simple*, whereby the state not only approves the appointment of teachers, but pays their salaries (initially this alternative was conceived as a provisional one);

(c) for the *contrat d'association*, whereby the state pays teachers, and also contributes to the school's running costs, based on the number of pupils (*forfait d'externat*). A school opting for this arrangement had to accept directives about timetable, curriculum, etc., as well as supervision in teaching methods and finance from the administration;

(d) for total liberty, in which case no subsidy was provided.

The law caused much controversy, being opposed by the parties of the left and also by the *Comité national d'action laïque* (CNAL). However, de Gaulle threatened the dissolution of the *assemblée nationale* if the proposed legislation were not passed, and this was sufficient to get it through both houses with a substantial majority. In spite of secular opposition to it, there was something essentially ambiguous about the *Loi Debré*. On the one hand, it gave the state the chance to take over private schools; but on the other, it gave the private sector the opportunity to profit financially from state resources whilst still retaining its separate identity. In 1965 the *Loi Debré* paid out in teachers' salaries the sum of 1,035,800 NF – a sum far greater than that provided by earlier legislation.[20]

However, in 1971, G. Pompidou personally imposed a solution to the provisional nature of some aspects of the *Loi Debré*, not only on parliament, but on his prime minister, J. Chaban-Delmas, apparently more favourable to secularist views. The *contrat simple*, initially envisaged as a temporary measure, was made permanent for Catholic primary schools, and the *contrat d'association* in the secondary schools. After 1979, the *contrat simple* would no longer be permitted to secondary schools. The result of this is that 90 per cent of Catholic primary schools have a *contrat simple* with the state and 94 per cent of Catholic secondary schools have a *contrat d'association*. It is equally worth noting that secular private schools have in the main chosen to remain totally independent (see *Le Monde*, 8 June 1977). Consequently, when the cost of private education represents 11.46 per cent of the 1978 education budget, with 96,647 persons in private education salaried by the state (*Projet de loi de finances pour 1978*, Paris, Imprimerie nationale, 1977, pp. 8, 10), it is almost exclusively Catholic education which benefits.

Although over ten million people signed the CNAL petition against the *Loi Debré* in 1960, a decrease in feeling against the law seems to have gone hand in hand with a waning of church influence, particularly in the urban and industrial areas.[21] Nevertheless, the parties of the left and the teaching unions have maintained a fairly consistent hostility to the Fifth Republic's subsidizing of private schools, with the promise of changes when the left comes to power. 'Le bénéfice des lois laïques sera étendu à tout le territoire (y compris Alsace-Moselle). Dès la première législature, les établissements privés . . . percevant les fonds publics seront en règle générale nationalisés.'[22] However, the hostility of the left to private schools gave rise to some political embarrassment. The last municipal elections brought to office in many areas a left-wing majority, which made possible the implementation of certain policies favoured by the left. The socialist mayor of Saint-Herblain (Loire-Atlantique), for example, decided to cut off credits to private schools in the town (see *Le Monde*, 17 June 1977); similar action was taken in Cherbourg (*Le Monde*, 7 September 1977), which looked like the shape of things to come (given a victory of the left at the parliamentary elections of March 1978). An unfortunate impression was also made by the first draft of a socialist plan for education, the so-called 'rapport Mexandeau', which had to be altered to tone down comments on socialist policy towards subsidized schools. The problem was not so crucial for the communists who, in the person of Georges Marchais, adopted a fairly moderate line on the issue (see *Le Monde*, 18 June 1977); whereas the socialist leadership had to contend in its own party with the traditionally secularist views of, on the one hand, the *Fédération Cornec*, whose president had been extremely outspoken on the subject at the federation's congress at Albi in June 1977 and on the other, of the FEN, whose secretary-general, André Henry, stated his position categorically: 'Nous serons intransigeants sur le principe de la nationalisation . . . Il faut montrer aux partis de la gauche qu'ils ne doivent pas céder sur l'essentiel: les fonds publics à l'école publique'

(*Le Monde*, 22 June 1977).[23] The socialists also needed to pay heed to the views of some of the newer members of the party, often of christian views. Whatever the party did in these circumstances could alienate a portion of its members, not to mention the electorate at large.

In September 1977, therefore, the socialist party issued a directive to all its municipal representatives not to cut off subsidies to private schools without negotiation, which would only inflame the controversy all over again, and provide the supporters of private education with electoral ammunition.

With the parties of the left 'back-pedalling', as it were, on the issue, it seemed a golden opportunity to Guy Guermeur, the RPR deputy for Finistère, and president of the parliamentary association for freedom of education, to press for yet greater advantages for private education. His proposals, as approved by the *assemblée nationale* (29 June) and *sénat* (25 October), allow for: state loans at reduced interest for the building of private secondary schools and of workshops required by the *réforme Haby*: an improvement of the *forfait d'externat*: financial aid from the state for the training of teachers, who are to have the same benefits as their counterparts in the state system. The choice of teachers will henceforth be the responsibility of the heads of private schools. The state thus has slightly less control than before, but pays substantially more. M. Guermeur had proposed one further measure, not accepted by the government, which would have provided for the public financing of the construction of new private schools! The cost of those measures which were accepted is reckoned to be in the order of 800 million francs (*Le Monde*, 14 July 1977). If this is added to an annually increasing proportion of the education budget, it contrasts very markedly, in the mind of the British reader, with state aid in Britain, provided now only for the few voluntary controlled schools, and the ever diminishing number of direct grant schools. In spite of the political left's low profile on the question of state subsidies to private education, the *Loi Guermeur*, opposed by the left in parliament, was received with hostility by the FEN, and by the *Fédération Cornec*. For J. Cornec indeed, the *Loi Guermeur* was yet another stage in the long war waged by the Catholic hierarchy against France's national education system. His description of their activities sounds, to put it mildly, far-fetched (see J. Cornec, 'Libres opinions', *Le Monde*, 7 July 1977). The implications of this view are, paradoxically, borne out by the leader of a far less radical organization, Antoine Lagarde,[24] who suggests that more and more parents are turning to private education, when faced with their children's failure at school (see editorial, 'Laïcité', by A. Lagarde, *La Voix des parents*, no. 198, May 1978). Both men, in their different ways, react to what they see as an increase in the numbers of children attending private schools. Yet this impression does not seem to be wholly borne out by the facts. Since the passing of the *Loi Debré* the overall proportion of the school population attending private schools has decreased steadily. Yet even so, it can scarcely be said that private education presents a serious threat to the state system, which claims even in relation to its size a much larger share of the school population (see Table 6.3).[25]

A British reader, accustomed to debates on the relative merits of comprehensive or grammar schools, might be tempted to take the issue out of context, and view it simply as a conflict between the freedom of choosing a school, which it is alleged parents should have (freedom of education), and the need to avoid a system which maintains a privilege which only wealthy parents can exercise (social justice). This would partly explain the problem, although it has been asserted that in 1974 nearly 30 per cent of pupils in Catholic schools received grants, and in some areas the percentage was twice as high. In 1975–6 there were 260,892 pupils to whom grants were awarded (at secondary level) in private schools, out of a total of 983,573.[26] It is sometimes suggested that Catholic schools are merely the instruments of capitalism and reactionary employers, but the purpose of Catholic education, according to the Roman Catholic church, is totally different: 'contribuer à la construction d'un monde nouveau nettement opposé à une mentalité caractérisée par la recherche du plaisir, de l'obsession de l'efficacité et de la tyrannie de la consommation' (*Le Monde*, 7 July 1977). Yet while there seems to be substantial support in France for the existence of Catholic schools, the motivation for such support seems less clear. In a recent opinion poll, 42 per cent of those asked were in favour of their children attending private (Catholic) schools;

Table 6.3   Percentage of children in private schools

Primary education

1958–9	18.6
1966	17.3
1972	16.4
1975	16.2
1976–7	15.9

Secondary education, 1976–7

1st cycle	18.5
2nd cycle (short)	21.6
2nd cycle (long)	23.4

Source: adapted from *Le Monde*, 8 June 1977.

the percentage went up to 64 per cent for ex-pupils of Catholic schools, and, surprisingly, only down to 35 per cent for ex-pupils of non-Catholic schools. Yet, according to other answers given, it is estimated that about five million people attend church regularly, while half the population of France rarely set foot inside a church. When questions were asked about political preferences, 59 per cent of ex-pupils from non-Catholic schools were pro-left, and 57 per cent from Catholic schools were pro-right (see *Témoignage chrétien*, 2 March 1978); in other words, Catholic schools *may* produce Catholics, but they have a much better chance of producing political conservatives. This is perhaps the root cause of the political controversy, since the right clearly benefit from the existence of Catholic education, and the left do not.[27] Consequently, the right vaunt its advantages and the left, when freed from constraints of the political conjuncture, denounce it as divisive and anti-national. In other words, in spite of the changes in Catholic opinion, particularly since Vatican II, it will receive its support from centre and right parties, and will face the hostility of the left; and, as in the second half of the nineteenth century, political allegiances may still be defined not, as in the past, by the issue of church and state, but by that of Catholic education.

The classics, and particularly Latin, have formed a substantial part of education in France for many centuries. This was brought about by both cultural and religious pressures: the use of Latiñ in Catholic services, although no longer current, and the view held that French culture is most closely related to that of ancient Rome. Consequently, since the Renaissance, a knowledge of Latin was looked upon as an essential part of the cultured man's intellectual equipment. In the eighteenth and nineteenth centuries it retained its importance, and may be said in general to have provided an education for the country's political leadership, although not without some attempt to introduce a greater degree of scientific education into the system.

    In secondary education, Latin became optional with the reform of 1902, which organized *lycée* courses as follows. The first cycle comprised Latin (and Greek on an optional basis in 4e and 3e), which gave the possibilities at 2e in preparation for a *baccalauréat*: (a) Latin-Greek; (b) Latin-modern Languages; (c) Latin-science. A fourth possibility (d), science and modern languages, could be taken by those who had not studied Latin during the first cycle of secondary education, and the idea behind this was to make secondary education minus Latin as reputable as the more classical options. However, the secondary teachers of the period, particularly attached to classical studies, guided their best pupils towards these disciplines, which meant that the weaker pupils were orientated towards non-classical studies.

An unsuccessful attempt was made in 1923 to suppress the first cycle minus Latin, leading to category (d).

Further changes were brought about in 1925, whereby the four sections were reduced to three: (a) Latin-Greek; (b) Latin-science; (c) Modern languages-science (with the same curriculum for all in science, French, history and geography). These courses of study led up to *baccalauréats* in either philosophy or mathematics. The idea here was to give the same weight to the sciences as to literary studies. This appears to have been unsuccessful since, under Vichy, the arrangements for secondary education reverted virtually to the situation of 1902 with four sections, Latin-Greek, Latin-modern languages having less science to study than the others.

The reforms of J. Berthoin in 1959 maintained the teaching of Latin, so that three of the options available in the second cycle of secondary education comprised Latin as an essential component. It took the events of May 1968 to make the learning of Latin less of a priority than in the past. In his speech of 24 July, E. Faure proposed to delay the teaching of Latin for two years at secondary level (until 4^e), in order to allow for a lengthier common programme. However, this was something announced, but not effected, and it was left to O. Guichard, Faure's successor, to decide what should be done. The decision arrived at was a compromise, whereby Latin was introduced at 5e level as an aid to French, although G. Pompidou, by then president of the republic, as an erstwhile teacher of Latin, would have preferred to have obligatory Latin taught from 6e to 4e inclusive.[28]

The present situation, i.e. the implementation of the *réforme Haby*, requires of teachers of French that they should use Latin as a point of reference not only at 6e and 5e, although the formal initiation begins at 5e,[29] and Latin is now an optional study for three of the courses of study at 2e.[30]

The question of Latin is more immediately political than might be supposed. The insistence, over many years, that it comprises an essential ingredient of the whole of secondary education, has held up the implementation of policies leading to a greater degree of comprehensive education in France. Consequently, those who favour the maintenance of Latin may consider themselves as the staunch upholders of the highest traditions of French education, but are viewed by their opponents as placing obstacles in the path of a more egalitarian type of education. The issue has been complicated by the fact that while students of the classics may indeed be preserving something which is crucial to French culture, they are not necessarily well equipped to lead politically a technological society. From two standpoints therefore, the position of Latin in school is vulnerable, and it is perhaps surprising that it has maintained itself as well as it has. There are still those who, like Pompidou, would prefer a return of Latin at 6^e.[31]

However, the question of Latin is symbolic, not merely of conservative and reforming tendencies in education, but also of attitudes to education in general. In the last century, there was a fairly large-scale prejudice in favour of literary studies, as opposed to those of a more scientific and technical nature, and *a fortiori* to 'mere' manual labour, which has persisted well into the twentieth century. It is only in comparatively recent years that efforts in favour of science and technology have been realized, and that mathematics has replaced the classics as a sure passport to higher education and high-income careers.

(3) Primary and secondary education

In view of the centralized organization of the French education system, the activities of the state have assumed, for well over a century, a primordial importance. The French Revolution may be said to have laid down the definitive principles for education in France; the subsequent 170-odd years can be viewed as a long, painful and often vain endeavour to put them into practice.

> Les grands principes scolaires de la Révolution apparaissent donc comme des anticipations. Leur fécondité n'est pas niable: l'affirmation des droits de l'Etat, de la gratuité, d'obligation, de l'égalité des enfants devant l'Ecole; la conception d'un service public indépendant des Eglises et facteur d'unité nationale, par l'usage systématique du français, notamment, inspireront toute l'évolution ultérieure. (A. Prost, *L'Enseignement en France, 1800–1967* (2nd ed.), Paris, Colin, 1970, p. 90)

Initially, it may seem as if little attempt was made in this direction, since Napoleon, while adapting the concept of state education to his own requirements, neglected the more egalitarian aspects of the revolution's educational principles, and his example was followed, with some modification, by subsequent governments.

While it is a fact that the *Loi Guizot* of 1833 reduced illiteracy,[32] progress was slow because primary education was not obligatory; nor was it free of charge, except for the children of destitute parents. This law, apparently of democratic tendencies, was not conceived by its author for such a purpose. In his view, education had to be appropriate to the social classes; consequently, primary education was divided into two parts to suit different strata of society. The first level (*instruction primaire élémentaire*) was to be sufficient for the lower classes, but the second level (*instruction primaire supérieure*) was aimed at 'une partie très nombreuse de la nation, qui, sans jouir des avantages de la fortune, n'est pas non plus réduite à une gêne sévère' (Guizot, speech of 2 January 1833, *Archives parlementaires*,

Paris, 1891, vol. 78, p. 465). Secondary education for these strata of society, was considered a positive danger, causing many to feel dissatisfied with their lot. Its task was to educate the middle classes for their role as leaders of society. 'C'est par l'instruction secondaire seulement que la classe moyenne peut se préparer aux professions libérales, aux industries scientifiques, aux travaux et aux fonctions de tout genre qui sont sa vocation naturelle' (Guizot, speech of 1 February 1836, *Archives parlementaires*, Paris, 1899, vol. 100, p. 85).

As long as education was viewed as a positive danger to the social order and a source of dissatisfaction, the question of free primary schooling was not likely to be a burning issue. The wealthier classes could afford to pay, and the poorer classes were not obliged to send their children to school. By the end of the Second Empire the idea of free education for all had become more widely accepted, and the legislation of 1881 was the last step in a series of advances from the 1860s onwards, when an increasing number of children attended school free of charge. This undoubted advance was assisted by the law of 1882, which made primary education obligatory for children of both sexes from the ages of six to thirteen. There is no doubt that the thinking behind these laws was essentially egalitarian, imbued with the desire to remove social inequalities by education, which had hitherto helped to maintain, rather than reduce, class differences. The task before the legislators of the 1880s was, in the words of Jules Ferry, the initiator of these reforms, to: 'faire disparaître la dernière, la plus redoutable des inégalités qui viennent de la naissance, l'inégalité d'éducation' (Jules Ferry, speech of 10 April 1870, quoted by A. Prost, op. cit., p. 14). Ferry was very much alive to the political consequences of an education system which maintained inequalities since, in his opinion, a genuine equality, as opposed to a merely theoretical one, would never be attained without the benefit of an adequate education for all.

Yet the changes brought about by Ferry were not sufficient to redress the balance. First of all, while primary education was obligatory up to the age of thirteen, and no fees were charged in the state primary schools, the parents of any child who wished to continue studying and go on to a secondary school had to find the money for school fees, since secondary education in state schools was still not free of charge, and it was thus more difficult for children of poorer families to benefit from further study. The poorer classes were consequently still at a disadvantage, however much equality was thought to exist at the obligatory primary stage. Moreover, the two areas of education still remained distinct, complete in themselves. Each, for example, has its own version of the other; primary education had its own type of secondary level with the *écoles primaires supérieures* and the *cours complémentaires*, whereas secondary education had its own elementary classes – the *petites classes* of the *lycées*. It was not until after the First World War that any solution to these problems was envisaged. One was financial; between 1929 and 1933, all classes in secondary education ceased to be fee-paying. However, this, together with a population increase, augmented to such an extent the numbers of children wishing to enter secondary education that an entrance examination was imposed in 1933–4.

However, the solution which might have solved the problem of the separation of primary and secondary levels was the concept of the *école unique*, which proposed a much less rigid barrier between the two, either by prolonging the primary stage, or by creating schools at an intermediate stage to, as it were, fill the gap. Also, incorporated into the concept of the *école unique* was the idea of *orientation* (educational guidance) that a child would receive after primary schooling, and before going on to any definitive courses of study. Depending on aptitude, these would be studies in either a *lycée*, a technical school, or workshop. The idea behind these views was democratic enough: 'Faire en sorte que les distinctions d'origine sociale cèdent le pas au seul mérite, afin que chaque Français accède à la culture sans autre considération que celle de ses aptitudes.'[33]

The man who came closest to implementing these views was Jean Zay, a Radical, who was minister of education from 1936 to 1939, in the government of the *Front Populaire* and in its successors. His proposed reform of 1937 provided for three elements of primary education:

(1) *enseignement primaire élémentaire*
(2) *enseignement primaire complémentaire*, for those not going on to secondary education
(3) *enseignement post-scolaire*, to be provided for those over fourteen years of age attending neither the complementary courses just mentioned, nor classes at secondary level.

The *certificat d'études primaires* (CEP), obtained after examination, and normally taken by children aged twelve-plus, could be taken a year earlier by those intending to continue their education at secondary school, for which it was obligatory. This hurdle overcome, the first year of secondary education (6e) was to be characterized by a *tronc commun* (a common syllabus), at the end of which pupils would be guided, according to their abilities and to parents' wishes, towards one of three courses of study: *classique, moderne* and *technique*. Since the reform also allowed pupils to switch from one section to another where this was considered advisable, all three sections had to run parallel to each other.

While the maintenance of the CEP meant that selection was applied, this proposed legislation tended to reduce the element of class discrimination which had hitherto existed. However, overall reform was never discussed in parliament, and Jean Zay was only able to bring éements of it into being on an experimental basis, notably the *classe d'orientation* at 6e.

These innovations had not been forgotten when René Capitant education minister in the provisional government at Algiers set up a commission to consider possible reforms in education. At that time, there was a serious preoccupation with the inadequacies of the education system as demonstrated not only by the collapse of France in 1940, but by subsequent collaboration.

> Il semble bien que, si les hommes du peuple, formés par l'école primaire se sont montrés . . . admirablement courageux et patients pendant la guerre ouverte et la guerre clandestine . . . les 'élites', compte tenu d'honorables exceptions individuelles, ont montré, elles, un manque lamentable de caractère . . . Ceux qui pouvaient se dire issus des sommets de notre enseignement sont ceux dont la lâcheté a été la plus éclatante (M. Durry, 'Rapport général sur les travaux de la commission pour la réforme de l'enseignement', *Bulletin officiel du ministère de l'éducation nationale*, 16 November 1944, p. 13).

The paradox of this state of affairs was thought to lie in the nature of French secondary education, 'enseignement de caste qui continuait à maintenir en France une féodalité de l'argent et des charges' (ibid.).

Equality in education was thus considered, at the liberation and after, to be of prime significance; and earlier efforts in this direction, although scarcely adequate in practice, were looked to for inspiration. Consequently a number of elements, such as the need for practical education, for guidance of pupils at secondary level towards the sections appropriate to their interests and abilities and the removal of the *petites classes* of the *lycées* were emphasized.

However, it is from the report of the Langevin-Wallon commission, set up by R. Capitant in November 1944, that the definitive plan for a renovated education system was to come. It proposed no more than two main sections: *second degré* (higher education) and *premier degré*, that is, compulsory school education from ages six to eighteen, divided into four stages:

(a) nursery schooling (*école maternelle*);
(b) a first cycle for children aged six to eleven, with a *tronc commun*;
(c) a second cycle (*cycle d'orientation*) for eleven- to fifteen-year-olds, where part of the syllabus would be for all, and part more specialized, relating to individual abilities. There would be, in the later years, options leading to differing types of education provided in the following cycle;
(d) *cycle de détermination* (for fifteen- to eighteen-year-olds), subdivided into: *section pratique*, for those whose manual competence

was greater than their intellectual abilities; *section professionnelle*, for those who were likely to form middle management and were less biased towards theoretical studies; and the *section théorique*, for those whose abilities were more specifically intellectual, whether scientific or literary, and who would take the *baccalauréat* or its equivalent.

However, it is perhaps less for its proposals which were fairly general, and were never implemented, than for its underlying ideology, that the Langevin–Wallon report is significant. Its views on the need for the democratization of education, based on social justice, have a strong affinity with those of Condorcet.

> Tous les enfants . . . ont un droit égal au développement maximum que leur personnalité comporte . . . la diversification des fonctions sera commandée non plus par la fortune ou la classe sociale, mais par la capacité à remplir une fonction. La démocratisation de l'enseignement, conforme à la justice, assure une meilleure distribution des tâches sociales. (Commission ministérielle d'étude, *La Réforme de l'enseignement*, Paris, Ministère de l'éducation nationale, n.d., p. 9)

Against the current prejudice in favour of intellectual pursuits, it also emphasized the equal importance of more practical types of work, including manual labour, in an endeavour to bring about a change of approach on this issue, thus going beyond the usual scope of educational reforms, in its desire to associate education and democracy.

> Le travail manuel, l'intelligence pratique sont encore trop souvent considérés comme de médiocre valeur. L'équité exige la reconnaissance de l'égale dignité de toutes les tâches sociales, de la haute valeur technique. Ce reclassement des valeurs réelles est indispensable dans une société démocratique moderne dont le progrès et la vie même sont subordonnés à l'exacte utilisation des compétences. (ibid., pp. 8–9)

Perhaps the breadth of vision and the idealism shown by the commission account for the lasting prestige of the report amongst those wishing to see far-reaching changes in the education system.[34] Consequently, later reforms may be regarded as more or less successful attempts to implement some of the proposals of Langevin–Wallon.

There seems little reason to doubt the good will of the Fourth Republic in the realm of education, since several vain attempts were made to introduce measures of reform (those of E. Depreux in 1948, of Y. Delbos in 1949 and J. Berthoin in 1955). One cause for this apparent stagnation was the inherent weakness of coalition government, which did not always give a minister sufficient time to work out and propose effective measures. Other difficulties related more to the opposition of teachers' unions, who felt their interests were threatened by changes. This seems to have been in part the reason for the failure of the reform bill proposed by René Billères, education minister in the government of G. Mollet. The main aim of these proposals was to deal with the class discrimination which obtained as between primary and secondary education. This problem was clearly indicated by the social origins of children entering secondary education of whatever kind. Billères estimated that 13 per cent of the children of agricultural workers went on to secondary level, as opposed to 21 per cent of industrial workers, 81 per cent management, 86 per cent officials and 87 per cent from the liberal professions.[35] To meet this flagrant inequality, he proposed to extend obligatory education up to age sixteen, and perhaps more importantly, to institute middle schools (*écoles moyennes*). The purpose of these was to do away with the sharp line drawn between primary and secondary education, which would permit a greater degree of social mobility in that secondary education might become less of a purely middle-class prerogative. Two years would be spent in these schools. During the first, the programme would be common to all pupils; in the second, it would be part common to all and part optional, depending on individual abilities. The two-year period in the middle schools was designed to prepare pupils for subsequent courses of study, whether practical, professional or leading to higher education.

While these proposals might have gone a long way towards solving the problem of the inequality in education, they were received with hostility by the unions of secondary teachers who did not wish to see any link between primary and secondary, where the latter might be reduced, to the former's benefit. Such hostility from the unions made it difficult for Radicals and socialists, and the government itself, to give the proposals strong support, and they were shelved. Clearly any attempt to bridge the gap between primary and secondary would have to be less than profound, if it were to have any hope of success.

Such were undoubtedly the conclusions drawn, in the early days of the Fifth Republic, by J. Berthoin, who introduced (significantly, by decree) in January 1959 a modified version of Billères's proposals. The school-leaving age was increased to sixteen, to come into effect in 1967; and the CEP, giving admittance to the *lycée*, was suppressed. The specially created *école moyenne* envisaged by Billères was rendered down into a two-year period (*cycle d'observation*) of which one term only had a teaching programme common to all pupils -- to take place in whatever school the pupils found themselves. This meant that the erstwhile *école moyenne* could be included in secondary education if the teaching took place in a *lycée*, or in primary if it took place in a *collège d'enseignement général*; yet it was indicated in the decree (article 8) that the courses of study during these two years should be as similar as possible. These provisions had the advantage of not upsetting the teaching unions, since there could be no suspicion either at primary or at secondary level that either side was poaching on the other's preserves. They equally had the disadvantage of rendering the 'bridging' quality of the genuine *école moyenne* null and void, since it now remained in one camp or the other.

Whatever the defects, 'the reform contained seeds of growth that could not be impeded'.[36] The fact that both primary and secondary teachers were involved in the *cycle d'observation* gave a greater possibility for primary teachers to move into the secondary level. Also the use of *conseils d'orientation*, originally proposed by Billères, added the counsellor to the school personnel. The greatest extension to the Berthoin reform was put into effect under the auspices of Christian Fouchet. In 1963, the two-year *cycle d'observation*, having been found inadequate, was extended to four years, and a new form of school was set up, the *collège d'enseignement secondaire* (CES) with three sections: Modern I (*lycée*-style course), Modern II (CEG-type course) and Transitional III, into which were placed those unable to cope with the more academic programmes.[37] The courses in the CES were to last four years – 6e to 3e – which thus constituted the first cycle of secondary education to be taken away from the *lycées*. The introduction of the CES has met with mixed response. The minister claimed, with some justice, that it was an important step towards the democratization of education, 'puisque, pour la première fois dans l'histoire des institutions scolaires françaises, tous les élèves quittant l'école élémentaire se trouvent réunis dans un même établissement' (Ministère de l'éducation nationale, *La Réforme de l'enseignement, août 1963–juin 1966*, Paris, n.d., p. 2). At all events, this was the ideal goal to be reached, and the creation of CES throughout France proceeded apace (1968 – 1,500; 1972-3 – 2,426; 1975-6 – 3,040).

While the CES brought comprehensive education from primary to secondary level, it brought also confusion when changes were effected, and led ultimately to resentment on the part of both pupils and teachers. A further target of criticism was the existence of the differing sections in the CES, into which pupils are divided according to ability (streaming). Those who are not capable of academic study are downgraded in relation to those who are in every sense, since, in due course, they are likely to find themselves in a subordinate role *vis-à-vis* their more successful colleagues. The orientation into these sectors consequently is not merely an academic distinction, but one which has an effect on the individual's place in society and, as a corollary, on the salary which he or she earns. As a result, the democratic purpose of the CES is regarded by some as more apparent than real.

The events of May 1968 brought about a definitive change in the climate of opinion, although the *Loi d'Orientation* of Edgar Faure was primarily concerned with higher education. In his speech to the *assemblée nationale*, Faure spelled out a number of fundamental principles relating to education in general: the need, for example, to do away with the centralized administration of education, and to introduce new relationships between the administration and educational establishments, on the one hand, and between teachers and taught on the other. This in turn would require different forms of teaching with less emphasis on the formal lesson, and more on pupil and student participation. There was also a need, in order to bring France nearer to that still elusive goal, democratization of education, to remove the disadvantages under which certain classes still laboured. This would be arrived at by providing grants at pre-*baccalauréat* stage, by a policy of *décloisonnement*, i.e. removing the breaks between the different parts of school education, by changes in the curriculum.

> Elle [democratization] est liée davantage aux programmes d'enseignement et aux méthodes d'examen qui favorisent inconsciemment certaines catégories et certains groupes. L'école ne doit pas supposer acquis ce que reçoivent de leur famille les seuls enfants des milieux culturellement favorisés. Elle doit se garder de confondre humanisme et humanités. (E. Faure, *L'Education nationale et la participation*, p. 21)

Thus, other forms of learning (scientific and technical), which would take from the culturally privileged classes the advantage which was theirs in the more literary sphere, would assume larger proportions in primary and secondary education. Such a renewal was in any case desirable given a society which was in a perpetual state of flux and which required an education more suited to modern life. 'Cette éducation nationale doit participer à la vie de toute la nation comme la nation tout entière doit contribuer à son devenir' (ibid., p. 19).

Since, in spite of criticisms, the *Loi d'Orientation* has acquired such eminence that all ministers of education have at the very least paid lip-service to it, we may expect to find, in the decade since 1968, changes introduced in line with the spirit of Faure's reform. The legislation of 16 July 1971 (three separate laws) is concerned with the organization of vocational and technological education, apprenticeship, and adult education (*formation continue*) for employed workers. The first provides for an initiation into technology and economics from 4e and 3e onwards. It also requires that adequate information be provided on the differeing branches of education, job possibilities and on 'les perspectives scientifiques, techniques et économiques dont dépend l'évolution de l'emploi' (article 3). The second, on apprenticeship, deals with its reorganization, in apprentice training centres, with training lasting from one to three years, and with the possibility of proceeding to further study and higher qualifications. These two laws clearly represent an attempt to induce a higher esteem on the part of the public for these areas of study, as well as an endeavour to provide appropriate training for work in a technological society. Yet it is perhaps the third law on *formation continue* which comes closest to the ideals of May 1968. This gives a worker in employment the right to have time off from work in order to pursue courses of study approved by the state, leading to further qualification. As a rule the maximum period of absence from work is either one year, or 1,200 hours, depending on the nature of the course. This is an innovation which seems to give education the possibility of achieving what many think of as its main task, the social (and consequently, financial) up-grading of the working classes. The number benefiting from *formation continue* has risen from 1,760,000 in 1972 to 2,550,000 in 1975; the financial involvement of the state has increased in the same period from 1.7 million francs to 3 million and that of private industry from 2.8 million to 5.5 million. Although the purpose of this legislation is social advance, there are inequalities as to the percentage of categories benefiting (cf. Table 6.4). Furthermore, the proportion of workers who seek a course of training on their own initiative is decreasing, while the overall numbers rise (88,000 out of 1,790,000 in 1974; 65,000 out of 2,550,000 in 1975). There is therefore a fear that what was intended as a mechanism for social advancement is turning purely and simply into a measure of convenience for employers; and consequently a greater degree of freedom for workers to choose further training outside the categories laid down is thought to be necessary.[38] At the same time, the figures show that the under-privileged categories (women, workers/white collars) are gradually increasing their share of the benefits of *formation continue*, even if it may be thought that the increase is too slow.

A further attempt to improve secondary education came during Joseph Fontanet's term of office as education minister. Although his reform proposals were nipped in the bud by Pompidou's death and his own consequent departure from the ministry, they are worth looking

Table 6.4   Categories benefiting from adult education, 1977
            (percentages)

Categories	1972	1975
Women	25	29
Engineers/management	16	13
Technicians	30	26
Workers/employees	54	61

Source: FEN Information, supplement 3 January 1977, pp. 12–13.

at, since they show areas where the Fouchet legislation required amendment. The system of three streams of ability in the first part of secondary education, although in theory permitting a pupil to pass from one to another, in fact allowed for very little mobility. To add to the rigid hierarchy system, the *lycée*-type stream (I) was taught only by *agrégés* and *certifiés*, and the other two streams by PEGC and *instituteurs* respectively. J. Fontanet's solution was to remove total streaming, and replace it by a compromise system: certain subjects would be taught in mixed ability classes, others in homogeneous or partly homogeneous classes, permitting pupils, however, to pass from one group to another, depending on progress. The teaching of the first part would, in due course, become the province of a specific type of teacher (*enseignement du premier cycle*) to which PEGC and *instituteurs* could accede; the *agrégés* and *certifiés* would in time teach only in the later cycle of secondary education. While remedial teaching could be provided where necessary, the practice of *redoublement*, i.e. the repeating of a whole year, would be done away with, requiring in turn a less rigid organization of classes and timetable. However, where it was thought that an extra year would be genuinely beneficial at the end of the first cycle, this would be allowed.

After the election of Giscard d'Estaing in 1974, it was the turn of René Haby to see how he could improve the system. He too has now left office, but the controversy and uncertainty surrounding his reforms still exist. It seems clear enough that the guiding principles of the legislation are to be found in the views of Giscard d'Estaing – views which Haby undoubtedly shares. In his *Démocratie française*,[39] the former states the importance of education in giving all children the opportunity to develop abilities to the full. 'La justice . . . est de faire en sorte que, quel que soit le milieu d'origine, les personnalités de nos enfants puissent se développer et trouver dans la vie sociale, à mérite égal, des chances équivalentes. Une démocratie sincère doit fixer cet objectif au premier de ses ambitions.' In other words, social origins should not prove a handicap to genuine ability. In presenting his proposals, R. Haby spoke of the need to create genuine equality of opportunity and therefore to ensure that late development, often a result of cultural deprivation, was not penalized: 'déculpabiliser le retard' (see *Le Monde de l'éducation*, March 1975).

The text of the law, as passed by the *assemblée nationale* on 11 July 1975, is, as befits a *loi cadre*, exceedingly vague; but it seems to be egalitarian in tendency. It provides for nursery education, which is not obligatory, but which any five-year-old child may attend if the family wishes. Nursery education is regarded as having a crucial role to play in the removal of disadvantages caused by class differences. 'Elle tend à prévenir les difficultés scolaires, à dépister les handicaps et à compenser les inégalités' (article 2). Primary education, with five successive levels, although the duration of the initial period may vary, remains as before, based on a common syllabus. After primary education, all children enter a *collège* (the distinction between CEG and CES having been removed) where a further four levels of common syllabus are taught; although in the two final levels, more vocational training may be comprised in the curriculum for those working towards this type of qualification. Further secondary education takes place in the *lycée*, and qualifications there obtained may lead on to higher education. The *filières* are dispensed with, and decisions taken as to the future are arrived at on the basis of observation and assessment, due heed being paid to the family's wishes, and with the possibility of appeal.

Alterations in the running of schools are also provided for by a measure of parent participation, with the election of parents' representatives to the *comité des parents* and the *conseil d'école* at nursery and primary level or to the *conseils d'établissement* at secondary level; parents' delegates also have the right to be present at the *conseil de classe*, one for each class of children.

With the total abolition of streaming, certain provisions have had to be made, in favour of those who progress either more quickly or more slowly than the norm. Further study -- *activités d'approfondissement* -- is provided for the quicker pupil, and remedial work for the pupil who finds it difficult to keep up.

It might have been thought that such a reform, introducing a more genuine form of the *collège unique*, with a common programme up to 3e level, and *orientation* thereafter, would have been sympathetically received by the left, and by the teaching unions. Hostility has been strong from the beginning; while Haby's purpose was to permit children to progress at their own speed, without penalty for late development, this purpose is considered to be no more and no less than a sham. 'Loin de combattre les difficultés scolaires qui ont pour source essentielle l'origine sociale des élèves, il se borne à les enregistrer et à en dissimuler les consequences: les retards scolaires sont officialisés par la prolongation de la scolarité primaire; l'enseignement du cycle d'observation est "allégé" pour les enfants en difficulté; le cycle d'orientation est explicitement fondé sur le caractère irréversible de cette sélection' (J. Chambaz, *Le Monde de l'éducation*, March 1975).

Such was the attitude of the left before the legislation was even voted; and union hostility has been maintained ever since, mainly on the grounds that selection is maintained even when, officially, it is being removed. The remedial help provided by the law was not thought to be sufficient (three hours per week) to be of any real assistance to backward children. Selection is still considered to be present in the system, with the middle classes, employers, and capitalism in general as the main beneficiaries. Part of the problem has also been that great quantities of instructions, advice, and guide-lines have been sent out to bewildered and resentful teachers.[40] Another worry for teachers is the extra help required for the remedial work, and for the more flexible timetable. Faced with pressure from the unions of the *instituteurs* and PEGC, Haby provided 4,200 extra teaching posts to cope with the first cycle teaching (see *Le Monde*, 7 September 1977), and this was the price of union co-operation at that level. Yet it should not be assumed that all criticism attacked the élitism of the reforms. The independent union of *lycée* teachers, SNALC, take the view that the *réforme Haby* is a form of confidence trick, designed to lower the standard of education in France, on the part of a technocracy (recruited from the bourgeoisie and the aris-tocracy).

> Pour pérénniser une puissance abusive et illégitime, la méthode la plus sûre ne consiste-t-elle pas à médiocriser l'enseignement destiné à la masse, sous couvert d'"égalité des chances'; à empêcher la pro-motion intellectuelle et sociale d'élites potentielles étrangères à l'intelligentsia? (G. Simon, *SNALC et la réforme de l'enseignement*, Paris, Livre Vert, 1976).

It is evident that, at the moment, the Haby reforms suit neither the left nor elements of the right. Nevertheless, the first *rentrée* in 1977 passed off with less difficulty than might have been expected, partly because of concessions which had been made, partly because there was still the hope of the law's repeal if the left won the legislative elections. The *rentrée* of 1978 was less tranquil, owing to dissatisfaction on the part of parents.

The Haby reforms will inevitably take a number of years to bring into effect. In 1977 the first secondary class – 6e – received its common syllabus; school books were made free of charge; in the first primary class, the *cycle préparatoire*, the inability to read and to count was not to hold back pupils from entering the next class. The various school councils, with parental participation, have also been installed, together with, in theory, the *dossier scolaire*, intended as a complete record of a pupil's development, from nursery school to 3e and hence as an aid to *orientation*; but this aroused such controversy and suspicion among teachers, that it has since been shelved by C. Beullac. For the *rentrée* of 1978 a common syllabus was introduced for the 5e, with the corresponding school-books again being rendered free of charge. In subsequent years, the common syllabus will be applied to 4e and 3e, which means that the second cycle of secondary education will not be reached until 1981-2, and the *baccalauréat* not until 1983-4. It is thus very difficult to say what success the reform will achieve, since its effects will not become evident for some time to come.

At this stage, it may be appropriate to give an indication as to how the system should function for a child beginning in nursery education at the earliest age – two years old. After four years, he/she passes into primary school where, in five or six years, he/she passes through the stages of *cours préparatoire, élémentaire* and *moyen*. Without any sanction or selection, the child begins a four-year course in a *collège*. The first two years are based on a common syllabus; the latter two (4e and 3e) may comprise more vocational training, some of which may take place away from the *collège*. It is at the end of 3e where the final decision as to *orientation* must be taken; either to opt for *lycée, baccalauréat* and, subsequently, higher education if appropriate; or to opt for the *lycée d'enseignement professionnel* (formerly technical college) and prepare for the various vocational qualifications – CEP (*certificat d'éducation professionnelle*), a one-year course without examination; or the more exacting BEP (*brevet d'études professionnelles*) and CAP (*certificat d'aptitude professionnelle*). This simplified description may make it possible to see that, in spite of the claims made for the *collège unique*, and a removal of *filières*, a measure of orientation inevitably takes place at 5e, and more decisively at 3e. Those who are either not considered suitable for the *lycée* cycle of secondary education, or who do not wish to enter it, begin some of their vocational training in their last two years of *collège*. It is, however, at 3e when many futures are settled; and it appears that it is on results gained in mathematics that they turn, since this leads to the *baccalauréat* C, which in turn provides greater chances of further success. 'Les mathématiques commandent l'entrée des grands concours, mais aussi des petits. Les mathématiques ouvrent les études de médecine, les carrières de l'Administration. Tous les métiers aux débouchés assurés . . .' (D. Granet, 'La gare de triage de la 3e', *L'Express*, 13–19 June 1977).

As already noted, the unions in the main tend to view the Haby reform as a masked form of selection, but it is difficult to see how selection can be entirely dispensed with, since at some point, an assessment must be given and a decision taken. It would perhaps be fairer to say that *orientation* is an attempt to do more positively what a more brutal form of selection-by-failure did in the past. Yet until there is a change of heart, and of salary structure, relating to manual and technical skills, there will still be an impression that those who take up these posts are, in some sense, second-class citizens. Until all classes can clear their minds of the distinction between 'noble' and 'non-noble' professions, the problem of social inequality maintained by education will remain.

In the long-term also, it depends to a large extent on the teaching unions as to how successful the reform is to be. If C. Beullac is able to provide the extra numbers of teachers and auxiliaries necessary to make the changes reasonably smoothly, then all may yet be well. However, the shortage of money and means is a constant problem, in spite of an ever-rising education budget.[41] While the government feels itself obliged to consider other national needs, education is regarded by the left as a number one priority, in part because of the pursuit of social equality. Whereas the problem of gearing education to the needs of the economy is of importance, it is not one which the left regards with favour, since it seems like the subjugation of education to more commercial priorities. Yet full employment is considered highly desirable, and, in a technological, post-industrial society, whether communist or capitalist, qualified workers at all levels, would undoubtedly be of vital significance for the country's future.

The problem of equality in education is not easy to resolve. Inasmuch as inequality has been thought to owe its continued existence to the type of education provided in schools, i.e. one where an aristocratic or bourgeois culture prevailed, alien to working-class children, and not one in which they were likely to make progress, it can be said that attempts have been made in recent years to set the balance straight.[42] 'Yet meritocracy is a form of élitism which . . . may be even more pernicious than one of wealth . . . That cruellest of yardsticks by which to judge a man, the accident of birth which determines how much brainpower he will possess, will inexorably determine social position and life expectancy, conferring a fixed status from which there is no possibility of escape.' There is, however, some doubt that education can bring about an effect whose desirability may seem, in the long run, questionable.[43] Whatever the solution to the problem, it is clear that it will be a long-term one, and may, in the final analysis, depend upon decisions taken as to the kind of society which the French people, as a whole, wish to see develop in France.

(4) Higher education

As with education at school level, so has higher education also been the subject of much thought over the last thirty-odd years. This has led to reform, and attempts at reform, both before and since the events of May. If we look at the higher education system as it existed in the immediate post-war period, we find the following elements.

(a) *Qualifications*: a *baccalauréat* giving automatic access to higher education: a *licence* composed, in arts, of four or five *certificats* (in different subjects, with a separate examination for each); three *certificats* were required in science. The *licence en droit* was not split up in this way, and medical studies followed a different pattern again. There were also the *agrégation* – a competitive examination taken after the *licence*, giving to the successful candidate entrance into teaching in higher education or into *lycée* teaching – and the *doctorat*: either a *doctorat d'université* or a *doctorat d'état* – the ultimate qualification in higher education.

(b) *Institutions*: the teaching for the university qualifications was dispensed in the *facultés*. Another path into higher education was to prepare for entrance into the *grandes écoles*, autonomous educational establishments providing courses leading to a professional qualification of the most prestigious kind. These *classes préparatoires*, lasting several years and leading to competitive examinations for entry, were themselves selective. Graduates from the *grandes écoles* were expected to provide an élite of the highest calibre, whose training would enable them to take on duties in many areas of activity, but all possessed of considerable influence. Some of these institutions date back to the eighteenth century, even before the Revolution, but the tradition of providing an élite of administrators was continued by Napoleon and his successors.

This was, in general terms, the system as it existed at the end of the Second World War. The most substantial reforms in higher education have been introduced since the establishment of the Fifth Republic, but some piecemeal changes brought in during the life of the Fourth have not been without influence. As indicated earlier, secondary and higher education was not thought to have covered itself with glory during the Second World War, as a result of the activities of many who had passed through the system. It was inevitable therefore that changes would be proposed, not only in relation to qualifications as such, but also to the training of teachers.

Among the innovations put forward by the Langevin–Wallon report was a year of study – *enseignement propédeutique ou préuniversitaire*, to be undertaken by all *bacheliers*. It was to have a dual role: preparation for further study, and also to provide the necessary help and guidance for school-leavers starting a career. Ideally, it should have taken place neither in the *lycées* nor in the *facultés*. A move in this direction, instituted before the publication of this report, provided for a *propédeutique* year in the *facultés*, which was to prepare the hopeful student for higher education, by providing suitable advice and guidance as to the type of studies to be undertaken, consolidating the knowledge already acquired, and introducing students to methods of study appropriate at university level. However, an examination at the end of the course acted as a hurdle allowing the successful student to prepare for the *licence*, but preventing the unsuccessful candidate (who was left with the *baccalauréat* as sole qualification) from pursuing further study.

It should also be borne in mind that, in the main, perhaps even more in literary studies than in others, the function of higher education had traditionally been to provide teachers. The term *licence* originally meant precisely that: a licence to teach. While the *agrégés* were auto-matically appointed to teaching posts in *lycées*, the *certifiés* — that is, teachers with a licence — were normally expected to teach in *collèges*, although they too could take up posts in a *lycée*. With the increase in numbers of pupils, more and more of the latter obtained *lycée* posts, and to ensure a maintenance of standards, a further qualification was required; from 1952 onwards, a competitive exam-ination gained for the successful candidate the *certificat d'aptitude à l'enseignement du second degré* (CAPES). This qualification, based on a competitive examination, may be said to typify in this respect much of higher education. The problem of numbers caused much of the system to seem more and more competitive. While every *bachelier* had the automatic right to a place in a *faculté* for the first year, the *propédeutique* examination was an obstacle in the path of further study. It could also be said with some justice, that while the preparation for certain *certificats* was not unduly onerous, the exam-ination in other disciplines was neither more nor less than a competition, allowing success to a fraction of the total candidates who had to pass in both written and oral. It was possible to resit the examination, but this was time-consuming, and made what might have been a two-year course last between three and five years. The problem was exacerbated by the fact that although student numbers were on the increase, staff numbers were not, and it was virtually impossible for teachers in higher education to give individual guidance and help, or indeed to do more than rely on the *cours magistral* (lecture), without any kind of back-up in the form of small-group teaching. Many students also were unable to work full-time at their studies, since they needed to earn money in order to make ends meet. Some were teaching part-time in schools which undoubtedly provided useful experience for a future career, but postponed the time when they would be fully qualified. It was not only the inefficiency of the system which was criticized, but also the relevance of the studies which were pursued. The country needed people with technological qualifications, but the branches of education providing these were much less popular than the letters and law faculties; yet job opportunities were less immediate in these areas.

These were, overall, the problems facing C. Fouchet, when he became education minister in 1962. We have already seen his en-deavours to increase the extent of the comprehensive principle at secondary level. This was to be crowned by a re-organization of the *baccalauréat*, which was to be divided up into five main sections. Although a *baccalauréat technique industriel* had existed since 1946 there would now be much less emphasis on literary studies, and a correspondingly greater one on science and technology. While Fouchet claimed that the aims of this reform were to preserve the role of secondary education as a provider of general culture, as well as to bring a more positive content to the concept of *orientation* by indicating precise possibilities to pupils in relation to their abilities, it provided one section for literary studies, one for social sciences, but two for science, and one for scientific and technical knowledge combined. This last provided for three *baccalauréats* of a more technical nature.

Another institution of higher education was established, the *institut universitaire de technologie* (IUT) to provide two-year courses for the training of highly qualified technicians: 'des cadres et techniciens supérieurs des activités industrielles et du secteur tertiaire, dont le rôle est de traduire dans le concret les conceptions abstraites ou les résultats des recherches théoriques. Ils doivent donc posséder une formation technique plus profonde et plus précise que celle des ingénieurs et, éventuellement, une vue générale des choses plus large que celle des simples techniciens' (Ministère de l'éducation nationale, *La Réforme de l'enseignement, août 1963–juin 1966*, Paris, n.d., p. 7). A qualification was obtained after the two-year course — the *diplôme universitaire de technologie* (DUT) — and instruction given not only by full-time teachers but also by people with practical experience in management.

The organization of the *baccalauréat* was further changed in that the examinations, instead of being staggered over two years, were in future to be taken at the end of the third year (*classes terminales*). However, the most important change was perhaps less in the *baccalauréat* itself than in the use which could be made of it. Traditionally the *baccalauréat* gave unrestricted entry into the *facultés*, according to the *bachelier*'s choice. Fouchet proposed to curtail this freedom by tying specific *baccalauréats* to specific university courses, and, by the same token, requiring prospective university candidates to make a firm decision as to their choice of discipline much earlier. This did not mean that it was wholly out of the question for a *bachelier* to consider pursuing a course to which his *baccalauréat* did not strictly entitle him; but in that case he would only be accepted by the *faculté* of his choice after consideration of his *dossier*, or after success in a special examination.

C. Fouchet also reorganized higher education, providing three cycles of study. Once the *bachelier* was duly admitted to a *faculté*, he would, instead of facing the *propédeutique* examination at the end of the first year, prepare for a qualification to be gained after a two-year course either in arts (*diplôme universitaire d'études littéraires* — DUEL), or in sciences (*diplôme universitaire d'études scientifiques* — DUES). Study for these diplomas was divided up into a number of sections, thought to be particularly appropriate for students preparing for a career in teaching. Once this initial qualification was obtained, the student could either seek employment or continue into the second cycle, in which one further year of study conferred the *licence* (still required as a qualification for teachers in secondary school), and two years further study after the DUEL or DUES led to the *maîtrise* (master's degree). The third cycle comprised the options of *agrégation* or *doctorat*.

The purpose behind the three-cycle system was to provide in the first cycle for the acquisition of basic knowledge, in the second for specialization, and in the third for research, or, in other words, to separate teaching from research work. Hitherto it had been possible to pass from teaching in secondary school to teaching and research in a *faculté*, but with the new system and the new qualification of the *maîtrise*, this flexibility would be less feasible, with secondary school teaching provided for by the *licence* and CAPES and higher education provided for by *maîtrise, agrégation* and *doctorat*. Such a change was welcome to scientists, but less so to teachers in the arts faculties.

A further criticism levelled at the reforms was that, although no selection existed in theory, in reality the creation of the IUT could well attract only the weaker *bacheliers*. The question of selection was, and still is, of vital importance. In Britain selection of university entrants, by a variety of means, is in the main accepted, if not wholly approved. Since for many years any *bachelier* had an automatic right to a place in a *faculté*, any curtailing of that right was inevitably viewed as a retrograde and reactionary step, contrary to the democratization of education. Unfortunately, the absence of selection at entry operated much more brutally, by failure, at the end of the first year. Fouchet's first cycle, DUEL and DUES, was an attempt to deal with that difficulty; but no attempt was made to deal with the underlying problem of a lack of selection, aggravated by the ever-increasing student numbers. At the *colloque de Caen* of 1966 one notable partisan of selection, M. Zamansky, then dean of the Paris science faculty, proposed a solution; namely to turn the *baccalauréat* into a genuine qualification of secondary education, which the large majority of pupils would obtain. Only then would any selection operate, not on the basis of failure, but on a positive approach to individual abilities. 'Au système actuel: vous êtes bon à ceci ou vous n'êtes bon à rien; il faut substituer le système, vous êtes bon à quelque chose et voici à quoi' (M. Zamansky in *colloque de Caen*). However, Fouchet had not felt it possible to adopt such a radical approach. It has been suggested that all the education reforms introduced by Fouchet were directly inspired by de Gaulle; yet in the matter of selection, the latter's influence did not prevail.[44]

These reforms were undoubtedly important, and attempted to provide for the French economy the greater number of scientific and technological experts which it needed for expansion. Yet the problem of numbers was not dealt with, save by the hasty construction of extra universities and overspill annexes, such as Nanterre, which within a few years were themselves overcrowded. The problems created by overcrowding were therefore permanent, and provided one of the causes of the dissatisfaction leading to the events of May 1968.

If the May events achieved no more, they forced the government to face up to the question of higher education and the radical views expressed as to the purpose of higher education, which could no longer be regarded either as the privileged domain of the upper classes, or as a high powered sausage-machine, geared to produce an appropriate number of managers, administrators, scientists, etc. as required by the state, the economy or the consumer society. Consequently other criteria had to be established with the participation of all those involved in higher education, whether as teachers, students or in some other capacity.

This was the task allotted to Edgar Faure in June 1968 – to produce a reform which would take into account the many views which had been expressed. His initial move was to intensify the arrangements made by his predecessor, F. Ortoli, by the use of *chargés de mission* to provide him with information, in co-operation with the *recteurs*, since many universities and faculties had produced proposals for reform.

His speech to the *assemblée nationale* of 24 July 1968 gave a clear enough indication of his reforming intentions. Society was in a state of constant change, and higher education had to keep pace with it, which it had hitherto signally failed to do. The old-style *université*, Napoleon's creation, was out-dated and all traces of it should be eradicated, whether in legislation, teaching methods, or relations between teachers, students and administration, whether central or local. One essential goal to aim for was (yet again) democratization of education from nursery school to university, whilst at the same time maintaining high cultural standards. In this context there would have to be, as well as financial assistance to poorer families, changes in the curriculum, in order that there should no longer be an in-built advantage to the culturally privileged classes.

To avoid the feeling of alienation experienced by many students at university, numbers should not be excessive. 'Les universités nouvelles doivent avoir une personnalité. Chacune d'elles . . . doit être à l'échelle humaine, c'est-à-dire accueillir dix mille ou douze mille étudiants.'[45] A limit of student numbers was also laid down for certain types of classes: small groups – 25 maximum; *travaux pratiques* (seminars) – 40 maximum; and no more than 250 students at the formal lecture.

With these very specific indications about suitable numbers in classes and in the ideal university it might have been expected that Faure would have embraced selection as a solution to the problem of student numbers. Yet a decision was taken not to adopt a selective system, the reasons being that the right of *bacheliers* to enter the faculties had been long accepted, and that any selective system should not be adopted hastily, merely to deal with an immediate problem of numbers; on the contrary, it should be weighed up, and if introduced thereafter, very carefully organized. These reasons were doubtless important, but there was one other far more powerful:[46]

Le droit est toujours, surtout dans une société aussi juridique que la nôtre, la traduction des situations de fait, mais d'un ensemble de dispositions d'esprit et d'habitudes mentales. C'est une donnée de la psychologie française universitaire que, à la différence des grandes écoles, recrutées par concours, les facultés sont ouvertes sur présentation du baccalauréat. Et la méconnaissance dans ces conditions, d'ailleurs bien délicates, à la fois de la règle du droit et de l'habitude de l'esprit ne pourrait manquer d'entraîner des réactions psychologiques tres inquiétantes.

This indicates clearly enough that student reaction to selection was feared, and with some reason, since the proposal to introduce it had been made in April 1968, and had not been well received. No one in the government wished to see a recrudescence of the events of May, and, whatever else was to be reformed, the open-door policy could not be touched. In other words, Faure's task was to produce a law which would assist in the shoring-up of a régime which had come near to collapse, by radically reforming higher education and consequently obtaining support from those who felt reforms to be essential.[47] Concessions already made, whatever troubles they might have caused, would not be rescinded.

Some of the most important changes would have to come in the administration of education, so much criticized during May 1968 for its excessive centralization. To bring about these changes, Faure proposed, in general, the remedy of *participation* to all levels and in varying ways, in new units of higher education, with a wider range of subjects (*pluri-disciplinarité*) than that encompassed by the out-dated *faculté*.

After a summer of consultations with all interested parties (except the extreme right and the *groupuscules* of the extreme left), the law came before the *assemblée nationale* in September 1968, and was passed by it on 11 October and by the *sénat* a fortnight later.

The *Loi d'Orientation* provided for a complete structural reorganization of higher education, with the abolition of *facultés* and the introduction of the *unité d'enseignement et de recherche* (UER) as the basic unit of the *université*. The UER is governed by an elected council, and a director elected thereby for three years. In the same way the council of the *université* is elected, and in turn, elects the president for five years. In each case the councils comprise not only teachers, researchers and students, but also non-teaching staff and people from outside the academic world. In mixed councils, the proportion of teachers' representatives was to be at least equal to that of the students. Student representation was to be related to the number of voters. If the latter fell to less than 60 per cent of the total registered, then the number of representatives would be proportionately reduced.

The principle of autonomy was also not wholly neglected. While it was stated that the state provides finance for the *université*, the latter also may enjoy the use of other resources, i.e. donations, bequests, etc. The *université* votes on its budget, which, says the law, must balance. The organization of teaching and research, again, is a matter for each *université*, as is the assessment of students' work, by examination or continuous assessment. Yet in this area of what is called *autonomie pédagogique*, the awarding of degrees is still the prerogative of the ministry of education, for although qualifications from specific establishments do exist, they lack the standing of the nationally recognized degree or diploma. It also became clear, once university institutions began to attempt their reorganization in the light of the *Loi d'Orientation*, that there was only one acceptable interpretation – that of the minister. Furthermore, one crucial element of the centralized system – namely the administration – in no wise came within the competence of the law, so that while the new universities were re-organized on a supposedly decentralized and participatory basis, the administrative framework remained essentially as before.

The concepts of participation and autonomy thus may be seen as less generous in scope than they seem at first glance. Centralization, or, at least, bureaucracy, could be suggested as being greater than before. The *Loi d'Orientation* provided for a *Conseil national de l'enseignement supérieur et de la recherche* (CNESR), to replace the previous CNES. This is presided over by the minister and has a total of ninety members, fifty-four elected university members including students, six from other establishments of higher education, and thirty representing national interests, i.e. politicians, union members, etc. It meets at least twice a year, but maintains a *section permanente*, whose members are elected by the whole council and a *commission scientifique permanente*, with the task of examining university research programmes, and teaching at the *troisième cycle* and *doctorat* level. The task of the CNESR seems to be essentially consultative; it is involved in the planning of higher education and research, in relation to the National Plan; it gives opinions as to university curricula, requests for credit, and the apportioning of budget resources, on national diplomas, and on decisions by an *recteur* to suspend the proceedings of the universities' councils within his *académie*. On a local level, regional councils have been set up, composed of elected representatives from universities and other institutions within the region, as well as representatives of regional activities. The task of these councils is to co-ordinate higher education and research in the region and, again, they have a consultative role on curricula and requests for credits from universities.

Doubtless this seems like an effort towards decentralization, but of a very cumbersome kind. 'Such an elaborate apparatus appears to be a heavy price to pay for participation',[48] particularly when the power to act, as opposed to the possibility of being consulted, seems so limited.

One further institution must be added to the list of bodies to which the *Loi d'Orientation* has, as it were, acted as midwife — namely the *conférence des présidents*, which was formally created by the decree of 24 February 1971. When the new universities came into being with their elected presidents, the need was felt to form a body on which every university would have a representative (which is not the case in the CNESR). During 1970 regular meetings were held. This body has, like the others, a consultative role, giving its opinion on matters submitted to it by the minister; yet it also has the right to study questions of interest to the universities and to put proposals and plans to the minister. With its regular meetings it is a powerful body wielding considerable influence.

The *conférence* could be viewed as the representative of active participation at the centre, and in general it could be asserted that a larger number of university teachers have a greater say in decisions which are taken. Participation, however, may be seen as very much less successful among students. This is most clearly evinced by the proportion of those who take the trouble to vote for student representatives on UER and university councils. Initially the quorum required was 60 per cent, which in July 1975 was reduced to 50. In general it can be said that student representation has never reached the requirement; just over half used their vote in 1969, and the proportion has not risen much above a quarter over the last few years. There are several reasons for this: many left-wing groups take the view that there should be no quorum and have as a rule boycotted the elections since these do not provide students with adequate participation. One other reason could simply be a lack of interest, of willingness to spend the necessary time on matters of this kind. While students might feel that the participation accorded to them was insufficient, they had gained a related right, namely to hold political meetings and to carry out political activity on university premises.

This change was probably less welcome to the university authorities who in the persons of the university president and the UER director, have the responsibility of keeping order, and the task of applying disciplinary sanctions where necessary. Since 1968, the problem of disorder has become a serious one, impinging to a considerable extent on the work of the universities. The disorder provoked by the ministerial decision of January 1976 on the second cycle of higher education led in a number of universities to a good deal of violence and to prolonged strikes which caused substantial reductions in the syllabus with a corresponding reduction of assessment and examination, which can have done little to raise the prestige of qualifications, when acquired under such conditions.

The university presidents were blamed for either their complicity or for their weakness, in their unwillingness to act firmly against violence. Yet while the presidents united in a body may appear to be powerful enough, it must be remembered that they are, when all is said and done, elected under highly political circumstances, and with clearly defined political allegiances. Violent acts may be deplored, but to repress them could be thought at times even more dangerous than the violence itself. Such a climate of opinion may make of university life at best a precarious and temporary activity – at worst a shambles. Yet whatever the motivation, political or other, behind a course of action (or lack of it) adopted by a university president, there can be little doubt of the fragility of the system and structures which the *Loi d'Orientation* called into being, inasmuch as they appear to have all the disadvantages of a participatory system which is considered too liberal by some, with too many opportunities for malpractice, and too limited by others and which clearly forces numbers of people to expend their energy for little return.

E. Faure, in office for scarcely a year, had little time to devote to other aspects of higher education. Subsequent ministers have not done away with the provisions of the *Loi d'Orientation*, although these may not have been interpreted as widely as he would have wished. The two most important changes introduced since 1968 have been:
(1) the replacement of the DUEL and the DUES, and
(2) the reform of the second cycle.

In 1973 J. Fontanet, then minister of education, changed the first cycle of university studies by introducing, in place of Fouchet's DUEL and DUES, the *diplôme d'études universitaires générales*, for law, economics, economics and social administration, social sciences, letters and science, each discipline consisting of a number of sections. The courses were to be multi-disciplinary – the principle subject to be studied for 60 per cent of the course, and the other 40 per cent to be devoted to optional work. The qualification would be awarded partly on assessment of work, and partly on the result of examinations and would lead either to employment or to further study. The reasons behind this change were twofold: to deal with the problems created by the existing system, over-specialization, and also wastage, with a good half of the students failing and leaving university without a qualification.

It was also thought that the DEUG would indicate the attainment of a reputable standard which would be acceptable to employers. Neither of these hopes have as yet been wholly realized. The percentage of failure is still very high — in some disciplines, 50 per cent, in others more than this (see for details G. Herzlich, 'Les chances de succès dans chaque discipline', *Le Monde de l'éducation*, June 1978). Also the continual difficulties of graduates in obtaining suitable employment have meant that higher qualifications are demanded than would have been the case five years ago. The basic DEUG therefore is insufficient, and in many cases the DUT is more immediately attractive to the prospective employer. The second major change since the *Loi d'Orientation* was even more controversial, the so-called *arrêté Soisson* of 16 January 1976, validated in June 1977 and signed in fact by J.-P. Soisson's successor, Mme Alice Saunier-Seïté, the second occupant of the autonomous *secrétariat d'état aux universités*, since raised to a full ministry. This measure dealt with the *licence* and *maîtrise*, to take one year each after the DEUG. In general the second cycle was to provide 'une formation scientifique de haut niveau qui prépare les étudiants à la vie active et à l'exercice de responsabilités profession-nelles' (Arrêté 16 January 1976, article 1). The various types of *licence* and *maîtrise* would be authorized as national diplomas by the secretary of state, after the consideration of detailed proposals by the various universities, by the *groupes d'étude technique* consisting not only of academics but also people from other professions. The idea behind this was to prevail upon universities to provide high-level courses with a bearing upon subsequent employment, that is, of a more technological nature. It seems hard to believe that there would have been any opposition to this, had it not been for the fact that as in theory all *licences* and *maîtrises* had to go before the *groupes d'étude* (which would inevitably have a bias towards the more vocational and less purely academic course), those teaching the more traditional courses felt their positions threatened if their second-cycle syllabus were not approved. Saunier–Seïté not only had to face opposition on the part of students but also that of the university presidents. In due course, concessions were made, in the sense that the *groupes d'étude technique* lost a good deal of its power, which the CNESR and the president's conference gained.

The opposition of the university presidents may not seem wholly surprising in view of the vested interests which required protection, in the shape of traditional courses of study, and also in view of some clashes of personality. The student position is, historically, possibly less consistent, particularly if we relate this problem to some of the ideas of May 1968. It will be remembered that one of the criticisms levelled by students at French higher education was that of the irrelevance of what was taught, since in many cases the qualifications gained led to teaching, and little else besides. While such a view might not commend itself to those who feel that a country's (or a civilization's) cultural heritage ought to be protected, cherished, and passed on from one generation to another, the unemployed graduate could not as a rule take such an elevated stand on the issue. It might therefore have been supposed that changes along these lines would have met with some approval; instead they met with hostility, violence and prolonged strikes. That being said, it should be borne in mind that eight years had passed since May 1968, the students were consequently of another generation. Equally, the views expressed then had not been quite consistent since, while on the one hand higher education had been criticized for turning out unemployable graduates, it was also criticized for its tendency to assist in the maintenance of a capitalist, consumer society, by training the leaders and managers for it.

It is perhaps this latter point that caused such a strong reaction amongst students, and only time will tell whether or not this innovation, which in its drive towards technology, may be likened to the Fouchet reforms, will have any long-term success.

Any student entering upon higher education at this point in time would begin with the first cycle, the two-year DEUG. If successful, he could then continue his studies into the second cycle, with the *licence* and *maîtrise* as a rule for those intending to enter the teaching profession. However, with the advent of the *arrêté Soisson*, he would also have the possibility of studying for more vocational *maîtrises*, in three categories: (a) *maîtrise de sciences et techniques* (MST), (b) *maîtrise d'informatique appliquée à la gestion* (MIAGE), or (c) *maîtrise de sciences de gestion* (MSG). On completion of the *maîtrise* he could enter the third cycle, where three possibilities present themselves: either to prepare for a *diplôme d'études supérieures spécialisées* (DESS), which, lasting only for a year, would prepare for some form of employment, with, as part of the training, vocational experience. If on the other hand our graduate was of more academic persuasions, he could prepare for a *doctorat de troisième cycle* (roughly M.Phil.), a three-year course at most, with a qualification at the end of the first year — the *diplôme d'études approfondies* — with initiation into research work and, as necessary, laboratory experience. The final stage is still the *doctorat d'état*, no longer of limitless duration, but to be completed in five years, unless any extension is granted. This qualification by thesis is still the most prestigious of the purely academic qualifications.

One endeavour which may be seen in ministers of education from Fouchet onwards was the endeavour to redress the balance, and arrive at a larger proportion of students preparing for science and technology qualifications. If we look at the figures of degrees awarded in 1976, at the level of the DEUG, it can be seen that the greatest number still come from arts and social sciences (14,715) as opposed to, for example, law (8,718) or science (7,475); although this in itself represents a certain stabilizing of the numbers qualifying on the arts side. The same picture is to be found at the *licence* level: law, 7,610; science, 6,746; arts and social sciences, 18,764. Clearly, the literary imbalance is far from being seriously corrected. This situation could stem from two factors, one that arts subjects, possibly easier, or considered so, attracted members of the poorer classes who had had more of a struggle to enter higher education, or that the prejudice in favour of literary studies has not yet died, and that another generation of school teachers may have to pass before a change in attitude comes about.

As already indicated, in spite of the numbers obtaining the DEUG, there are many students who fail to obtain it even after the second attempt. Yet the competitive element, solidly entrenched even in the newer qualifications of higher education, is even more savage in the competitive examinations for the *agrégation* and the CAPES. For the former, in 1977, 23,900 people competed for 1,600 posts and overall 1,481 persons were successful; for the latter, over 44,000 registered for the examination, with about one thousand posts available. However, the starkest competition is that which obtains the *classes préparatoires*, and the entrance examination into one of the *grandes écoles*. Only those with excellent results at the *baccalauréat* are admitted to these classes, with prepare for three categories: (a) scientific establishments such as the *école des mines* or *polytechnique*, (b) literary, essentially the *écoles normales supérieures*, such as Sèvres or Saint-Cloud, or the *école des chartes*; (c) commercial, the most prestigious being the *hautes études commerciales*. The newest addition to these is the *école nationale d'administration*, founded in 1945. In this case only, the *classes préparatoires* take place, not as for the others, in the fifty most important *lycées* in Paris and the provinces, but at the *institut d'études politiques*, and many graduates from other *grandes écoles* proceed from there to ENA.

Even those candidates who fail to enter a *grande école* after the *classes préparatoires* invariably benefit when they enter the universities, from the training received there. While the standard achieved in the *grandes écoles* is exceedingly high, and those who come out at the top of the examination list at the end of the course have a choice to enter directly into, for example, the *inspectorat de finances* (as often happens with graduates of ENA), nevertheless the system 'creams off' the best brains and guides them away from the universities and a possible career in research, and into what are extremely high-powered vocational courses. This means that, however democratic the rest of the system may become, the process will never be complete while the *grandes écoles* maintain their system of selection and, it must be admitted, their high standard, and while they keep themselves totally separate from the rest of higher education. They still may be said to fulfil the role for which they were created, to supply the state with its leaders, both political and administrative, with results at once beneficial perhaps to the planning of the economy, but also harmful to the democratic process.

The universities thus at present are in an ambiguous position, since they have to accept those whom the *grandes écoles* reject, and may make no selection other than that permitted by the differentiated *baccalauréats*. The increase of numbers in general has brought about a considerable expansion in the numbers and categories of teachers, which gives rise to great insecurity for those who are not *titularisés* (i.e. do not have tenure). A further problem arising from the question of numbers is inevitably that of finance, in a period of inflation. The difficulty relates in part to the way in which the budget is organized: the *budget de fonctionnement et de recherche*, running from January to December, and the *budget pédadogique*, which covers the academic year from October to June. It must also be admitted that those who have, as it were, grown up under a régime of tight administrative control, are not perhaps the best suited to cope with such complexities in a budget, which must always balance and which the state verifies after the event. In recent years, it is no secret that some universities have been on the verge of bankruptcy. The fact is also that some of the Parisian universities are housed in several buildings, with a resultant doubling or trebling of expenses. At the moment, the Parisian universities manage to gain a greater proportion of the funds available (40 per cent) with 33 per cent of the total student population.

While selection would present a solution to the problems of wastage and possible insolvency, it is not formally envisaged, yet it undoubtedly exists, taking two main forms: (a) the type of *baccalauréat* obtained, category C (mainly scientific) being the one which, overall, is most advantageous for future success in higher education, and (b) the system adopted recently in the Paris area to restrict the number of applicants, whereby Paris universities may only take in the same number as they were allowed in the previous year. The result, in 1977 and 1978, was what was caustically, but aptly, named 'la selection par le sprint', in other words — first come, first served. This is the ultimate absurdity: the government, rather than face up to what is a political taboo, obliges Parisian universities to take the first applicants who present themselves, regardless of suitability, and provincial universities to operate the 'open-door' system. There are exceptions to this, such as medicine, but in the main selection is not formally permitted. One Parisian university, Paris VIII — Vincennes, accepts candidates who do not have the *baccalauréat*, but who are at least twenty years old, having been in employment and paid social security for two years at least. If the candidate is over twenty-four, no conditions obtain. The idea behind Vincennes, a creation of E. Faure, was to make higher education more available to the working classes, who are still under-privileged in this respect (see Table 6.5), with liberal professions and higher management still taking the lion's share of university places. Vincennes has always been controversial, for its politics, its qualifications, and its life-style. Over the last few years the press has abounded with allegations of open drug-pushing and addiction, a situation highly displeasing to Mme Saunier-Seïté, who had other reasons for deploring the Vincennes approach. Part of the problem lies in the fact that the numbers are too great, but in spite of instructions from the minister as to the numbers in general and the proportion of foreigners admitted, the situation remains the same. Mme Saunier-Seïté's plans for Vincennes are undoubtedly drastic: its removal to a suburban site; the reduction of its numbers from 32,000 to 15,000; the abolition of its experimental nature, and its conversion into a university like any other. While such plans may be viewed as draconian, questions must also be asked about the validity of certain of its qualifications. The problem is not whether the means used by the teaching staff at Vincennes to assess student ability and competence are adequate, but whether or not the qualifications awarded are acceptable to the world at large. If they are, then the problem is solved, and national diplomas from Vincennes or elsewhere have equal value. If, however, this is not the case, and the view appears to be widely held, particularly in academic circles, that it is not, then, however idealistic and generous the concept, Vincennes is not providing the unqualified worker with what he should expect to gain, namely a qualification of an adequate standard, which will allow him to make the social and financial advance to which his abilities entitle him.

In conclusion it must be said that in spite of some serious attempts to cope with the problems of numbers without imposing selection and to introduce a more democratic system, much more needs to be done if this is to be accomplished; but also some time must elapse before the effects of the last ten years are to be observed.

As a general conclusion to this chapter, it is perhaps worth accentuating again the paradoxical admixture of old and new, of reform and tradition, which is very clearly to be seen in matters of controversy, rooted in the past but with shifts of emphasis (as in the case of Catholic education), which make them into exceedingly contemporary matters. The influence of tradition is equally to be observed in the administrative system, which, although in some ways encumbered by superimposed structures, still pursues its task of the organization of education in as much detail and as much uniformity as is possible.

Under these circumstances it is perhaps vain even to suggest that participation, autonomy, decentralization, and genuine equality of

Table 6.5   University students according to CSP of parents, 1975–6 (percentages)

	Law	Economics	Arts	Sciences	Medicine	Pharmacy	Dentistry	Combined courses	Polytechnic (IUT)	Total or average
Percentage of students per discipline										
Agriculteur exploitant	15.6	7.0	26.2	19.4	12.0	5.5	0.7	2.2	11.4	100
Salarié agricole	15.9	5.3	37.3	16.1	9.1	3.1	0.8	2.1	10.3	100
Patron de l'industrie et du commerce	16.2	7.1	30.0	13.2	18.6	5.1	1.8	2.0	6.0	100
Profession libérale, cadre supérieur	15.5	6.3	26.6	13.2	26.8	5.4	2.1	1.5	2.6	100
Cadre moyen	15.2	6.4	31.8	17.0	16.9	3.6	1.2	2.3	5.6	100
Employé	17.1	6.1	33.0	15.6	14.7	3.5	1.2	2.4	6.4	100
Ouvrier	14.7	5.7	35.5	17.1	10.5	2.0	0.7	2.5	11.4	100
Personnel de service	20.6	7.5	33.2	13.6	9.7	2.0	0.4	2.5	10.5	100
Ensemble	**15.9**	**6.4**	**30.9**	**14.9**	**18.6**	**4.0**	**1.5**	**2.1**	**5.7**	**100**
Percentage of students in relation to total student-age population										
Agriculteur exploitant	5.0	5.6	4.3	6.7	3.3	7.0	2.6	5.5	10.2	5.1
Salarié agricole	0.4	0.4	0.5	0.5	0.2	0.3	0.2	0.4	0.8	0.4
Patron de l'industrie et du commerce	10.5	11.6	10.1	9.2	10.4	13.2	12.5	10.0	10.8	10.4
Profession libérale, cadre supérieur	29.6	29.9	26.1	26.8	43.7	40.5	42.7	22.4	13.6	30.3
Cadre moyen	14.8	15.5	15.9	17.7	14.1	13.8	12.8	17.1	15.1	15.5
Employé	9.1	8.1	9.1	8.8	6.7	7.4	6.9	10.0	9.6	8.5
Ouvrier	10.4	10.0	13.0	13.0	6.4	5.7	5.1	13.5	22.6	11.3
Personnel de service	1.0	0.9	0.8	0.7	0.4	0.4	0.2	0.9	1.5	0.8
Autres catégories	19.2	18.0	20.2	16.6	14.8	11.7	17.0	20.2	15.8	17.7

Source: INSEE, *Données sociales, 1978.*

opportunity exist in any degree. Nevertheless, the moves made towards these first three goals by Faure, however superficial they may seem, represent an attempt to alter an entire age-old historical tendency. It has indeed been suggested that decentralization and autonomy already existed in that the *recteur* was in many ways an autonomous official, even in matters of finance, and that the *recteur*'s approval was necessary for any appointment made by the minister in the former's *académie*.

Yet this could not in any sense be regarded as participation, which is evidently a difficult ideal to realize, particularly in view of the polarization of French society. Whereas education and politics are now recognized as being more closely linked than was once thought, the problem of politicization is another matter altogether, not only because of the violence which it can engender, but also because of the impossibility of any kind of compromise consensus being arrived at, and consequently French society is not a society without values, but one where one group may have values antagonistic to those of others.

This means that when the question of the teaching of values is discussed, in relation to education, there is uncertainty as to what should be taught. A code of conduct which, for example, respects the right of others to own property, would be viewed by some as a form of indoctrination imposed by the dominant class on those classes it was exploiting, whereas by others it would be viewed as a form of decency which all children, regardless of religious beliefs, should learn.

When education was in the hands of the church and when, in the main, the values of the church were widely held, it was accepted that these would have their place in education. Even when the church's dominance was removed, it was still accepted by nineteenth-century legislators that some form of moral instruction should be taught. If we look at Jules Ferry's classic circular of 17 November 1883 on the subject of moral and civic instruction, there is no doubt at all as to the confidence with which he describes that which is to be taught:

> ces règles élémentaires de la vie morale qui ne sont pas moins universellement acceptées que celles du langage et du calcul . . . cette bonne et antique morale que nous avons reçue de nos pères . . . une de ces idées d'ordre universel que plusieurs siècles de civilisation ont fait entrer dans le patrimonie de l'humanité (J. Ferry, *Discours et opinions*, Paris, Colin, 1893-8, vol. IV, pp. 261-2).

This confidence is no longer to be found and, on a code of morality, modern society would have no more than a consensus of uncertainty. It may still be possible to reproduce a form of culture and of class dominance, but the teaching of a code of morality no longer forms a part of it. Moral and civic instruction has given way to an instruction which is purely civic, dealing with subjects such as the *commune*, the *département*, etc. Yet the primary teachers' handbook expresses itself in language which is almost Victorian in its decorum.

> L'éducateur être irréprochable, dans sa tenue et dans sa conduite privée. Insister sur ce point serait, semble-t-il, superflu . . . il ne peut oublier un seul instant . . . qu'il est impossible que toute sa vie privée ne soit pas l'illustration de la leçon de morale ou de civisme qu'il donne à l'école . . . L'institutrice, surtout, aura à se surveiller . . . elle ne saurait . . . se prêter à des fréquentations douteuses. (*Code Soleil* (48th ed.), pp. 23-4)

This in itself shows the difficulty which French society is facing, since, while such views would seem entirely appropriate in the nineteenth century, they are less obviously appropriate in the latter half of the twentieth century, however regrettable this may be. Yet until these questions are answered, an important element — the educating of *citizens* — will be a significant omission from the curriculum, and this problem may not be resolved until a consensus on the nature of French society has finally been arrived at.

Notes

Chapter 1

1 Marshall Aid was in effect money transferred by the US government to west European governments, so as to finance the recovery of the western European economies after the war. As such it also served to check the spread of communist and socialist influence in that area.

2 M. Parodi, *L'Economie et la société française de 1945 à 1970*, p. 149.

3 G. Wright, *Rural Revolution in France*, Stanford University Press, 1964, p. 115.

4 The whole episode of collaboration/resistance is equivocal and complex. Many collaborators were executed at the liberation – thirty to forty thousand, according to Robert Aron (*Histoire de la libération*, Fayard, 1959, p. 655). Many others were imprisoned or barred from public life for several years. Some of these were, however, almost certainly innocent; and on the other side of the coin, many whose responsibilities in the crimes of the occupation were undoubtedly great escaped with impunity, sometimes without even having to leave France. As regards the resistance, while the bravery and fortitude of many thousands of authentic resisters is well documented, it is also true that many people only joined in by 1943 or later, when it was fairly clear who was going to win the war and equally plain that a good resistance record would be vital as a passport to success in politics or any other field, once hostilities were over. As can be imagined, this whole episode aroused strong passions and indeed continues to do so – logically enough, given that many of the resistance generation still occupy important positions in French society. No study of life in postwar France can ignore the long-term effects of this phenomenon.

5 Laos and Cambodia were 'associated states', not colonies, which would make it slightly easier for the French to concede independence in 1953. Today's Vietnam was divided into three: Tonkin in the north and Cochin–China in the south were colonies, and Annam was a protectorate.

6 The best overall description and analysis of French politics in this period is P. Viansson-Ponté, *Histoire de la république gaullienne*, 2 vols, 1970, 1971.

7 A good analysis of the politics of the Algerian crisis is D. Pickles, *Algeria and France*, pp. 60–120; for texts of policy statements and

documents relating to the Algerian crisis, see the relevant annual
volumes of *L'Année politique*, Paris, PUF.

8   A good account of election and referendum campaigns and their
results is in P.M. Williams, *French Politicians and Elections, 1951–
69*, pp. 94–225; details of all referendum and election campaigns
and results are in relevant annual volumes of *L'Année politique*.

9   A good description and analysis of French foreign and defence
policies under de Gaulle is in G. de Carmoy, *Les Politiques étrangères de la France, 1944–67*, Paris, La Table Ronde, 1967, pp. 251–
503. The English translation, *The Foreign Policies of France, 1944–
68*, Chicago University Press, 1970, has the one distinct advantage
that it takes the study up to 1968; texts of treaties, policy statements and press conferences referred to in this section on foreign
affairs can be found in the relevant annual volumes of *L'Année
politique*.

10   A good account of economic affairs in this period is in Parodi, op.
cit., pp. 52–78; another brief but perceptive analysis is in J. Sheahan,
An Introduction to the French Economy, Columbus, Merrill, 1969.

11   For a description of its inadequacies, see P. Seale and M. McConville,
French Revolution, 1968, pp. 25–6.

12   A. Touraine, *Le Mouvement de mai ou le communisme utopique*,
p. 103.

13   Daniel Cohn-Bendit is reported as having castigated the minister
over his unwillingness to consider the sexual problems of young
people. Missoffe's answer was to advise a cold dip in the swimming-
pool. 'C'est une réponse fasciste' was the student reaction. This
exchange of amenities made him a 'personality' on the campus.

14   In many accounts of the May events, it is stated that six students
from Nanterre were required to appear before the disciplinary
council. However the fullest and most authoritative account,
L. Rioux and R. Backmann, *L'Explosion de mai*, points out em-
phatically that eight students and not six were convoked (see p. 91
and p. 94 n.).

15   B.E. Brown suggests that the student revolutionaries had agreed to
have their papers checked at the local police stations and were
taken away in police vans for that purpose. The bystanders outside
the Sorbonne, unaware of this agreement, assumed that the students
were being arrested, and the violence began as a result of the
apparent provocation (see B.E. Brown, *Protest in Paris: the Anatomy
of a Revolt*, p. 9). The then *préfet de police*, M. Grimaud, has
stated that this verification of identity at police stations was
common police practice (and presumably no one ought to have
been surprised by it). See M. Grimaud, *En Mai, fais ce qu'il te plaît*,
pp. 15 and 18.

16   On the question of police violence, see the letter from Maurice
Grimaud sent to all members of the police force, dated 29 May
1968, in P. Labro *et al.*, *Mai–juin '68: ce n'est qu'un début*. See
also Grimaud, op.cit., pp. 200–2, and letters to the editor of
Le Monde, 7 and 9 May 1968. On the state of mind of the police

during the events of May, see Rioux and Backmann, op.cit., pp. 371–2.
17 See A. Kastler's account in Labro *et al.*, pp. 80–4.
18 Op.cit., p. 156.
19 There also had to be some negotiations with the police, against whom the demonstration was being held. For example, M. Grimaud, in discussions with M. Herzberg, representative of SNESup, prevailed upon the organizers not to have the demonstration pass in front of the Hôtel de Ville, which has always been the traditional goal in every French revolution. Curiously enough, the police were also asked if loud-hailers and the like could be provided for the *service d'ordre*. See Grimaud, op.cit., p. 181.
20 Seale and McConville, op.cit., p. 106.
21 The number of workers on strike during May and June 1968 is difficult to assess. According to J. Gretton, *Students and Workers*, p. 181, the accepted figure is ten million out of a total working population of fourteen million. However, a more likely figure appears to be around six or seven and a half million at the most. See G. Adam, 'Etude statistique des grèves de mai–juin 1968' *Revue française de science politique*, vol. 20, no. 1, February 1970.
22 Gretton (op.cit., p. 194) suggests that not only was the rally at the Charléty stadium much less significant politically than was thought at the time, but also that the presence of Mendès-France made it seem as if the rally was to be used to make political propaganda for him and his party. An expression of this view – a resentful one – can be found in D. Bensaid and H. Weber, *Mai 1968: une répétition générale*, p. 184, where it is further stated that Mendès-France's reception was in fact a very modest one.
23 Figures taken from A. Prost, *L'Enseignement en France, 1800–1967*, Paris, Colin, 1968, p. 461, and *L'Education nationale en chiffres*, Paris, Institut Pédagogique National, 1969, p. 29.
24 Figures taken from D. Singer, *Prelude to Revolution*, p. 52.
25 E. Cahm, *Politics and Society in Contemporary France, 1789–1971*, p. 460.
26 Op.cit., pp. 105–7.
27 See R. Aron, *La Révolution introuvable*.
28 P. Crisol and Y. Lhomeau, *La Machine RPR*, Paris, Intervalle Fayolle, 1978, p. 43.

Chapter 2

1 The best historical introduction to the French economy is T. Kemp, *Economic Forces in French History*.
2 *Nouvel Observateur, Faits et Chiffres, 1977*, Paris, 1978, p. 12.
3 C.P. Kindleberger, 'The French Economy' in S. Hoffmann (ed.), *In Search of France*, pp. 118–59.
4 R.O. Paxton, *Vichy France: Old Guard and New Order*, Barrie & Jenkins, 1972, pp. 330–52.

5 M. Parodi, *L'Economie et la société française de 1945 à 1970*, Colin, 1971, pp. 41 ff.
6 The PME are firms employing from 6 to 249 employees (in commerce) or 6 to 499 employees (in industry). Firms with 5 employees or fewer are usually counted as artisanal — see below.
7 *Fortune*, August 1977, pp. 226 ff.
8 In December 1977 Giscard d'Estaing announced his objective of a 20 milliard franc surplus for agriculture within France's balance of payments. At the same time he spoke of the 'modernization' necessary to achieve such a result. It is hard to imagine the small farmer fitting readily into such a grand design (*Le Monde*, 18–19 December 1977).
9 INSEE, *Les Agriculteurs: clés pour une comparaison sociale*, Paris, 1977, p. 82.
10 Value added is the base of the VAT. It is equivalent to the difference in price between the costs that have gone into the making of a product or service and the sales price of the latter. The GDP of a country could thus be said to be the sum of the value added by the work of its population.
11 The half million artisans in France are of course direct producers of commodities, but own their means of production; hence they cannot be considered as part of the working class. Their class-situation is closest to that of the small independent peasantry.
12 A medium-sized firm, it will be recalled, employs up to 500 workers.
13 F. Morin, *La Structure financière du capitalisme français*, Paris, Calmann-Lévy, 1974, pp. 92–3.
14 A girl in a typing pool or on a supermarket checkout, for instance, performs a very arduous kind of manual labour. But would either necessarily see herself as part of a 'proletariat' or working class?
15 These figures apply to male workers only.
16 G. Mathieu, in *L'Année économique et sociale: 1977, la langueur*, Paris, *Le Monde*, 'Dossiers et documents', 1978, p. 120.
17 A. Vernholes, *Le Monde*, 11 December 1972.
18 Mathieu, op.cit., p. 125.
19 F. Parkin, *Class, Inequality and Political Order*, London, Granada, 1972, p. 56.
20 X. Debonneuil and M. Gollac, 'Structure sociale des villes', *Economie et statistique*, 98, March 1978, pp. 51–66.
21 J. Marceau, *Class and Status in France*, Oxford University Press, 1977, p. 62.
22 Ideology: a system of beliefs and values, common to a class or group, which enables it to identify itself and situate itself in relation to other segments of society.
23 *Notable*: during the July Monarchy the term designated the few thousand property-holders who formed the political class. They had a strong local base, plus influence in Paris. Nowadays the term refers more loosely to anyone well placed in local affairs (mayor, *conseiller général*, etc.) or in a party machine.
24 Problematic: a *series* of questions, some of them apparently dis-

parate, but in fact linked by an underlying (and implicit) set of assumptions. This determines the way in which the questions are put.

25 V. Wright, *The Government and Politics of France*, London, Hutchinson, 1978, pp. 173–212; H. Machin, *The Prefect in French Public Administration*, London, Croom Helm, 1977.
26 S. Hoffmann, 'Paradoxes of the French Political Community' in *In Search of France.*
27 M. Crozier, *Société bloquée.*

Chapter 3

1 It could also be asserted that the régime of Marshal Pétain fitted likewise into the authoritarian tradition of France. However, the influence of the fascist dictatorships also had a role to play here; furthermore, there was no pretence at any kind of popular consultation.
2 Jean Casimir–Périer in 1895; Alexandre Millerand in 1924.
3 Vincent Wright, *The Government and Politics of France*, London, Hutchinson, 1978, p. 109.
4 The uproar over this decision stemmed from the fact that there was an article (no. 89) which provided for constitutional reforms. It stated that a proposed revision should be passed in identical terms by the two legislative bodies, and only thereafter put to referendum. Another method required that the two houses of parliament in a congress should vote on proposed changes, when a three-fifths majority was necessary for the reform to become law. No referendum was necessary in this case. The proposed election of the president of the republic by universal suffrage was put to referendum according to article 11 of the constitution, which allowed a referendum to be called on 'tout projet de loi portant sur l'organisation des pouvoirs publics'. It must be admitted that this interpretation of article 11 is not wholly unjustifiable, but in that case article 89 seems to be totally superfluous. At all events, the *conseil constitutionnel*, when asked to pronounce on the constitutional propriety of de Gaulle's decision, alleged that it was not competent to do so.
5 During his electoral campaign of 1974, V. Giscard d'Estaing announced that he would endeavour to change the regulations concerning *suppléants*, so that representatives should have the right to take up their seats on leaving the ministry if they so desired. The two attempts made in this direction have met with no success, the last one having been quashed by the *conseil constitutionnel* (see *Le Monde* of 27–28 May, 16 June and 7 July 1977).
6 M. Debré and J.-L. Debré, *Le Pouvoir politique*, pp. 30–1.
7 See the following editions of *Le Monde* for these exchanges: Debré–de Gaulle, 12 July 1962; Pompidou–de Gaulle, 12 July 1968; Chaban-Delmas–Pompidou, 7 July 1972; Chirac–Giscard

d'Estaing, 27 August 1976.
8 P. Mendès-France, interviewed by I. Allier and J. Julliard in *Nouvel Observateur*, no. 695, 4 March 1978.
9 See J.-L. Debré, *La Constitution de la Ve République*, pp. 17–19.
10 R. Pleven described the narrow interpretation of article 40 as 'talmudique'. He cited an example where a proposal inviting the government to ratify an international convention (on the increased repression of prostitution) was deemed unacceptable, on the grounds that it would have brought about an increase in police expenditure! See *Journal officiel*, Débats, 29 May 1959.
11 The Chirac government contained 24.32 per cent of ministers without a previous career in parliament, and 75.67 per cent of ministers who were deputies or senators at the time of their appointment. This compares with the overall percentage from January 1959 to June 1974: 23.5 per cent non-parliamentarians, 76.5 per cent parliamentarians. For further details and statistics, see P. Antoni and J.-D. Antoni, *Les Ministres de la Ve République*.
12 See F. Giroud, *La Comédie du pouvoir*, Paris, Fayard, 1977, pp. 25–34.
13 *The One and Indivisible French Republic*, London, Weidenfeld & Nicolson, 1973.
14 See Giroud, op.cit., p. 198.
15 J. Whale, *The Politics of the Media*, Glasgow, Fontana, 1977, p. 122.
16 P. Pascallon, *L'Auvergne face à son avenir*, Nonette, Editions Créer, 1978, p. 75.

Chapter 4

1 P. Crisol and Y. Lhomeau, *La Machine RPR*, p. 187.
2 J.-P. Soisson (ed.), *Le Parti républicain*, p. 31.
3 C. Ysmal, 'Le chemin difficile du PR', *Projet*, no. 118, September–October 1977.
4 A. Campana, *L'Argent secret: le financement des partis politiques*, p. 60.
5 Le Matin, *Dossier des législatives 1978*, Paris, 1978, pp. 32–3.
6 V. Wright, *The Government and Politics of France*, p. 150.
7 Campana, op.cit., p. 122.
8 C. Ysmal, *Politique-Hebdo*, no. 305, 18–24 March, 1978.
9 Wright, op.cit., p. 173.
10 G. Ross, 'Party and mass organization: the changing relationship of PCF and CGT' in D. Blackmer and S. Tarrow (eds), *Communism in France and Italy*, Princeton U.P., 1975, pp. 504–40.
11 B. Brizay, *Le Patronat*, pp. 243–4.
12 CIDUNATI resents bitterly being linked with Poujade, whom it despises not for his ideas but for his inefficacy: a recent number of its journal *Libre Entreprise* referred to a press conference given by Poujade, 'no doubt in a telephone-box!'

Chapter 5

1 C. de Gaulle, *Mémoires de guerre*, vol. 3, p. 52.
2 ibid., vol. 1, p. 1.
3 Televised broadcast by de Gaulle, 27 April 1965, printed in *L'Année politique, 1965*, pp. 431–2.
4 K.J. Holsti, *International Politics: a framework for analysis*, pp. 83–96; see also J. Frankel, *National Interest*, London, Macmillan, 1970, pp. 70–1.
5 R. Aron, *Paix et guerre entre les nations*, Paris, Calmann-Lévy, 1962, pp. 730–4; and *La République impériale*, Paris, Calmann-Lévy, 1973, pp. 323–8.
6 R.O. Keohane and J.S. Nye, *Power and Interdependence*, Boston, Little, Brown, 1977, pp. 140–3.
7 S. Hoffmann, *Decline or Renewal? France since the 1930s*, pp. 430–3.
8 Y. Delahaye, *La Frontière et le texte: pour une sémiotique des relations internationales*, pp. 222–3.
9 J. Hayward, *The One and Indivisible French Republic*, London, Weidenfeld & Nicolson, 1973, p. 236.
10 G. de Carmoy, 'The last year of de Gaulle's foreign policy', *International Affairs*, vol. 45, no. 3, July 1969, pp. 424–35.
11 *L'Année politique*, 1976, pp. 259–60, 274.
12 J.-M. Lech, 'L'évolution de l'opinion des Français sur la défense à travers les sondages de 1972 à 1976' *Défense nationale*, January 1977, pp. 47–56.
13 These and subsequent details of French forces are taken mainly from *The Military Balance, 1978–9*, London, International Institute for Strategic Studies, 1978, pp. 22–24.
14 Special report (anon.), *Africa*, no. 83, July 1978, p. 81.
15 J. Klein, 'Commerce des armes et politique: le cas français', *Politique étrangère*, no. 6, 1976, pp. 563–85.
16 G.M. Bailly-Cowell, 'Focus on French armament' in *NATO's Fifteen Nations*, February–March 1977.
17 R. Aron, *The Great Debate: theories of nuclear strategy*, pp. 135–43; cf. also W.L. Kohl, *French Nuclear Diplomacy*, pp. 169–77; also L. Ruehl, *La Politique militaire de la Ve République*, pp. 158–89.
18 Cf. P.M. Gallois, *Le Renoncement*, pp. 11–14.
19 F. Lewis, article in *International Herald Tribune*, 25 February 1978; cf. also *Le Monde* article, 18 July 1978.
20 L. Mandeville, J.-L. Loubet del Bayle and A. Picard, 'Les forces de maintien de l'ordre en France', *Défense nationale*, July 1977, pp. 59–76.
21 The text of the memorandum was published, not at the time but long after de Gaulle's death, in *Espoir* (review of the *Institut Charles de Gaulle*), no. 15, June 1976, together with a commentary by Couve de Murville, the French foreign minister in 1958.
22 See J. Newhouse, *De Gaulle and the Anglo-Saxons*, p. 129.

23   F.C. Bergsten and L.B. Krause (eds), *World Politics and Inter-national Economics*, Washington DC, Brookings Institution, 1975, pp. 50–51, 184, 192.
24   R.O. Keohane and J.S. Nye, *Power and Interdependence*, pp. 84–6.
25   Details of the agreement were meant to be secret, but the West German chancellor, Schmidt, leaked them to American journalists on 16 July. See *L'Année politique, 1976*, pp. 234–5.
26   Report in *Guardian*, 31 October 1978, p. 7.
27   L. Dollot, *Les Relations culturelles internationales*, Paris, PUF, 1968, pp. 36–60.
28   M. McQueen, *Britain, the EEC and the Developing World*, London, Heinemann, 1977, pp. 48–54.
29   M. Sauldie, 'France's military intervention in Africa', *Africa*, no. 77, January 1978, pp. 43–9.
30   Général Méry, Conférence à l'Institut des Hautes Etudes de Défense Nationale et au Centre des Hautes Etudes de l'Armement, 3 April 1978, printed in *Défense nationale*, June 1978, pp. 17–42.
31   Z. Cervenka and B. Rogers, *The Nuclear Axis*, London, Friedmann, 1978, pp. 165–70.

Chapter 6

1   *Education, Culture and Politics in Modern France*, Oxford, Pergamon, 1976, p. vii.
2   For more detailed statistics, see A. Trognon, *L'Equipement des ménages en biens durables au début de 1977*, Paris, INSEE, coll. M61, 1978, pp. 28–29 and Ministère de la culture et de l'environnement, *Annuaire statistique de la culture: données de 1970 à 1974*, Paris, Documentation française, 1977, pp. 62–4.
3   See C. Baudelot and R. Establet, *L'Ecole capitaliste en France*.
4   See P. Bourdieu and J.-C. Passeron, *La Réproduction*.
5   The limitations of this 'liberalizing measure' are clearly illustrated by the references made to the financing of faculty library facilities: 'La bibliothèque universitaire est et reste un service commun par excellence. Elle n'est pas plus la bibliothèque de telle Faculté que de telle autre. Elle est la bibliothèque du corps universitaire. Mais, si elle a en soi une individualité incontestable, elle n'a pas la personnalité civile. Il était donc impossible de lui constituer, comme à chaque Faculté prise à part, un budget particulier . . .', *Bulletin administratif du ministère de l'instruction publique*, vol. 47, Paris, Imprimerie Nationale, 1890, p. 246.
6   Here too the same type of limitation prevails; article 4 indicates very precisely what financial resources come to the universities and what the latter may do with them. 'A dater du 1er janvier 1898, il sera fait recette, au budget de chaque Université, des droits d'études, d'inscription, de bibliothèque et de travaux pratiques acquittés par les étudiants conformément aux règlements. Les ressources proven-

ant de ces recettes ne pourront être affectées qu'aux objets suivants: dépenses des laboratoires, bibliothèques et collections; construction et entretien des bâtiments; création de nouveaux enseignements; œuvres dans l'intérêt des étudiants. Les droits d'examen, de certificat d'aptitude, de diplôme ou de visa acquittés par les aspirants aux grades et titres prévus par les lois, ainsi que les droits de dispense et d'équivalence, continueront d'être perçus au profit du Trésor' (A. de Beauchamp, *Lois et règlements sur l'enseignement supérieur* (5 vols), Paris, Delalain frères, 1880-98, vol. 5, p. 591).

7 G. Vedel, 'Les exigences du service public' in AUPEL, *Pour que l'Université ne meure*, Paris, Le Centurion, 1977, p. 31.

8 P. Seale and M. McConville, *French Revolution, 1968*, Penguin, 1968, p. 27.

9 See P. Bourdieu and J.-C. Passeron, *Les Héritiers*, pp. 48-58.

10 E. Faure, *L'Education nationale et la participation*, p. 18.

11 Although the 1944 Education Act gave to the British minister of education wide powers which are apparently increasing (see W.O. Lester-Smith, *Government of Education* (rev. ed.), Penguin, 1971, pp. 133-7), these are limited by comparison with those of the French minister. For a description of the British education minister's powers see Edward Boyle and Anthony Crosland in conversation with M. Kogan, *The Politics of Education*, Penguin, 1974, pp. 124-8, 159-60.

12 N. Delanoë, *La Faute à Voltaire*, p. 20.

13 Halls, op. cit., p. 49.

14 ed. A. Dansette, Paris, Flammarion, 1969.

15 See J. Godechot, *Les Institutions de la France sous la révolution et l'empire* (2nd ed.), Paris, PUF, 1968, pp. 735-6.

16 The following statistics are given by R.D. Anderson, in *Education in France, 1848-70*, Oxford, OUP, 1975, p. 112. In 1850, the Catholic teaching orders ran a total of 10,312 primary schools (public and private); by 1863, this had risen to 17,206. In 1850, the teaching orders taught at primary level 15 per cent of all boys, 45 per cent of all girls; in 1863, 22 and 54 per cent respectively. Over all, 1,600,000 pupils attended Catholic schools in 1863 (see E. Cahm, *Politics and Society in Contemporary France*, London, Harrap, 1972, p. 521).

17 See A. Prost, *L'Enseignement en France, 1808-1967*, pp. 172-89.

18 See on this question, A. Werth, *France, 1940-1955*, London, Robert Hale, 1956, pp. 57-65.

19 For greater detail, see W.R. Fraser, *Reforms and Restraints in Modern French Education*, p. 63. J. Hayward, *The One and Indivisible French Republic* (London, Weidenfeld & Nicolson, 1973) puts the proportion of Catholic schools in the private sector at 91 per cent, whereas *Le Monde* of 8 June 1977 puts it at 93.17 per cent (p. 193).

20 See Fraser, op.cit., p. 69.

21 See the figures given by H. Ehrmann, *Politics in France* (2nd ed.),

Boston, Little, Brown, 1971, pp. 47–50. It is generally assumed that anti-clericalism is no longer a force to be reckoned with, but in the view of René Rémond, such a view is premature. See his article 'L'anti-cléricalisme n'est pas mort', *Projet*, September–October 1977. One is tempted to agree with this view when the presence of the president of the republic, the government and the presidents of both houses of parliament at a religious service on 11 November 1977, to commemorate France's war dead, is noted with hostility. See P. Avril and J. Gicquel, 'Chronique constitutionelle française', *Pouvoirs*, no. 4, 1978.

22 *Programme commun de gouvernement* (préf. G. Marchais), Paris, Editions sociales, 1973, p. 77.

23 Its full title being *Fédération des conseils de parents d'élèves des écoles publics*, for brevity known as the *Fédération Cornec*, after its president Jean Cornec, a veteran secularist from the CNAL.

24 President of the *Fédération des parents d'élèves de l'enseignement public* – known, for brevity, as PEEP or *Fédération Lagarde*.

25 Figures for 1977–8 on private education at primary level indicate that private nursery schools receive 13.4 per cent of school-children, a diminution from the previous year; the primary school population has also increased by 1 per cent, whereas the number of schools has decreased by 1.7 per cent (see Ministère de l'éducation, *Note d'information*, no. 78–02, 13 January 1978).

26 See *Le Figaro*, 14 January 1977, and *Tableaux des enseignements et de la formation*, Paris, Service central des statistiques et sondages, 1977, p. 539, p. 9.

27 The party political undertones of this issue may account for the illiberal tendencies displayed at times by both sides, who each claim to speak in the name of freedom of thought. In fairness it should be said that there is an ambiguity in the French political tradition, since the republic is *laïque* (see Constitution, article 2), and the *Déclaration des droits de l'homme et du citoyen* states (article 10) that 'nul ne doit être inquiété pour ses opinions, même religieuses'. See on this point P. Arrighi, 'A l'université, les élections et l'avenir de l'école libre', *Revue des deux mondes*, March 1978, pp. 662–3.

There seems little doubt that the left would be happy to see the end of private education as such; the CPG of 1972 refers to the absorption of subsidized and, eventually, unsubsidized schools into the national system (*Programme commun de gouvernement*, p. 77). It also seems clear that at least some partisans of Catholic education are equally happy to prevent the existence of state schools where possible. An example of this is the small town of Plogonnec (Finistère), where a state primary school has only recently been opened, in the face of strong Catholic opposition, including apparently G. Guermeur himself. See *Le Nouvel Observateur*, no. 620, 27 September–3 October 1976.

28 See O. Guichard, *Un Chemin tranquille*, Paris, Flammarion, 1975, p. 137.

29 See Ministère de l'Education, *Réforme du système éducatif, classes de sixième et cinquième* (2nd ed.), Paris, CNDP, 1977, pp. 19, 39–41.
30 *Apres la Troisième*, Paris, ONISEP, année scolaire 1977–8, pp. 18–21.
31 See *Actes du colloque national sur l'éducation*, Paris, Documentation française, 1974, vol. 2, pp. 367–8.
32 See Anderson, op. cit., p. 31.
33 M. Chavardès, *Un Ministre éducateur: Jean Zay*, Paris, SEVPEN, 1965, p. 43.
34 The FEN has always accorded great respect to the report, and has reprinted it four times, the latest impression being included in the supplement *L'Ecole de l'éducation permanente* to *FEN-Informations* of 16 February 1977. Λ. Prost (op. cit., p. 420) writes of the 'référence liturgique' constituted by the report for supporters for a more democratic education system, and of its 'prestige quasi sacral'.
35 See R. Billères, 'Exposé des motifs' in the supplement to *L'Education nationale*, no. 35, 13 December 1956, p. 135.
36 Fraser, op. cit., p. 127.
37 Initially there was one other section — classical (*lycée*-type) — which no longer obtains.
38 These categories are: change of employment, retraining, preparation for a job obtained, promotion, refresher courses and training for a first job.
39 Paris, Fayard, 1976, pp. 65–6.
40 The collection of very detailed instructions for 6e and 5e runs to no less than 410 pages.
41 The proportions of the total state budget taken by education are as follows: 1950: 8 per cent; 1964: 15.9 per cent; 1968: 16.4 per cent; 1971: 19.5 per cent; 1978: 17.5 per cent (plus a separate budget for higher education).
42 Halls, op.cit., p. 258.
43 See C. Jencks, *Inequality*, Penguin, 1975.
44 Guichard, op.cit., pp. 13–14.
45 Faure, op.cit., p. 29.
46 ibid., p. 33.
47 There is little doubt that E. Faure's radical intentions provoked some alarm among the more conservative Gaullists, and that his reform might never have been realized but for de Gaulle's continued support. As a sop to conservative opinion, a Gaullist deputy was appointed *secrétaire d'état*, but during his term of office was allowed virtually no areas of responsibility which had not previously been approved by Faure himself.
48 Halls, op. cit., p. 211.

Bibliographical essay

Books in English are published in London and books in French are published in Paris, unless otherwise stated.
Books asterisked thus * contain particularly useful hints on further reading.

Chapter 1

1944–58: The best general history of the period is **G. Dupeux**, *La France de 1945 à 1965* (3rd ed., Colin, 1972). **A. Werth**, *France 1940–55* (Hale, 1956) is more impressionistic, but full of insights. **P.-M. de la Gorce**, *L'Après-guerre* (Grasset, 1978) is very detailed.

On social and economic change, the best introduction is **M. Parodi**, *L'Economie et la société française de 1945 à 1970* * (Colin, 1971) which is excellently documented and goes much deeper than a mere introduction. **J. Ardagh**, *The New France* (3rd ed., Penguin, 1977) is full of information but is rather eclectic and apolitical. **J. Lecerf**, *La Percée de l'économie française* (Arthaud, 1963) evokes well the 'technocratic' nature of post-war growth. The reactions of victims of change are clinically analysed in **S. Hoffmann** (ed.), *Le Mouvement Poujade* (Colin, 1956) and in a more general study by **D. Borne**, *Petits Bourgeois en révolte – le mouvement Poujade* (Flammarion, 1977). **L. Wylie**, *Village in the Vaucluse* (Cambridge, Harvard University Press, 1957) catches the change in lifestyle at grass-roots level.

On the politics of the Fourth Republic, no one has surpassed **P. Williams**, *Crisis and Compromise* * (Longmans, 1964) which is exhaustive and very readable. **D. MacRae jun.**, *Parliament, Parties and Society in France, 1946–58* (New York, St Martin's Press, 1967) uses much more abstract political science techniques. **J. Fauvet**, *La Quatrième République* (Fayard, 1959) concentrates particularly on the parliamentary scene. **G. Elgey**, *La République des illusions, 1945–51* (Fayard, 1965) is massively detailed, as is its companion *La République des contradictions, 1951–4* (Fayard, 1968). Defences of 'the system' are put up by **J. Barsalou**, *La Mal-Aimée* (Plon, 1964) and, more discursively, by **F. Fontvieille-Alquier**, *Plaidoyer pour la IVe République* (Laffont, 1976). A critical socialist account is **J. Julliard**, *La IVe République* (Calmann-Lévy, 1968). **N. Leites**, *On the Game of Politics in France* (Stanford UP, 1959) is good on the psychology of the professional

politician.
General accounts of foreign policy are given in the notes to chapter 5.
On colonial matters, **R.E.M. Irving**, *The First Indo-China War*
(Croom Helm, 1975) is concise and well written, to be supplemented by
a lengthier study, **D. Lancaster**, *The Emancipation of French Indo-
China* (New York, Octagon, 1975). As for Algeria, **G. Andrews**, *French
Politics and Algeria* (New York, Appleton, 1962) is a concise account
of the impact of the war on domestic politics. The role of the army in
politics has been studied illuminatingly by **J.S. Ambler**, *The French
Army in Politics, 1945-62* (Ohio State UP, 1966). See also **G. Kelley**,
Lost Soldiers: the French Army and Empire in Crisis, 1947-62 (MIT
Press, 1965); **R. Girardet**, *La Crise militaire française, 1945-62* (Colin,
1964). The general work by **H. Grimal**, *La Décolonisation, 1919-63*
(Colin, 1965; translated as *Decolonization*, Routledge & Kegan Paul,
1978) fits French policy into the international context.

1958-68: As with other periods, a very useful brief narrative in
English supported by documents in French is provided in **E. Cahm**,
Politics and Society in Contemporary France, 1789-1971 (Harrap,
1972). Otherwise the best full narrative and analysis of the period is
P. Viansson-Ponté, *Histoire de la république gaullienne* (2 vols, Fayard,
1970, 1971) which is eminently readable and reliable partly because of
its size — with French books very often the longer they are the easier
they are to read. On the Algerian war the same point applies, and to
understand a complex period the best work is **Y. Courrière**, *La Guerre
d'Algérie* (4 vols, Fayard, 1970-2); the most recent work is **A. Horne**,
A Savage War of Peace: Algeria 1954-62 (Macmillan, 1977) which is
more descriptive than analytical, perhaps overdoing the linkages
between stormy skies and stormy politics; the most clear-cut guide to
the political implications at each stage of the war is still provided by
D. Pickles, *Algeria and France* (Methuen, 1963). For description and
analysis of developments in France particularly after the war ended, the
best work is **P.M. Williams** and **M. Harrison**, *Politics and Society in de
Gaulle's Republic* available in paperback (New York, Doubleday, 1973),
to be supplemented by **P.M. Williams**, *French Politicians and Elections,
1951-69* (Cambridge UP, 1970) which is particularly useful for insight
into electoral campaign issues as well as the results. For an understanding of the socio-economic structures of France under de Gaulle and for
an explanation of why he faced increasing opposition and unrest in the
years leading up to 1968 the indispensable work is **M. Parodi**, *L'Economie et la société française de 1945 à 1970* (Colin, 1971).

The events of May 1968: The most detailed and authoritative account
is undoubtedly **L. Rioux** and **R. Backmann**, *L'Explosion de mai* (Laffont,
1968), but a fairly extensive description may also be found in **P. Labro**
et al., *Mai-juin '68: ce n'est qu'un début* (Denoël, 1968). For a more
specifically Trotskyist approach, see **D. Bensaid** and **H. Weber**, *Mai 1968:
une répétition générale* (Maspéro, 1968). Among books in English on
the subject, the following may be consulted with profit: **P. Seale** and
M. McConville, *French Revolution, 1968* (Penguin, 1968), lively, with
some vivid descriptions, if at times a little gushing; **D. Singer**, *Prelude to*

Revolution (Cape, 1970) – a sympathetic account; **B.E. Brown**, *Protest in Paris: the Anatomy of a Revolt* (Morristown, NJ, General Learning Press, 1974), for a more conservative approach to the events; **J. Gretton**, *Students and Workers* (MacDonald, 1969) possibly the best work on the subject in English. For the events of May and their effect on the political parties of the left, see **A. Barjonet**, *La Révolution trahie de 1968* (John Didier, 1968), explaining in doctrinal terms the reasons for the failure of the communist party to back up the student revolt; **R. Johnson**, *The French Communist Party versus the Students* (Yale UP, 1972); **J. Poperen**, *L'Unité de la gauche, 1965–73* (Fayard, 1975), particularly parts 2 and 3. There seems to be little available on the *lycéens*, but a collection of their views and proposals has been published: Comités d'action lycéens, *Les Lycéens gardent la parole* (Seuil, 1968).

The political aspects are adequately covered in **P. Viansson-Ponté**, *Histoire de la république gaullienne*, vol. 2 (Fayard, 1971) which is particularly good on de Gaulle's 'disappearance'. One recent book which well repays study is that of **M. Grimaud**, *En Mai, fais ce qu'il te plaît* (Stock, 1977), which looks at the events from the standpoint of the *préfet de police*. There have been a number of reflections and analyses of the events: **E. Morin** *et al.*, *Mai 1968: la brèche* (Fayard, 1968), sympathetic to the student revolt, with **R. Aron**, *La Révolution introuvable* (Fayard, 1968), profoundly hostile. A more sustained interpretation is that of **A. Touraine**, *Le Mouvement de mai ou le communisme utopique* (Seuil, 1968), while a useful summing-up of the main interpretations is provided by **P. Beneton** and **J. Touchard**, 'Les interprétations de la crise de mai–juin 1968', *Revue française de science politique*, vol. 20, June 1970. Finally, there is a valuable collection of documents, tracts, posters, etc. produced during May 1968 in *Le Mouvement social* (July–September 1968) entitled 'La Sorbonne par elle-même'.

1969 to the present: There is obviously little in the way of general works for so recent a period. **P. Alexandre**, *Le Duel de Gaulle–Pompidou* (Grasset, 1970) deals especially with the politics of Pompidou's accession to power. **J.-D. Bredin**, *La République de Monsieur Pompidou* (Fayard, 1974) is a polemical view from a leading left-Radical. **G. Martinet**, *Le Système Pompidou* (Seuil, 1973) is a brilliant and hostile account of his presidency. **C. Debbasch**, *La France de Pompidou* (PUF, 1974) is more of a socio-economic cross-section of France than anything else.

General books on the politics of the Fifth Republic abound. **F. Goguel** and **A. Grosser**, *La Politique en France* (5th ed., Colin, 1975) is well written. There are two very clear American works: **H. Ehrmann**, *Politics in France* (3rd ed., Boston, Little, Brown, 1976) and the earlier **J.S. Ambler**, *The Government and Politics of France* (Boston, Houghton Mifflin, 1971). **P. Williams** and **M. Harrison**, *Politics and Society in de Gaulle's Republic* (Longman, 1971) is very informative.

D. Pickles, *The Government and Politics of France* (2 vols, Methuen, 1973) marshals many examples to support a rather pro-Gaullist analysis. The most recent British works are **V. Wright**, *The Government and Politics of France** (Hutchinson, 1978) which stresses well the nature of presidential decision-making and **J. Hayward,** *The One and Indivisible French Republic* * (Weidenfeld & Nicolson, 1973) which is more critical and harder to read; both books are very good on the relationship between politics and administration. To keep up with the rapid movement of French politics it is important to become familiar with the political press. Any selection of this is likely to be arbitrary, so at the risk of disappointing some readers, the following are suggested: *Le Monde* (daily) is distinguished for the perspicacity of its political analyses and its discreetly oppositional stance. *Le Monde* publishes documentary specials on all major elections, and also periodic selections of relevant articles in its *Dossiers et documents* series. *Le Matin* (daily) is pro-socialist and readable. Among the weeklies, *Le Nouvel Observateur* caters for the more intellectual socialist reader, whereas *L'Express* and *Le Point* are of liberal persuasion. *L'Expansion* is aimed at *cadres* and is invaluable for its reporting of the social and economic conjuncture. Annual summaries of developments in the major areas of French society come in *L'Année politique, économique, sociale et diplomatique,* edited by **E. Bonnefous** and **J.B. Duroselle** and published by PUF and Editions du Grand Siècle. The main regular publications of political organizations as such are given in the text of chapter 4.

Chapter 2

Economy: The best historical introductions are **T. Kemp,** *Economic Forces in French History* (Dobson, 1971) and *The French Economy, 1913–39* (Longmans, 1972). See also the clear study of **C. Kindleberger,** *Economic Growth in France and Britain* (Harvard UP, 1964). On postwar growth, **B. Guibert,** *La Mutation industrielle de la France* (2 vols, INSEE, 1976), is wide-ranging and well-documented. **J.-J. Carré, P. Dubois** and **E. Malinvaud,** *French Economic Growth* (Stanford UP, 1976) is a more technical discussion.

On introductions to contemporary economic structures, **P. Maillet,** *La Structure économique de la France* (PUF, 1975) is brief; **J. Sheahan,** *Introduction to the French Economy* (Columbus, Merrill, 1969) brings a more political analysis. **J. Albertini,** *L'Economie française – initiation* (Editions Ouvrières, 1978) presents the topic in a novel and provocative way.

The relationship between economy and state has received much treatment, most of it centring on the theme of planning. **P. Bauchet,** *La Planification française* (5th ed., Seuil, 1966) seems aware of the political dimension of planning, as does **J. Sheahan,** *Promotion and Control of Industry in Post-war France* (Harvard UP, 1963). Of accounts by planners, **Y. Ullmo,** *La Planification en France* (Dalloz, 1975) is readable.

As regards left-orientated critiques of contemporary structures, **F. Morin,** *La Structure financière du capitalisme français* (Calmann-Lévy, 1974) is a sophisticated neo-marxist analysis. The PCF view is in **P. Boccara** (ed.), *Etudes sur le capitalisme monopoliste d'état, sa crise et* *son issue* (Editions Sociales, 1973). Cf. also PCF, *Le Capitalisme monopoliste d'état* (2nd ed., Editions Sociales, 1976).

Invaluable instruments for keeping up with developments in all fields of the economy are the ongoing INSEE collections, with a wealth of documentation and analyses that are more accessible to non-specialists than might be supposed. The main series are D — Démographie; E — Entreprises; C — Comptabilité; M — Ménages and R — Régions. *Le Monde* now publishes early each year its *Année économique et sociale*, analysing in detail the past year in the French and international economies.

Social stratification: The best historical introduction is **G. Dupeux**, *French Society, 1789–1970* (Methuen, 1976). There are interesting documents, but a rather shallow presentation, in a work dealing with the contemporary period: **G. Vincent**, *Les Français, 1945–75: chronique et structures d'une société* (Masson, 1977). **C. Quin**, *Classes sociales et union du peuple de France* (Editions Sociales, 1976) gives the PCF line. **A. Granou**, *La Bourgeoisie financière au pouvoir* (Maspéro, 1977) is from a more leftist viewpoint. **J. Marceau**, *Class and Status in France** (Oxford UP, 1977) is vastly informative and rather eclectic in its leftish approach.

On particular classes or fractions **P. Birnbaum** *et al., La Classe dirigeante française* (PUF, 1978) tries to demonstrate empirically the nature of the ruling class. Cf. also here his *Sommets de l'état* (Seuil, 1977). **C. Baudelot, R. Establet** and **J. Malemort**, *La Petite Bourgeoisie en France* (Maspéro, 1974) is a provocative study, hostile to its subject. **M. Roy**, *Les Commerçants: entre la révolte et la modernisation* (Seuil, 1971) pinpoints with no great sympathy the plight of the *petit commerçant*. **J.P. Bachy**, *Les Cadres en France* (Colin, 1971) has concise analysis and documents. **M. Faure**, *Les Paysans dans la société française** (Colin, 1966) is a good introduction. **B. Lambert**, *Les Paysans dans la lutte des classes* (Seuil, 1970) presents the articulate view of a leftist farmer and union leader.

On the working class **P. Gavi**, *Les Ouvriers* (Mercure de France, 1970) is an impressionistic, leftist view, very much inspired by 1968. A more sober scientific analysis comes in **G. Adam** *et al., L'Ouvrier français en 1970* (Colin, 1970). Access to the debate about the changing nature of the working class can be had through the writings of **S. Mallet**, notably *La Nouvelle Classe ouvrière* (4th ed., Seuil, 1969) and **A. Touraine**, *La Société post-industrielle* (Denoël, 1969).

Political culture: Most of the general works on the Fifth Republic listed in chapter 1 have some pages on this, but book-length studies are rare. The best start is **S. Hoffmann** (ed.), *In Search of France** (Harper & Row, 1963), especially Hoffmann's own essay on 'Paradoxes of the French Political Community'. Hoffmann has further developed his ideas in *Decline or Renewal? France since the 1930s* (New York, Viking, 1974). Other studies include **E. Deutsch, D. Lindon** and **P. Weil**, *Les Familles politiques* (Editions de Minuit, 1966), brief, but brings out ideological cleavages, and the provocative, pro-Gaullist view of **C. Morazé**, *Les Français et la république* (Colin, 1956), written at the apogee of the Fourth Republic and catching well the attitudes of the day. **P. Fougey-**

rollas, *La Conscience politique dans la France contemporaine* (Denoël, 1963) insists on the tension between national consensus and partisan values. H. Waterman, *Political Change in Contemporary France* (Columbus, Merrill, 1969) sees political culture with an 'end of ideology' problematic and thus produces a very ideological, transatlantic view. P. Avril, *Politics in France* (Penguin, 1969) has some lucid insights from this Mendesist analyst.

On relations between state and citizen, the most authoritative work is by M. Crozier, notably his *Société bloquée* (Seuil, 1970) and *Le Phénomène bureaucratique* (Seuil, 1963). On religious cleavages there is both sharp analysis and plentiful documentation in A. Coutrot and F.-G. Dreyfus, *Les Forces religieuses dans la société française** (Colin, 1965) and R. Rémond (ed.), *Forces religieuses et attitudes politiques dans la France contemporaine** (Colin, 1965). A special tradition is historically studied in depth in Rémond's *L'Anticléricalisme en France: de 1815 à nos jours* (Fayard, 1976).

Chapter 3

Central government: The works of a general nature on the Fifth Republic listed above all contain useful accounts of the topic dealt with in these sections. Works of an autobiographical nature mentioned in the text or notes may also be consulted with profit. An interesting discussion on the nature of the Fifth Republic is to be found in a special number of *Pouvoirs* (no. 4) *20 Ans après: la Ve République*, and an excellent analysis in F. de Baecque, *Qui gouverne la France?* (PUF, 1976) which also contains a selection of key documents. The Gaullist view of the constitution is typified by M. Debré and J.-L. Debré, *Le Pouvoir politique* (Seghers, 1976) and J.-L. Debré, *La Constitution de la Ve République* (PUF, 1975). Among the many works of M. Duverger, see in particular *La Ve République* (5th ed., PUF, 1974); see also an informative study by L. Hamon, *Une République présidentielle* (2 vols, Bordas, 1975, 1977).

On the role of the president of the republic, a useful introduction is provided by J. Baguenard, J.-Ch. Maout and R. Muzellec, *Le Président de la Ve République** (Colin, 1970) and a succinct, up-to-date account in *Documents d'études* (ed. G. Burdeau), *Le Président de la Ve République* (Documentation française, 1977, no. 1.06). J. Massot, *La Présidence de la république en France* (Documentation française, 1977) situates the presidency in its historical context. B. Tricot *et al.*, *De Gaulle et le service de l'état* (Plon, 1977) give a fascinating, if discreet, account of the General's presidency.

For basic introductions on the role of parliament, see J.-Ch. Maout and R. Muzellec, *Le Parlement sous la Ve République* (Colin, 1971) and *Documents d'études*, no. 14, *Le Contrôle parlementaire* (Documentation française, 1970).

The constitutional vicissitudes of de Gaulle's republic are covered by Ph. Braud, *Les Crises politiques de la Ve République* (Colin, 1970).

For an introduction to a study of the *conseil constitutionnel* see
G. Dupuis, J. Georgel and **J. Moreau**, *Le Conseil constitutionnel* (Colin,
1970) or a more recent publication, **L. Favoreu** and **L. Philip**, *Le Conseil
constitutionnel* (PUF, 1978); a more detailed study by the same
authors, *Les Grandes Décisions du conseil constitutionnel* (Sirey, 1975)
makes clear the political implications of the *conseil*'s activities. On the
conseil d'etat, the most up-to-date study in English is that of **M. Rendel**,
The Administrative Functions of the French Conseil d'Etat (Weidenfeld
& Nicolson, 1970). A collective historical study, **A. Parodi** (ed.), *Le
Conseil d'état, 1799-1974* (CNRS, 1974) provides a clear account
of its controversial decisions. See also, **M.-C. Kessler**, *Le Conseil d'état*
(Colin, 1968) and **P. Escoube**, *Les Grands Corps de l'état* (2nd ed.,
PUF, 1977).

On the central administration (ministries, etc.), the clearest (and best
set out) introduction is **L. François**, *Les Institutions politiques et administratives de la France* (Hachette, 1976). At a higher level, see
B. Gournay *et al.*, *Administration publique** (PUF, 1967), **G. Belorgey**,
*Le Gouvernement et l'administration de la France** (2nd ed., Colin,
1970). **F. de Baecque**, *L'Administration centrale de la France* (Colin,
1973) is a highly technical study. Since the finance ministry is being
reorganized, only two indications will be given: **X. Beauchamps**, *Un
Etat dans l'état? le ministère de l'économie et des finances* (Bordas,
1976); *Les Notices de la documentation française: Finances publiques*
(Documentation française, 1974). For a brilliant essay on the governing
élites, see **P. Birnbaum**, *Les Sommets de l'état* (Seuil, 1977); see also
P. Antoni and **J.-D. Antoni**, *Les Ministres de la Vᵉ République* (PUF,
1976) for a detailed sociological study of the Fifth Republic's political
class.

On the media, a useful account is to be found in **J. Ardagh**, *The New
France* (3rd ed., Penguin, 1977). A highly technical and comprehensive
exposition of the problems, the legal situation and the main theories
of communication is provided by **F. Balle**, *Institutions et publics des
moyens d'information* (Montchrestien, 1973). See also **R. Cayrol**, *La
Presse écrite et audiovisuelle* (PUF, 1973). On radio and television, see
G. Dupuis and **J. Raux**, *l'ORTF** (Colin, 1970) for a good introduction
to the ORTF before the last two reforms; **J. Chevallier**, *La Radio-télé-
vision française entre deux réformes** (LGDJ, 1975) and **R. Thomas**,
*Broadcasting and Democracy in France** (Bradford UP, 1976) for an
excellent analysis of the political dimensions. On the press, the most up-
to-date account is **P. Albert**, *La Presse française** (Documentation
française, 1978); but **B. Voyenne**, *La Presse dans la société contemporaine* (Colin, 1970) is still very well worth reading, together with his
L'Information en France (McGraw-Hill-France, 1972).

Local government: There are good introductory works in English,
notably **F. Ridley** and **J. Blondel**, *Public Administration in France**
(Routledge & Kegan Paul, 1969). Two older works which are still of
interest are **B. Chapman**, *Introduction to French Local Government*
(Allen & Unwin, 1953) and *The Prefects and Provincial France* (Allen &
Unwin, 1955), the latter to be supplemented with a well-researched and

clear study, **H. Machin**, *The Prefect in French Public Administration* (Croom Helm, 1977). **M. Kesselman**, *The Ambiguous Consensus* (New York, Knopf, 1967) shows up the realities of small communes, while **J. Lagroye**, *Société et politique: J. Chaban-Delmas à Bordeaux* (Pedone, 1973) is an excellent study of a large town. **P. Bernard**, *Le Grand Tournant des communes de France* (Colin, 1969) gives a lengthy but informative prefect's point of view.

Inevitably, in the logic of centralization, there are many works on public administration which have substantial sections on local (subaltern) government. **C. Debbasch**, *L'Administration au pouvoir* (Calmann-Lévy, 1969) is brief but telling. **B. Gournay** *et al.*, *Administration publique** (PUF, 1967) is a thorough textbook, as is **G. Belorgey**, *Le Gouvernement et l'administration de la France** (2nd ed., Colin, 1970), which brings out well the weight of centralization.

On regions, one needs to approach the problem from an economic as well as from a political angle; much pioneer work was done by **J.-F. Gravier**, notably *L'Aménagement du territoire et l'avenir des régions françaises* (Flammarion, 1964). There is a readable general study by an economic geographer: **I. Thompson**, *Modern France: a Social and Economic Geography* (Butterworth, 1970). **N. Hansen**, *French Regional Planning* (Edinburgh UP, 1968) is written from a planner's point of view, but is rewarding if at times fairly technical. On a more polemical level, **J.-J. Servan-Schreiber**, *Le Pouvoir régional* (Grasset, 1970) presents a reformist view; a socialist-cum-autonomist viewpoint is developed in a series of works by **R. Lafont**, notably *Autonomie: de la région a l'autogestion* (Gallimard, 1976). On particular regions, **R. Dulong**, *La Question bretonne* (FNSP, 1975) is a sophisticated marxist treatment: Corsica has attracted a plethora of review articles, of which the series in the leftish *Les Temps modernes* are particularly interesting (cf. nos. 357, April 1976; 366 and 367, January–February 1977; 385 and 386, August–September 1978).

Chapter 4

The most useful introductions to French parties are **F. Borella**, *Les Partis politiques** (2nd ed., Seuil, 1975) which is lucid and critical, and **J. Frears**, *Political Parties and Elections in the Fifth French Republic** (Hurst, 1978) which is well documented but less incisive. **M. Steed's** chapter in **S. Henig** and **J. Pinder** (eds), *European Political Parties* (PEP/Allen & Unwin, 1969) is still valuable for its crispness and clarity. **P. Campbell**, *French Electoral Systems and Elections since 1789* (Faber, 1966) is a concise outline. On party finance **A. Campana**, *L'Argent secret: le financement des partis politiques* (Arthaud, 1976) has extracted much information on a very obscure topic. The major parties have produced small-format introductory handbooks, published by Marabout of Verviers (Belgium) in 1977. These are: *Le Parti républicain* (ed. **J.-P. Soisson**); *Le Rassemblement pour la république* (ed. **J. Chirac**); *Le Mouvement des radicaux de gauche* (ed. **R. Fabre**); *Le Parti socialiste* (ed. F. Mitterrand); *Le Parti communiste français* (ed. G. Marchais) and a collective work, *Les Ecologistes*.

The most important recent party publications, which state theoretical and current policy stances, are: Rassemblement pour la République, *Propositions pour la France* (Stock, 1977); Parti Républicain, *Le Projet républicain* (Flammarion, 1978); Centre des démocrates sociaux, *L'Autre Solution* (CDS, 1977); Parti communiste français, *Un Socialisme pour la France* (Editions Sociales, 1976); Parti socialiste, *Propositions socialistes pour l'actualisation* (Flammarion, 1978). There is a handy version of the CPG introduced by G. Marchais: Parti communiste français, *Programme commun de gouvernement* (Editions Sociales, 1972).

The right: An essential introduction is R. Rémond, *The French Right Wing from 1815 to de Gaulle* (Pennsylvania UP, 1969), which is absolutely lucid and should be followed by M. Anderson, *Conservative Politics in France* (Allen & Unwin, 1973).

On Gaullism the most authoritative work is that of J. Charlot, notably *Le Gaullisme* (Colin, 1970) and *The Gaullist Phenomenon* (Allen & Unwin, 1971). A. Hartley, *Gaullism* (Routledge & Kegan Paul, 1972) offers a sympathetic view. Earlier works, of a more introductory character but still worth looking at, are: P. Avril, *UDR et Gaullistes* (PUF, 1971) and P. Viansson-Ponté, *Les Gaullistes* (Seuil, 1963). J. Touchard, *Le Gaullisme, 1940–69* (Seuil, 1978) sets Gaullism, approvingly, in the context of French nationalism. An early PCF view is in H. Claude, *Gaullisme et grand capital* (Editions Sociales, 1961). A Trotskyist viewpoint is in J.-M. Brohm *et al.*, *Le Gaullisme et après: état fort et fascisation* (Maspéro, 1974). P. Crisol and Y. Lhomeau, *La Machine RPR* (Intervalle Fayolle, 1978) has much up-to-date and solid information on Gaullism under Chirac.

On Giscardism, literature is beginning to grow. J.-C. Colliard, *Les Républicains indépendants* (PUF, 1971) is a thorough early study, to be supplemented by a brilliant sociological interpretation of the differences within the right, P. Birnbaum, *Les Sommets de l'état* (Seuil, 1977). V. Giscard d'Estaing defines his own position in *Démocratie française* (Fayard, 1976). M. Poniatowski, *Conduire le Changement* (Fayard, 1975) is more energetic and technocratic. B. Lecomte and C. Sauvage, *Les Giscardiens* (Albin Michel, 1978) has much up-to-date information. R.E.M. Irving, *Christian Democracy in France* (Allen & Unwin, 1973) is clear and thorough.

Radicalism has had several studies, starting with the brief introduction by a supporter: C. Nicolet, *Le Radicalisme* (PUF, 1974). J.-T. Nordmann, *Histoire des Radicaux, 1820–1973* (Table Ronde, 1974) is by a collaborator of J.-J. Servan-Schreiber, whose own *Le Manifeste* (Firmin-Didot, 1977) is a concise statement of current positions.

The left: G. Lefranc, *Les Gauches en France, 1789–1972* (Payot, 1973) is a long-term study. Studies covering more recent time-spans include J. Touchard, *La Gauche en France depuis 1900* (Seuil, 1977), with its vast grasp of detail and lack of sympathy; F.-G. Dreyfus, *Histoire des Gauches en France, 1940–74* (Grasset, 1975) from a hostile, fairly pro-Gaullist viewpoint, and two works by socialists: **J. Poperen**, *L'Unité de la gauche, 1965–73* (Fayard, 1975), a work of meticulous detail and **R. Verdier**, *PS–PC: une lutte pour l'entente** (Seghers, 1976). G. **Lichtheim**, *Marxism in modern France* (Columbia UP, 1966) attempts to situate the development of the left in the context of marxist political theory. **J. Charlot** (ed.), *Quand la Gauche peut gagner* (Moreau, 1973) is vital to the understanding of the dynamics of left unity.

On socialism, it is useful to start with an historical account of the SFIO. **G. Lefranc**, *Le Mouvement socialiste sous la Troisième République* (Payot, 1963) is a sound study by an SFIO and trade-union activist. **R. Quilliot**, *La SFIO et l'exercice du pouvoir* (Fayard, 1972) by a socialist senator is essential for understanding the party's decay after 1945. The dilemmas of the 1960s are studied in detail by two US scholars: **F. Wilson**, *The French Democratic Left, 1963–9* (Stanford UP, 1971) and **H. Simmons**, *French Socialists in Search of a Role, 1956–67* (Cornell UP, 1970). The 'new' PS has drawn many studies. **C. Hurtig**, *De la SFIO au nouveau parti socialiste* (Colin, 1970) has documents and concise commentary. The structures and leaders of the PS are studied briefly, but penetratively, by **T. Pfister**, *Les Socialistes* (Albin Michel, 1977) and more discursively by **J.-F. Bizot**, *Au Parti des socialistes* (Grasset, 1975). **F.-O. Giesbert's** biography *François Mitterrand ou la tentation de l'histoire* (Seuil, 1977) is full of insight into the development of the post-war left. The CERES group present their views in a resolute and readable analysis by **M. Charzat, J.-P. Chevènement** and **G. Toutain**, *Le CERES, un combat pour le socialisme** (Calmann-Lévy, 1975). **Chevènement** has also produced *Le Vieux, la crise, le neuf* (Flammarion, 1974) and *Les Communistes, les socialistes et les autres* (Aubier-Montaigne, 1977).

The PCF has several historical studies devoted to it, the most penetrating being **J. Fauvet**, *Histoire du parti communiste** (2nd ed., Fayard, 1977). **R. Tiersky**, *French Communism, 1920–72** (Columbia UP, 1974) is very clear. On party structures the work of **A. Kriegel**, especially *Les Communistes* (Seuil, 1970) is very well informed, and hostile – not unsurprisingly, perhaps, for an ex-communist. There are essays on varied aspects of party activity in **F. Bon** (ed.), *Le Communisme en France* (Colin, 1969) and **D. Blackmer** and **S. Tarrow**, *Communism in Italy and France* (Princeton UP, 1975). **A. Laurens** and **T. Pfister**, *Les Nouveaux Communistes* (Stock, 1973) charts the party's recent evolution. A brief study by **A. Stiefbold**, *The French Communist Party in Transition* (Praeger, 1977) situates the PCF with regard to the Soviet Union.

The leadership's view is given in the writings of **G. Marchais**, notably *Le Défi démocratique* (Grasset, 1973) and *Parlons franchement* (Grasset, 1977). **J. Elleinstein**, *Le PC* (Grasset, 1976) is by the 'official liberal' of the party, and has interesting documents; a more oblique and prudent line of dissent comes in **G. Molina** and **Y. Varga**, *Dialogue à l'intérieur du parti communiste français* (Maspéro, 1978).

On fringe parties, **B. Brigouleix**, *L'Extrême Droite en France* (Intervalle-Fayolle, 1977) is well-informed and clear. There is a good guide to the theoretical foundations of much French leftism in **R. Gombin**, *Les*

Origines du gauchisme (Seuil, 1971) and **T. Pfister**, *Le Gauchisme* (Filippachi, 1972). **Y. Craipeau**, *Le Mouvement trotskiste en France* (Syros, 1971) by a veteran Trotskyite, traces the movement in its fissiparousness down to 1968. On the PSU, **M. Rocard**, *Le PSU et l'avenir de la France* (Seuil, 1969) is still readable, if slightly dated. For the ecologists, see *Le Monde: L'Ecologie – enjeu politique* (supplement aux 'Dossiers et documents du monde', 1978).

Interest groups: A good start, in terms of a general approach to the problem, is **J. Meynaud**, *Nouvelles Etudes sur les groupes de pression en France* (Colin, 1962). On unions, **J.-D. Reynaud**, *Les Syndicats en France** (2 vols, Seuil, 1975) is an excellent textbook with many documents. **G. Caire**, *Les Syndicats ouvriers** (PUF, 1971) is very detailed and informative. **G. Lefranc** is sound on trade-union history, see notably his brief *Le Syndicalisme en France* (8th ed, PUF, 1973) and the two-volume *Le Mouvement syndical* (Payot, 1969) which goes up to 1968. A handy documentary introduction is **J. Capdevielle** and **R. Mouriaux**, *Les Syndicats ouvriers en France** (Colin, 1970). Pro-CGT views are expressed in the brief **H. Krasucki**, *Syndicats et socialisme* (Editions Sociales, 1972) and the more scholarly **J. Bruhat** and **M. Piolo**, *Esquisse d'une histoire de la CGT* (CGT, 1966). A critical view, from a communist disillusioned by 1968, is **A. Barjonet**, *La CGT* (Seuil, 1969).

The CFDT presents its views in *La CFDT* (Seuil, 1971) and in the committed work by **E. Maire** and **J. Julliard**, *La CFDT aujourd'hui* (Seuil, 1975). **M. Schifres**, *La CFDT des militants* (Stock, 1972) is impressionistic, but conveys much of the ethos of the organization.

On FO, **A. Bergounioux**, *Force ouvrière* (Seuil, 1975) is a critical left-socialist view. **A. Bergeron**, *FO* (Force ouvrière, 1973) gives an official view.

On the CNPF, **H. Ehrmann**, *Organized Business in France* (Princeton UP, 1957) is a thorough history, to be brought up to date by the well-informed **B. Brizay**, *Le Patronat** (Seuil, 1975).

On farmers' groups **G. Wright**, *Rural Revolution in France** (Stanford UP, 1964) is an admirable historical introduction. **Y. Tavernier**, *Le Syndicalisme paysan – FNSEA: CNJA** (Colin, 1969) is an excellent study of the structures of farmers' organizations.

CIDUNATI has attracted little book-length study, but its ideology comes across clearly in the autobiographical **G. Nicoud**, *Au Risque de déplaire* (Bourg de Péage, L'Objectif, 1977). A sober and concise assessment of the movement is **A. Bonnet**, 'Un nouveau groupe de pression', *Revue politique et parlementaire*, no. 843, June–July 1973, pp. 44–61.

The FEN has two historical studies: **J. Clark**, *Teachers and Politics in France: a Pressure-group Study of the FEN* (Syracuse UP, 1967) and a more recent and more pro-FEN view **R. Chéramy**, *La Fédération de l'éducation nationale: 25 ans d'unité syndicale* (Epi, 1974).

Chapter 5

The best introduction to the theory of international relations is **K.J.**

Holsti, *International Politics: a framework for analysis* (2nd ed., Prentice-Hall, 1974); this can be supplemented by a brief and readable work **W. Wallace,** *Foreign Policy and the Political Process* (Macmillan, 1971) which situates foreign policy in the socio-political context; a new approach to international relations from a semiotic point of view is **Y. Delahaye,** *La Frontière et le texte: pour une sémiotique des relations internationales* (Payot, 1977) though it provides a new angle of observation rather than an interpretation complete in itself. For the impact of French political culture on foreign policy the best work is still **J.-B. Duroselle** (ed.), *La Politique étrangère et ses fondements* (Colin, 1954). For the organization of foreign policy, one should begin with **A. Outrey,** 'Histoire et principes de l'administration française des affaires étrangères', *La Revue française de science politique* (3 articles): I, April–June 1953, pp. 298–318; II, July–September 1953, pp. 491–510; III, October–December 1953, pp. 714–35; to bring one up to date, there is an anonymous article by a practising diplomat: **XXX,** 'La réforme du Quai d'Orsay: des choix difficiles', *Défense nationale*, November 1977, pp. 103–33; an overview of organization and some main currents of policy is **H. Tint,** *French Foreign Policy since the Second World War* (Weidenfeld & Nicolson, 1972). For the main values and motivations behind foreign policy but with emphasis on judgment rather than on explanation, one may consult **S. Hoffmann,** *Decline or Renewal? France since the 1930s* (New York, Viking, 1974); for de Gaulle's policy aims and motivations, see **E.L. Morse,** *Foreign Policy and Interdependence in Gaullist France* (Princeton UP, 1973); and a committed discussion of a key concept is in **D. Colard** 'La conception française de l'indépendance nationale', *Studia Diplomatica*, no. 1, 1975; the best overall description and analysis of foreign policy is **G. de Carmoy,** *Les Politiques étrangères de la France, 1944–66* (La Table Ronde, 1967) translated and up-dated as *The Foreign Policies of France, 1944–68* (Chicago UP, 1970); the same author provides an interesting focus on changes in 1968–9 in 'The last year in de Gaulle's foreign policy', *International Affairs*, vol. 45, no. 3, July 1969, pp. 424–35; description and analysis is provided for at least part of the period since de Gaulle in **R. Macridis,** *French Politics in Transition* (Cambridge, Winthrop, 1975). It is important to understand the motivations of successive presidents through their speeches and writings, beginning with **C. de Gaulle,** *Mémoires de guerre* (3 vols, Plon, 1954–9) and *Mémoires d'espoir* (2 vols, Plon, 1970, 1971); a convenient collection of de Gaulle's most important speeches is in **A. Passeron,** *De Gaulle parle*, vol. 1, 1958–62; vol. 2, 1962–66 (Plon, 1962; Fayard, 1966). The memoirs of the longest-serving foreign minister in recent times are worth reading: **M. Couve de Murville,** *Une Politique étrangère, 1958–69* (Plon, 1971); for Pompidou, the most useful collection of his important speeches is in **P.-B. Cousté** and **F. Visine,** *Pompidou et l'Europe* (Librairies techniques, 1974); for presidential motivations after 1974 see **V. Giscard d'Estaing,** *Démocratie française* (Fayard, 1976), and the critique in **C. Zorgbibe,** 'La diplomatie giscardienne', *Le Monde diplomatique*, March 1978, p. 3.

For an introduction to the fundamental considerations of defence policy as well as a useful overview of recent international issues in the military field, see **O. Pick** and **J. Critchley**, *Collective Security* (Macmillan, 1974); a historical account of military organization is in **R.D. Challener**, *The French Theory of the Nation-in-Arms, 1866–1940* (Columbia UP, 1955), and the role of the army is discussed in **J.S. Ambler**, *The French Army in Politics, 1945–62* (Ohio State UP, 1966); moreover a particularly illuminating and sympathetic study is by **R. Girardet**, *La Crise militaire française 1945–62* (Colin, 1964). For a discussion of the origins, development and purpose of the *'force de frappe'*, see **W.L. Kohl**, *French Nuclear Diplomacy* (Princeton UP, 1971), to be supplemented indispensably with **B. Goldschmidt**, *Les Rivalités atomiques, 1939–66* (Fayard, 1967); to situate advanced technology in France within the socio-political context a fundamental work is **R. Gilpin**, *France in the Age of the Scientific State* (Princeton UP, 1968). For French defence policy and organization as a whole, the most up-to-date account is **L. Ruehl**, *La Politique militaire de la Ve République* (Presses de la Fondation nationale des sciences politiques, 1976), and government policy is explained in the text of **R. Barre**, 'Discours prononcé au camp de Mailly le 18 juin 1977', *Défense nationale*, April 1978, pp. 7–19, while from the general staff point of view, details are given in Général **Méry**, 'Conférence à l'Institut des Hautes Etudes de Défense Nationale et au Centre des Hautes Etudes de l'Armement, lundi 3 avril 1978', *Défense nationale*, June 1978, pp. 17–42. For French defence policy in an international context see **F. de Rose**, *La France et la défense de l'Europe* (Seuil, 1976), and **J. Klein**, 'France, NATO and European security', *International Security* (winter 1977, pp. 21–41). The strategy of massive retaliation is defended by **P.M. Gallois**, *Paradoxes de la paix* (Presses du Temps Présent, 1967) and with regret at its demise in *Le Renoncement: de la France défendue à l'Europe protégée* (Plon, 1977), while French thought is discussed in an Atlantic context in **R. Aron**, *Le Grand Débat: théories de la stratégie nucléaire* (Calmann-Lévy, 1963), translated as *The Great Debate: theories of nuclear strategy* (New York, Doubleday, 1965). French arms sales policy is discussed in **J. Klein**, 'Commerce des armes et politique: le cas français', *Politique étrangère*, no. 6, 1976, pp. 562–8. The civil-military tensions endemic in French society are analysed historically in **J. Rabaut**, *L'Antimilitarisme en France, 1810–1975* (Hachette, 1975); recent trends in public opinion are discussed in **J.-M. Lech** 'L'évolution de l'opinion des Français sur la défense à travers les sondages de 1972 à 1976', *Défense nationale*, January 1977, pp. 47–56, and with less optimism by **R. Girardet**, 'Opinion et politique de défense' in the same publication, pp. 21–7. The call for a stronger political and civilian control over the army is made in **J. Marrane**, *L'Armée de la France démocratique* (Editions Sociales, 1977) and by the PS spokesman, **C. Hernu**, *Soldat-citoyen* (Flammarion, 1975). The internal security forces are described in **L. Mandeville, J.-L. Loubet del Bayle** and **A. Picard**, 'Les forces de maintien de l'ordre en France', *Défense nationale* (July 1977, pp. 59–76).

French relations with the super-powers are described in **A. Fontaine**,

Histoire de la guerre froide, vol. 1, 1917–50; vol. 2, 1950–67 (Fayard, 1966–7); American pressure for German rearmament and French reactions are discussed in **P. Melandri**, 'Les Etats-Unis et le plan Pleven: octobre 1950–juillet 1951', *Relations internationales*, no. 11, autumn 1977, pp. 201–29. The friction between statesmen is described by **J. Newhouse**, *De Gaulle and the Anglo-Saxons* (Deutsch, 1970); the question of American decline or otherwise is given structured analysis in **J. Petras** and **R. Rhodes**, 'The reconsolidation of US hegemony' in *New Left Review*, no. 7, May–June 1976, pp. 37–53, and the diplomatic evidence of US resilience is in **J. Freymond**, 'L'Europe dans la politique extérieure de Henry Kissinger', *Relations internationales*, no. 11, autumn 1977, pp. 249–64; foreign policy is situated in politico-economic structures in **P.J. Katzenstein**, 'International relations and domestic structures: foreign economic policies of advanced industrial states', *International Organization*, vol. 30, 1976, pp. 1–45. French relations with the Soviet Union are discussed in **R. Levgold** 'The Franco–Soviet *rapprochement* after de Gaulle', *Survey*, autumn 1974, pp. 67–93.

For French relations with European neighbours, the best overall account is by **H. Brugmans**, *L'Idée européenne, 1920–70* (Bruges, De Tempel, 3rd ed., 1970); a brief factual survey of EEC institutions is in **J.-F. Deniau**, *Le Marché commun* (PUF, 11th ed., 1974), with complex economic aspects treated effectively in **D. Swann**, *The Economics of the Common Market* (Penguin, 3rd ed., 1975); cross-Channel relations are described in **N. Waites** (ed.), *Troubled Neighbours: Franco–British Relations in the Twentieth Century* (Weidenfeld & Nicolson, 1971) and recalled by a retired key participant, **R. Massigli**, *Une Comédie des erreurs, 1943–56* (Plon, 1978); relations with Germany are described in **F.R. Willis**, *France, Germany and the New Europe, 1945–63* (Stanford UP, 1965), and recalled by an important participant, **F. Seydoux**, *Dans l'Intimité allemande* (Editions Albatros, 1977). The most complete account of French relations with the EEC is **J. Rideau** *et al.*, *La France et les communautés européennes* (Librairie générale de droit et de jurisprudence, 1975); an equally fundamental analysis of de Gaulle and the EEC is **E. Jouve**, *Le Général de Gaulle et la construction de l'Europe, 1940–66* (Librairie générale de droit et de jurisprudence, 2 vols, 1967, 1969), a subject synthesized coherently in **S. Serfaty**, *France, de Gaulle and Europe* (Johns Hopkins Press, 1968). For the debate in France regarding the EEC during its formative period, see **B. Criddle**, *Socialists and European Integration: a study of the French Socialist Party* (Routledge & Kegan Paul, 1969), also evocative in a more optimistic way is **J.J. Servan-Schreiber**, *Le Défi américain* (Denoël, 1967), translated as *The American Challenge* (Penguin, 1969). The years after de Gaulle are best approached through **P.-B. Cousté** and **F. Visine**, *Pompidou et l'Europe* (Librairies techniques, 1974), to be followed by the penetrating analysis provided by **A. Grosser** *et al.*, *Les Politiques extérieures européennes dans la crise* (Presses de la Fondation nationale des sciences politiques, 1976). Atlanticism and neo-colonialism *vis-à-vis* the 'third world' are discussed in **S.E.M. Charlton** 'European unity and the politics of the French left', *Orbis*, winter 1976, pp. 1448–69, and in **A. Hodgart**,

The Economics of European Imperialism (New York, Norton, 1977).
French relations with the 'third world' are situated in a wider context in **H. Grimal**, *La Décolonisation* (Colin, 1965; translated as *Decolonization*, Routledge & Kegan Paul, 1978); post-independence
problems for ex-French colonies are revealed in **R. Dumont**, *L'Afrique
noire est mal partie* (Seuil, 1962), translated as *False Start in Africa*
(Deutsch, 1966). French aid programmes are described in **F. Luchaire**,
L'Aide aux pays sous-développés (PUF, 3rd ed., 1971), the educational
and cultural links are described in **L. Dollot**, *Les Relations culturelles
internationales* (PUF, 2nd ed., 1968); EEC aid programmes including
the Lomé convention are penetratingly analysed in **M. McQueen**,
Britain, the EEC and the Developing World (Heinemann, 1977) and the
structural relationship between the 'third world' and developed nations
such as France is analysed in **F. Partant**, 'Gauche et droite devant les
grands déséquilibres', *Le Monde diplomatique*, October 1977, pp. 2–4;
finally, French pursuit of trade in arms and nuclear energy-producing
equipment is discussed, along with that of West Germany and other
countries, in **Z. Cervenka** and **B. Rogers**, *The Nuclear Axis* (Friedmann,
1978) while more overt French military activities are discussed in
M. Sauldie, 'France's military intervention in Africa', *Africa*, no. 77,
January 1978, and in an anonymous article entitled 'Africa's French
gendarme', *Africa*, no. 81, May 1978.

To keep up to date with recent and current developments it is advisable to consult regular issues of *Défense nationale, L'Année politique,
Le Monde diplomatique, Regards sur l'actualité* (Documentation
française) and *The World Today* (the Royal Institute of International
Affairs).

Chapter 6

Education is so complex a subject, and in such a constant state of flux,
that regular study is necessary to keep up-to-date with changes.

Reading the daily and periodical press indicated above will provide
information on the current situation. *Le Monde de l'éducation*, which
goes into greater detail, is indispensable. The FEN publish two periodicals, both of with provide useful information on union feeling, *FEN–
Informations, L'Enseignement public*.

Useful basic material is contained in *Le Courrier de l'éducation*, published by the ministry for the benefit of teachers. Statistics are published
either in the frequent *Notes d'information*, and the annual *Tableaux
des enseignements et de la formation* (both by the *Service central des
statistiques et sondages*).

The best history of French education is undoubtedly that of **A. Prost**,
L'Enseignement en France, 1800–1967 (2nd ed., Colin, 1970), but
A. Léon, *Histoire de l'enseignement en France* (PUF, 1967) is a useful
short introduction, while further information is provided by **F. Ponteil**,
Histoire de l'enseignement en France, 1789–1964 (Sirey, 1965), **P.
Chevallier** *et al.*, *L'Enseignement français de la Révolution à nos jours*

(2 vols, Mouton, 1968–71) and **L. Decaunes** and **M.L. Cavalier** (eds), *Réformes et projets de réforme de l'enseignement français de la Révolution à nos jours* (IPN, 1962).

Most accounts of French education contain more than a fleeting reference to the administrative system. One overall account is Cahiers de documentation, *L'Organisation de l'enseignement en France* (INRDP, 1976). A more exhaustive study is **J.-L. Crémieux-Brilhac**, *L'Education nationale* (PUF, 1965).

On higher education, **C. Fourrier**, *Les Institutions universitaires* (PUF, 1971) gives good basic guidance; for an updated description, see **I. Boussard**, **M.-J. Guédon** and **D. Wolf**, *Les Institutions universitaires françaises* (Documentation française, 1977). The *Cahiers de l'INAS* have published some useful information with the relevant texts on aspects of university structures; *Conférence des présidents d'universités*, 1975; *Conseil national de l'enseignement supérieur et de la recherche*, 1975. On the financing of universities, see the report entitled, *Le Financement des universités* (Documentation française, 1976) which describes the present method and considers how it might be improved.

On the issue of Catholic education, a short history of the church/ state problem is provided by **B. Mégrine**, *La Question scolaire en France* (PUF, 1963), see also **A. Coutrot** and **F.-G. Dreyfus**, *Les Forces religieuses dans la société française* (Colin, 1965), **R. Rémond** (ed.), *Forces religieuses et attitudes politiques dans la France contemporaine* (Colin, 1965) and **R. Rémond**, *L'Anticléricalisme en France de 1815 à nos jours* (Fayard, 1976). For a particularly vivid insight into the anticlerical mentality, see **J. Cornec**, *Pour l'Ecole libre* (Laffont, 1977).

There are some good general studies on French education, notably **W.D. Halls**, *Education, Culture and Politics in Modern France* (Oxford, Pergamon, 1976); **W.R. Fraser**, *Reforms and Restraints in Modern French Education** (Routledge & Kegan Paul, 1971) and **J. Majault**, *L'Enseignement en France* (McGraw-Hill, 1973) are well worth study, in spite of their less recent date of publication.

Books by teachers, containing an account of their experiences, give a considerable insight into the workings (effective or otherwise) of the education system, for example, **R. Bréchon**, *La Fin des lycées* (Grasset, 1970), gives a perceptive account of life in a school in the immediate post-1968 period; **N. Delanoë**, *La Faute à Voltaire* (Seuil, 1972) deals with some of the same problems, but from a more specifically leftist approach. **S. Citron**, *L'Ecole bloquée* (Bordas, 1971) concentrates more on the extent to which the education system is unadapted to educational needs; **C. Duneton**, *Je suis comme une Truie que doute* (Seuil, 1976) gives a practical example of this.

A mine of information on primary education is the *Code Soleil* (48th ed., Sudel, 1978). See also, Intensive Study Visits–France, *Aspects of the French Education System seen through British eyes* (Central Bureau for Educational Visits and Exchanges, n.d.). **E. Faure**, *L'Education nationale et la participation* (Plon, 1968) is clearly a key text in any consideration of the *Loi d'orientation*. **J. de Chalendar**, *Une Loi pour l'université* (Desclée de Brouwer, 1970) gives an interesting account of the preparation of the law. Two books of particular interest in any consideration of the future of higher education are AUPEL, *Pour que l'Université ne meure* (Le Centurion, 1977) – a moderate view – and M. Duffour, D. Monteux and Y. Schwartz, *L'Université de la crise au changement* (Editions Sociales, 1978) for a PCF view of higher education. On the IUTs, see M. Domenc and J.-P. Gilly, *Les IUT, ouverture et idéologie* (Cerf, 1977) – a left-wing view – and on Vincennes M. Debeauvais, *L'Université ouverte: les dossiers de Vincennes* (PUF de Grenoble, 1976) – a committed approach.

On the possibilities of *éducation permanente*, see D. Chevrolet, *L'Université et la formation permanente* (Brussels, Casterman, 1977) and on the position today, P. Besnard and B. Lietard, *La Formation continue* (PUF, 1976).

On the purposes of education, C. Baudelot and R. Establet, *L'Ecole capitaliste en France* (Maspéro, 1971) giving a marxist viewpoint, attacks the education system as a means of reproducing social class-structures. P. Bourdieu and J.-C. Passeron, *La Réproduction* (Editions de Minuit, 1970) considers a similar problem, that of the continuing social and cultural dominance exercised by the upper classes. See also J. Fournier, *Politique de l'éducation* (Seuil, 1971), J. Capelle, *Education et politique* (PUF, 1974) and for an account of the realization of experimental approaches to education, R. Gloton (ed.), *L'Etablissement scolaire: unité éducative* (Brussels, Casterman, 1977).

The class structure of higher education is well illustrated by P. Bourdieu and J.-C. Passeron, *Les Héritiers* (Editions de Minuit, 1964).

Finally, three more specialized works, useful for reference: A. Charlot, *Les Universités et le marché du travail* (CEREQ-Documentation française, 1977); Commissariat du plan, *Rapport de la Commission éducation et formation: Préparation du 7e Plan* (Documentation française, 1976); B. Lemennicier *et al.*, *L'Aide aux étudiants en France* (CNRS, 1977).

Index

académie, 233, 235, 237, 238, 276
accords de Grenelle, 34, 37
Action française, 29
Adam, G., 289n
Adenauer, K., 21, 22, 26, 223
Africa, 11, 13, 48, 59, 70, 191, 203, 206, 211-30 *passim*
agrégation, 269, 273, 281
agrégés, 243, 265, 271
aid, 17, 195, 226-30
Ailleret, General, 210, 217
Alain (pseudonym of E. Chartier), 95
Algeria, 8, 13-14, 15-22, 26, 71, 102, 119, 138, 144, 154, 168, 190, 194-5, 197, 212-13, 226
Allier, 140
Allier, I., 292n
Alsace-Lorraine, 42, 142, 151, 165, 249
ambassadors, 196, 197, 199
Ambite, V., 238
Ancien Régime, 89-90, 93-4, 117, 118, 126, 246, 247
Anderson, R.D., 295, 297
Antoni, P. and J.-D., 292
apprenticeship, 263-4
Aquitaine, 55
Arabs, 195, 219, 224
Ardagh, J., 121
armed forces, 15, 16, 17, 21, 22, 187, 191, 196-7, 201-15
Aron, R., 193, 289
Arrighi, P., 296
arrondissement, 126
assemblée nationale, see under different Republics
Association des Maires de France, 129
Atlantic alliance, 10, 23, 211, 217
Atlanticism, 191, 210, 221, 223, 226
Aubert, A., 141, 181
autogestion, 37, 95, 155-7, 178
autonomie, 33, 37; of education, 276-7, 283, 285

Auvergne, 63, 131, 151
Avril, P. and Gicquel, J., 296

baccalauréat, 84, 233, 254-5, 260, 263, 267, 268, 269, 271-2, 273, 281, 282
bacheliers, 270, 271, 272, 275
Bao Dai, 12
Barjonet, A., 34
Barre, R., 47, 51, 105, 114, 115, 199
Barrès, M., 94
Barrot, J., 151
Baudelot, C. and Establet, R., 78, 83, 294
Bayeux speech (1946), 102-8 *passim*, 114-21 *passim*
Belgium, 189, 192, 217
Ben Bella, A., 14
Benin, 228
Bensaïd, D. and Weber, H., 289
BEP, 268
Bergeron, A., 177, 179
Berlin, 21, 206, 211
Berthoin, J., 255, 260, 261, 262
Beullac, C., 237, 268
Bigeard, General, 203
Billères, R., 261, 262, 297
bipolarization, 92, 133, 135, 155, 161
Birnbaum, P., 110
Blanc, J., 146
Blum, L., 109, 154
Bolshevik, 160, 171
Bonapartism, 89, 90-1, 108, 137, 139-40, 146, 188
Bordeaux, 55, 159
Bouches-du-Rhône, 157, 165, 238
Bourbon Restoration, 100, 247
Bourdieu, P. & Passeron, J.-C., 83, 294, 295
Brandt, W., 220
Bretton Woods, 23, 218
Brezhnev, L., 38, 220
Briand, A., 222
Britain, 14, 40, 43, 47, 52, 59, 61, 88,

Britain (*cont.*)
 92, 94, 95, 97, 176; Education Act
  (1944), 295; minister of education,
  295; *see also* United Kingdom
Brittany, 63, 130–1, 142, 148, 151,
 165
Brizay, B., 292
Brousse, P., 182
Brown, B.E., 288
Brudain, C., 194
Brussels treaty, 211, 222
Brussels Treaty Organization, *see*
 Western European Union
Budapest, 163
Burgundy, 159

Caen, 55; *colloque de*, 235, 273
Cahm, E., 289, 295
CAL, 28
Cambodia, 11, 287
Cameroon, 228
Campana, A., 147, 159, 292
Canal, M., 116
canton, 126
CAP (*certificat d'aptitude profession-
 nelle*), 268
CAPES, 238, 271, 273, 281
Capitant, R., 259
Casimir-Périer, J., 291
Catholic (church), 90, 92–3, 96, 142,
 148–51, 153, 159, 167, 222, 246,
 247, 248, 249, 253, 285
Cayrol, R., 158
CD, 149–50
CDS, 123, 148–52
CEG, 261, 266
censeur, 238
censorship, 118, 125
Central Intelligence Agency, 175
Centralization, 37, 89, 94–5, 113, 118,
 128, 178, 188; in education, 27,
 233 ff., 256, 263, 275, 276, 283; in
 PCF, 161
centre parties, 9, 19, 25, 40, 45, 135,
 149–52, 193–4, 210, 212, 225, 254
CEP (*certificat d'éducation profession-
 nelle*), 268
CEP (*certificat d'études primaires*),
 258, 261
CERES, 157–9, 160, 171
certificats, 269, 271
certifiés, 265, 271
CES, 83, 238, 262, 266
Ceyrac, F., 180
CFDT, 32, 34, 37, 159, 175–9, 182–3

CFTC, 175, 177
CGC, 6, 177, 182–3, 185
CGT, 32, 33, 34–5, 36, 38, 69, 164,
 174–9, 183, 185, 212
Chaban-Delmas, J., 41–5, 49, 106,
 140, 178, 198, 250, 291
Chad, 206, 226, 228
Challe, General, 16
Chambaz, J., 266
Chapot, V., 147
Charbonnel, J., 167
Charléty stadium rally, 34–5, 289
Charpentié, Y., 182
Charpy, P., 140
Chavardès, M., 297
Cherbourg, 251
Chevallier, J., 123
Chevènement, J.-P., 158
Chinaud, R., 147
Chinese People's Republic, 22, 191,
 195, 216, 221, 228
Chirac, J., 45, 49, 105, 106, 112, 128,
 137, 140–1, 145, 169–70, 291, 292
christian democracy, 3, 7, 9, 13–14,
 19, 93, 149–52, 154, 161, 222–3,
 250
Churchill, W., 190
CIDUNATI, 41, 181–2, 292
CIR, 155
Citron, S., 238, 246
classes préparatoires, 270, 281
classes terminales, 272
Clausewitz, K. von, 201
CNAL, 250, 251, 296
CNES, 276
CNESR, 276, 277, 279
CNIP, 19, 123, 139, 144, 152–3, 184
CNJA, 184
CNPF, 33, 179–80, 183
Cochard, J., 213
code civil, 115
Cohn-Bendit, D., 28, 29, 32, 34, 288
Cold War, 7, 10, 21, 144, 161, 190,
 195, 212, 216, 222
collège, 233, 266, 268, 271
colonialism (neo-), *see* imperialism
colons, 13–15, 16, 17
Comintern, 160
comité d'entreprise, 2, 47, 177
comité des parents, 266
committees of public safety, 15, 16
commune, 113, 126–9, 150, 235, 285;
 (1871), 188
commune étudiante, 32–3
communism, 3, 7, 9, 13, 18, 19, 20,

communism (*cont.*)
  25, 40, 44, 46, 50, 92-3, 133-4,
  138, 150, 152-6, 159, 166, 175,
  185, 194, 203, 211-12, 217, 219,
  222, 223, 225, 250, 287; PCF, 31,
  36, 77-8, 160-5, 167, 170-1, 178,
  184-5; eurocommunism, 162, 219
community, 195, 197
*Compagnie internationale pour
  l'informatique*, 49, 219
Compagnies républicaines de sécurité,
  213, 215
concentration (economic), 5, 6, 55,
  58-9, 68, 78, 138
Concordat (1802), 247, 249
Condorcet, marquis de, 233, 260
Congo, 216, 228
conseil académique, 233
conseil de classe, 266
conseil d'école, 266
conseil de l'université, 234
conseil d'établissement, 266
conseil d'orientation, 262
conseil du roi, 115
conseil général, 126, 151, 290
Constantine Plan, 16, 17
constitution: importance, 97; im-
  permanence, 98
consulate, 100
Conte, A., 122
contestation, 37
contrat d'association, 250, 251
contrat simple, 250, 251
Converse, P., 134
CORAN, 160
Cornec, J., 252, 296
corps intermédiaires, 145
Corrèze, 128
Corsica, 14, 130-1
cour des comptes, 117
cour de sûreté de l'état, 203
cours complémentaires, 257
cours élémentaire, 268
cours magistral, 246, 271
cours moyen, 268
cours préparatoire, 268
Couve de Murville, M., 107, 167,
  200
CPDM, 149-50.
CPG, 44, 50, 58, 105, 153, 155, 166-7,
  170, 179-80, 184, 296
Crépeau, M., 166
Creys-Malville, 169
Crisol, P. and Lhomeau, Y., 141, 289, 291
Crozier, M., 95, 291

CSEN, 236
CSP, 71, 75-7, 79-80, 82, 148
Cuba, 21, 190, 195
CVN, 28
cycle d'observation, 261, 262
cycle préparatoire, 267
Czechoslovakia, 38, 155, 162, 196,
  210, 216, 217, 220, 221

Dakar, 228-9
DATAR, 131, 140
Dayan, G., 158
Debatisse, M., 184-5
Debré, J.-L., 109, 291, 292
Debré, M., 16, 18-20, 25, 41, 105,
  106, 108, 131, 140, 202-3, 250,
  251, 253, 291
debudgetization, 111
decentralization, 39, 95, 125, 137, 145,
  151, 156, 179, 235, 276, 277, 283,
  285
*Déclaration des droits de l'homme et
  du citoyen* (26 August 1789), 99,
  100, 296
defence policy, 19, 21, 22, 25, 187-230
Defferre, G., 13, 40, 154, 158
deflation, 5, 47
Denanoë, N., 243, 295
Delbos, Y., 260
délégué syndical, 2
département, 113, 126-31, 235, 285
Depreux, E., 260
désistement, 104, 134
DESS, 280
détente, 21, 190, 195, 216, 220, 221
deterrence, 210-12
DEUG, 278-9, 280, 281
Devaquet, A., 140
developing countries, *see* third world
Development Assistance Committee,
  226
Diaz, M., 166
Dien Bien Phu, 12
Diligent report, 122
diplôme d'études approfondies, 280
directeur de publication, 124
directoire de surveillance du territoire,
  212
dirigisme, 3
Divini Illius Magistri, 249
Djibouti, 206, 228
doctorat, 233, 270, 273, 280
dossier scolaire, 267
Doumeng, J.-B., 164
Draguignan, 203

Dreyfus, A., 201
Duchet, R., 144
Duclos, J., 40
DUEL, 272, 273, 278
DUES, 272, 273, 278
Duhamel, J., 149-50
Dumas, R., 158
Dunkirk treaty, 222
Dupeux, G., 134
Durafour, M., 182
DUT, 272, 279
Dutschke, R., 29
Duveau, G., 248

eastern Europe, 10, 23, 26, 191,
    196, 216, 219, 220, 221
eclecticism, 248
école moyenne, 261, 262
école nouvelle, 38
école parallèle, 38
école primaire supérieure, 257
école unique, 258
ecologists, 169
Economic and Social Council, 126,
    139, 177
economic policy: Fifth Republic, 19,
    21, 24-6, 40, 42-3, 46-8, 51, 187,
    192-4, 196, 206, 208, 217-25,
    228-9; Fourth Republic, 2-5,
    54
EDC, 10-11
education: *activités d'approfondiss-
    ement*, 266; adult (*see formation con-
    tinue*); budget, 236, 269, 282,
    297n; catholic, 233, 248, 250-1,
    253, 254, 283, 285, 295n; choice
    of, 248, 253; comprehensive, 262;
    décloisonnement, 263; democrat-
    ization, 262, 263, 274; dualism in,
    247, 248, 250; equality in, 259,
    261, 269, 283; female, 233, 246;
    free, 257, 258; higher, 233, 246,
    247, 263, 266, 268, 269 ff.; *in-
    specteur départemental*, 237;
    inspecteur général, 234; inspection,
    problems of, 238-9; legislation
    (1971), 263-4; monopoly, 233;
    obligatory, 257; *pluri-disciplin-
    arité*, 275; primary, 233, 246, 247,
    248, 250, 251, 256ff.; private, 233,
    247, 249, 250, 251; purposes, 22,
    26, 202, 227, 231-2, 234, 246-7,
    253, 256-7, 274, 280, 282, 285-6;
    redoublement, 265; remedial, 266;
    rentrée (1977, 1978), 267; second-

ary, 233, 246, 247, 248, 250, 251,
    256ff.; selection in, 258, 268, 273,
    274-5, 281-2, 283; technological,
    263-4; *tronc commun*, 258, 259
EEC, 5, 15, 19, 21-3, 26, 40, 43-4,
    48, 59, 63, 157, 184, 191, 193, 194,
    195, 196, 198, 199, 212, 216, 219,
    220, 221, 222, 223, 224, 225, 226,
    227, 228; assembly, 48, 151, 225;
    commission, 225; Common Agri-
    cultural Policy, 23, 26, 43, 62, 184,
    194, 224; enlargement, 48, 51, 146,
    169, 185, 224, 226; integration, 9,
    23, 48, 146, 149, 151, 179, 191,
    193-4, 212, 220-3; monetary
    union, 224-6
Egypt, 14
Ehrmann, H., 295n
Eisenhower, General, 217
elections, 9, 51, 132, 133-4; depart-
    mental (April 1976), 50; legislative,
    Fourth Republic, 6, 7, 8; Fifth
    Republic (November 1958), 18;
    (November 1962), 20-1, 155,
    (March 1967), 25-6, 155, (June
    1968), 33-6, 155, (March 1973),
    44, 155, (March 1978), 50-1, 92,
    93, 161, 203, 211, 225, 230;
    municipal (March 1977), 50;
    presidential (December 1958),
    19, (December 1965), 20, 23, 25,
    155, (June 1969), 40, 167, (May
    1974), 45
Elleinstein, J., 171
Empire, 18, 188, 190, 223, 227
ENA, 158, 281
entreprise de presse, 124
Epinay congress, 155
Etats-Généraux, 99
Eurogroup, 209
European Coal and Steel Community,
    5, 190, 222
Europe No. 1, 124
events of May, 26-39; causes, 26-8,
    36-7; consequences, 37-8; edu-
    cation and, 26-8, 36-7, 38; government
    reaction, 31-6; interpretations, 38-
    9; *lycéen* involvement, 28; opposi-
    tion and, 34-5; police and, 28,
    30-2, 210, 213, 217, 220, 236, 262,
    269, 274, 279, 280; student in-
    volvement, 26-33; worker involve-
    ment, 33-6
Evian, 16, 17
Express, l', 221, 268

Fabius, L., 158
Fabre, R., 166
facultés, 233, 270, 272, 273
fascism, 7, 154, 168
Faure, E., 9, 39, 236, 255, 261-2,
    274, 275, 278, 283, 295, 297
Faure, M., 203
Fédération Cornec, 251, 252, 296
Fédération Lagarde, 296
FEN, 30, 32, 34, 177, 185-6, 251, 252
FER, 29
Ferry, J., 143, 249, 257, 285
FFA, 184
FGDS, 25, 35-6, 155
Fifth Republic, 188, 230; agricultural
    policy, 184; *assemblée nationale*,
    19, 20, 22, 25, 31, 35, 102, 104,
    106, 107, 109, 110, 194, 197,
    199-200, 217, 250, 252, 265, 274,
    275; budget, 110, 114; *cabinet* (minis-
    ter's collaborators), 113; cabinet
    meetings, 112; censure motions, 18,
    20, 22, 34, 103-4, 197; choice of
    ministers, 112; *conseil constitution-
    nel*, 51, 103, 115, 116-17, 291n;
    conseil d'état, 115-17, (*commission
    permanente*), 115, (de Gaulle and),
    116; constitution of, 14, 15, 17-21,
    25, 37, 102, 103, 104, 105, 108,
    197, (ambiguity of, 108, 109);
    decision-making in, 112-13; *députés*
    in, 104-5, 110, 111, 117; electoral
    legislation in, 104, 105; govern-
    mental stability in, 42, 104; in-
    compatibility principle, 105, 107,
    112, 117; ministers, 111, 112, 113,
    114; minister of commerce, 43,
    182; minister of defence, 206, 207,
    213, 214, 227; minister of education,
    107, 127, 234, 235, 236-7, 238,
    250, 285, (secrétaire d'état in, 237);
    minister of finance, 24, 43, 45, 47,
    50, 51, 112, 114-15, 127, 181,
    198-9, 207, 227; minister of foreign
    Affairs, 107, 112, 197-200, 207,
    227; minister of the interior, 46,
    112, 126, 127, 207, 212-5; minis-
    ter of universities, 237; ministerial
    counter-signature, 108; ministerial
    decrees, 111; Orleanist interpret-
    ation of, 108; parliament, 103, 105,
    110, 120, 133, (weakness), 110-11,
    118; parliamentary committees,
    110-11; parliamentary responsibilit,
    in, 103-4, 106-7, 108; political

parties, 103, 104, 136, 166, (broad-
    casting time for, 123); president,
    domaine réservé, 19, 197, (irres-
    ponsibility), 108-9, 112, 114,
    116-18, (powers), 18-21, 25, 44,
    102-3, 106-8, 195, 197-200,
    206-7, (use of special powers), 18-
    19, 197; presidential nature of, 92,
    109, 117-18, 133-4; prime minister,
    18-20, 102, 103, 106-8, 109, 112,
    114, 116, 117-18, 197-9, 206-7;
    secrétaires d'état in, 112; *secrétariat
    d'état aux universités*, 237, 279;
    sénat, 19, 39, 102, 252; *suppléant*,
    104-5, 117, 291n; television, uses
    of, 120-1; votes of confidence, 18,
    19, 103-4, 197
Figaro, le, 124, 296
filières, 266, 268
Finistère, 252
First Empire, 100
First Republic, 101
Flandin, P.-E., 143
FLN, 13-14, 16, 17
FLNC, 130
FNSEA, 183-4
FO, 175-9
Foccart, J., 41
Fontanet, J., 237, 264-5, 278
Ford, G., 199
foreign policy, 19, 20, 21, 22, 24, 25,
    187-230
forfait d'externat, 250, 252
formation continue, 263-4, 297
Fos, 42
Fouchet, C., 31; and EEC, 23, 223;
    and education, 27, 235, 262, 265,
    271-3, 278, 280
Fourcade, J.-P., 47, 147
Fourquet, General, 217
Fourth Republic, 7-15, 18, 22, 24,
    102, 136, 138, 188, 249, 260,
    270; collapse, 14-5, 154; instability,
    103, 132; minister of interior, 13;
    premier, 9; president, 9, 102-3;
    proportional representation, 104;
    senate, 9
FRAMATOME, 220, 230
France-Culture, 122
France-Soir, 124
François-Poncet, J., 200
francophonie, 194, 227
franc zone, 195, 226, 227
Fraser, W.R., 295, 297
Frears, J., 147

Free French (forces), 1, 7
Front national, 168
FRP, 167

Gabon, 206, 226, 228
Gaillard, F., 14
Gallet, D., 167
Garaud, M.-F., 44, 140
Gaulle, General C. de Gaullism, 3, 7-9,
    10-12, 14, 15-26, 31-8, 39-41,
    43-6, 48, 51, 59, 93, 131, 135-50
    passim, 154, 161-2, 167-8, 189-99,
    202, 204, 206, 209-12, 215-20,
    223, 250, 273, 291
Gaullist party, 10, 18-20, 25, 42, 43-6,
    49, 51, 105, 106, 111, 120, 123,
    136-43, 145-6, 148, 152, 169-70,
    203, 217, 225, 250
Geismar, A., 30
gendarmerie nationale, 205, 208, 213,
    214
General Electric, 216
General Motors, 217
Geneva conference, 12
German Federal Republic, 10-11, 21-2,
    26, 40, 52, 81, 188-227 *passim*
Gers, 71
Giap, V.N., 12
Gingembre, L., 181
Ginott, H., 201
Girardet, R., 202
Giroud, F., 112, 292
Giscard d'Estaing, O., 122
Giscard d'Estaing, V., 24-5, 39-40,
    43, 45-51, 62, 95, 107, 111, 112,
    114, 122-4, 131, 135, 140, 143-8,
    150, 152-3, 166-7, 169-71, 194,
    196, 198-200, 203, 208, 211-12,
    218-19, 221, 225-6, 228-30, 265,
    290, 291
Codechot, J., 295
Gramsci, A., 77
grandes écoles, 117, 270, 281-2
Granet, D., 268
Grappin, P., 27, 28, 29
Greece, 48, 226
Gretton, J., 29, 30, 289
Grimaud, M., 32, 39, 288, 289
Grosser, A., 211
Group of Ten, 217
groupes d'étude technique, 279
groupuscules, 275
Guéna, Y., 140, 203
Guinea, 18
Guermeur, G., 252, 296

Guichard, O., 129, 255, 296, 297
Guiringaud, L. de, 107, 199, 200
Guizot, F., 46, 235, 247, 248, 256,
    257

Haby, R., 107, 186, 237, 243, 246,
    252, 265-7
Halls, W.D., 231, 295, 297
haute cour de justice, 117
Haute-Provence, 204
Hayward, J., 114, 295
Heath, E., 224
hegemony, 75, 77, 88, 91, 133, 138,
    164, 191-3, 215, 223, 228
Helsinki conference, 221
Henry, A., 185, 251
Hernu, C., 203
Herriot, E., 222
Hersant, R., 124
Herzberg, M., 289
Herzlich, G., 279
Hintermann, E., 152
Hiroshima, 204, 206
Ho Chi Minh, 11-12
Hoffmann, S., 95, 289, 291
Holland, 189, 192, 224
Holsti, K., 192
Hugo, V., 222
Humanité, l', 31, 164, 203
Hungary, 221
Huntziger, J., 211

imperialism, 12, 13-14, 23, 59, 61,
    190, 219
independence, 11, 20-3, 37-8, 48-9,
    93, 137, 151, 162, 188-9, 191-7,
    204, 209-12, 216-17, 220, 223
Independent Programme Group, 209
Indo-China, 12-13, 190
inflation, 2, 4, 47, 50-1
INSEE, 51, 59, 70-1
inspecteur d'académie, 233, 237, 246
inspectorat des finances, 117, 281
instituteur, 248, 265, 267
instruction; civic, 285; moral, 247,
    285; religious, 247
intelligence organizations, 212
intendant, 238
International Energy Agency, 219, 224
International Monetary Fund, 218
International Labour Office, 69
Iraq, 209
Ireland, 63, 92, 224
Isère, 182
Israel, 195

Italy, 63, 70, 192, 219, 224
IUT, 272, 273
Ivory Coast, 206, 228

Jacobinism, 89, 125, 131, 137, 145,
    152, 188
Japan, 11, 52
Jaurès, J., 153, 202
Jeanneney report, 226
JCR, 28, 29
JDS, 151
Jencks, C., 297
Jobert, M., 38, 98, 198, 199, 219,
    220, 221
Jordan, 21
Jospin, L., 158
Jouhaud, General, 16
Joxe, L., 31
Juillet, P., 44, 140
Julliard, J., 15, 292
July Monarchy, 90–1, 100, 234, 247,
    248, 290
Juppé, A., 140

Kanapa, J., 171
Karlsruhe, 203
Kastler, A., 289
Kindleberger, C., 54, 289
Kissinger, H., 219
Korea, 5, 10, 55
Krasucki, H., 178
Kriegel, A., 171
Krivine, A., 29, 168, 202

Labro, P., 288, 289
Lacoste, R., 14
Lagarde, A., 252
Laguiller, A., 45, 168
laïcité, 249
Landes, 159
Langevin-Wallon report, 259–60, 270,
    297
Languedoc, 159, 165
Lannuzel, Admiral, 206
Laos, 11, 216, 287
Larzac, 169
Latin, 254–6
Laurent, P., 171
Lebanon, 21, 206
Lecanuet, J., 25, 45, 49, 149–51, 154,
    166, 194, 221
left parties, 9, 13, 24–5, 40, 44, 46,
    49, 50, 51, 58, 92, 95, 105, 108,
    117, 131, 133–5, 153–71, 169–71,
    184, 194, 203, 210–11, 250, 251,

254, 266
left union, 44–5, 50, 153–6, 166,
    170–1, 179
Lenin, V., 160–2, 167
Leroy, R., 171
Lester-Smith, W.O., 295
liberation, 1, 189, 215
Libya, 209, 228
licence, 233, 269, 273, 279, 280, 281
Lille, 128, 158–9
Limousin, 63, 165
loi Barangé, 250
loi cadre, 111, 236, 265
Loi d'Orientation, 37, 236, 238, 262,
    263, 275ff
Loi Falloux (1850), 248, 249
Loi Marie, 250
Loire, 159
Loire-Atlantique, 184, 251
Lomé convention, 227–8
Lot, 6
Lot-et-Garonne, 63
Louis XIV, 94
Lozère, 71, 128
Luxembourg, 192; agreements (January
    1966), 23
lycée, 28, 238, 254, 258, 259, 261,
    266, 268, 270, 271
lycée d'enseignement professionnel,
    268
Lyon, 32, 159

Machin, H., 291
MacMahon, P., 101
Maginot Line, 211
Maire, E., 177, 183
maîtrise, 273, 279, 280
Malaud, P., 121, 122
Malterre, A., 182
malthusianism, 5, 58, 70, 90
manoeuvres, 76
Mansholt Plan, 43, 62
Maoism, 168
Marceau, J., 86, 290
Marcellin, R., 144
Marchais, G., 162–3, 165, 251
Marseille, 32, 42, 55, 128
Marshall Aid, 5, 10, 189, 222, 287
marxism, 138, 153–4, 161, 164, 168,
    170
Maspéro, F., 168
mass media (radio and television), 25,
    118ff, 232; advertising, 121, com-
    mercialization of, 123, 124; law of
    August 1974, 122, 123, 124; state

mass media (*cont.*)
  monopoly, 118–24
Massif Central, 71, 131, 142
Massu, General, 15, 35
Mathieu, G., 58, 290
Matin, le, 159, 291
MAU, 29
Maurin, General, 210
Mauritania, 48, 228
Maurras, C., 94
Mauroy, P., 158
mayor, 46, 126, 128–9, 151, 290
Mayotte, 229
MDSF, 152
Méhaignerie, P., 151, 184
Mendès-France, P., 11, 12, 25, 35, 38, 166–7, 289, 292
Mermaz, L., 158
Méry, General, 211, 212, 229
Messmer, P., 41, 44, 203, 217
Mexandeau, L., 251
MIAGE, 280
Middle East, 195, 221, 224
Midi-Pyrénées, 55
Millerand, A., 291n
ministry of information, 119, 120; abolition (1969), 121; resurrection, 121
Missoffe, F., 28, 288
Mitterrand, F., 25, 35–6, 45, 112, 117, 155, 157–8, 167, 180, 182
mixed ability classes, 265
Mobutu, J., 48, 203, 229
MODEF, 164, 184
Mollet, G., 14, 154, 167, 261
monarchy; absolute, 99, 100, 117, 188, 222; *chambre des députés* in, 100–1; constitutional, 100
Monde, le, 34, 37, 38, 107, 117, 122, 238, 243, 251, 253, 267, 291
Monde de l'éducation, le, 185, 265, 266, 279
mondialisme, 226, 230
Monnet, J., 3, 222
Monod, J., 140–1
monopoly (capitalism), 77–8, 139, 156, 162
Monory, R., 51, 115
Morin, F., 77, 290
Morocco, 13–14, 48, 190, 203, 226, 229
Mouvement du 22 mars; 29
MRG, 165–7, 203
MRP, *see* christian democracy
MSG, 280

MST, 280
Muller, E., 152
municipal elections, 49, 126

Nanterre, 27–9, 274, 288
Nantes, 32
Napoleon I, 94, 100, 138, 231, 233, 234, 237, 246–7, 249, 256, 270, 274
Napoleon III (Louis–Napoleon Bonaparte), 100, 101, 109, 201
nationalism, 188, 192, 193, 194, 195, 222
nationalization, 2, 9, 44, 50, 54, 145
NATO, 10–11, 15, 21–3, 44, 49, 190, 191, 194, 195, 196, 209, 210, 212, 216, 220, 221
neocolonialism, *see* imperialism
Newhouse, J., 191
Nicoud, G., 181–2
Nixon, R., 217–18
Nord, 55, 157, 159, 165
Normandy, 63, 148
notables, 90–1, 128, 143, 148, 151, 165–6, 290
note administrative, 238
Nouvelle Revue socialiste, la, 159
Nouvel Observateur, le, 38, 289, 292
nuclear weapons, 191, 204–12, 216, 221

OAS, 17, 20, 116, 168
Occident, 29, 30
Occitania, 130
Odéon theatre, 32, 33, 36
OECD, 52, 55
oil, 17, 195, 199, 219, 220, 224, 229
OP, 75, 164
OPEC, 47, 59
OQ, 75
orientation, 258, 266, 267, 268
Orleanism, 100, 137, 143
Ornano, M. d', 49, 147
ORTF: *conseil d'administration*, 120; creation, 120; *directeur-général*, 120; disbanding, 122ff; financial difficulties, 121; *président-directeur-général*, 121–2; reform (1971), 121–2; strike (1968), 33, 121
Ortoli, F., 274
OS, 75–6
overseas territories, 18, 227

papacy, 247, 249
Papon, M., 115

Paris, 14, 43, 46, 49, 55, 61, 63, 91,
    125-8, 130-1, 139, 142, 164-5,
    181, 184, 290
Parkin, F., 82, 290
Parodi, M., 5, 54, 287, 290
Parti populaire européen, 151
participation, 37, 38, 42, 137, 275,
    277, 283, 285
Pas-de-Calais, 55, 157, 159, 165
Pasqua, C., 140
Pasquier, N., 147
patente, 127
Pau congress, 158
Paye report, 122
Paxton, R., 54, 289
PCF, *see* communism
PCMLF, 168
PEGC, 265, 267
Pelletier, J., 237
Pelletier, M., 147
Perspectives et réalités, 147
Pétain, P., 7, 291
Petit-Clamart, 20
petites classes, 258, 259
Peugeot factories at Sochaux, 35
Peyrefitte, A., 30, 31
Pflimlin, P., 14
PFN, 168-9
Philip, A., 194
Piaget, C., 167
pieds-noirs, *see colons*
Pinay, A., 10, 19, 139, 144
'pirate' radio stations, 124
planning, 2-3, 24, 26, 44, 51, 54, 131,
    145, 156, 179, 276
Pleven, R., 10, 292
Plogonnec, 296
Plyutsch, L., 162
PME, 58, 180
Poher, A., 40
Poincaré, R., 143
Poing et la rose, le, 159
Point, le, 147
Poland, 26
police, 28, 30-2; *see also* events of May
Polisario, 48, 228
political traditions, 100-1, 109
politicization, 285
Pompidou, G., 20, 31-3, 40-5, 49, 104,
    105, 106, 107, 114, 121, 122,
    135-6, 139, 141, 144, 149, 167,
    196, 198-9, 208, 217-22, 224-5,
    228, 250, 255, 264, 291
Poniatowski, M., 46, 112
Popular Front, 154, 160, 258

population, 2, 26, 37, 69-71, 187,
    195, 205
Portugal, 11, 48, 50, 71, 219, 226
Poujade, P., 6, 8-9, 140, 168, 181-2,
    292
Poulantzas, N., 78, 82, 138
PR, 123, 143-8, 150
Prague, 10
prefect, 113, 126-9, 146, 156; regional
    prefect, 113, 127
press: freedom of, 124; ordinances
    (1944), 124; state assistance for,
    124-5 (dangers), 125; state's
    relations with, 124-5
pressure groups, 10, 93, 95, 169,
    172-86
propédeutique, 270, 271, 272
Prost, A., 256, 257, 289n, 297
Provençal, le, 159
proviseur, 238
PS, *see* socialism
PSD, 152
PSU, 34, 35, 155, 167
publicité compensée, 121
Puerto Rico, 219
Puy-de-Dôme, 144

Quatar, 209
Quebec, 26
Quin, C., 77-8

Radicals, 7, 13, 19, 25, 123, 136, 152,
    153-5, 165-7, 194, 223, 250, 261
Radio Monte-Carlo, 124
recteur, 233, 235, 237, 238, 246, 274,
    276
Referendum (May 1945), 7, (October
    1945), 7, (September 1958), 18,
    102, (January 1961), 16, (April
    1962), 17, (October 1962), 20, 39,
    105, 116, 144, (April 1969), 39,
    110, (April 1972), 43-4, 224
réformateurs, 149
régime concordataire, 249
regions/regional development, 3, 46,
    51, 55, 126-31, 146, 150, 152,
    156; law (1972), 42
Rémond, R., 135, 137, 296n
Renault factories: at Boulogne-
    Billancourt, 33; at Flins, 35
Rennes, 150
resistance, 1, 3, 9, 93, 136, 149, 160,
    189, 202, 287
Réunion, 227, 228, 229
Revolution: (1789), 88-90, 92-3, 99,

Revolution (*cont.*)
135, 148, 188, 201, 233, 234, 246, 247, 256, 270, (1830), 100; (1848), 100, 201, 248
Revue des deux mondes, 296
Reynaud, J.-D., 177
Rhône, 55, 159
RI, 20, 24–5, 40, 144, 146, 194
right parties, 7, 9, 45, 46, 49, 51, 92, 94, 131, 133–5, 135–53, 169–71, 254
Rioux, L. and Backmann, R., 288, 289
Rocard, M., 158, 167, 183
Roche, J., 30
Rolland, H., 140
Romania, 221
Rome treaty, 23, 190, 224, 225
Ross, G., 178, 292
Rouen, 151
Royer, J., 43, 45, 182
RPF/RPR, *see* Gaullist party
RTF, 118–19; *comité de surveillance*, 119; *conseil supérieur*, 119; *directeur-général*, 119; reform of, 119
RTL, 124

Sadat, A., 199
Saint-Herblain, 251
Sainteny, J., 11
Sakhiet, 14
saisine, 116
Salan, General, 15, 16, 35
Sanguinetti, A., 46
Saunier-Seïté, A., 107, 279, 283
Sauvageot, J., 29
Sauvagnargues, J., 107, 199, 200
Schmidt, H., 48, 225
Schuman, R., 222
Schumann, M., 198
scrutin d'arrondissement, 133
Seale, P. and McConville, M., 288, 289, 295
Second Empire, 52, 91, 100, 109, 117, 174, 234, 248, 257
Second Republic, 100; *assemblée nationale*, 101
security, 187–9, 191–2, 196, 201, 203–4, 210–13, 216, 221–2, 226, 228–9
Séguy, G., 24, 176, 178
Senegal, 206, 226, 228
Senghor, L., 228
separation of church and state (1905), 92, 165, 249

Serpell, C., 37
Servan-Schreiber, J.-J., 131, 149, 152, 166, 194, 221
service de documentation extérieure et de contre-espionnage, 212
services extérieurs (field services), 113, 127
Simeoni, M. and E., 130
Simon, G., 267
Singer, D., 289
SMAG, 34
SMIG, 34, 42
SNALC, 267
SNES, 164, 185
SNESUp, 30, 164, 289
SNI, 185
socialism/socialists, 3, 7–9, 13, 17, 40, 44, 46, 49, 50, 92, 94, 133, 137, 149–50, 152, 160–1, 166, 175, 183, 188, 194, 202, 222–3, 250, 261, 287; PS, 153–60, 161, 163, 165, 167, 170–1, 175, 178–9, 185, 203, 211; SFIO, 15, 19, 20, 25, 153–6, 158–61, 174, 185
Sofirad, 124
Soisson, J.-P., 147–8, 279, 280, 291
Sonnenfeldt, H., 219
Sorbonne, 27, 29, 30–1, 32, 33, 36
South Africa, 229–30
South America, 191, 216, 226
Soutou, J.-M., 200
Spain, 48, 71, 209, 226
Stalinism, 50, 161; destalinization, 171
Stoléru, L., 47
students: clashes with police, 30–2, 36; criticism of education system, 36–7, 271, 276, 277, 279–80; demonstrations, 29–30, 32, 35, 36; at Nanterre, 27–9; unrest before May 1968, 26–7
Sud-Radio, 124
Sudan, 209
Sudreau, P., 47, 181
Suez, 14, 154, 190
syndicat, 174, 176–7

Taiwan, 55
Tautin, G., 35
taxation, 4–5, 47, 78, 81–2, 111, 127, 129, 183
taxe professionnelle, 127
Technocrats, 41, 54, 107, 117, 139, 181
Témoignage chrétien, 254
Tet offensive, 28

Theodorakis, M., 160
Thierry d'Argenlieu, 12
Third Republic, 52, 92, 100, 101, 132,
143, 165, 188, 201, 249; *chambre
des députés*, 101; fall of, 6, 8, 102;
instability, 101–2, 103; powers of
president, 101, 103; *président du
conseil*, 101; senate, 101
third world, 26, 48, 59, 199, 219,
223, 226–30
Thorez, M., 161, 164
Tocqueville, A. de, 145
Togo, 228
Toubon, J., 140
Toulouse, 32, 55, 159
Touraine, A., 39, 84, 288
Tours congress, 160
Tricot, B., 108
tripartisme, 7
Trotskyism, 45, 168
Tunisia, 14, 190, 229
tutelle, 127, 146

UCC, 183
UDF, 145, 152, 170, 183, 203
UDR/UDT, *see* Gaullist party
UER, 275, 277
UGITC, 183
UJP, 167
UNEF, 29, 34, 35
unemployment, 24, 37, 43, 47, 51,
68–9, 169, 183
Union of Societ Socialist Republics,
10, 21–3, 26, 94, 154–6, 162–3,
171, 189, 190, 192, 193, 195,
196, 205, 208, 209, 210, 211, 215,
216, 217, 220–1, 223, 226, 228
unions, 24, 44, 46, 51, 160, 174–85,
203, 213
Unité, l', 159
United Kingdom, 21, 22, 23, 26, 81,
90, 132, 174, 185, 189–90, 192,
198, 205–6, 209, 216, 219, 222–7
United Nations, 14, 199, 206
United States of America, 5, 10–12,

21, 22, 23, 24, 25, 40, 48, 52,
58–9, 63, 90, 94, 132, 137, 189–
96, 198–9, 205, 208–12, 215–27
université impériale, 233, 234, 246,
247, 274
universités, 235, 238, 275, 276
university presidents, 276, 277, 278,
279
UNR, *see* Gaullist party
UPC, 130

Vatican II, 254
Vedel, G., 235, 295
Viansson-Ponté, P., 37, 122
Vichy, 7, 54, 70, 91, 94, 122, 168,
175, 183, 249
Vietminh, 11–12
Vietnam, 11–12, 14, 23, 27, 28, 191,
193, 217–8, 287
Vincennes, 282–3
Voix des parents, la, 252
Vosges, 42
VRTS (*Versement représentatif de
la taxe sur les salaires*), 127

Warsaw Pact, 196, 210, 216
Watergate, 218
Werth, A., 295
Western European Union, 223
Westinghouse, 219
Whale, J., 292
World War, First, 188, 189, 202, 215
World War, Second, 188, 189, 202,
215
Wright, G., 287
Wright, V., 94–5, 111, 147, 172, 291,
292

Yalts, 10, 192, 215
Ysmal, C., 147, 165, 292

Zaïre, 48, 203, 221, 229
Zamansky, M., 273
Zay, J., 258–9, 297
Zeller, General, 16